Greenberg's GUIDES®

LIONEL® TRAINS

POCKET PRICE GUIDE

Editor: Kent J. Johnson
with assistance from Roger Carp

KALMBACH
BOOKS

Twenty-fourth Edition

For more information, visit our website at
www.kalmbachbooks.com

Manufactured in the United States of America
Lionel® and American Flyer are the registered trademarks of Li
LLC, Chesterfield, Michigan

Cover design: Kristi Ludwig
Book layout: Julia Gerlach

Cover photo: Provided by Jack Sommerfeld, model no. 13004
Milwaukee Road *Hiawatha* Passenger set was produced betw
2001 and 2002.

We are constantly striving to improve *Greenberg's Pocket Price
Guide*. If you find any missing items or detect any misinform
please write to us at the following address:

Editor—Lionel Pocket Price Guide (10-8704)
Kalmbach Publishing Co.
21027 Crossroads Circle
P.O. Box 1612
Waukesha, WI 53187-1612

Or via e-mail

books@kalmbach.com

*This edition involved the participation of many people who
generously gave of their time and knowledge. Although we appr
the contributions of everyone involved with this publication, w
especially indebted to the late Chris Rohlfing for the diligent eff
put forth this year.*

　　　　　　　　　　　　　　　　　　　　　　　　　—Kent J. Jc

CONTENTS

INTRODUCTION 4
    What Products Are Listed 4
    How Products Are Listed 4
    How Product Values Are Listed 4
    How Product Values Are Determined 5
    How to Read This Guide 6

TOY TRAIN COLLECTING 8
    100 Years of Lionel Electric Trains Timeline 10

ANNUAL MARKET REPORT 11
    ATI Top Ten 11
    ATI Composite Trading Ticker 12
    ATI Composite Value 13
    ATI Composite Summary 13
    CTT Market Basket Recap 14
    The Lionel Marketplace 16

PRODUCTS OF DISTINCTION 18

SECTION 1: Prewar 1901–1942 25

SECTION 2: Postwar 1945–1969 63

SECTION 3: Modern Era:
1970–2004 (MPC/LTI/LLC) 98

SECTION 4: Modern Tinplate 281

SECTION 5: Large Scale 286

SECTION 6: Club Cars and Special Production 293

SECTION 7: Catalogs 311

ABBREVIATIONS 315

This handy reference is divided into seven major sections: Prewar 1901–1942, Postwar 1945–1969, Modern Era (MPC/LTI/Lionel LLC) 1970–2004, Modern Tinplate, Large Scale, Special Production, and Catalogs. In the first five sections and in the Large Scale section, production is listed numerically, using the item's catalog number. In the Prewar section, equipment is further described by gauge—Standard, O, OO, or 2⅞. The gauge type is within the parentheses.

    Steam locomotives in all sections include value with tender, even if tenders are not listed in detail. Be advised that the value of steam locomotives, particularly those of the Prewar period, may be significantly affected by the type of tender the item came with. For detailed information on tenders, consult the relevant comprehensive guides.

INTRODUCTION

What Products Are Listed

This Pocket Price Guide lists nearly every Lionel toy train product produced between the years 1901–1942 and 1945–2003 (there was no Lionel production during World War II). This list of items also includes Lionel products tentatively planned for production in 2004, but not yet released at the time of publication. Subsequent additions and deletions to the 2004 product line will be reported in the next edition of this pocket guide.

How Products Are Listed

This guide is divided into seven major sections, each representing a significant era or type of production: Prewar, 1901–1942; Postwar, 1945–1969; Modern Era, 1970–2004 (including MPC, LTI, and Lionel LLC production); Modern Tinplate; Large Scale; Special Production; and Catalogs.

In the first five sections and in the Large Scale section, production is listed **numerically**, using the item's catalog number. In some cases, Lionel numbered products with a number different from the catalog number. In these cases we also list this number, enclosed in parentheses, and refer the reader to the published catalog number for the full product description.

In the Prewar section, equipment is further described by gauge—Standard, O, OO, or 2⅞. The gauge type is within the parentheses. Steam locomotives in all sections include value with tender, even if tenders are not listed in detail. Be advised that the value of steam locomotives, particularly those of the Prewar period, may be significantly affected by the type of tender the item came with. For detailed information on tenders, consult the relevant comprehensive guides.

Dates cited in this guide are cataloged dates. If there is no catalog date, production dates are listed, if known. While many products are frequently marked with "Built" or "New" dates, these dates often reflect the dates that company artists picked up from prototype photographs or the date when the artists prepared their drawings. These dates may or may not have any relation to catalog dates or actual production dates.

How Product Values Are Listed

We have provided three columns for items listed in Sections 1 through 5. The first two columns give the current market values for each piece. In the Prewar and Postwar sections, values are denoted for items in Good and Excellent condition. In the Modern Era sections, the Large Scale section, and the Catalog section, values are given for items in Excellent and New condition. The "Cond/$" column is for noting the condition and cost of items you acquire.

How Product Values Are Determined

The values presented in this Pocket Price Guide are meant to serve only as a guide to collectors. They are an averaged reflection of prices for items bought and sold across the country, and are intended to assist the collector in making informed decisions concerning purchases and sales.

Values listed herein are based on values obtained at train meets held throughout the nation during the Spring and Summer of 2003, and from private transactions reported by members of our nationwide review panel. Values in your area may be consistent with values published in this guide, or higher or lower, depending upon the relative availability, scarcity, or desirability of a particular item. General economic conditions in your area may also affect values. Even regional preferences for specific roadnames may be a factor.

If you are selling a train to an individual who is planning to resell it—a retailer, for example—you will NOT obtain the values reported in this book. Rather, you may expect to receive about 50 percent of these prices. For your item to be of interest to such a buyer, it must be purchased for considerably less than the price listed here. But if you are dealing one-to-one with another private collector, values may be expected to be more consistent with this guide.

Our studies of train values indicate that mail order and retail store prices are generally higher than prices found at train meets because of the cost and effort of running a retail establishment or producing and distributing a price list, as well as packing and shipping trains.

The values quoted in this guide are for the most common variety of each item. Some rare variations are worth considerably more, and a few of the more significant ones are cited. For more detailed information about variations, please refer to our comprehensive line of collector guides described at the back of this guide.

Note that new products usually enter the list at their suggested retail price, since most have yet to sell regularly on the secondary market.

WE STRONGLY RECOMMEND THAT NOVICE COLLECTORS SEEK THE ADVICE AND ASSISTANCE OF FRIENDS OR ASSOCIATES WHO HAVE EXPERIENCE IN BUYING, SELLING, AND TRADING TRAINS.

How to Read This Guide

PRODUCT NUMBER
- **(#)** Numbers that have been put in parentheses by us do not appear on the actual items.
- **[#]** means decorations which make this item unique were not done by Lionel.
- **No Number** means item may have lettering, but lacks an item number.
- **(no letters)** means no lettering or number appears on the item.
- ***** means excellent reproductions have been made.

2343 Santa Fe F-3 AA Units, *50–52*
2343C Santa Fe F-3 B Unit, *50–55*
    (A) Screen roof vents
    (B) Louver roof vents
2344 NYC F-3 AA Units, *50–52*
2344C NYC F-3 B Unit, *50–55*
2345 Western Pacific F-3 AA Units, *52*
2346 B&M GP-9, *65–66*

DESCRIPTION
The text description for most items identifies the road (railroad) name, equipment type, equipment number (indicated in quotes), notable color or lettering data, and the year the item was first cataloged or produced (those dates followed by a "u" denote uncataloged items).

6

CONDITION

Trains and related items are usually classified by condition relating to appearance. The following definitions apply for this guide:

- **FAIR**—well-scratched, chipped, dented, rusted, or warped condition.
- **GOOD**—scratched, small dents, and dirty.
- **VERY GOOD**—few scratches, no dents, rust or warpage; very clean.
- **EXCELLENT**—minute scratches or nicks; no dents or rust; exceptionally clean.
- **LIKE NEW**—free of blemishes, nicks or scratches; original condition throughout, with vibrant colors; only faint signs of handling or use; price includes original box.
- **NEW**—brand new, absolutely unmarred, all original and unused, in original packaging with all paperwork provided by the manufacturer.
- **CP (C**urrent **P**roduction**)** means that the item is now being advertised, manufactured, or is currently available from retail stores.
- **NRS (N**o **R**ecorded **S**ales**)** means that we do not know the current market value of the item. The item may be very scarce and bring a substantial premium over items in its general class, or it may be relatively common but unnoticed. Usually NRS listings occur when an older and previously unknown item is first reported, although we are still discovering relatively common variations that have not been previously reported. If you have confirmable information about the value of an NRS item, please write to us.
- **NM (N**ot **M**anufactured**)** means that the item may have been cataloged or otherwise advertised, but it was not produced.

● Good	Exc	
160	365	_____ 3
100	195	_____ 1
115	215	_____ 1
270	640	_____ 3
130	275	_____ 2
810	1450	_____ 2
175	315	_____ 1 ●

ACTIVE TRADING INDEX

The Active Trading Index is a measurement of how often a particular train is offered for sale on the open market. The Greenberg's Toy Train Active Trading Index is based on a five-point scale: an Active Trading Index value of "5" indicates that a train has appeared for sale in various advertisements, lists, and at shows/auctions with a frequency that places it in the top 20% of all toy trains. (To borrow a little terminology from the stock and bond markets, we can say that pieces with an Active Trading Index of "5" are among the most actively traded among collectors.) An Active Trading Index value of "4" indicates that the piece was offered for sale less frequently (i.e., in the next 20%), and so on, down to an Active Trading Index of "1."

Excerpted from the Kalmbach Book *Toy Train Collecting and Operating: An Introduction to the Hobby*, by John Grams

How to Start Collecting Toy Trains

Who collects toy trains? Most of today's toy train collectors have simply retained their love of trains from youth and continued to build upon it, going through various stages, changes, or specializations along the way. Others have experienced a rekindling of their childhood enthusiasm later in life, when they had children or grandchildren to share in the hobby.

As few hobbyists can afford to purchase everything produced by a particular manufacturer, most collectors choose a specific concentration of toy trains to collect. Collectors often narrow their focus to:

One particular gauge or scale

A specific manufacturer's products

A certain era of toy train production

One class of locomotive, rolling stock, accessory, or an individual road name

Where to Buy and Sell Toy Trains

The following suggested sources of old toy trains are tried and true. They are presented as starting points as you enter this fascinating and engrossing hobby.

Private homes, garage sales, estate sales

Classified ads in newspapers and magazines

Mail order

Hobby shops

Swap meets and train shows

Auctions

Antique shops

Trades with other collectors

How to Buy Toy Trains

While geared to the basic circumstances of swap meets, these guidelines will serve the uninitiated train buyer in other places and situations as well. Although they resemble flea markets and gypsy camps on the surface, these train events usually have rules governing them. Most are sponsored by groups or organizations that have a vested interest in promoting the hobby, and they are concerned about scam artists bilking their customer-guests.

Most regular dealers are fairly honest, or at least try to be fair. Many are there primarily because they enjoy the hobby, too. Don't expect trade-ins, unlimited return privileges, layaways, or gift wrap. Few dealers are equipped to handle credit card purchases. And don't be surprised if they refuse to take your check. The first rule of the swap meet game: CASH AND CARRY.

What you see is what you get. All swap meet merchandise is sold as-is. While flaws and malfunctions should be noted, don't assume anything. Look over the merchandise carefully. Note the flaws. Ask questions about it before you start negotiating. Is it all original or does it include reproduced or remanufactured parts? Does it come with an original box? Does it work? Ask to take it to the test track so you can check the performance. Your best assurance is to buy from a dealer who has a good reputation or attends the meets regularly.

That brings us to the negotiation. Some dealers hold firmly to their ticket prices, considering them to be fair appraisals of market value. Others believe that dickering is part of the process of selling. A third group doesn't believe in ticket prices at all and will give you oral quotes if you ask. Give these dealers a wide berth unless you really know what you are doing.

The key to successful bargaining is in making a reasonable offer. Chiseling 10 to 15 percent from the ticket price in good-faith negotiation will probably be acceptable to most dealers. Some will consider larger discounts, but that is hard to predict. Package deals are good. Volume buying will often get you a few more total percentage points.

A dealer's willingness to negotiate on price can be contingent on many variables. Here's a list of the more common ones:

Price of the item
Rarity of the item
Length of time the dealer has carried the item
Volume of traffic at the meet
Length of time into the meet
Season of the year

One final bit of advice: Don't walk around a swap meet thumbing through your pocket price guide. That's a sure sign you're either ripe for picking or looking for an argument. The most vulnerable buyer is a neophyte with a book in his hand.

Preserving Toy Trains

As your collection grows, you will undoubtedly take more interest in maintaining its condition and value. How you choose to deal with this issue may well be one of the most important decisions you make regarding your collection.

Many would have you believe that toy trains should be kept only in a temperature- and humidity-controlled environment, free of dust and pollution, and away from direct sunlight. These trains were produced as toys. Although not indestructible, they are inherently tough.

High humidity can cause rust, but it is easily controlled using a small dehumidifier. Temperature, too, is only a factor in the extreme. And as far as dust, pollution, and direct sunlight are concerned, you need only look for practical solutions such as soft brushes, cans of compressed air, or in worst cases, mild soap and water or furniture polish.

Years of Lionel Trains Timeline

100

1900
1901—Lionel trains are born with the 2⅞-inch scale train no. 200 Electric Express.

1905
1907—Standard gauge trains running on 3-rail tubular track replace 2⅞-inch scale trains.

1910

1915
1915—The no. 700, based on New York Central electric prototype, debuts as the first O gauge Lionel locomotive.

1920
1920 to 1930—Lionel rises to the top during the Classic Period of Standard gauge trains.

1925

1930
1934—The $1 Mickey Mouse handcar helps Lionel stay afloat during the Great Depression.

1935
1937—Lionel creates a masterpiece: the magnificent 700E scale Hudson steam locomotive.

1940

1945
1948—Lionel, in conjunction with General Motors, the Santa Fe Railway, and the New York Central Railroad, produces its landmark no. 2333 F3 diesels.

1950

1955
1957—Lionel introduces its last and largest new steam locomotive of the Postwar era, the no. 746 Norfolk and Western J-class 4-8-4.

1960
1969—The Postwar era ends. Lionel Corp. sells its train line to General Mills.

1965

1970
1970—General Mills sets up train production in Michigan, and then briefly shifts production to Mexico in the early 1980s.

1975
1974—Fundimensions issues the GE U36B, its first new locomotive that is not a Postwar reissue.

1980

1985
1986—Richard Kughn buys Lionel from General Mills, forming Lionel Trains Inc.

1990
1994—Lionel announces its high-tech TrainMaster wireless control system.

1995
1995—Richard Kughn sells Lionel to Wellspring Associates, an investment firm that creates Lionel LLC.

2001
2001—A century after it started, American production of Lionel electric trains moves offshore to China.

ANNUAL MARKET REPORT

In this report you'll find a number of features we've devised to help you gather an accurate assessment of the current market for Lionel Trains.

The **ATI® Top Ten** lists rank the ten products (within each production era) most regularly offered for sale on the open market. Whether you're buying or selling, these lists will help you see what items hold the most competitive positions. Additionally, the **ATI Composite**, a chart indicating the annual conglomerate value of a selected set of common and actively traded items, helps you evaluate the direction of product values in the overall market.

With the growing popularity of on-line auctions, you'll certainly want to read through the **CTT Market Basket Recap** for review and analysis of both conventional and on-line auction prices. And to wrap up the report, we've included **The Lionel Marketplace** segment to bring you dealer's feedback and comments regarding the latest product offerings and announcements.

ATI Top Ten lists

Lionel Prewar			Good	Exc
1.	**2817**	Caboose (O), *36–42*		
		(A) Light red body and roof	90	145
		(B) Flat red, tuscan roof	140	225
2.	**58**	Lamp Post, 7⅞" high, *22–42*	34	48
3.	**92**	Floodlight Tower, *31–42**	120	265
4.	**700E**	Steam 4-6-4, Scale Hudson, 5344 (O), *37–42**	1400	2550
5.	**513**	Cattle Car (Std.), *27–38*		
		(A) Olive green	70	145
		(B) Orange	70	110
		(C) Cream, maroon roof	70	135
6.	**253**	Electric 0-4-0 (O), *24–32*		
		(A) Maroon	180	430
		(B) Dark green	105	195
		(C) Mohave	105	235
		(D) Terra-cotta	180	430
		(E) Peacock	95	195
		(F) Red	210	475
7.	**654**	Tank Car (O), *34–42*		
		(A) Orange of aluminum finish	35	60
		(B) Gray	42	75
8.	**814**	Boxcar (O), *26–42*		
		(A) Cream, orange roof	46	105
		(B) Cream, maroon roof	115	140
		(C) Yellow, brown roof	115	120
9.	**97**	Coal Elevator, *38–42*	145	285
10.	**164**	Log Loader, *40–42*	125	225

Lionel Postwar

			Good	Exc
1.	**3927**	Lionel Lines Track Cleaner, *56–60*	55	100
2.	**ZW**	Transformer, 275 watts, *50–66*	155	240
3.	**736**	Steam 2-8-4, 2671WX/2046W/736W Tender, *50–66*	295	370
4.	**50**	Lionel Gang Car, *54–64*	38	65
5.	**KW**	Transformer, 190 watts, *50–65*	100	130
6.	**364**	Conveyor Lumber Loader, *48–57*	95	110
(Tie)				
	2321	Lackawanna Train Master, *54–56*		
		(A) Gray roof	290	420
		(B) Maroon roof	390	630
	2332	Pennsylvania GG-1, *47–49*		
		(A) Black	880	1750
		(B) Green	325	600
9.	**60**	Lionelville Rapid Transit Trolley, *55–58*	110	180
(Tie)				
	6414	Evans Auto Loader w/ 4 cars, *55–66*		
		(A) Early premium cars	44	110
		(B) Four cheap cars w/o trim	300	540
		(C) Four red cars w/ gray bumpers	50	160
		(D) Four yellow cars w/ gray bumpers	150	365
		(E) Dark yellow, gray bumpers		NRS
		(F) Dark brown, chrome bumpers		NRS
		(G) Four brown cars w/ gray bumpers	315	710
		(H) Medium green, chrome bumpers		NRS
		(I) Four green cars w/ gray bumpers	405	890

Lionel Modern Era

			Exc	New
1.	(11711)	Santa Fe F-3 ABA set "8100", "8101", "8102", *91*	450	550
2.	(28052)	N&W Class A 2-6-6-4 Articulated Steam Locomotive "1218", *00*	—	1100
3.	(8606)	B&A 4-6-4 "784", *86 u*	890	1000
4.	(18303)	Amtrak GG-1 "8303", *89*	405	475
5.	(18045)	"777" Commodore Vanderbilt, *96*	—	780
6.	(18007)	Southern Pacific 4-8-4 "4410", *91*	590	620
7.	(29294)	Hellgate Bridge Boxcar "1900-2000", *99 u*	—	80
8.	(18000)	PRR 0-6-0 "8977" *89, 91*	420	475
9.	(18205)	Union Pacific Dash 8-40C "9100", *89*	190	230
10.	(28029)	UP Big Boy 4-8-8-4 Articulated Steam Locomotive "4006", *99–00*	—	1550

ATI Composite Trading Ticker

`Catalog No.•Description•Current price`

Prewar **116 Station** •$1,450 . . . . . .Prewar **400E Steam**
Postwar **455 Operating Oil Derrick** •$190 . . . . . .Postwar
. . . . Postwar **2344 NYC F-3 AA units** $640 . . . . . .
6907 NYC Wood-sided Caboose •$90 . . . . . . Modern **11711**
Steam Turbine Locomotive •$1,350 . . . .

ATI Composite Value

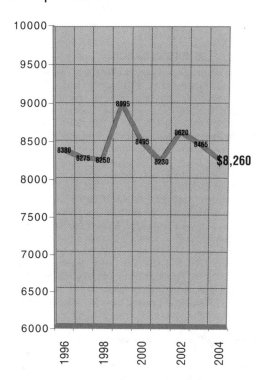

ATI Composite Summary

	Current Value	2003	1996	MSRP
				Percentage change from
2004 Composite	**$8,260**	**-2.4%**	**-1.4%**	**402.6%**
Prewar	$3,600	0.0%	5.9%	6445.5%
Postwar	$2,670	-1.7%	1.5%	1829.2%
Modern	$1,990	-11.2%	-15.3%	37.2%

Locomotive •$2,150 . . . . . . Postwar ZW •$240. . . . .
773 LL 4-6-4 Steam Locomotive w/ 2426W Tender •$1,500 . .
Postwar 3927 Track Cleaning Car •$100 . . . . . .Modern
AT&SF F-3 ABA set •$550 . . . . . . Modern 18010 PRR 6-8-6
. . . .

CTT MARKET BASKET RECAP

by Bob Keller, associate editor of *Classic Toy Trains*

AUCTIONS
Conventional auctions

There are still plenty of auctions going on where you can see (if not touch) the trains you're interested in. What is even better, is that many of these now have the option of permitting you to place absentee bids or even "live" bids via computer. These venerable auction houses include Lloyd Ralston Toys of Stratford, Conn., Stout Auctions of Indianapolis, Ind., and New England Toy Train Exchange of Bridgeport, Conn., among others.

PREWAR: *Engines, rolling stock, accessories & sets*
No. 173E 48x42 layout with original crate $23,500; No. 303 trolley $9,000; No. 890W set with 226E $9,000; No. 251B set with 227 $8,000; No. 29 trolley $7,100; No. 763 Hudson with gray coal pile, no boxes, $6,750; No. 151W set with 225E $5,500; No. 269W set with 225E $5,500; No. 755W Hiawatha set $4,000; No. 400E/400T black locomotive and tender $3,500; No. 318E locomotive $3,500; No. 390E locomotive $2,300; No. 422 Blue Comet Pullman, sealed box dated 1937, $2,200; No. 116 double station, ivory body red roof $2,000; No. 515 Shell tank car, box incomplete $1,750; No. 785W City of Portland set $1,400; No. 44 racing boat $1,100; No. 916 tunnel with original box $900; Lionel executive catalog for 1938 $525

POSTWAR: *Engines, rolling stock, accessories & sets*
No. D-54 crossing signal display $5,250; No. D1601 4x6-foot dealer display $800; No. 6015 Sunoco tank car $3,600; No. 264 lumber loader $225; No. 746 4-8-4 Northern $1,200; No. 773 Hudson (1950) $1,050; No. 773 Hudson (1964 version) with box and inserts $1,000; No. 908 cardstock station (unasembled) $2,800; No. 1464W Anniversary set, MN with boxes $5,600; No. 1587S "Girl's Set" MN $14,500; No. 2031 Rock Island Alcos with original boxes $275; No. 2219W Lackawanna Diesel Freight set $3,200; No. 2245 Texas Special A-B, EX for $1,700; No. 2330 GG-1 EX with box $2,500; No. 2332 GG-1 $1,400; No. 2359 Boston & Maine GP, never run, $875; No. 2373 Canadian Pacific set with original boxes $3,000; No. 2373 Canadian Pacific F3 A-B set $1,550; No. 2368 Baltimore & Ohio F3 A-B set $1,500; No. 2523W Santa Fe set $1,350; No. 4110WS electronic set $1,500; Nos. 8767 and 8768 B&O RDC cars $125; Lionel illuminated dealer's sign $5,300

MODERN: *Engines, rolling stock, accessories & sets*
Lionel Smithsonian seven-car passenger set, MN/OB $4,750; No. 13803 Lionel Classics auto race set $1,050; No. 52018 TCA 1993 3M boxcar $700; No. 18023 Western Maryland shay $700; No. 18043 Chesapeake & Ohio Hudson $650; No. 51000 Lionel Classic Hiawatha set $500; No. 13101 Lionel Classics 384-E locomotive $450; No. 8615 L&N "Big Emma" Berkshire $400; No. 18045

Commodore Vanderbilt MN/OB $400; No 18006 Atlantic Coast Line Hudson with display case $625; No. 13100 Lionel Classics 390-E $400; No. 18016 Northern Pacific 4-8-4 Northern $375; No. 11718 Norfolk Southern unit train set $325

Internet auctions

The digital revolution has changed the way we find and buy toy trains and there's no way we're going to get the genie back in the bottle. While it is still possible to make the buy of a lifetime, more and more sellers are placing reserves, or first bids that effectively establish a reserve bid.

Still, if you live in the middle of Montana and you can't get off to the East coast to attend a major train show or an auction, the internet will make finding those few of a kind items much easier.

PREWAR: *Engines, rolling stock, accessories & sets*
Nos. 412, 413, and 416 State cars (yellow windows) $6,000; Nos. 424, 425, 426 passenger set $4,650; No. 400E locomotive black/brass, w/OB s $3,200; No. 701 0-6-0 switcher $2,751; No. 216 dark green hopper, nickel trim $2,386; No. 213 cream and maroon cattle car $1,815; No. 100 trolley $1,424; No. 217 red caboose, nickel trim $1,376; No. 227 B6 switcher $919; No. 773 Hudson (1950, motor from 763 and re-painted) $919

POSTWAR: *Engines, rolling stock, accessories & sets*
No. 1587 Girl's set $2,650; No. 2360-25 green GG1 w/OB $2,200; No. 2223W Lackawanna freight set w/OB $1,800; No. 2358 Great Northern EP5 $1,799; No. 2360 Tuscan GG-1 $1,375; No. 2367 Wabash set w/OB $1,226; No. 6464-325 B&O Sentinel boxcar $1,199; No. 2373 Canadian Pacific F3 A-A $959; No. 2235W Milwaukee Road set w/OB $954; No. 2322 Virginian Train Master diesel $925

MODERN: *Engines, rolling stock, accessories & sets*
No. 18027 Smithsonian Dreyfuss Hudson $1,600; No. 21876 100th anniversary set $1,500; No. 28011 C&O 2-6-6-6 Allegheny $1,500; No. 28012 Commodore Vanderbilt,red $1,481; No. 28099 Union Pacific 4-6-6-4 Challenger $1,259; No. 38052 Pere Marquette 2-8-4 $1,130; No. 28062 Gold Hudson $1,136; Nos. 14536 and 14539 Santa Fe Fe A-B-A set $1,125; No. 38029 Union Pacific 4-12-2 $1,075; Nos. 38153 F3 A-A set and matching 39109 passenger car set $1,105; No. 38009 Rio Grande 4-6-6-4 $1,100; No. 18043 C&O Hudson $1,099; No. 38066 Elkhorn Lumber Shay $1,030; No. 18027 Smithsonian Dreyfuss Hudson $998; No. 18023 Western Maryland shay $970; No. 21759 Canadian Pacific set $898; No. 28051 B&O EM-1 2-8-8-4 for $897

Market report

In last year's market comments, I wrote that I believed that we were pulling out of the poor conditions that plagued the hobby for the past few years, and I believe that this has proven to be the case.

Although nationally, the overall economy may be starting to slowly spring back; the primary driver for the calming of the waves in our hobby may be the return of more limited production by both Lionel and MTH Electric Trains.

Ergo, if you don't order an item from your local retailer when the catalog comes out, when the catalog comes out, you may not get it at all. This may seem like a return to the "bad old days" of the 80s and 90s where demand was high and prices are higher, but restricting the quantity of product on the market will help the retail network (and the core of the hobby) and Lionel simultaneously.

The dynamics are already in place. Most retailers that I've spoken with over the past year book their preorders and a limited number of "safe" items (hometown roads, always-in-demand accessories, etc.) and order fewer items on speculation. While, as a hobbyist, that might limit my impulse buys, it helps strengthen the model railroading dealer network. Why? Dealers don't buy a lot of merchandise that they end up "blowing out" below cost, just to make their electric bill.

Generally, as with last year's report, top condition or genuinely rare vintage items continue to be hot. Sets, mint locomotives (prewar and postwar), and lionel "doo-dads" like dealer window stickers and shop signs, have robust sales.

More recent production is tougher to gauge. The locomotives in the J. L. Cowen line generally command retail or better, you can still manage to score one with a deep discount if you look hard enough. Diesel locomotives such as the SD40-2 can be a challenge to locate in the right road name, and the recent ultra-detailed F3s are the bright spot of the year—but only if you got your complete A-B-A Santa Fe set via early ordering!

What looks good in the catalogs?

The 2003 Lionel catalogs were pretty darned nice. A variety of products in all price ranges, from el-cheapo $99 steamers to deluxe steam monsters. Limited editions like the nos. 38024 Pennsylvania S1 6-4-4-6 Duplex, the 38053 New York Central 4-8-2 Mohawk, and the newly redesigned F3 diesel will make the competition take note.

Starter sets: The coupling of starter sets with Lionel's new FasTrack is a terrific idea. We received a no. 31928 Great Train Robbery set for review and the first thing I did was grab the track and begin to test it. It has great connectivity, it is fairly easy to assemble, and best of all, it stays together well enough that you can actually lift the loop off the floor (or train table) and it won't pop apart. This is one of those "value-added" elements that should pay off for the Michigan train company.

Upscale sets: I still give the no. 21788 Missile launch Train set two thumbs up. It is well made and is all any postwar kid who wanted one, but didn't get one, could ask for. I was initially put off by the no. 31711 Wabash freight set, but after thinking about it, I concluded it was a pretty good idea. From everything I've seen, this outfit is as close to being "just like the original" as possible. Pullmor motors and Magne-Traction. What more could you ask for. Last but not least, "everyone" is doing a Freedom Train, but only Lionel is doing the original Freedom Train. This will be great for sitting on a shelf, or better, running lickety-split around your layout.

O gauge: The LionMaster line is a brilliant effort to counter the MTH RailKing line, which is becoming more oriented toward scale size. The 38020 T-1 is a superb miniaturization and the variety of 4-6-6-4 Challengers. Comparing the tooling of these locomotives with those of just a few years ago, you're getting $1,000 detail for 2/3 the price! I will be very interested in seeing the no. 38045 New York Central Hudson which, presumable, priced at $599.99, is targeting the crowd attracted by K-Line's economy priced, but big on detail, Hudson. The PA is one of my favorite locomotives and Lionel's investment in new tooling for this baby may set a new standard for detail.

I thought that the H-16-44 diesels looked dopey in the catalog, but in a hands-on setting, I love them. The rounded body, the oval cab windows, and an appearance that is businesslike made this one of my faves for 2003.

Accessories: I'm scratching my head about the "Historic Layout series" (I mean, does anyone care that accessory "A" is based on something on layout "B"? I don't think so. However, this has proven to be a fertile ground for some creative products like the nos. 24137 "Mr. Spiff and Puddles," the 24138 "Playtime playground," 24139 "Duck shooting gallery," and 24140 (with mother walking back and fourth with the baby in the bedroom) are certainly things that you wouldn't expect to see. You may also find yourself wanting to squeeze in "just one more" structure on your layout.

Things I didn't like: For me, at least, Lionel's recent catalogs seem to be on target, there wasn't anything that stood out as excessively "dumb," or way overpriced. The only candidate I had was the $1,500 Union Pacific PA passenger set, but when I did the math, it was no worse than buying separate sale pieces. Great looking set if you can pony up the bucks for it!

Products of Distinction

Attractive middle-weight

Lionel's Ten-wheeler 4-6-0 is one of the most attractive mid-range models on the market. The no. 38042 Chicago & North Western version would be at home on a layout modeling the 1920s through the late 1950s—later if you're modeling a shortline! This rig is also available in the nos. 38043 Frisco, 28098 New York Central, and 38004 Virginian road names.

Missle away!

Stand up and salute our victory in the Cold War with Lionel's no. 18456 Minuteman motorized unit. Offering as part of the Postwar Celebration series, the diminutive switcher heralds back to the train-maker's attempt to get layouts around the nation ready for WW3! Old Nikita only wished he had O Gauge trains like this!

Pastels or primary colors?

The no. 31701 "Boy's" set has fun with the "suggested but rejected" concept of a Boy's train set to complement the 1957 Girl's set. I mean, really, the regular Lionel product line was in "boy's" colors for goodness sake. This is a case where the postwar Lionel Corp. was smart enough to not throw good money after bad. Fast forward 40 years, however, and Lionel LLC targets the collecting community—as well as operators with a sense of humor—with this neat set.

Get ready to rumble!

As hot as today's headlines is the no. 18298 Union Pacific Desert Victory SD40-2. Lionel's superb rendition of the General Motors SD40-2 done up in the Union Pacific's camouflage paint scheme, made it to store shelves in time for the US-Iraq rematch. If you have a less martial disposition, this model is also available in the no. 18299 CP Railroad name.

My breaking back!

Who'd have thought there would be a battle for
Standard gauge supremacy in the year 2004?
Lionel's massive *Hiawatha* and Vanderbilt train
sets showed that there was both room for inno-
vation—and a market—for these total behemoths
of the rails. The locomotives feature first rate
operating capability and the cars have interior
illumination and are detailed down to the seats
in the lavatory!

Shark in the water!

While the execution of the LionMaster T-1 wasn't
quite my cup of tea, the concept and quality of the
model was apparent. It also was a hallmark,
allowing fans of both the Pennsy and art deco-
style streamliners to have one of the most distinc-
tive-looking engines of the late-steam era that
would run on tighter-radius track.

Don't cut yourself on that nose!

The nose of the Lionel E-6 diesel looks sharp enough to slice your finger, and the Southern Railway paint scheme on no, 14544 A-A set looks terrific. The model features first rate operation and an innovative system to channel smoke through all of the locomotive's exhaust stacks!

Up to the challenge?

Lionel's LionMaster series locomotives are first rate products and the firm's rendition of the Union Pacific's Challenger is a top quality product. While the Western Maryland did have 4-6-6-4 Challengers, they didn't quite look like the Union Pacific version. Would that stop me from buying one? No way, because you are getting a great value, good performance, and superb detail in one nice package.

Incoming!

Lionel's no. 21788 missile launch set once more turns the page back to an earlier time when we were "Us" and the Russkies were "Them." From the time I saw this gear advertised on Captain Kangaroo a thousand years ago, I wanted it. Well, this set gives you that thrill with the benefits of modern production and decoration techniques.

Award winner!

You may have a ton of Lionel F3s, but until you have one of the new Lionel F3 rigs, your collection isn't complete. The no. 14536 Santa Fe F3 is astonishing in its level of detail and, thanks to limited production, it is in hot demand. It looks great, runs well, and the largest gripe I could find is the overly bright cab lightbulb. This one is a keeper.

Proof positive

I don't normally get excited by either $60 freight cars or refrigerator cars, but the new series of ultra-detailed reefers, commencing with the no. 17331 Hood's Milk Car are something special. This is proof positive that Lionel is eager to branch out and take some of the turf away from outfits offering ultra-detailed rolling stock.

A moving box with sound

Kinda boxy. Kinda ugly. Kinda cool. That is the Lionel Fairbanks-Morse FM16-44 switcher. With rounded cab windows and a smoother design than the standard Trainmaster body, this switcher managed to look business-like and art-deco-ish at the same time.

Feel the heat

Over the last 50 years, Lionel has produced some pretty anemic models of the Alco FA. This model, however, makes up for that. It is packed with detail, it runs very, very well, and is offered in a striking red freight scheme for the Missouri-Kansas-Texas railroad (no. 38182). If the burnings sands of the great southwest aren't your cup of tea, it also comes in the no. 38147 Great Northern, and 38176 Pennsylvania road names.

Back to basics

Alco cranked out more than 2,200 of its 1,000 horsepower S-2 and S-4 diesel switchers and Lionel is offering a terrific model of it in O gauge. The no. 28530 Northern Pacific S-4 packs heft and some great features into a small package. It is also available as an S-2 switcher in the nos. 28531 Santa Fe, 28532 Lehigh Valley, and 28533 Seaboard road names.

Stick'em up!

My original disposition toward this set was, well, disdain. "Not another general set?" I asked myself. But the no. 31928 Great Train Robbery set has a twist. It is a train robbery set where the robbers can chase the train with a handcar! Cool. And the track is Lionel's new FasTrack. Way cool. And it packs a new 80-watt transformer with accessory outlets! Chillin'. And proving that Lionel "gets it," the firm includes a video for beginner operation.

Section 1
PREWAR 1901–1942

		Good	Exc	Cond/$
001	Steam 4-6-4 (OO), *38–42*	195	410	____[1]
1	Bild-A-Motor, *28–31*	60	140	____[1]
1	Trolley (Std.), *06–14*			
	(A) Cream body, orange band/roof	1900	4750	____[1]
	(B) White body, blue band/roof	1750	4750	____[1]
	(C) Cream body, blue band/roof	1300	3150	____[1]
	(D) Cream body, blue band/roof	2150	5550	____[1]
	(E) Blue, cream band, blue roof	1450	3150	____[1]
1/111	Trolley Trailer (Std.), *06–14*	1000	2700	____[1]
002	Steam 4-6-4 (OO), *39–42*	160	315	____[1]
2	Bild-A-Motor, *28–31*	100	180	____[1]
2	Countershafting, *04–11*		NRS	____
2	Trolley (Std.), *06–16**			
	(A) Yellow, red band	1200	2250	____[1]
	(B) Red, yellow band	1200	2250	____[1]
2/200	Trolley Trailer (Std.), *06–16*	1000	1800	____[1]
003	Steam 4-6-4 (OO), *39–42*			
	(A) With 003W whistling tender	190	395	____[1]
	(B) With 003T non-whistling tender	175	355	____[1]
3	Trolley (Std.), *06–13*			
	(A) Cream, orange band	1400	3100	____[1]
	(B) Cream, dark olive green band	1400	3100	____[1]
	(C) Orange, dark olive green band	1400	3100	____[1]
	(D) Dark green, cream windows	1400	3100	____[1]
	(E) Green, cream window, "BAY SHORE"	1650	3700	____[1]
3/300	Trolley Trailer (Std.), *06–13*	1500	3500	____[1]
004	Steam 4-6-4 (OO), *39–42*			
	(A) With 004W whistling tender	210	345	____[1]
	(B) With 004T non-whistling tender	190	315	____[1]
4	Electric 0-4-0 (O), *28–32**			
	(A) Orange, black frame	550	900	____[1]
	(B) Gray, apple green stripe	580	1050	____[1]
4	Trolley (Std.), *06–12*			
	(A) Cream, dark olive green band	3000	4950	____[1]
	(B) Green or olive green, cream roof	3000	4950	____[1]
4U	#4 Kit form (O), *28–29*	1050	1600	____[1]
5	Electric (2⅞") (See 100)			

		Good	Exc	Cond/$
5	Steam 0-4-0, no tender, Early (Std.), *06–07*			
	(A) "N.Y.C. & H.R.R."	1000	1450	___[1]
	(B) "PENNSYLVANIA"	1400	2300	___[1]
	(C) "N.Y.C. & H.R.R.R." (3 Rs)	1250	2050	___[1]
	(D) "B. & O. R.R."	1500	2400	___[1]
5	Steam 0-4-0, w/ tender, Early Special (Std.), *06–09*	1150	1500	___[1]
5	Steam 0-4-0, no tender, Later (Std.), *10–11*	750	1150	___[1]
5	Steam 0-4-0, w/ tender, Later Special (Std.), *10–11*	830	1400	___[1]
5/51	Steam 0-4-0, w/ tender, Latest (Std.), *12–23*	800	1100	___[1]
6	Steam 4-4-0 (Std.), *06–23*	750	1100	___[1]
6	Steam 0-4-0 Special (Std.), *08–09*	2050	2950	___[1]
7	Steam 4-4-0 (Std.), *10–23**	1850	2300	___[1]
7	Steam 4-4-0 (Std.), *10–23**	1850	2300	___[1]
	Variation 1	—	20	___[1]
	Variation 2	—	30	___[1]
8	Electric 0-4-0 (Std.), *25–32*			
	(A) Maroon, brass windows/trim	235	250	___[1]
	(B) Olive green or mojave w/ brass	155	205	___[1]
	(C) Red, brass or cream window	195	250	___[1]
	(D) Peacock, orange windows	520	750	___[1]
8	Trolley (Std.), *08–14**			
	(A) Cream, orange band and roof	3000	5400	___[1]
	(B) Dark green, cream windows	3000	5400	___[1]
8E	Electric 0-4-0 (Std.), *26–32*			
	(A) Mojave, brass windows/trim	175	240	___[1]
	(B) Red, brass or cream window	130	205	___[1]
	(C) Peacock, orange windows	370	590	___[1]
	(D) Pea green, cream stripe	465	670	___[1]
9	Electric 0-4-0 (Std.), *29**	1200	2150	___[1]
9	Trolley (Std.), *09*	3000	5400	___[1]
9E	Electric 0-4-0 (Std.), *28–35**			
	(A) 0-4-0	700	1250	___[1]
	(B) 2-4-2, two-tone green	880	1600	___[1]
	(C) 2-4-2, gun-metal gray	820	1300	___[1]
9U	Electric 0-4-0 Kit (Std.), *28–29*	1050	2050	___[2]
9	Motor Car (Std.), *09–12*		NRS	___
10	Electric 0-4-0 (Std.), *25–29**			
	(A) Mojave, brass trim	150	215	___[1]
	(B) Gray, brass trim	125	205	___[1]
	(C) Peacock, brass inserts	125	205	___[1]
	(D) Red, cream stripe	580	880	___[1]

		Good	Exc	Cond/$
10	Interurban (Std.), *10–16*			
	(A) Maroon	3000	5750	___[1]
	(B) Dark olive green	1200	2150	___[1]
10E	Electric 0-4-0 (Std.), *26–30*			
	(A) Olive green, black frame		NRS	___
	(B) Peacock, dark green or black frame	345	470	___[1]
	(C) State brown, dark green frame	435	630	___[1]
	(D) Gray, black frame	165	220	___[1]
	(E) Red, cream stripe	610	890	___[1]
011	Switches, pair (O), *33–37*	20	35	___[1]
11	Flatcar, Early (Std.), *06–11*	150	360	___[1]
11	Flatcar, Later (Std.), *11–16*	50	90	___[1]
11	Flatcar, Latest (Std.), *16–18*	50	90	___[1]
11	Flatcar, Lionel Corp. (Std.), *18–26*	50	80	___[1]
012	Switches, pair (O), *27–33*	21	38	___[1]
12	Gondola, Early (Std.), *06–11*	600	720	___[1]
12	Gondola, Later(Std), *11–16*	50	90	___[1]
12	Gondola, Latest (Std.), *16–18*	45	70	___[1]
12	Gondola, Lionel Corp. (Std.), *18–26*	50	70	___[1]
013	(2) 012 Switches and 439 Panel Board, *27–33*	120	190	___[1]
13	Cattle Car, Early (Std.), *06–11*	300	450	___[1]
13	Cattle Car, Later (Std.), *11–16*	150	225	___[1]
13	Cattle Car, Latest (Std.), *16–18*	65	115	___[1]
13	Cattle Car, Lionel Corp. (Std.), *18–26*	65	115	___[1]
0014	Boxcar (OO), *38–42*			
	(A) Yellow, "Lionel Lines"	80	145	___[1]
	(B) Tuscan body, "PENNSYLVANIA"	50	90	___[1]
14	Boxcar, Early (Std.), *06–11*	195	435	___[1]
14	Boxcar, Later (Std.), *11–16*	80	105	___[1]
14	Boxcar, Latest (Std.), *16–18*	80	105	___[1]
14	Boxcar, Lionel Corp. (Std.), *18–26*	80	105	___[1]
0015	Tank Car (OO), *38–42*			
	(A) Silver, "SUN OIL"	40	70	___[1]
	(B) Black, "SHELL"	40	70	___[1]
15	Oil Car, Early (Std.), *06–11*	200	360	___[1]
15	Oil Car, Later (Std.), *11–16*	75	115	___[1]
15	Oil Car, Latest (Std.), *16–18*	75	115	___[1]
15	Oil Car, Lionel Corp. (Std.), *18–26*	75	115	___[1]
0016	Hopper Car (OO), *38–42*			
	(A) Gray	75	145	___[1]
	(B) Black	75	125	___[1]
16	Ballast (Dump) Car, Early (Std.), *06–26*	245	395	___[1]
16	Ballast (Dump) Car, Later (Std.), *11–16*	95	175	___[1]

		Good	Exc	Cond/$
16	Ballast (Dump) Car, Latest (Std.), *16–18*	95	175	___ [1]
16	Ballast (Dump) Car, Lionel Corp. (Std.), *18–26*	95	175	___ [1]
0017	Caboose (OO), *38–42*	48	90	___ [1]
17	Caboose, Early (Std.), *06–11*	220	440	___ [1]
17	Caboose, Later (Std.), *11–16*	70	135	___ [1]
17	Caboose, Latest (Std.), *16–18*	70	135	___ [1]
17	Caboose, Lionel Corp. (Std.), *18–26*	50	90	___ [1]
18	Pullman (Std.), *08*			
	(A) Dark olive green, unremovable roof	700	2150	___ [1]
	(B) Dark olive green, removable roof	90	195	___ [1]
	(C) Yellow-orange, removable roof	275	870	___ [1]
	(D) Orange, removable roof	80	180	___ [1]
	(E) Mojave, removable roof	275	870	___ [1]
18	Pullman (Std.), *11–13*		NRS	___
18	Pullman (Std.), *13–15*	150	270	___ [1]
18	Pullman (Std.), *15–18*	150	270	___ [1]
18	Pullman (Std.), *18–22*	80	135	___ [1]
18	Pullman (Std.), *23–26*	270	530	___ [1]
19	Combine (Std.), *08*			
	(A) Dark olive green, unremovable roof	1100	2600	___ [1]
	(B) Dark olive green, removable roof	80	125	___ [1]
	(C) Yellow-orange, removable roof	225	375	___ [1]
	(D) Orange, removable roof	100	180	___ [1]
	(E) Mojave, removable roof	275	870	___ [1]
19	Combine (Std.), *11–13*		NRS	___
19	Combine (Std.), *13–15*	200	270	___ [1]
19	Combine (Std.), *15–18*	200	270	___ [1]
19	Combine (Std.), *18–22*	80	135	___ [1]
19	Combine (Std.), *23–26*	265	520	___ [1]
020	90° Crossover (O), *15–42*	2	5	___ [1]
020	90° Crossover (O), *15–42*	2	5	___ [1]
020X	45° Crossover (O), *17–42*	2.50	7	___ [1]
20	90° Crossover (Std.), *09–32*	4	9	___ [1]
20	Direct Current Reducer, *06*	—	195	___ [1]
20X	45° Crossover (Std.), *28–32*	5	9	___ [1]
021	Switches, pair (O), *15–37*	20	46	___ [1]
21	Switches, pair (Std.), *15–25*	40	70	___ [2]
21	90° Crossover (Std.), *06*	10	18	___ [1]
022	Switches, pair, Remote (O), *38–42*	35	70	___ [1]
22	Switches, pair (Std.), *06–25*	47	75	___ [1]
023	Bumper (O), *15–33*	15	37	___ [1]
23	Bumper (Std.), *06–23*	18	34	___ [1]

		Good	Exc	Cond/$
0024	PRR Boxcar (OO), *39–42*	45	80	____[1]
24	Railway Station (Std.), *06*		NRS	____
025	Bumper (O), *28–42*	25	31	____[1]
0025	Tank Car (OO), *39–42*			
	(A) Black, "SHELL"	40	80	____[1]
	(B) Silver, "SUNOCO"	40	80	____[1]
25	Open Station (Std.), *06*		NRS	____
25	Bumper (Std.), *27–42*	26	38	____[1]
26	Passenger Bridge (Std.), *06*	—	45	____[1]
0027	Caboose (OO), *39–42*	40	80	____[1]
27	Lighting set, *11–23*	15	41	____[1]
27	Station (Std.), *09–12*		NRS	____
28	Double Station w/ dome, *09–12*		NRS	____
29	Day Coach (Std.), *07–22*			
	(A) Dark olive green, 9-window	1500	3000	____[2]
	(B) Maroon, 10-window body	1200	1500	____[2]
	(C) Dark green, 10-window body	3000	4500	____[2]
	(D) Dark olive green, 10-window	680	1000	____[2]
	(E) Dark green, 10-window body	500	900	____[2]
29	(See #3 Trolley)			
31	Combine (Std.), *21–25*			
	(A) Maroon	70	90	____[1]
	(B) Orange	115	170	____[1]
	(C) Dark olive green	70	90	____[1]
	(D) Brown	75	95	____[1]
32	Mail Car (Std.), *21–25*			
	(A) Maroon	85	110	____[1]
	(B) Orange	105	160	____[1]
	(C) Dark olive green	65	85	____[1]
	(D) Brown	70	90	____[1]
32	Miniature Figures, *09–18*	75	135	____[1]
33	Electric 0-6-0, Early (Std.), *13*			
	(A) Dark olive green, NYC in oval	90	175	____[1]
	(B) Black, NYC LINES in oval	440	950	____[1]
	(C) Dark olive green, NYC	440	950	____[1]
	(D) "PENNSYLVANIA RAILROAD"	580	1250	____[1]
33	Electric 0-4-0, Later (Std.), *13–24*			
	(A) Dark olive green or black, NYC	85	150	____[1]
	(B) Black, lettered "C & O"	395	720	____[1]
	(C) Maroon, red, or peacock	340	620	____[1]
34	Electric 0-6-0, Early (Std.), *12*	450	810	____[1]
34	Electric 0-4-0 (Std.), *13*	200	385	____[1]

35	Blvd. Lamp, 6⅛" high, *40–42*	23	45	___[1]
35	Pullman (Std.), *12–13*			
	(A) Dark blue	470	900	___[1]
	(B) Dark olive green	150	205	___[1]
35	Pullman (Std.), *14–16*			
	(A) Dark olive green, maroon windows	50	70	___[1]
	(B) Maroon, green windows	85	105	___[1]
	(C) Orange, maroon windows	125	170	___[1]
35	Pullman (Std.), *15–18*	50	70	___[1]
35	Pullman (Std.), *18–23*			
	(A) Dark olive green, maroon windows	36	50	___[1]
	(B) Maroon, green windows	30	45	___[1]
	(C) Orange, maroon windows	110	195	___[1]
	(D) Brown, green windows	36	50	___[1]
35	Pullman (Std.), *24*	40	55	___[1]
35	Pullman (Std.), *25–26*	40	55	___[1]
36	Observation (Std.), *12–13*			
	(A) Dark blue	315	810	___[1]
	(B) Dark olive green	125	180	___[1]
36	Observation (Std.), *14–16*			
	(A) Dark olive green, maroon windows	70	95	___[1]
	(B) Maroon, green windows	50	70	___[1]
	(C) Orange, maroon windows	180	290	___[1]
	(D) Brown, green windows	60	75	___[1]
36	Observation (Std.), *15–18*	60	80	___[1]
36	Observation (Std.), *18–23*			
	(A) Dark olive green, maroon windows	40	55	___[1]
	(B) Maroon, green windows	40	55	___[1]
	(C) Orange, maroon windows	120	205	___[1]
	(D) Brown, green windows	40	55	___[1]
36	Observation (Std.), *24*	40	55	___[1]
36	Observation (Std.), *25–26*	40	55	___[1]
38	Electric 0-4-0 (Std.), *13–24*			
	(A) Black	100	120	___[1]
	(B) Red	475	680	___[1]
	(C) Mojave or pea green	405	540	___[1]
	(D) Dark green	270	360	___[1]
	(E) Brown	270	315	___[1]
	(F) Red, cream trim	405	540	___[1]
	(G) Maroon	170	270	___[1]
	(H) Gray	110	125	___[1]
40	(See #4 Trolley)			

		Good	Exc	Cond/$
41	Accessory Contactor, *37–42*	1	3	___¹
042	Switches, pair (O), *38–42*	17	39	___¹
42	Electric 0-4-4-0, square hood, Early (Std.), *12**	900	1450	___¹
42	Electric 0-4-4-0, round hood, Later (Std.), *13–23*			
	(A) Black or gray	280	475	___¹
	(B) Maroon	1250	2050	___¹
	(C) Dark gray	375	600	___¹
	(D) Dark green or mojave	500	800	___¹
	(E) Peacock	1100	1800	___¹
	(F) Olive or dark olive green	750	1200	___¹
043/43	Bild-A-Motor Gear set, *29*	—	85	___¹
43	Boat, Runabout, *33–36, 39–41*	435	640	___¹
0044	Boxcar (OO), *39–42*	32	70	___¹
0044K	Boxcar Kit (OO), *39–42*	75	120	___¹
44	Boat, Speedster, *35–36*	500	780	___¹
0045	Tank Car (OO), *39–42*			
	(A) Black, "SHELL"	40	80	___¹
	(B) Silver, "SUNOCO"	40	80	___¹
0045K	Tank Car Kit (OO), *39–42*	75	120	___¹
45/045/45N	Automatic Gateman, *35–42*	40	70	___¹
0046	Hopper Car (OO), *39–42*	45	80	___¹
0046K	Hopper Car Kit (OO), *39–42*			
	(A) "SOUTHERN PACIFIC"	75	135	___¹
	(B) "READING"		NRS	___
46	Crossing Gate, *39–42*	75	120	___¹
0047	Caboose (OO), *39–42*	35	70	___¹
0047K	Caboose Kit (OO), *39–42*	75	135	___¹
47	Crossing Gate, *39–42*	85	150	___²
48W	Whistle Station, *37–42*	32	75	___¹
49	Lionel Airport, *37–39*	160	410	___¹
50	Airplane, *36–39*	120	280	___¹
50	Electric 0-4-0 (Std.), *24*			
	(A) Dark green or dark gray	125	225	___¹
	(B) Maroon	315	600	___¹
	(C) Mojave	155	300	___¹
50	Cardboard Train, Cars, Accessory (O), *43**	200	360	___¹
51	Steam 0-4-0, 5 Late eight-wheel (Std.), *12–23*	800	1150	___¹
51	Lionel Airport, *36, 38*	155	395	___¹
52	Lamp Post, *33–41*	40	75	___¹
53	Electric 0-4-4-0, Early (Std.), *12–14*	1200	2450	___¹

		Good	Exc	Cond/$
53	Electric 0-4-0, Later (Std.), *15–19*			
	(A) Maroon	500	900	___[1]
	(B) Mojave	670	1350	___[1]
	(C) Dark olive green	560	1150	___[1]
53	Electric 0-4-0, Latest (Std.), *20–21*	200	450	___[1]
53	Lamp Post, *31–42*	30	43	___[1]
53	Electric 0-6-6-0, Early (Std.), *11*		NRS	___
54	Electric 0-4-4-0, Early (Std.), *12**	2500	4050	___[1]
54	Electric 0-4-4-0, Late (Std.), *13–23*	1800	2700	___[1]
54	Lamp Post, *29–35*	45	80	___[1]
55	Airplane w/ stand, *37–39*	165	450	___[1]
56	Lamp Post, removable lens and cap, *24–42*	34	60	___[3]
57	Lamp Post w/ street names, *22–42*	45	85	___[1]
58	Lamp Post, 7⅜" high, *22–42*	34	48	___[4]
59	Lamp Post, 8¾" high, *20–36*	38	70	___[2]
60/060	Telegraph Post (Std./O), *29–42*	11	23	___[1]
60	Electric 0-4-0, F.A.O.S. (Std.), *15 u*		NRS	___
61	Electric 0-4-4-0, F.A.O.S. (Std.), *15 u*		NRS	___
61	Lamp Post, one globe, *14–36*	40	65	___[2]
62	Electric 0-4-0, F.A.O.S. (Std.), *24–32 u*		NRS	___
62	Semaphore, *20–32*	25	50	___[1]
63	Lamp Post, two globes, *33–42*	135	230	___[1]
63	Semaphore, *15–21*	25	50	___[1]
64	Lamp Post, *40–42*	36	65	___[2]
64	Semaphore, 6¾" high, *15–21*	30	60	___[1]
65	Semaphore, one-arm, *15–26*	30	60	___[1]
65	Whistle Controller, *35*	5	7	___[1]
66	Semaphore, two-arm, *15–26*	35	70	___[1]
66	Whistle Controller, *36–39*	9	10	___[1]
67	Lamp Post, *15–32*	85	145	___[1]
67	Whistle Controller, *36–39*	4	8	___[1]
68/068	Crossing Sign, *25–42*	11	17	___[1]
69/069/69N	Electric Warning Signal, *21–42*	33	70	___[1]
70	Outfit: (2) 62s (1) 59 (1) 68, *21–32*	55	130	___[1]
071	(6) 060 Telegraph Poles (Std.), *24–42*	70	160	___[1]
71	(6) 60 Telegraph Poles (Std.), *29–42*	70	160	___[1]
0072	Switches, pair (OO), *38–42*	170	310	___[1]
0074	Boxcar (OO), *39–42*	40	80	___[1]
0075	Tank Car (OO), *39–42*	50	100	___[1]
076/76	Block Signal, *23–28*	25	75	___[1]
76	Warning Bell and Shack, *39–42*	60	250	___[1]
0077	Caboose (OO), *39–42*	40	70	___[1]
77/077/77N	Automatic Crossing Gate, *23–39*	28	55	___[1]

		Good	Exc	Cond/$
78/078	Train Signal (Std.), *24–32*	40	100	___¹
79	Flashing Signal, *28–40*	115	130	___¹
80	Automobile, *12–16*	550	900	___¹
80/080/80N Semaphore (Std), *26–42*		48	125	___¹
81	Automobile, *12–16*	720	1450	___¹
81	Controlling Rheostat, *27–33*	2	5	___¹
82/082/82N Semaphore, *27–42*		55	110	___¹
83	Flashing Traffic Signal, *27–42*	60	200	___¹
084	Semaphore, *28–32*	60	100	___¹
84	Semaphore, *27–32*	55	85	___¹
84	(2) Automobiles, *12–16*	1400	2900	___¹
85	Telegraph Pole (Std.), *29–42*	15	27	___¹
85	(2) Automobiles, *12–16*	1400	2900	___¹
86	(6) Telegraph Poles, *29–42*	65	120	___¹
87	Flashing Crossing Signal, *27–42*	75	165	___¹
88	Battery Rheostat, *15–27*	3	7	___¹
88	Rheostat Controller, *33–42*	3	5	___¹
89	Flag Pole, *23–34*	38	75	___¹
90	Flag Pole, *27–42*	39	85	___¹
91	Circuit Breaker, *30–42*	34	60	___²
092	Signal Tower, *23–27*	120	190	___¹
92	Floodlight Tower, *31–42**	120	265	___⁴
93	Water Tower, *31–42*	70	135	___¹
94	High Tension Tower, *32–42**	130	270	___¹
95	Controlling Rheostat, *34–42*	2.50	6	___¹
96	Coal Elevator, manual, *38–40*	170	230	___¹
097	Telegraph set (O)	50	75	___¹
97	Coal Elevator, *38–42*	145	285	___³
98	Coal Bunker, *38–40*	200	385	___¹
99/099/99N Train Control, *32–42*		44	145	___¹
100	Electric Loco (2⅞"), *03–05**	2900	5200	___¹
100	Trolley (Std.), *10–16*			
	(A) Blue, white windows	1300	2700	___¹
	(B) Blue, cream windows	1850	3600	___¹
	(C) Red, cream windows	1300	2700	___¹
100	(2) Bridge Approaches (Std.), *20–31*	20	36	___¹
100	Wooden Gondola (2⅞"), *01*		NRS	___
101	Bridge Span (2) Approaches (Std.), *20–31*	60	115	___¹
101	Summer Trolley (Std.), *10–13*	1300	2700	___¹
102	(2) Bridge Spans (2) Approaches (Std.), *20–31*	65	155	___¹
103	Bridge (Std.), *13–16*	50	70	___¹
103	(3) Bridge Spans (2) Approaches (Std.), *20–31*	60	145	___¹
104	Bridge Span (Std.), *20–31*	20	41	___¹

		Good	Exc	Cond/$
104	Tunnel (Std.), *09–14*	50	135	___[1]
105	Bridge (Std.), *11–14*	40	70	___[1]
105	(2) Bridge Approaches (O), *20–31*	50	70	___[1]
106	Bridge Span, (2) Approaches (O), *20–31*	30	65	___[1]
107	DC Reducer, 110V, *23–32*		NRS	___
108	(2) Bridge Spans, (2) Approaches (O), *20–31*	50	90	___[1]
109	(3) Bridge Spans, (2) Approaches (O), *20–32*	50	115	___[1]
109	Tunnel (Std.), *13–14*	30	70	___[1]
110	Bridge Span (O), *20–31*	12	23	___[1]
111	Box of 50 Bulbs, *20–31*	50	90	___[1]
112	Gondola, Early (Std.), *10–12*	195	350	___[1]
112	Gondola, Later (Std.), *12–16*	40	65	___[1]
112	Gondola, Latest (Std.), *16–18*	40	65	___[1]
112	Gondola, Lionel Corp. (Std.), *18–26*	40	65	___[1]
112	Station, *31–35*	155	285	___[1]
113	Cattle Car, Later (Std.), *12–16*	50	70	___[1]
113	Cattle Car, Latest (Std.), *16–18*	50	70	___[1]
113	Cattle Car, Lionel Corp. (Std.), *18–26*	40	55	___[1]
113	Station, *31–34*	150	295	___[1]
114	Boxcar, Later (Std.), *12–16*	50	90	___[1]
114	Boxcar, Latest (Std.), *16–18*	40	70	___[1]
114	Boxcar, Lionel Corp. (Std.), *18–26*	40	70	___[1]
114	Station, *31–34*	530	1200	___[1]
115	Station, *35–42**	220	385	___[1]
116	Station, *35–42**	640	1450	___[2]
116	Ballast Car, Early and Later (Std.), *10–16*	75	100	___[1]
116	Ballast Car, Latest (Std.), *16–18*	55	95	___[1]
116	Ballast Car, Lionel Corp. (Std.), *18–26*	55	95	___[1]
117	Caboose, Early (Std.), *12*	60	70	___[1]
117	Caboose, Later (Std.), *12–16*	50	70	___[1]
117	Caboose, Latest (Std.), *16–18*	50	70	___[1]
117	Caboose, Lionel Corp. (Std.), *18–26*	43	70	___[1]
117	Station, *36–42*	110	285	___[1]
118	Tunnel, 8" long (O), *22–32*	20	55	___[1]
118L	Tunnel, 8" long, *27*	20	55	___[1]
119	Tunnel, 12" long, *20–42*	25	60	___[1]
119L	Tunnel, 12" long, *27–33*	20	55	___[1]
120	Tunnel, 17" long, *22–27*	27	75	___[1]
120L	Tunnel, *27–42*	60	125	___[1]
121	Station (Std.), *09–16*			
	(A) 14" x 10" x 9"		NRS	___
	(B) 13" x 9" x 13"	150	300	___[1]

		Good	Exc	Cond/$
121	Station (Std.), *20–26*	75	150	____[1]
121X	Station (Std.), *17–19*	110	255	____[1]
122	Station (Std.), *20–30*	85	165	____[2]
123	Station (Std.), *20–23*	75	205	____[1]
123	Tunnel, 18½" long (O), *33–42*	85	205	____[1]
124	Station, "Lionel City", *20–36**			
	(A) Tan or gray base, pea green	90	180	____[1]
	(B) Pea green base, red roof	200	360	____[1]
125	Station, "Lionelville", *23–25*	85	195	____[1]
125	Track Template, *38*	1	4	____[1]
126	Station, "Lionelville", *23–36*	85	185	____[1]
127	Station, "Lionel Town", *23–36*	80	160	____[1]
128	124 Station & Terrace, *31–34**	900	1900	____[1]
128	115 Station & Terrace, *35–42**	900	1900	____[1]
129	Terrace, *28–42**	600	1100	____[1]
130	Tunnel, 26" long, *20–36*	100	450	____[1]
130L	Tunnel, 26" long, *27–33*	150	450	____[1]
131	Corner Display, *24–28*	125	295	____[1]
132	Corner Grass Plot, *24–28*	125	295	____[1]
133	Heart Shaped Plot, *24–28*	125	295	____[1]
134	Oval Shaped Plot, *24–28*	125	300	____[1]
134	Station, "Lionel City", w/ stop, *37–42*	200	340	____[1]
135	Circular Plot, *24–28*	125	295	____[1]
136	Large Elevation, *24–28*		NRS	____
136	Station, "Lionelville", w/ stop, *37–42*	75	180	____[1]
140L	Tunnel, 37" long, *27–32*	400	900	____[1]
150	Electric 0-4-0, Early (O), *17*	90	160	____[1]
150	Electric 0-4-0, Late (O), *18–25*			
	(A) Brown, brown or olive windows	95	150	____[1]
	(B) Maroon, dark olive windows	90	135	____[1]
152	Electric 0-4-0 (O), *17–27*			
	(A) Dark green	90	135	____[1]
	(B) Gray	115	160	____[1]
	(C) Mojave	340	680	____[1]
	(D) Peacock	340	680	____[1]
152	Crossing Gate, *40–42*	19	45	____[2]
153	Block Signal, *40–42*	23	45	____[2]
153	Electric 0-4-0 (O), *24–25*			
	(A) Dark green	100	160	____[1]
	(B) Gray	100	160	____[1]
	(C) Mojave	100	160	____[1]
154	Electric 0-4-0 (O), *17–23*	100	180	____[1]

		Good	Exc	Cond/$
154	Highway Signal, *40–42*	21	47	___¹
	(A) Black Base	21	47	___¹
	(B) Orange base	35	90	___¹
155	Freight Shed, *30–42**			
	(A) Yellow base, orange floor	180	320	___²
	(B) White base, terra-cotta floor	240	400	___²
156	Electric 4-4-4 (O), *17–23*			
	(A) Dark green	475	810	___¹
	(B) Maroon	540	890	___¹
	(C) Olive green	600	1050	___¹
	(D) Gray	670	1200	___¹
156	Electric 0-4-0 (O), *17–23*	400	720	___¹
156	Station Platform, *39–42*	90	155	___²
156X	Electric 0-4-0 (O), *23–24*			
	(A) Maroon	380	495	___¹
	(B) Olive green	440	550	___¹
	(C) Gray	530	710	___¹
	(D) Brown	470	600	___¹
157	Hand Truck, *30–32*	25	41	___¹
158	Electric 0-4-0 (O), *19–23*			
	(A) Gray, red windows	75	205	___¹
	(B) Black	95	250	___¹
158	(2) 156s and (1) 136, *40–42*	110	280	___¹
159	Block Actuator, *40*	10	27	___¹
161	Baggage Truck, *30–32**	44	85	___¹
162	Dump Truck, *30–32**	40	75	___¹
163	(2) 157 (1) 162 (1) 161, boxed, *30–42**	190	310	___¹
164	Log Loader, *40–42*	125	225	___³
165	Magnetic Crane, *40–42*	220	310	___³
166	Whistle Controller, *40–42*	3	7	___¹
167	Whistle Controller, *40–42*	5	15	___²
167X	Whistle Controller (OO), *40–42*	5	12	___¹
169	Controller, *40–42*	3	7	___¹
170	DC Reducer, 220V, *14–38*	3	7	___¹
171	DC to AC Inverter, 110V, *36–42*	3	15	___¹
172	DC to AC Inverter, 229V, *39–42*	3	7	___¹
180	Pullman (Std.), *11–13*			
	(A) Maroon body and roof	125	180	___¹
	(B) Brown body and roof	125	235	___¹
180	Pullman (Std.), *13–15*	80	160	___¹
180	Pullman (Std.), *15–18*	80	160	___¹
180	Pullman (Std.), *18–22*	80	135	___¹

		Good	Exc	Cond/$
181	Combine (Std.), *11–13*			
	(A) Maroon, dark olive doors	125	180	___1
	(B) Brown, dark olive doors	125	180	___1
	(C) Yellow-orange, orange door	350	495	___1
181	Combine (Std.), *13–15*	80	160	___1
181	Combine (Std.), *15–18*	80	160	___1
181	Combine (Std.), *18–22*	80	135	___1
182	Observation (Std.), *11–13*			
	(A) Maroon, dark olive doors	125	180	___1
	(B) Brown, dark olive doors	125	180	___1
	(C) Yellow-orange, orange door	350	495	___1
182	Observation (Std.), *13–15*	80	160	___1
182	Observation (Std.), *15–18*	80	160	___1
182	Observation (Std.), *18–22*	80	135	___1
183	Pullman (Std.)		NM	___
184	Bungalow, Illuminated, *23–32**	65	110	___1
184	Combine (Std.), *11*		NM	___
185	Bungalow, *23–24*	50	115	___1
185	Observation (Std.), *11*		NM	___
186	(5) 184 Bungalows, *23–32*	195	610	___1
186	Log Loader Outfit, *40–41*	130	340	___1
187	(5) 185 Bungalows, *23–24*	165	590	___1
188	Elevator and Car set, *38–41*	115	370	___1
189	Villa, Illuminated, *23–32**	170	195	___1
190	Observation (Std.), *08*			
	(A) Dark olive green, unremovable roof	1150	2600	___1
	(B) Dark olive green, removable roof	100	180	___1
	(C) Yellow-orange, removable roof	280	540	___1
	(D) Orange, removable roof	100	180	___1
	(E) Mojave, removable roof	345	870	___1
190	Observation (Std.), *11–13*		NRS	___
190	Observation (Std.), *13–15*	200	295	___1
190	Observation (Std.), *15–18*	200	295	___1
190	Observation (Std.), *18–22*	80	135	___1
190	Observation (Std.), *23–26*	230	475	___1
191	Villa, Illuminated, *23–32**	140	275	___1
192	Villa set, Illuminated: (1) 189; (1) 191; (2) 184, *27–32*	—	800	___1
193	Accessory set, boxed, *27–29*	150	325	___1
194	Accessory set, boxed, *27–29*	100	325	___1
195	Terrace, *27–30*	350	740	___1
196	Accessory set, *27*	200	335	___1
200	Electric Express (2⅞"), *03*	4150	5600	___1

No.	Description	Good	Exc	Cond/$
200	Turntable, *28–33**	85	190	___¹
200	Wooden Gondola (2⅞"), *01–02*		NRS	___
200	Trailer, matches #2 Trolley (Std.), *11–16*	—	2400	___¹
200	Electric Express (2⅞"), *03–05**	4000	6300	___¹
201	Steam 0-6-0 (O), *40–42*			
	(A) With 2201B tender w/ bell	375	760	___¹
	(B) With 2201T tender w/o bell	345	690	___¹
202	Summer Trolley (Std.), *10–13*			
	(A) "ELECTRIC RAPID TRANSIT"	1300	2700	___¹
	(B) "PRESTON ST."	3250	4500	___¹
203	Armored 0-4-0 (O), *17–21*	1100	1800	___¹
203	Steam 0-6-0 (O), *40–42*			
	(A) With 2203B tender w/ bell	400	590	___¹
	(B) With 2203T tender w/o bell	365	550	___¹
204	Steam 2-4-2 (O), *40–42 u*			
	(A) Black locomotive	55	105	___¹
	(B) Gun-metal gray locomotive	80	165	___¹
205	(3) Merch. Containers, *30–38**	130	290	___¹
206	Sack of Coal, *38–42*	5	16	___¹
208	Tool set, boxed, *34–42**	55	150	___¹
0209	Barrels, *34–42*	5	14	___¹
209	Wooden Barrels, *34–42*	8	19	___¹
210	Switches, pair (Std.), *26, 34–42*	42	75	___¹
211	Flatcar (Std.), *26–40**	110	190	___¹
212	Gondola (Std.), *26–40**			
	(A) Gray or green	100	205	___¹
	(B) Maroon	75	135	___¹
213	Cattle Car (Std.), *26–40**			
	(A) Mojave, maroon roof	180	400	___¹
	(B) Terra-cotta, green or maroon roof	130	285	___¹
214	Boxcar (Std.), *26–40**			
	(A) Terra-cotta, green roof	195	295	___¹
	(B) Cream body, orange roof	150	270	___¹
	(C) Yellow, brown roof	300	495	___¹
214R	Refrigerator Car (Std.), *29–40**			
	(A) Ivory or white, peacock roof	325	495	___¹
	(B) White, light blue nickel roof	435	720	___¹
215	Tank Car (Std.), *26–40**			
	(A) Pea green	150	215	___¹
	(B) Ivory	220	360	___¹
	(C) Silver	315	720	___¹
216	Hopper Car (Std.), *26–38**			
	(A) Brass plates	195	335	___¹

		Good	Exc	Cond/$
	(B) Nickel plates	445	1100	____1
217	Caboose (Std.), *26–40* *			
	(A) Orange, maroon roof	250	510	____1
	(B) Red, peacock roof	120	245	____1
	(C) Red body/roof, white door	150	320	____1
217	Lighting set, *14–23*		NRS	____
218	Dump Car (Std.), *26–38* *	210	350	____2
219	Crane (Std.), *26–40* *			
	(A) Peacock, red boom	135	240	____3
	(B) Yellow, light green boom	270	400	____3
	(C) Ivory, light green boom	270	435	____3
	(D) Cream, red boom	130	305	____3
	(E) White, green boom	300	470	____3
220	Floodlight Car (Std.), *31–40* *			
	(A) Terra-cotta base	225	385	____2
	(B) Green base	340	485	____2
220	Switches, pair (Std.), *26* *	25	90	____1
222	Switches, pair (Std.), *26–32*	40	100	____1
223	Switches, pair (Std.), *32–42*	40	100	____1
224/224E	Steam 2-6-2 (O), *38–42*			
	(A) Black, die-cast 2224 tender	155	290	____1
	(B) Black, plastic 2224 tender	110	195	____1
	(C) Gun-metal, die-cast 2224 tender	385	950	____1
	(D) Gun-metal, 2689 tender	120	210	____1
225	222 Switches, 439 Panel, *29–32*	105	235	____2
225/225E	Steam 2-6-2 (O), *38–42*			
	(A) Black, 2235 or 2245 tender	210	370	____1
	(B) Black, 2235 plastic tender	185	320	____1
	(C) Gun-metal, 2225 or 2265 tender	200	360	____1
	(D) Gun-metal, 2235 die-cast tender	285	730	____1
226/226E	Steam 2-6-4 (O), *38–41*	345	670	____1
227	Steam 0-6-0 (O), *39–42*			
	(A) With 2227B tender w/ bell	600	1250	____2
	(B) With 2227T tender w/o bell	600	1150	____2
228	Steam 0-6-0 (O), *39–42*			
	(A) With 2228B tender w/ bell	600	1250	____1
	(B) With 2228T tender w/o bell	600	1150	____1
229	Steam 2-4-2 (O), *39–42*			
	(A) Black or gun-metal w/ 2689W	155	280	____2
	(B) Black or gun-metal w/ 2689T	120	200	____2
	(C) Black w /2666W whistle tender	155	280	____2
	(D) Black w /2666T non-whistle tender	120	200	____2
230	Steam 0-6-0 (O), *39–42*	1000	2050	____1

		Good	Exc	Cond/$
231	Steam 0-6-0 (O), *39*	1000	1800	____[1]
232	Steam 0-6-0 (O), *40–42*	1000	1800	____[1]
233	Steam 0-6-0 (O), *40–42*	1000	1800	____[1]
238	Steam 4-4-2 (O), *39–40 u*	400	710	____[2]
238E	Steam 4-4-2 (O), *36–38*			
	(A) W/265W or 2225W whistle tender	280	365	____[1]
	(B) W/265 or 2225T non-whistling tender	275	360	____[1]
248	Electric 0-4-0 (O), *27–32*	130	240	____[1]
249/249E	Steam 2-4-2 (O), *36–39*			
	(A) Gun-metal, 265T or 265W tender	100	200	____[1]
	(B) Black, 265W tender	110	210	____[1]
250	Electric 0-4-0, Early (O), *26*	125	220	____[1]
250	Electric 0-4-0, Late (O), *34*			
	(A) Yellow-orange, terra-cotta frame	145	245	____[1]
	(B) Terra-cotta body, maroon frame	160	275	____[1]
250E	Steam 4-4-2 Hiawatha (O), *35–42**	470	1100	____[1]
251	Electric 0-4-0 (O), *25–32*			
	(A) Gray body, red windows	190	340	____[1]
	(B) Red body, ivory stripe	215	410	____[1]
	(C) Red body, w/o ivory stripe	200	380	____[1]
251E	Electric 0-4-0 (O), *27–32*			
	(A) Red body, ivory stripe	225	425	____[1]
	(B) Red body, w/o ivory stripe	215	395	____[1]
	(C) Gray, red trim	195	350	____[1]
252	Electric 0-4-0 (O), *26–32*			
	(A) Peacock or olive green	95	190	____[2]
	(B) Terra-cotta or yellow-orange	125	255	____[2]
252E	Electric 0-4-0 (O), *33–35*			
	(A) Terra-cotta	145	250	____[1]
	(B) Yellow-orange	125	205	____[1]
253	Electric 0-4-0 (O), *24–32*			
	(A) Maroon	180	430	____[3]
	(B) Dark green	105	195	____[3]
	(C) Mojave	105	235	____[3]
	(D) Terra-cotta	180	430	____[3]
	(E) Peacock	95	195	____[3]
	(F) Red	210	475	____[3]
253E	Electric 0-4-0 (O), *31–36*			
	(A) Green	150	205	____[1]
	(B) Terra-cotta	190	305	____[1]
254	Electric 0-4-0 (O), *24–32*	210	260	____[1]
254E	Electric 0-4-0 (O), *27–34*	155	220	____[1]
255E	Steam 2-4-2 (O), *35–36*	440	880	____[1]

		Good	Exc	Cond/$
256	Electric 0-4-4-0 (O), *24–30**			
	(A) Rubber-stamped lettering	470	1250	___3
	(B) (A) w/o outline and "LIONEL..."	425	770	___3
	(C) "LIONEL" and "256" on brass	450	1050	___3
257	Steam 2-4-0 (O), *30–35 u*			
	(A) Black tender	145	305	___1
	(B) Black crackle-finish tender	240	435	___1
258	Steam 2-4-0, Early (O), *30–35 u*			
	(A) With 4-wheel 257 tender	85	170	___1
	(B) With 8-wheel 258 tender	100	195	___1
258	Steam 2-4-2, Late (O), *41 u*			
	(A) Black	60	90	___1
	(B) Gun-metal	85	135	___1
259	Steam 2-4-2 (O), *32*	60	120	___1
259E	Steam 2-4-2 (O), *33–42*	75	125	___2
260E	Steam 2-4-2 (O), *30–35**			
	(A) Black, green or black frame	385	520	___2
	(B) Dark gun-metal body and frame	440	640	___2
261	Steam 2-4-2 (O), *31*	150	215	___1
261E	Steam 2-4-2 (O), *35*	170	250	___1
262	Steam 2-4-2 (O), *31–32*	215	315	___2
262E	Steam 2-4-2 (O), *33–36*			
	(A) Gloss black, copper/brass trim	100	210	___2
	(B) Satin black, nickel trim	125	265	___2
263E	Steam 2-4-2 (O), *36–39**			
	(A) Gun-metal gray	315	610	___2
	(B) 2-tone blue, from Blue Comet	415	950	___2
264E	Steam 2-4-2 (O), *35–36*			
	(A) Red, "RED COMET"	150	295	___1
	(B) Black	220	380	___1
265E	Steam 2-4-2 (O), *35–40*			
	(A) Black or gun-metal	170	330	___2
	(B) Light blue, "BLUE STREAK"	460	800	___2
267E/267W	Sets: 616, (2) 617s, 618, *35–41*	—	560	___1
270	Bridge, 10" long (O), *31–42*	23	55	___1
270	Lighting set, *15–23*		NRS	___
271	(2) 270 Spans (O), *31–33, 35–40*	65	150	___1
271	Lighting set, *15–23*		NRS	___
272	(3) 270 Spans (O), *31–33, 35–40*	55	165	___1
280	Bridge, 14" long (Std.), *31–42*	50	115	___1
281	(2) Bridge Spans (Std.), *31–33, 35–40*	85	205	___1
282	(3) Bridge Spans (Std.), *31–33, 35–40*	105	240	___1
289E	Steam 2-4-2 (O), *37 u*	120	305	___1

		Good	Exc	Cond/$
300	Electric Trolley Car (2⅞"), 01–05	2000	3600	___ [1]
300	Hell Gate Bridge (Std.), 28–42*			
	(A) Cream towers, green trusses	800	1350	___ [2]
	(B) Ivory towers, aluminum truss	700	1600	___ [2]
300	(See #3 Trolley)			
301	Batteries, set of 4 (2⅞"), 03–05		NRS	___
302	Plunge Battery (2⅞"), 01–02		NRS	___
303	Summer Trolley, 10–13	1500	3150	___ [1]
303	Carbon Cylinders (2⅞"), 02		NRS	___
304	Composite Zincs (2⅞"), 02		NRS	___
306	Glass Jars (2⅞"), 02		NRS	___
308	(5) Signs (O), 40–42	26	70	___ [1]
309	Electric Trolley Trailer (2⅞"), 01–05	2500	4050	___ [1]
309	Pullman (Std.), 26–39			
	(A) Maroon body/roof, mojave window	100	160	___ [1]
	(B) Mojave body/roof, maroon window	100	160	___ [1]
	(C) Light brown body, dark brown roof	120	185	___ [1]
	(D) Medium blue body, dark blue roof	170	260	___ [1]
	(E) Apple green body, dark green roof	170	260	___ [1]
	(F) Pale blue body, silver roof	100	160	___ [1]
	(G) Maroon body, terra-cotta roof	130	185	___ [1]
310	Baggage (Std.), 26–39			
	(A) Maroon body/roof, mojave window	100	160	___ [1]
	(B) Mojave body/roof, maroon window	100	160	___ [1]
	(C) Light brown body, dark brown roof	115	185	___ [1]
	(D) Medium blue body, dark blue roof	170	260	___ [1]
	(E) Apple green body, dark green roof	170	260	___ [1]
	(F) Pale blue body, silver roof	100	160	___ [1]
310	Rails and Ties, complete section (2⅞"), 01–02	5	14	___ [1]
312	Observation (Std.), 24–39			
	(A) Maroon body/roof, mojave window	100	160	___ [1]
	(B) Mojave body/roof, maroon window	100	160	___ [1]
	(C) Light brown body, dark brown roof	120	185	___ [1]
	(D) Medium blue body, dark blue roof	170	260	___ [1]
	(E) Apple green body, dark green roof	170	260	___ [1]
	(F) Pale blue body, silver roof	100	160	___ [1]
	(G) Maroon body, terra-cotta roof	130	185	___ [1]
313	Bascule Bridge (O), 40–42			
	(A) Silver bridge	235	500	___ [1]
	(B) Gray bridge	250	590	___ [1]
314	Girder Bridge (O), 40–42	17	40	___ [1]
315	Trestle Bridge (O), 40–42	28	80	___ [1]
316	Trestle Bridge (O), 40–42	21	48	___ [1]

Good Exc Cond/$

		Good	Exc	Cond/$
318	Electric 0-4-0 (Std.), *24–32*			
	(A) Gray, dark gray, or mojave	150	250	___[1]
	(B) Pea green	150	250	___[1]
	(C) State brown	250	395	___[1]
318E	Electric 0-4-0, *26–35*			
	(A) Gray, mojave, or pea green	150	250	___[1]
	(B) State brown	275	440	___[1]
	(C) Black	550	990	___[1]
319	Pullman (Std.), *24–27*	105	175	___[1]
320	Baggage (Std.), *25–27*	100	175	___[1]
320	Switch and Signal (2⅞"), *02–05*		NRS	___
322	Observation (Std.), *24–27, 29–30 u*	100	175	___[1]
330	Crossing, 90° (2⅞"), *02–05*		NRS	___
332	Baggage (Std.), *26–33*			
	(A) Red body and roof, cream doors	80	120	___[2]
	(B) Peacock body/roof, orange doosr	75	115	___[2]
	(C) Gray body/roof, maroon doors	75	115	___[2]
	(D) Olive green body/roof, red doors	90	145	___[2]
	(E) State brown body, dark brown roof	165	375	___[2]
337	Pullman (Std.), *25–32*			
	(A) Red body/roof, cream doors	95	190	___[1]
	(B) Mojave body/roof, maroon doors	95	190	___[1]
	(C) Olive green body/roof, red doors	105	225	___[1]
	(D) Olive green body/roof, maroon doors	95	190	___[1]
	(E) Pea green body/roof, cream doors	210	500	___[1]
338	Observation (Std.), *25–32*			
	(A) Red body/roof, cream doors	95	190	___[1]
	(B) Mojave body/roof, maroon doors	95	190	___[1]
	(C) Olive green body/roof, red doors	105	225	___[1]
	(D) Olive green body/roof, maroon doors	95	190	___[1]
339	Pullman (Std.), *25–33*			
	(A) Peacock body/roof, orange doors	55	100	___[1]
	(B) Gray body/roof, maroon doors	55	100	___[1]
	(C) State brown body, dark brown roof	120	330	___[1]
	(D) Peacock body, dark green roof	75	130	___[1]
	(E) Mojave body, maroon roof/doors	145	230	___[1]
340	Suspension Bridge (2⅞"), *02–05* *		NRS	___
341	Observation (Std.), *25–33*			
	(A) Peacock body/roof, orange doors	50	70	___[1]
	(B) Gray body/roof, maroon doors	50	70	___[1]
	(C) State brown body, dark brown roof	110	240	___[1]
	(D) Peacock body, dark green roof	65	95	___[1]
	(E) Mojave body, maroon roof/doors	135	165	___[1]

		Good	Exc	Cond/$
350	Track Bumper (2⅞"), *02–05*	—	550	___ [1]
370	Jars and Plates (2⅞"), *02–03*		NRS	___
380	Electric 0-4-0 (Std.), *23–27*	310	440	___ [1]
380	Elevated Pillars (2⅞"), *04–05**	30	70	___ [1]
380E	Electric 0-4-0 (Std.), *26–29*			
	(A) Mojave	445	630	___ [1]
	(B) Maroon	295	400	___ [1]
	(C) Dark green	370	460	___ [1]
381	Electric 4-4-4 (Std.), *28–29**	1600	2100	___ [1]
381E	Electric 4-4-4 (Std.), *28–36**			
	(A) State green, apple green sub-frame	1500	2500	___ [1]
	(B) State green, red sub-frame	1900	2850	___ [1]
381U	Electric 4-4-4 Kit (Std.), *28–29*	1600	3600	___ [1]
384	Steam 2-4-0 (Std.), *30–32**	395	580	___ [1]
384E	Steam 2-4-0 (Std.), *30–32**	360	570	___ [1]
385E	Steam 2-4-2 (Std.), *33–39**	435	790	___ [1]
390	Steam 2-4-2 (Std.), *29**	415	720	___ [1]
390E	Steam 2-4-2 (Std.), *29–31**			
	(A) Black, w/ or w/o orange stripe	460	690	___ [1]
	(B) 2-tone blue, cream-orange stripe	590	1200	___ [1]
	(C) 2-tone green, orange or green stripe	990	2050	___ [1]
392E	Steam 4-4-2 (Std.), *32–39**			
	(A) Black, 384 tender	750	1250	___ [1]
	(B) Black, large 12-wheel tender	1050	1800	___ [1]
	(C) Gun-metal gray	1000	1800	___ [1]
400	Express Trail Car (2⅞"), *03–05**	3500	5850	___ [1]
400E	Steam 4-4-4 (Std.), *31–39**			
	(A) Black or dark gun-metal	1400	2150	___ [2]
	(B) Medium blue boiler	1550	2400	___ [2]
	(C) Crackle black finish	1550	2450	___ [2]
402	Electric 0-4-4-0 (Std.), *23–27*	300	495	___ [1]
402E	Electric 0-4-4-0 (Std.), *26–29*	300	495	___ [1]
404	Summer Trolley (Std.), *10*		NRS	___
408E	Electric 0-4-4-0 (Std.), *27–36**			
	(A) Apple green or mojave, red pilots	700	1150	___ [1]
	(B) 2-tone brown, brown pilots	2100	2650	___ [1]
	(C) Dark green, red pilots	1850	3400	___ [1]
412	Pullman, "California" (Std.), *29–35**			
	(A) Light green body, dark green roof	590	1750	___ [1]
	(B) Light brown body, dark brown roof	620	2100	___ [1]
413	Pullman, "Colorado" (Std.), *29–35**			
	(A) Light green body, dark green roof	590	1750	___ [1]
	(B) Light brown body, dark brown roof	620	2100	___ [1]

		Good	Exc	Cond/$
414	Pullman, "Illinois" (Std.), *29–35**			
	(A) Light green body, dark green roof	590	2050	___1
	(B) Light brown body, dark brown roof	590	1750	___1
416	Observation, "New York" (Std.), *29–35**			
	(A) Light green body, dark green roof	590	1750	___1
	(B) Light brown body, dark brown roof	620	2100	___1
418	Pullman (Std.), *23–32**	205	320	___1
419	Combination (Std.), *23–32**	205	280	___1
420	Pullman, "Faye" (Std.), *30–40**	520	900	___1
421	Pullman, "Westphal" (Std.), *30–40**	550	900	___1
422	Observation, "Tempel" (Std.), *30–40**	520	900	___1
424	Pullman, "Liberty Belle" (Std.), *31–40**			
	(A) Brass trim	350	530	___1
	(B) Nickel trim	385	650	___1
425	Pullman, "Stephen Girard" (Std.), *31–40**			
	(A) Brass trim	350	530	___1
	(B) Nickel trim	385	650	___1
426	Observation, "Coral Isle" (Std.), *31–40**			
	(A) Brass trim	350	530	___1
	(B) Nickel trim	385	650	___1
427	Diner (Std.), *30*		NM	___
428	Pullman (Std.), *26–30**			
	(A) Dark green body and roof	250	385	___1
	(B) Orange body/roof, apple green window	390	890	___1
429	Combine (Std.), *26–30**			
	(A) Dark green body and roof	250	385	___1
	(B) Orange body/roof, apple green window	390	890	___1
430	Observation (Std.), *26–30**			
	(A) Dark green body and roof	250	385	___1
	(B) Orange body/roof, apple green window	390	890	___1
431	Diner (Std.), *27–32**			
	(A) Mojave body, screw-mounted roof	350	540	___1
	(B) Mojave body, hinged roof	465	720	___1
	(C) Dark green body, orange windows	410	720	___1
	(D) Orange body, apple green window	410	720	___1
	(E) Apple green body, red window	410	720	___1
435	Power Station, *26–38**	180	400	___1
436	Power Station, *26–37**			
	(A) "POWER STATION" plates	135	265	___1
	(B) "EDISON SERVICE" plate	270	610	___1
437	Switch/Signal Tower, *26–37**	190	370	___1

		Good	Exc	Cond/\$
438	Signal Tower, 27–39*			
	(A) Mojave base, orange house	215	425	___1
	(B) Gray base, ivory house	325	640	___1
	(C) Black base, white house	325	640	___1
439	Panel Board, 28–42*	80	125	___1
440/0440/440N	Signal Bridge, 32–42*	180	445	___1
440C	Panel Board, 32–42	90	145	___1
441	Weighing Station (Std.), 32–36	495	1400	___1
442	Landscape Diner, 38–42	165	265	___2
444	Roundhouse (Std.), 32–35*	1350	2850	___1
444-18	Roundhouse Clip, 33		NRS	___
450	Electric 0-4-0, Macy's (O), 30 u			
	(A) Red, black frame	295	700	___1
	(B) Apple green, dark green frame	415	880	___1
450	Set: 450; matching 605; (2) 606s, 30 u	750	1800	___1
455	Electric Range, 30, 32–33	355	1000	___1
490	Observation (Std.), 23–32*	195	260	___1
500	Dealer Display, 27–28		NRS	___
500	Electric Derrick Car (2⅞"), 03–04*	5000	6750	___1
501	Dealer Display, 27–28		NRS	___
502	Dealer Display, 27–28		NRS	___
503	Dealer Display, 27–28		NRS	___
504	Dealer Display, 24–28		NRS	___
505	Dealer Display, 24–28		NRS	___
506	Dealer Display, 24–28		NRS	___
507	Dealer Display, 24–28		NRS	___
508	Dealer Display, 24–28		NRS	___
509	Dealer Display, 24–28		NRS	___
510	Dealer Display, 27–28		NRS	___
511	Flatcar (Std.), 27–40	65	120	___2
512	Gondola (Std.), 27–39			
	(A) Peacock	38	70	___1
	(B) Green	50	90	___1
513	Cattle Car (Std.), 27–38			
	(A) Olive green	70	145	___3
	(B) Orange	70	110	___3
	(C) Cream, maroon roof	70	135	___3
514	Boxcar (Std.), 29–40			
	(A) Cream yellow, orange roof	85	155	___2
	(B) Yellow, brown roof	115	270	___2
514	Refrigerator Car (Std.), 27–28			
	(A) White, peacock roof	240	540	___3
	(B) Cream, peacock roof	215	340	___3

		Good	Exc	Cond/$
	(C) Ivory, peacock roof	285	800	___3
	(D) Cream, green roof	265	680	___3
514R	Refrigerator Car (Std.), *29–40*			
	(A) Ivory, peacock roof, brass plates	140	180	___3
	(B) Ivory, light blue roof, nickel plate	440	600	___3
	(C) White, light blue roof, brass plates	140	180	___3
515	Tank Car (Std.), *27–40*			
	(A) Ivory or terra-cotta	90	160	___3
	(B) Light tan	110	170	___3
	(C) Silver	90	160	___3
	(D) Orange, red "SHELL" decal	340	520	___3
516	Hopper Car (Std.), *28–40*	155	250	___3
517	Caboose (Std.), *27–40*			
	(A) Pea green, red roof	50	100	___1
	(B) Red body and roof	105	155	___1
	(C) Red, black roof, orange windows	355	610	___1
520	Floodlight Car (Std.), *31–40*			
	(A) Terra-cotta base	95	185	___1
	(B) Green base	95	215	___1
529	Pullman (O), *26–32*			
	(A) Olive green body and roof	25	45	___1
	(B) Terra-cotta body and roof	25	60	___1
530	Observation (O), *26–32*			
	(A) Olive green body and roof	25	45	___1
	(B) Terra-cotta body and roof	25	60	___1
550	Miniature Figures, boxed (Std.), *32–36**	175	305	___1
551	Engineer (Std.), *32*	25	45	___1
552	Conductor (Std.), *32*	25	38	___1
553	Porter (Std.), *32*	25	38	___1
554	Male Passenger (Std.), *32*	25	45	___1
555	Female Passenger (Std.), *32*	25	45	___1
556	Red Cap Figure (Std.), *32*	25	45	___1
600	Derrick Trailer (2⅞"), *03–04**	5000	8550	___1
600	Pullman, Early (O), *15–23*			
	(A) Dark green	65	170	___1
	(B) Maroon or brown	48	85	___1
600	Pullman, Late (O), *33–42*			
	(A) Light red or gray; red roof	50	90	___1
	(B) Light blue, aluminum roof	70	120	___1
601	Observation, Late (O), *33–42*			
	(A) Light red body and roof	50	90	___1
	(B) Light gray, red roof	50	90	___1
	(C) Light blue body, aluminum roof	70	120	___1

		Good	Exc	Cond/$
601	Pullman, Early (O), *15–23*	50	70	___[1]
602	Baggage, Lionel Lines, Late (O), *33–42*			
	(A) Light red or gray; red roof	60	110	___[1]
	(B) Light blue body, aluminum roof	90	150	___[1]
602	Baggage, NYC (O), *15–23*	30	45	___[1]
602	Observation (O), *22 u*	30	36	___[1]
603	Pullman, Early (O), *22 u*	40	70	___[1]
603	Pullman, Later (O), *20–25*	20	45	___[1]
603	Pullman, Latest (O), *31–36*			
	(A) Light red body and roof	45	85	___[1]
	(B) Red body, black roof	35	60	___[1]
	(C) Stephen Girard green, dark green roof	35	60	___[1]
	(D) Maroon body/roof, "MACY SPCL"	60	125	___[1]
604	Observation, Later (O), *20–25*	35	60	___[1]
604	Observation, Latest (O), *31–36*			
	(A) Light red body and roof	44	85	___[1]
	(B) Red body, black roof	35	60	___[1]
	(C) Yellow-orange body, terra-cotta roof	35	60	___[1]
	(D) Stephen Girard green, dark green roof	35	60	___[1]
	(E) Maroon body and roof	70	150	___[1]
605	Pullman (O), *25–32*			
	(A) Gray, "LIONEL LINES"	85	170	___[1]
	(B) Gray, "ILLINOIS CENTRAL"	85	170	___[1]
	(C) Red, "LIONEL LINES"	170	255	___[1]
	(D) Red, "ILLINOIS CENTRAL"	255	340	___[1]
	(E) Orange, "LIONEL LINES"	170	255	___[1]
	(F) Orange, "ILLINOIS CENTRAL"	300	430	___[1]
	(G) Olive green, "LIONEL LINES"	255	340	___[1]
606	Observation (O), *25–32*			
	(A) Gray, "LIONEL LINES"	130	215	___[1]
	(B) Gray, "ILLINOIS CENTRAL"	90	170	___[1]
	(C) Red, "LIONEL LINES"	170	255	___[1]
	(D) Red, "ILLINOIS CENTRAL"	255	340	___[1]
	(E) Orange, "LIONEL LINES"	170	255	___[1]
	(F) Orange, "ILLINOIS CENTRAL"	170	255	___[1]
	(G) Olive green, "LIONEL LINES"	255	340	___[1]
607	Pullman (O), *26–27*			
	(A) Peacock, "LIONEL LINES"	50	70	___[1]
	(B) Peacock, "ILLINOIS CENTRAL"	75	115	___[1]
	(C) 2-tone green, "LIONEL LINES"	50	75	___[1]
	(D) Red, "LIONEL LINES"	75	110	___[1]
608	Observation (O), *26–37*			
	(A) Peacock, "LIONEL LINES"	50	70	___[1]

FREE TRIAL ISSUE!

BUSINESS REPLY MAIL
FIRST-CLASS MAIL   PERMIT NO. 16   WAUKESHA, WI

POSTAGE WILL BE PAID BY ADDRESSEE

**CLASSIC
TOY TRAINS**®

PO BOX 1612
WAUKESHA WI 53187-9950

		Good	Exc	Cond/$
	(B) Peacock, "ILLINOIS CENTRAL"	75	115	___1
	(C) 2-tone green, "LIONEL LINES"	50	75	___1
	(D) Red, "LIONEL LINES"	75	110	___1
609	Pullman (O), *37*	55	75	___1
610	Pullman, Early (O), *15–25*			
	(A) Dark green body and roof	50	65	___1
	(B) Maroon body and roof	60	95	___1
	(C) Mojave body and roof	60	95	___1
610	Pullman, Late (O), *26–30*			
	(A) Olive green body and roof	60	80	___1
	(B) Mojave body and roof	50	80	___1
	(C) Terra-cotta body, maroon roof	100	155	___1
	(D) Pea green body and roof	70	115	___1
	(E) Light blue body, aluminum roof	130	260	___1
	(F) Light red, aluminum finish roof	100	155	___1
611	Observation (O), *37*	55	90	___1
612	Observation, Early (O), *15–25*			
	(A) Dark green body and roof	50	60	___1
	(B) Maroon body and roof	70	90	___1
	(C) Mojave body and roof	70	90	___1
612	Observation, Late (O), *26–30*			
	(A) Olive green body and roof	50	80	___1
	(B) Mojave body and roof	50	80	___1
	(C) Terra-cotta body, maroon roof	100	155	___1
	(D) Pea green body and roof	70	115	___1
	(E) Light blue body, aluminum roof	130	260	___1
	(F) Light red, aluminum finish roof	100	155	___1
613	Pullman (O), *31–40**			
	(A) Terra-cotta, maroon/terra-cotta roof	85	195	___1
	(B) Light red, light red/aluminum roof	175	350	___1
	(C) Blue, two-tone blue roof	115	225	___1
614	Observation (O), *31–40**			
	(A) Terra-cotta, maroon/terra-cotta roof	100	190	___1
	(B) Light red, light red/aluminum roof	175	350	___1
	(C) Blue, two-tone blue roof	115	225	___1
615	Baggage (O), *33–40**	130	260	___1
616E/616W Diesel only (O), *35–41*		90	215	___1
616E/616W Set: 616, (2) 617s, 618		310	570	___1
617	Coach (O), *35–41*			
	(A) Blue and white	55	85	___1
	(B) Chrome, gun-metal skirts	55	85	___1
	(C) Chrome, chrome skirts	55	85	___1
	(D) Silver finish	55	85	___1

		Good	Exc	Cond/$
618	Observation (O), *35–41*			
	(A) Blue and white	55	85	___¹
	(B) Chrome, gun-metal skirts	55	85	___¹
	(C) Chrome, chrome skirts	55	85	___¹
	(D) Silver finish	55	85	___¹
619	Combine (O), *36–38*			
	(A) Blue, white window band	100	205	___¹
	(B) Chrome, chrome skirts	100	205	___¹
620	Floodlight Car (O), *37–42*	50	85	___¹
629	Pullman (O), *24–32*			
	(A) Dark green body and roof	30	40	___¹
	(B) Orange body and roof	30	40	___¹
	(C) Red body and roof	20	32	___¹
	(D) Light red body and roof	40	55	___¹
630	Observation, *24–32*			
	(A) Dark green body and roof	30	40	___¹
	(B) Orange body and roof	30	40	___¹
	(C) Red body and roof	20	32	___¹
	(D) Light red body and roof	40	55	___¹
636W	Diesel only (O), *36–39*	90	175	___¹
636W	Set: 636W, (2) 637s, 638, *36–39*	350	640	___¹
637	Coach (O), *36–39*	70	105	___¹
638	Observation (O), *36–39*	70	105	___¹
651	Flatcar (O), *35–40*	28	55	___²
652	Gondola (O), *35–40*	28	55	___²
653	Hopper Car (O), *34–40*	35	65	___¹
654	Tank Car (O), *34–42*			
	(A) Orange or aluminum finish	35	60	___³
	(B) Gray	42	75	___³
655	Boxcar (O), *34–42*			
	(A) Cream, maroon roof	35	60	___¹
	(B) Cream, tuscan roof	47	75	___¹
656	Cattle Car (O), *35–40*			
	(A) Light gray, vermilion roof	40	75	___¹
	(B) Burnt orange, tuscan roof	65	125	___¹
657	Caboose (O), *34–42*			
	(A) Red body and roof	20	34	___²
	(B) Red, tuscan roof	25	42	___²
659	Dump Car (O), *35–42*	40	75	___²
700	Electric 0-4-0 (O), *15–16*	360	690	___¹
700	Window Display (2⅞"), *03–05*		NRS	___
700E	Steam 4-6-4, Scale Hudson, 5344 (O), *37–42**	1400	2550	___⁴
700K	Steam 4-6-4, unbuilt (O), *38–42*	4400	5950	___¹

		Good	Exc	Cond/$
701	Electric 0-4-0 (O), *15–16*	390	660	___[1]
701	Steam 0-6-0 (See 708)	—	2350	___[1]
702	Baggage (O), *17–21*	115	305	___[1]
703	Electric 4-4-4 (O), *15–16*	1400	2350	___[1]
706	Electric 0-4-0 (O), *15–16*	375	630	___[1]
708	Steam 0-6-0, "8976" on boiler front (O), *39–42**	1450	2850	___[1]
710	Pullman (O), *24–34*			
	(A) Red, "LIONEL LINES"	200	300	___[2]
	(B) Orange, "LIONEL LINES"	150	225	___[2]
	(C) Orange, "NEW YORK CENTRAL"	200	225	___[2]
	(D) Orange, "ILLINOIS CENTRAL"	300	450	___[2]
	(E) 2-tone blue, "LIONEL LINES"	300	415	___[2]
	(F) Orange, "NEW YORK CENTRAL"	200	260	___[2]
711	R.C. Switches, pair (O72), *35–42*	75	175	___[3]
712	Observation (O), *24–34*			
	(A) Red, "LIONEL LINES"	185	355	___[1]
	(B) Orange, "LIONEL LINES"	140	265	___[1]
	(C) Orange, "NEW YORK CENTRAL"	185	310	___[1]
	(D) Orange, "ILLINOIS CENTRAL"	280	530	___[1]
	(E) 2-tone blue, "LIONEL LINES"	280	485	___[1]
	(F) Orange, "NEW YORK CENTRAL"	185	310	___[1]
714	Boxcar (O), *40–42**	390	710	___[1]
714K	Boxcar, unbuilt (O), *40–42*	—	650	___[1]
715	Tank Car (O), *40–42**			
	(A) "S.E.P.S. 8124" decal	340	610	___[1]
	(B) "S.U.N.X. 715" decal	435	880	___[1]
715K	Tank Car, unbuilt (O), *40–42*	—	530	___[1]
716	Hopper Car (O), *40–42**	305	570	___[1]
716K	Hopper, unbuilt (O), *40–42*	—	730	___[1]
717	Caboose (O), *40–42**	390	590	___[1]
717K	Caboose, unbuilt (O), *40–42*	—	590	___[1]
720	90° Crossing (O72), *35–42*	21	40	___[1]
721	Manual Switches, pair (O72), *35–42*	50	105	___[1]
730	90° Crossing (O72), *35–42*	20	36	___[1]
731	R.C. Switches, pair, T-rail (O72), *35–42*	80	135	___[1]
751E/751W	Set: 752; (2) 753s; 754 (O), *34–41**	640	1050	___[1]
752E	Diesel only (O), *34–41*			
	(A) Yellow and brown	190	355	___[1]
	(B) Aluminum finish	180	340	___[1]
753	Coach (O), *36–41*			
	(A) Yellow and brown	100	185	___[1]
	(B) Aluminum Finish	95	180	___[1]

		Good	Exc	Cond/$
754	Observation (O), *36–41*			
	(A) Yellow and brown	100	185	___¹
	(B) Aluminum Finish	95	180	___¹
760	16-piece Curved Track (O72), *35–42*	41	80	___¹
761	Curved Track (O72), *34–42*	1	2.50	___¹
762	Straight Track (O72), *34–42*	1	2.50	___¹
762	Inside Straight Track (O72), *34–42*	2	5	___¹
763E	Steam 4-6-4 (O), *37–42*			
	(A) Gun-metal, 263 or 2263W tender	1200	2650	___²
	(B) Gun-metal, 2226X or 2226WX	1350	2950	___²
	(C) Black, 2226WX tender	1200	2650	___²
771	Curved Track, T-rail (O72), *35–42*	3	9	___¹
772	Straight Track, T-rail (O72), *35–42*	4	12	___¹
773	Fishplate Outfit (O72), *36–42*	25	32	___¹
782	Hiawatha Combine (O), *35–41* *	270	380	___¹
783	Hiawatha Coach (O), *35–41* *	155	290	___¹
784	Hiawatha Observation (O), *35–41* *	205	445	___¹
792	Rail Chief Combine (O), *37–41* *	290	800	___¹
793	Rail Chief Coach (O), *37–41* *	290	800	___¹
794	Rail Chief Observation (O), *37–41* *	290	800	___¹
800	Boxcar (O), *15–26*			
	(A) Light orange, brown-maroon roof	45	70	___¹
	(B) Orange body/roof, "PENN RR"	30	50	___¹
800	Boxcar (2⅞"), *04–05* *	2500	4050	___¹
801	Caboose (O), *15–26*	36	46	___¹
802	Stock Car (O), *15–26*	43	60	___¹
803	Hopper Car, Early (O), *23–28*	32	47	___¹
803	Hopper Car, Late (O), *29–34*	35	60	___¹
804	Tank Car (O), *23–28*	27	47	___¹
805	Boxcar (O), *27–34*			
	(A) Pea green, terra-cotta roof	35	60	___¹
	(B) Pea green, maroon roof	44	115	___¹
	(C) Orange, maroon roof	44	95	___¹
806	Stock Car (O), *27–34*			
	(A) Pea green, terra-cotta roof	42	75	___¹
	(B) Orange; various color roof	35	60	___¹
807	Caboose (O), *27–40*			
	(A) Peacock, dark green roof	20	35	___¹
	(B) Red, peacock roof	20	35	___¹
	(C) Light red body and roof	23	40	___¹
809	Dump Car (O), *31–41*			
	(A) Orange bin	40	75	___¹
	(B) Green bin	40	85	___¹

		Good	Exc	Cond/$
810	Crane (O), *30–42*			
	(A) Terra-cotta cab, maroon roof	190	200	____ 2
	(B) Cream cab, vermilion roof	125	180	____ 2
811	Flatcar (O), *26–40*			
	(A) Maroon	40	70	____ 2
	(B) Aluminum finish	47	100	____ 2
812	Gondola (O), *26–42*	42	85	____ 2
812T	Tool Set, *30–41*	40	85	____
813	Stock Car (O), *26–42*			
	(A) Orange, pea green roof	65	145	____ 2
	(B) Orange, maroon roof	55	135	____ 2
	(C) Cream, maroon roof	100	225	____ 2
	(D) Tuscan body and roof	—	1600	____ 2
814	Boxcar (O), *26–42*			
	(A) Cream, orange roof	46	105	____ 3
	(B) Cream, maroon roof	115	140	____ 3
	(C) Yellow, brown roof	115	120	____ 3
814R	Refrigerator Car (O), *29–42*			
	(A) Ivory, peacock roof	100	190	____ 1
	(B) White, light blue roof	120	265	____ 1
	(C) Flat white, brown roof	600	900	____ 1
815	Tank Car (O), *26–42*			
	(A) Pea green, maroon frame	250	510	____ 1
	(B) Pea green, black frame	70	155	____ 1
	(C) Aluminum, black frame	50	115	____ 1
	(D) Orange-yellow, black frame	150	255	____ 1
816	Hopper Car (O), *27–42*			
	(A) Olive green	85	155	____ 1
	(B) Red body	65	135	____ 1
	(C) Black body	370	680	____ 1
817	Caboose (O), *26–42*			
	(A) Peacock, dark green roof	45	80	____ 3
	(B) Red, peacock roof	45	80	____ 3
	(C) Light red body and roof	45	80	____ 3
820	Boxcar (O), *15–26*			
	(A) Orange, "ILLINOIS CENTRAL"	45	80	____ 1
	(B) Orange, "UNION PACIFIC"	65	105	____ 1
820	Floodlight Car (O), *31–42*			
	(A) Terra-cotta	100	175	____ 2
	(B) Green	100	175	____ 2
	(C) Light green	105	180	____ 2
821	Stock Car (O), *15–16, 25–26*	45	85	____ 1
822	Caboose (O), *15–26*	35	70	____ 1

		Good	Exc	Cond/$
831	Flatcar (O), *27–34*	22	41	___[1]
840	Industrial Power Station, *28–40**	1200	3050	___[1]
900	Ammunition Car (O), *17–21*	120	340	___[1]
900	Box Trail Car (2⅞"), *04–05**	2000	3600	___[1]
901	Gondola (O), *19–27*	27	44	___[1]
902	Gondola (O), *27–34*	27	45	___[1]
910	Grove of Trees, *32–42*	70	155	___[1]
911	Country Estate, *32–42*	175	360	___[1]
912	Suburban Home	225	540	___[1]
913	Landscaped Bungalow, *40–42*	140	285	___[1]
914	Park Landscape, *32–35*	90	205	___[1]
915	Tunnel, *32, 34–35*	160	435	___[1]
916	Tunnel, 29¼" long, *35*	95	180	___[1]
917	Scenic Hillside, *32–36*	90	205	___[1]
918	Scenic Hillside, *32–36*	90	205	___[1]
919	Park Grass, bag, *32–42*	8	17	___[1]
920	Village, *32–33*	600	1600	___[1]
921	Scenic Park, 3 pieces, *32–33*	980	2600	___[1]
921C	Park Center, *32–33*	400	1050	___[1]
922	Terrace, *32–36*	80	155	___[1]
923	Tunnel, 40¼" long, *33–42*	90	225	___[1]
924	Tunnel, 30" long (O72), *35–42*	50	135	___[1]
925	Lubricant, *35–42*	1	2.50	___[1]
927	Flag Plot, *37–42*	70	135	___[1]
1000	Passenger Car (2⅞"), *05**	4500	6750	___[1]
1000	Trolley Trailer (Std.), *10–16*	1400	2250	___[1]
1010	Electric 0-4-0, Winner (O), *31–32*	90	160	___[1]
1010	Interurban Trailer (Std.), *10–16*	1000	1800	___[1]
1011	Pullman, Winner (O), *31–32*	55	75	___[1]
1011	Interurban (Std.), *10*		NM	___
1012	Station, *32*	50	70	___[1]
1012	(See #1011 Interurban)			
1015	Steam 0-4-0 (O), *31–32*	100	205	___[1]
1017	Winner Station, *33*	25	70	___[1]
1019	Observation (O), *31–32*	50	70	___[1]
1020	Baggage (O), *31–32*	65	110	___[1]
1021	90° Crossover (O27), *32–42*	1	4	___[1]
1022	Tunnel, 18¾" long (O), *35–42*	15	32	___[1]
1023	Tunnel, 19" long, *34–42*	20	41	___[1]
1024	Switches, pair (O27), *37–42*	4	15	___[1]
1025	Bumper (O27), *40–42*	12	25	___[1]
1027	Transformer, Tin Station, *34*	50	115	___[1]
1028	Transformer, 40 watts, *39*	3	11	___[1]

		Good	Exc	Cond/$
1030	Electric 0-4-0 (O), *32*	75	135	___[1]
1035	Steam 0-4-0 (O), *32*	75	115	___[1]
1045	Watchman, *38–42*	15	60	___[2]
1050	Passenger Car Trailer (2⅞"), *05**	5000	7200	___[1]
1100	Handcar, Mickey Mouse, *35–37**			
	(A) Red base	400	640	___[1]
	(B) Apple green base, orange shoes	500	880	___[1]
	(C) Orange base	600	1200	___[1]
1100	Summer Trolley Trailer (Std.), *10–13*		NRS	___
1103	Handcar, Peter Rabbit (O), *35–37**	330	820	___[1]
1105	Handcar, Santa Claus (O), *35–35**			
	(A) Red base	580	1250	___[1]
	(B) Green base	630	1400	___[1]
1107	Transformer, Tin Station, *33*	25	70	___[1]
1107	Handcar, Donald Duck (O), *36–37**			
	(A) White dog house w/ red roof	475	1200	___[1]
	(B) White dog house w/ green roof	450	1100	___[1]
	(C) Orange dog house w/ green roof	640	1850	___[1]
1121	Switches, pair (O27), *37–42*	15	34	___[1]
1506L	Steam 0-4-0 (O), *33–34*	95	125	___[1]
1506M	Steam 0-4-0 (O), *35*	250	430	___[1]
1508	Steam 0-4-0, Commodore Vanderbilt	335	620	___[1]
	w/ Mickey in 1509 Stoker Tender, *35*			
1511	Steam 0-4-0 (O), *36–37*	110	160	___[1]
1512	Gondola (O), *31–33, 36–37*	29	47	___[1]
1514	Boxcar (O), *31–37*	25	41	___[1]
1515	Tank Car (O), *33–37*	25	41	___[1]
1517	Caboose (O), *31–37*	25	41	___[1]
1518	Mickey Mouse Diner (O), *35*	105	235	___[1]
1519	Mickey Mouse Band (O), *35*	105	235	___[1]
1520	Mickey Mouse Animal (O), *35*	105	235	___[1]
1536	Circus: 1508, 1509, 1518, 1519, 1520, *15–20*	700	1550	___[1]
1550	Switches, pair, windup, *33–37*	2	5	___[1]
1555	90° Crossover, windup, *33–37*	1	2.50	___[1]
1560	Station, *33–37*	15	34	___[1]
1569	Accessory set, 8 pieces, *33–37*	35	70	___[1]
1588	Steam 0-4-0 (O), *36–37*	150	250	___[1]
1630	Pullman (O), *38–42*			
	(A) Aluminum windows	35	70	___[1]
	(B) Light gray windows	47	80	___[1]
1631	Observation (O), *38–42*			
	(A) Aluminum windows	35	70	___[1]
	(B) Light gray windows	47	80	___[1]

		Good	Exc	Cond/$
1651E	Electric 0-4-0 (O), *33*	130	240	___[1]
1661E	Steam 2-4-0 (O), *33*	75	160	___[1]
1662	Steam 0-4-0 (O27), *40–42*	270	445	___[1]
1663	Steam 0-4-0 (O27), *40–42*	200	385	___[1]
1664/1664E	Steam 2-4-2 (O27), *38–42*			
	(A) Gun-metal	55	100	___[1]
	(B) Black	55	95	___[1]
1666/1666E	Steam 2-6-2 (O27), *38–42*			
	(A) Gun-metal	115	170	___[1]
	(B) Black	95	145	___[1]
1668/1668E	Steam 2-6-2 (O27), *37–41*			
	(A) Gun-metal	75	125	___[1]
	(B) Black	70	130	___[1]
1673	Coach (O), *36–37*			
	(A) Aluminum windows	35	75	___[1]
	(B) Light gray windows	47	90	___[1]
1674	Pullman (O), *36–37*	35	75	___[1]
1675	Observation (O), *36–37*	30	70	___[1]
1677	Gondola (O), *33–35, 39–42*			
	(A) "IVES/R.R. LINES", light blue	40	60	___[1]
	(B) "LIONEL", blue or red	21	37	___[1]
1679	Boxcar (O), *33–42*			
	(A) Cream, "IVES" on side	23	38	___[2]
	(B) Cream, "LIONEL" on side	23	38	___[2]
	(C) Cream or yellow, "BABY RUTH"	23	38	___[2]
1680	Tank Car (O), *33–42*			
	(A) Aluminum, "IVES TANK LINES"	80	95	___[2]
	(B) Aluminum, no "IVES" lettering	19	34	___[2]
1681	Steam 2-4-0 (O), *34–35*			
	(A) Black, red frame	55	120	___[1]
	(B) Red, red frame	110	145	___[1]
1681E	Steam 2-4-0 (O), *34–35*			
	(A) Black, red frame	65	130	___[1]
	(B) Red, red frame	130	165	___[1]
1682	Caboose (O), *33–42*			
	(A) Vermilion, "IVES" on side	34	70	___[1]
	(B) Red or tuscan, "LIONEL"	17	40	___[1]
1684	Steam 2-4-2 (O27), *41–42*	50	80	___[2]
1685	Coach (O), *33–37 u*			
	(A) Gray, maroon roof	240	495	___[1]
	(B) Red, maroon roof	170	335	___[1]
	(C) Blue, silver roof	170	315	___[1]

		Good	Exc	Cond/$
1686	Baggage (O), *33–37 u*			
	(A) Gray, maroon roof	240	495	___[1]
	(B) Red, maroon roof	170	335	___[1]
	(C) Blue, silver roof	170	315	___[1]
1687	Observation (O), *33–37 u*			
	(A) Gray, maroon roof	170	315	___[1]
	(B) Red, maroon roof	170	315	___[1]
	(C) Blue, silver roof	170	315	___[1]
1688/1688E	Steam 2-4-2 (027), *36–46*	50	85	___[1]
1689E	Steam 2-4-2 (027), *36–37*			
	(A) Gun-metal	75	115	___[1]
	020 Variation 1	—	20	___[1]
	020 variation 2	—	30	___[1]
	(B) Black	60	100	___[1]
1690	Pullman (O), *33–40*	35	60	___[1]
1691	Observation (O), *33–40*	35	60	___[1]
1692	Pullman (027), *39 u*	45	70	___[1]
1693	Observation (027), *39 u*	45	70	___[1]
1700E	Diesel, power unit only (027), *35–37*	45	70	___[1]
1700E	Set: 1700 (2) 1701s, 1702 (027), *35–37 u*			
	(A) Aluminum and light red	140	250	___[1]
	(B) Chrome and light red	140	250	___[1]
	(C) Orange and gray	155	285	___[1]
1701	Coach (027), *35–37*			
	(A) Chrome sides and roof	20	46	___[1]
	(B) Silver sides and roof	30	55	___[1]
	(C) Orange and gray	75	150	___[1]
1702	Observation (027), *35–37*			
	(A) Chrome sides and roof	20	46	___[1]
	(B) Silver sides and roof	30	55	___[1]
	(C) Orange and gray	75	150	___[1]
1703	Observation w/ hooked coupler, *35–37 u*	41	95	___[1]
1717	Gondola (O), *33–40 u*	27	42	___[1]
1717X	Gondola (O), *40 u*	25	48	___[1]
1719	Boxcar (O), *33–40 u*	30	50	___[1]
1719X	Boxcar (O), *41–42 u*	30	50	___[1]
1722	Caboose (O), *33–42 u*	25	50	___[1]
1722X	Caboose (O), *39–40 u*	26	41	___[1]
1766	Pullman (Std.), *34–40**			
	(A) Terra-cotta, maroon roof, brass trim	300	650	___[2]
	(B) Red, maroon roof, nickel trim	300	540	___[2]

		Good	Exc	Cond/$
1767	Baggage Car (Std.), *34–40**			
	(A) Terra-cotta, maroon roof, brass trim	295	850	____¹
	(B) Red, maroon roof, nickel trim	295	700	____¹
1768	Observation (Std.), *34–40**			
	(A) Terra-cotta, maroon roof, brass trim	300	650	____¹
	(B) Red, maroon roof, nickel trim	300	540	____¹
1811	Pullman (O), *33–37*	32	70	____¹
1812	Observation (O), *33–37*	30	65	____¹
1813	Baggage Car (O), *33–37*	60	135	____¹
1816/1816W Diesel (O), *35–37*		100	240	____¹
1817	Coach (O), *35–37*	22	50	____¹
1818	Observation (O), *35–37*	22	50	____¹
1835E	Steam 2-4-2 (Std.), *34–39*	520	900	____¹
1910	Electric 0-6-0, Early (Std.), *10–11*	800	1800	____¹
1910	Electric 0-6-0, Late (Std.), *12*	550	1350	____¹
1910	Pullman (Std.), *09–10 u*	1000	1800	____¹
1911	Electric 0-4-0, Early (Std.), *10–12*	1000	2000	____¹
1911	Electric 0-4-0, Late (Std.), *13*	700	1100	____¹
1911	Electric 0-4-4-0, Special (Std.), *11–12*	1000	2500	____¹
1912	Electric 0-4-4-0 (Std.), *10–12**			
	(A) NY, New Haven & Hartford	1800	3200	____¹
	(B) "NEW YORK CENTRAL LINES"	1500	2700	____¹
1912	Electric 0-4-4-0 Special (Std.), *11**	2500	4500	____¹
2200	Summer Trolley Trailer (Std.), *10–13*	1100	2250	____¹
2600	Pullman (O), *38–42*	100	180	____¹
2601	Observation (O), *38–42*	80	135	____¹
2602	Baggage Car (O), *38–42*	85	185	____¹
2613	Pullman (O), *38–42**			
	(A) Blue, 2-tone blue roof	100	270	____²
	(B) State green, 2-tone green roof	200	440	____²
2614	Observation (O), *38–42**			
	(A) Blue, 2-tone blue roof	100	270	____¹
	(B) State green, 2-tone green roof	200	440	____¹
2615	Baggage Car (O), *38–42**			
	(A) Blue, 2-tone blue roof	115	270	____¹
	(B) State green, 2-tone green roof	200	420	____¹
2620	Floodlight Car (O), *38–42*	49	105	____²
2623	Pullman (O), *41–42*			
	(A) "IRVINGTON"	170	335	____²
	(B) "MANHATTAN"	155	295	____²
2624	Pullman (O), *41–42*	750	1700	____¹
2630	Pullman (O), *38–42*	30	70	____¹

		Good	Exc	Cond/$
2631	Observation (O), *38–42*	30	70	___1
2640	Pullman Illuminated (O), *38–42*			
	(A) Light blue, aluminum roof	30	70	___1
	(B) State green, dark green roof	28	70	___1
2641	Observation Illuminated (O), *38–42*			
	(A) Light blue, aluminum roof	30	70	___1
	(B) State green, dark green roof	28	70	___1
2642	Pullman (O), *41–42*	42	80	___1
2643	Observation (O), *41–42*	30	65	___1
2651	Flatcar (O), *38–42*	30	50	___1
2652	Gondola (O), *38–41*	24	50	___2
2653	Hopper Car (O), *38–42*			
	(A) Stephen Girard green	38	65	___1
	(B) Black	60	100	___1
2654	Tank Car (O), *38–42*			
	(A) Aluminum finish, "SUNOCO"	35	60	___3
	(B) Orange, "SHELL"	35	60	___3
	(C) Light gray, "SUNOCO"	41	70	___3
2655	Boxcar (O), *38–42*			
	(A) Cream, maroon roof	35	65	___1
	(B) Cream, tuscan roof	38	75	___1
2656	Stock Car (O), *38–41*			
	(A) Light gray, red roof	45	75	___1
	(B) Burnt orange, tuscan roof	75	115	___1
2657	Caboose (O), *40–41*	19	34	___3
2657X	Caboose (O), *40–41*	25	41	___1
2659	Dump Car (O), *38–41*	40	70	___1
2660	Crane (O), *38–42*	75	100	___1
2672	Caboose (O27), *41–42*	21	39	___1
2677	Gondola (O27), *39–41*	23	37	___1
2679	Boxcar (O27), *38–42*	17	30	___1
2680	Tank Car (O27), *38–42*			
	(A) Aluminum finish, "SUNOCO"	15	41	___1
	(B) Orange, "SHELL"	15	41	___1
2682	Caboose (O27), *38–42*	18	32	___1
2682X	Caboose (O27), *38–42*	22	35	___1
2717	Gondola (O), *38–42 u*	21	41	___1
2719	Boxcar (O), *38–42 u*	25	50	___1
2722	Caboose (O), *38–42 u*	25	50	___1
2755	Tank Car (O), *41–42*	60	115	___1
2757	Caboose (O), *41–42*	26	37	___1
2757X	Caboose (O), *41–42*	25	36	___1
2758	Automobile Boxcar (O), *41–42*	47	65	___1

		Good	Exc	Cond/$
2810	Crane (O), *38–42*	165	230	___²
2811	Flatcar (O), *38–42*	65	115	___¹
2812	Gondola (O), *38–42*			
	(A) Green	40	90	___¹
	(B) Dark orange	42	95	___¹
2813	Stock Car (O), *38–42*	110	250	___¹
2814	Boxcar (O), *38–42*			
	(A) Cream, maroon roof	85	210	___³
	(B) Orange, brown roof	85	205	___³
2814R	Refrigerator Car (O), *38–42*			
	(A) White, light blue roof, nickel plates	150	250	___¹
	(B) White, brown roof, no plates	375	660	___¹
2815	Tank Car (O), *38–42*			
	(A) Aluminum finish	85	165	___¹
	(B) Orange	135	250	___¹
2816	Hopper Car (O), *35–42*			
	(A) Red	100	190	___²
	(B) Black	110	205	___²
2817	Caboose (O), *36–42*			
	(A) Light red body and roof	90	145	___⁵
	(B) Flat red, tuscan roof	140	225	___⁵
2820	Floodlight Car (O), *38–42*			
	(A) Stamped nickel searchlight	110	235	___¹
	(B) Gray die-cast searchlights	120	260	___¹
2954	Boxcar (O), *40–42**	150	410	___²
2955	Sunoco Tank Car (O), *40–42**			
	(A) "SHELL" decal	225	560	___¹
	(B) "SUNOCO" decal	340	780	___¹
2956	Hopper Car (O), *40–42**	180	470	___¹
2957	Caboose (O), *40–42**	155	385	___²
3300	Summer Trolley Trailer (Std.), *10–13*	1400	2250	___¹
3651	Operating Lumber Car (O), *39–42*	22	55	___²
3652	Operating Gondola (O), *39–42*	29	75	___³
3659	Operating Dump Car (O), *39–42*	22	35	___²
3811	Operating Lumber Car (O), *39–42*	35	70	___¹
3814	Operating Merchandise Car (O), *39–42*	150	250	___³
3859	Operating Dump Car (O), *38–42*	44	110	___¹
4351	(See 14, 17, 117)			
4400	(See #404 Summer Trolley)			
5344	(See 700E)			
5906	(See 14, 17)			
8118	(See 14)			

		Good	Exc	Cond/$
8976	(See 227, 228, 229, 230, 706, 708)			
19050	(See 14)			
51906	(See 17)			
54078	(See 14, 114)			
62976	(See 114)			
65784	(See 12, 16, 112)			
76399	(See 16, 112)			
98237	(See 14, 114)			
342715	(See 17)			
A	Miniature Motor, *04*	50	95	___¹
A	Transformer, 40, 60 watts, *27–37*	8	24	___¹
B	New Departure Motor, *06–16*	75	135	___¹
B	Transformer, 50, 75 watts, *16–38*	6	24	___¹
C	New Departure Motor, *06–16*	100	180	___¹
D	New Departure Motor, *06–14*	100	180	___¹
E	New Departure Motor, *06–14*	100	180	___¹
F	New Departure Motor, *06–14*	100	180	___¹
G	Battery Fan Motor, *06–14*	100	180	___¹
K	Power Motor, *05*	100	180	___¹
K	Transformer, 150, 200 watts, *13–38*	26	95	___¹
L	Power Motor, *05*	50	100	___¹
L	Transformer, 50, 75 watts, *13–38*	7	24	___¹
M	Battery Motor, *15–20*	30	80	___¹
N	Transformer, 50 watts, *41–42*	7	23	___¹
Q	Transformer, 50, 75 watts, *14–15*	16	37	___¹
R	Battery Motor, *15–20*	30	75	___¹
R	Transformer, 100 watts, *38–42*	25	60	___¹
S	Transformer, 50, 80 watts, *14–17*	18	37	___¹
T	Transformer, 75, 100,150 watts, *19–28*	10	30	___¹
U	Transformer, Aladdin, *32–33*	6	16	___¹
V	Transformer, 150 watts, *39–42*	60	125	___¹
W	Transformer, 75 watts, *32–33*	7	26	___¹
Y	Battery Motor, *15–20*	40	80	___¹
Z	Transformer, 250 watts, *39–42*	120	165	___¹

Other Transformers and Rheostats made by Lionel

		Good	Exc	Cond/$
106	Rheostat, *11–14*	3	9	___¹
1029	25 watts, *36*	6	18	___¹
1030	40 watts, *35–38*	6	23	___¹
1031	Rheostat, circa 1938, *38*	2	4	___¹
1036	Rheostat, circa 1941, *40*	2	5	___¹

		Good	Exc	Cond/$
1037	Transformer, 40 watts, *40–42*	7	23	___[1]
1038	Rheostat, circa 1940, *40*	2	4	___[1]
1039	Transformer, 35 watts, *37–40*	7	18	___[1]
1040	Transformer, 60 watts, *37–39*	12	27	___[1]
1041	Transformer, 60 watts, *39–42*	13	30	___[1]

Track, Lockons, and Contactors

	Good	Exc	Cond/$
O Straight	0.25	0.70	___[1]
O Curve	0.25	0.70	___[1]
O72 Straight	1	2	___[1]
O72 Curve	1	2	___[1]
O27 Straight	0.10	0.50	___[1]
O27 Curve	0.10	0.45	___[1]
Standard Straight	0.70	2.50	___[1]
Standard Curve	0.60	2	___[1]
O Gauge Lockon	0.10	0.50	___[1]
Standard Gauge Lockon	0.30	1	___[1]
UTC Lockon	0.30	0.85	___[1]
145C Contactor	0.85	3	___[1]
153C Contactor	0.75	3	___[1]

Section 2
POSTWAR 1945–1969

		Good	Exc	Cond/$
011-11	Fiber Pins (O), *46–50*	0.10	0.15	___¹
011-43	Insulating Pins, dz. (O), *61*	1	1.50	___¹
020	90° Crossover (O), *45–61*	5	10	___¹
020X	45° Crossover (O), *46–59*	7	10	___¹
022	R.C. Switches, pair (O), *45–69*	25	44	___²
022-500	Adapter set (O), *57–61*	1	3	___¹
022A	R.C. Switches, pair (O), *47*	70	120	___¹
025	Bumper (O), *46–47*	8	19	___¹
026	Bumper, *48–50*	9	18	___¹
027C-1	Track Clips, dz. (O27), *47, 49*	0.55	0.90	___¹
30	Water Tower, *47–50*	70	115	___²
31	Curved Track (Super O), *57–66*	1	1.50	___¹
31-7	Power Blade Con. (Super O), *57–61*	—	0.35	___¹
31-15	Ground Rail Pin (Super O), *57–66*	—	0.60	___¹
31-45	Power Blade Connection (Super O), *61–66*	—	0.60	___¹
32	Straight Track (Super O), *57–66*	0.75	2.50	___¹
32-10	Insulating Pin (Super O), *57–60*	—	0.35	___¹
32-20	Power Blade Ins. (Super O), *57–60*	—	0.15	___¹
32-25	Insulating Pin (Super O), *57–61*	—	0.15	___¹
32-30	Ground Pin (Super O), *57–61*	—	0.15	___¹
32-31	Power Pin (Super O), *57–61*	—	0.15	___¹
32-32	Insulating Pin (Super O), *57–61*	—	0.15	___¹
32-33	Ground Pin (Super O), *57–61*	—	0.15	___¹
32-34	Power Pin (Super O), *57–61*	—	0.15	___¹
32-45	Power Blade Insulators, dz. (Super O), *61–66*	0.85	1.50	___¹
32-55	Insulating Pins, dz. (Super O), *61–66*	1	2	___¹
33	Half Curved Track (Super O), *57–66*	1	2.50	___¹
34	Half Straight Track (Super O), *57–66*	1	2.50	___¹
35	Boulevard Lamp, *45–49*	14	34	___¹
36	Remote Control set (Super O), *57–66*	10	14	___¹
37	Uncoupling Track set (Super O), *57–66*	7	15	___¹
38	Water Tower, *46–47*	180	405	___¹
38	Accessory Adapter Track (Super O), *51–61*	5	11	___¹
39	Operating set (Super O), *57*	4	8	___¹
39-5	Operating set (Super O), *57–58*	4	8	___¹
39-10	Operating set (Super O), *58*	4	8	___¹
39-15	Operating set, w/ blade (Super O), *57–58*	4	8	___¹
39-20	Operating set (Super O), *57–58*	4	8	___¹
39-25	Operating set (Super O), *61–66*	4	9	___¹

		Good	Exc	Cond/$
39-35	Operating set (Super O), *59*	4	9	___ [1]
40	Hookup Wire, *50–51, 53–63*	4	19	___ [1]
40-25	Conductor Wire, *56–59*	5	18	___ [1]
40-50	Cable Reel, *60–61*	4	8	___ [1]
41	Contactor (Super O)	0.50	1.50	___ [1]
41	U.S. Army Switcher, *55–57*	95	125	___ [3]
42	Picatinny Arsenal Switcher, *57*	170	260	___ [2]
042/42	Manual Switches, pr. (O), *46–59*	15	35	___ [1]
43	Power Track (Super O), *59–66*	4	7	___ [1]
44	U.S. Army Mobile Launcher, *59–62*	135	250	___ [1]
44-80	Missiles, *59–60*	10	21	___ [1]
45	U.S. Marines Mobile Launcher, *60–62*	125	220	___ [1]
45	Automatic Gateman, *46–49*	29	46	___ [1]
45N	Automatic Gateman, *45*	32	65	___ [2]
48	Insl. Straight Track (Super O), *57–66*	4	8	___ [1]
49	Insl. Curved Track (Super O), *57–66*	4	8	___ [1]
50	Lionel Gang Car, *54–64*	38	65	___ [4]
51	Navy Yard Switcher, *56–57*	115	185	___ [2]
52	Fire Car, *58–61*	95	190	___ [2]
53	Rio Grande Snowplow, *57–60*			
	(A) Backwards "a" in Rio Grande	180	275	___ [2]
	(B) Correctly printed "a"	370	650	___ [2]
54	Ballast Tamper, *58–61, 66, 68–69*	100	185	___ [2]
54-6446	(See 6446 or 6446-25), *54–55*			
55	Tie-jector, *57–61*	155	245	___ [3]
55-150	Ties, *57–60*	5	15	___ [1]
56	Lamp Post, *46–49*	26	49	___ [1]
56	M&St L Mine Transport, *58*	305	495	___ [1]
57	AEC Switcher, *59–60*	345	680	___ [1]
58	Lamp Post, *46–50*	23	60	___ [1]
58	GN Snowplow, *59–61*	385	590	___ [2]
59	Minuteman Switcher, *62–63*	300	460	___ [1]
60	Lionelville Rapid Transit Trolley, *55–58*	110	180	___ [4]
61	Ground Lockon (Super O), *57–66*	0.25	0.45	___ [1]
62	Power Lockon (Super O), *57–66*	0.25	0.45	___ [1]
64	Street Lamp, *45–49*	25	49	___ [1]
65	Lionel Lines Handcar, *62–66*	165	305	___ [1]
68	Executive Inspection Car, *58–61*	195	275	___ [3]
69	Lionel Maintenance Car, *60–62*	155	225	___ [1]
70	Yard Light, *49–50*	27	50	___ [1]
71	Lamp Post, *49–59*	9	24	___ [2]
75	Goose Neck Lamp, set of 2, *61–63*	12	21	___ [1]
76	Blvd. Street Lamp, *59–66, 68–69*	10	19	___ [1]

		Good	Exc	Cond/$
80	Controller	11	20	___[1]
88	Controller, *46–60*	4	7	___[1]
89	Flagpole, *56–58*	20	47	___[1]
90	Controller	3	7	___[1]
91	Circuit Breaker, *57–60*	12	25	___[1]
92	Circuit Breaker, *59–66, 68–69*	8	16	___[1]
93	Water Tower, *46–49*	22	41	___[1]
96C	Controller	3	5	___[1]
97	Coal Elevator, *46–50*	135	205	___[1]
100	Multivolt-DC/AC, Trans., *58–66*	—	70	___[1]
108	Trestle set	25	36	___[1]
109	Partial Trestle set, *61*	—	30	___[1]
110	Graduated Trestle set, *55–69*	12	21	___[2]
111	Elevated Trestle set, *56–69*	9	20	___[1]
111-100	Two Elevated Trestle Piers, *60–63*	10	18	___[1]
112	R.C. Switches, pr. (Super O), *57–66*	55	80	___[2]
114	Newsstand w/ horn, *57–59*	50	105	___[1]
115	Passenger Station, *46–49*	170	350	___[1]
118	Newsstand w/ whistle, *57–58*	45	95	___[1]
119	Landscaped Tunnel, *57–58*		NRS	___
120	90° Crossing (Super O), *57–66*	6	10	___[1]
121	Landscaped Tunnel, *59–66*		NRS	___
122	Lamp Assortment	—	170	___[1]
123	Lamp Assortment, *55–59*	85	185	___[1]
123-60	Lamp Assortment, *60–63*	—	150	___[1]
125	Whistle Shack, *50–55*	28	48	___[1]
128	Animated Newsstand, *57–60*	90	170	___[1]
130	60° Crossing (Super O), *57–61*	7	13	___[1]
131	Curved Tunnel, *59–66*		NRS	___
132	Passenger Station, *49–55*	50	90	___[2]
133	Passenger Station, *57, 61–62, 66*	32	80	___[1]
137	Passenger Station (See Prewar section), *46*	75	135	___[1]
138	Water Tower, *53–57*	85	130	___[1]
140	Automatic Banjo Signal, *54–66*	21	34	___[1]
142	Man. Switches, pr. (Super O), *57–66*	28	55	___[1]
145C	Contactor, *50–60*	1	6	___[1]
145	Automatic Gateman, *50–66*	27	46	___[3]
147	Whistle Controller, *61–66*	1	4	___[1]
148	Dwarf Trackside Signal, *57–60*	21	49	___[1]
150	Telegraph Pole set, *47–50*	29	75	___[1]
151	Auto. Semaphore, *47–69*	21	43	___[2]
152	Auto. Crossing Gate, *45–49*	13	32	___[1]
153	Auto. Block Control, Signal, *45–59*	15	40	___[2]

		Good	Exc	Cond/$
153C	Contactor	1	6	___¹
154	Auto. Highway Signal, *45–69*	15	40	___²
155	Blinking Light Signal w/ bell, *55–57*	30	65	___¹
156	Station Platform, *46–49*	39	95	___²
157	Station Platform, *52–59*	23	55	___¹
160	Unloading Bin, *52–57*	1	3	___¹
161	Mail Pickup set, *61–63*	38	95	___¹
163	Single Target Block Signal, *61–69*	17	30	___¹
164	Log Loader, *46–50*	115	220	___²
167	Whistle Controller, *45–46*	6	13	___¹
175	Rocket Launcher, *58–60*	110	300	___¹
175-50	Extra Rocket, *59–60*	5	18	___¹
182	Magnetic Crane, *46–49*	125	230	___¹
192	Oper. Control Tower, *59–60*	105	205	___¹
193	Industrial Water Tower, *53–55*	90	115	___²
195	Floodlight Tower, *57–69*	34	55	___²
195-75	Eight-Bulb Extension, *58–60*	18	35	___¹
196	Smoke Pellets, *46–47*	—	37	___¹
197	Rotating Radar Antenna, *57–59*	55	105	___¹
199	Microwave Relay Tower, *58–59*	33	75	___¹
202	UP Alco A Unit, *57*	55	90	___¹
204	Santa Fe Alco AA Units, *57*	115	185	___¹
205	Missouri Pacific Alco AA Units, *57–58*	70	115	___¹
206	Artificial Coal, large bag, *46–68*	—	10	___¹
207	Artificial Coal, small bag, *46–48*	—	8	___¹
208	Santa Fe Alco AA Units, *58–59*	100	230	___¹
209	New Haven Alco AA Units, *58*	315	650	___¹
209	Wooden Barrels, set of 4, *46–50*	8	18	___¹
210	Texas Special Alco AA Units, *58*	100	140	___¹
211	Texas Special Alco AA Units, *62–66*	80	160	___¹
212	USMC Alco A Unit, *58–59*	85	155	___¹
212	Santa Fe Alco AA Units, *64–66*	80	160	___¹
212T	USMC Dummy A Units, *58–59 u*	300	550	___¹
213	Railroad Lift Bridge, *50*		NM	___
213	M&StL Alco AA Units, *64*	75	160	___¹
214	Plate Girder Bridge, *53–69*	9	25	___¹
215	Santa Fe Alco Units, *65 u*			
	(A) AB Units	80	165	___¹
	(B) Double A Units (usually w/ 212T)	80	160	___¹
216	Burlington Alco A Unit, *58*	95	305	___¹
216	M&StL Alco AA Units, (usually w/ 213T), *64 u*	90	180	___¹
217	B&M Alco AB Units, *59*	85	190	___¹

No.	Description	Good	Exc	Cond/$
218	Santa Fe Alco Units, *59–63*			
	(A) Double A Units	65	145	___1
	(B) AB Units	70	150	___1
219	Missouri Pacific Alco AA Units, *59 u*	75	140	___1
220	Santa Fe Alco Units, *60–61*			
	(A) A Unit only	75	115	___1
	(B) AA Units	100	205	___1
221	2-6-4, 221T/221W Tender, *46–47*			
	(A) Gray die-cast body	75	150	___1
	(B) Black die-cast body	75	140	___1
221	Rio Grande Alco A Unit, *63–64*	50	80	___1
221	USMC Alco A Unit, *63–64 u*	125	345	___1
221	Santa Fe Alco A Unit, *63–64 u*	180	400	___1
222	Rio Grande Alco A Unit (adv. cat.), *62*	35	70	___1
223	218C Santa Fe Alco AB Units, *63*	85	165	___1
224	Steam 2-6-2, 2466T/2466W Tender, *45–46*	90	115	___1
224	U.S. Navy Alco AB Units, *60*	125	225	___1
225	C&O Alco A Unit, *60*	65	90	___1
226	B&M Alco AB Units, *60 u*	85	185	___1
227	CN Alco A Unit, *60 u*	80	155	___1
228	CN Alco A Unit, *61 u*	70	145	___1
229	M&StL Alco Units, *61–62*			
	(A) A Unit only, *61*	60	110	___1
	(B) AB Units, *62*	95	205	___1
230	C&O Alco A Unit, *61*	55	105	___1
231	Rock Island Alco A Unit, *61–63*	65	125	___1
232	New Haven Alco A Unit, *62*	65	125	___1
233	Steam 2-4-2, 233W Tender, *61–62*	55	95	___1
235	Steam 2-4-2, 1130T/1060T Tender, *60 u*	65	165	___1
236	Steam 2-4-2, 1130T/1050T Tender, *61–62*			
	(A) 1050T slope-back tender	18	41	___1
	(B) 1130T tender	18	41	___1
237	Steam 2-4-2, *63–66*			
	(A) w/ 1060T Tender	25	55	___1
	(B) w/ 234W Tender	45	90	___1
238	Steam 2-4-2, 234W Tender, *63–64*	55	115	___1
239	Steam 2-4-2, 234W Tender, *65–66*	45	75	___1
240	Steam 2-4-2, 242T, *64 u*	140	235	___1
241	Steam 2-4-2 w/ 234W Tender, *65 u*	70	135	___1
242	Steam 2-4-2 w/ 1060T Tender or 1062T Tender, *62–66*	20	46	___1
243	Steam 2-4-2, 243W Tender, *60*	85	135	___1
244	Steam 2-4-2, 244T/1130T Tender, *60–61*	25	36	___1

		Good	Exc	Cond/$
245	Steam 2-4-2, w/ 1060T Tender, *59–60 u*	49	110	___¹
246	Steam 2-4-2, 244T/1130T Tender, *59–61*	26	42	___¹
247	Steam 2-4-2, 247T Tender, *59*	30	60	___¹
248	Steam 2-4-2, 1130T Tender, *58*	30	70	___¹
249	Steam 2-4-2, 250T Tender, *58*	20	45	___¹
250	Steam 2-4-2, 250T Tender, *57*	21	48	___¹
251	Steam 2-4-2, 1062T Tender, *66 u*			
	(A) Slope-back tender	145	305	___¹
	(B) 250T-type tender	145	280	___¹
252	Crossing Gate, *50–62*	22	35	___²
253	Block Control Signal, *56–59*	17	31	___¹
256	Illuminated Freight Station, *50–53*	25	55	___²
257	Freight Station w/ diesel horn, *56–57*	35	85	___¹
260	Bumper, *51–69*			
	(A) Die-cast	9	15	___¹
	(B) Black plastic	19	39	___¹
262	Highway Crossing Gate, *62–69*	25	60	___¹
264	Operating Forklift Platform w/ 6264, *57–60*	200	315	___²
270	Metal Bridge (O), *46*	18	38	___¹
282	Gantry Crane, *54–57*	110	210	___²
282R	Gantry Crane, *56–57*	125	210	___¹
299	Code Transmitter Beacon set, *61–63*	75	155	___¹
308	Railroad Sign set, die-cast, *45–49*	17	33	___¹
309	Yard Sign set, plastic, *50–59*	13	27	___²
310	Billboard set, *50–68*	11	24	___¹
313	Bascule Bridge, *46–49*	325	500	___²
313-82	Fiber Pins, *46–60*	—	0.05	___¹
313-121	Fiber Pins, dozen, *61*	—	1.50	___¹
314	Scale Model Girder Bridge, *45–50*	12	22	___¹
315	Trestle Bridge, *46–48*	50	90	___¹
316	Trestle Bridge, *49*	17	41	___¹
317	Trestle Bridge, *50–56*	15	37	___¹
321	Trestle Bridge, *58–64*	11	37	___¹
332	Arch-Under Bridge, *59–66*	20	44	___¹
334	Operating Dispatching Board, *57–60*	145	285	___¹
342	Culvert Loader, *56–58*	145	245	___²
345	Culvert Unloader, *57–59*	195	345	___¹
346	Manual Culvert Unloader, *65*	80	175	___¹
347	Cannon Firing Range set, *64 u*	170	520	___¹
348	Manual Culvert Unloader, *66–69*	80	190	___¹
350	Engine Transfer Table, *57–60*	160	315	___²
350-50	Transfer Table Extension, *57–60*	75	190	___¹
352	Ice Depot, includes 6352, *55–57*	125	190	___¹

		Good	Exc	Cond/$
353	Trackside Control Signal, *60–61*	15	40	___¹
356	Operating Freight Station, *52–57*	44	95	___¹
362	Barrel Loader, *52–57*	50	105	___³
362-78	Wooden Barrels, *52–57*	5	17	___¹
364	Conveyor Lumber Loader, *48–57*	95	110	___⁴
364C	On/Off Switch, *48–64*	3	7	___¹
365	Dispatching Station, *58–59*	65	120	___¹
375	Turntable, *62–64*	170	265	___¹
390C	Switch, d.p.d.t., *60–64*	8	13	___¹
394	Rotary Beacon, *49–53*	25	35	___²
395	Floodlight Tower, *49–56*	26	50	___¹
397	Diesel Operating Coal Loader, *48–57*	100	140	___³
400	B&O RDC Passenger, *56–58*	185	235	___³
404	B&O RDC Baggage-Mail, *57–58*	205	375	___¹
410	Billboard Blinker, *56–58*	29	55	___¹
413	Countdown Control Panel, *62*	44	80	___¹
415	Diesel Fueling Station, *55–57*	95	130	___²
419	Heliport Control Tower, *62*	160	410	___¹
443	Missile Launch Platform, w/ 943 Ammo Dump, *60–62*	17	41	___¹
445	Switch Tower, lighted, *52–57*	38	70	___²
448	Missile Firing Range set, w/ 6448, *61–63*	85	165	___¹
450	Signal Bridge, two-track, *52–58*	31	60	___³
450L	Signal Light Head, *52–58*	15	38	___¹
452	Signal Bridge, single-track, *61–63*	70	130	___¹
455	Operating Oil Derrick, *50–54*	150	190	___²
456	Coal Ramp w/ 3456 Hopper, *50–55*	110	195	___²
460	Piggyback Transportation, includes 3460, *55–57*	85	150	___²
460P	Piggyback Platform, *55–57*	30	70	___¹
461	Platform w/ truck and trailer, *66*	75	160	___¹
462	Derrick Platform set, *61–62*	175	325	___¹
464	Lumber Mill, *56–60*	95	160	___²
465	Sound Dispatching Station, *56–57*	55	105	___¹
470	Missile Launching Platform w/ 6470, *59–62*	95	130	___²
480-25	Conversion Coupler, *50–60*	1	3	___¹
480-32	Conv. Magnetic Coupler, *61–69*	1	2.50	___¹
494	Rotary Beacon, *54–66*	21	44	___¹
497	Coaling Station, *53–58*	115	180	___¹
520	Lionel Lines Box Cab Electric, *56–57*	70	105	___¹
600	MKT NW-2 Switcher, *55*			
	(A) Black frame and end rails	80	145	___²
	(B) Gray frame and yellow end rails	220	360	___²
601	Seaboard NW-2 Switcher, *56*	90	200	___¹

		Good	Exc	Cond/$
602	Seaboard NW-2 Switcher, *57–58*	95	210	___¹
610	Erie NW-2 Switcher, *55*			
	(A) Black frame	85	145	___¹
	(B) Yellow frame	285	540	___¹
611	Jersey Central NW-2 Switcher, *57–58*	125	160	___¹
613	UP NW-2 Switcher, *58*	125	335	___¹
614	Alaska NW-2 Switcher, *59–60*			
	(A) Plastic bell, no brake	115	175	___¹
	(B) No bell, yellow brake/air	135	205	___¹
	(C) (B) w/ "BUILT BY LIONEL"	195	390	___¹
616	Santa Fe NW-2 Switcher, *61–62*	115	185	___²
617	Santa Fe NW-2 Switcher, *63*	135	255	___¹
621	Jersey Central NW-2 Switcher, *56–57*	75	165	___¹
622	Santa Fe NW-2 Switcher, *49–50*			
	(A) Large "GM" decal on cab	190	320	___²
	(B) Small "GM" decal on cab	145	290	___²
623	Santa Fe NW-2 Switcher, *52–54*	115	200	___²
624	C&O NW-2 Switcher, *52–54*	110	210	___²
625	LV GE 44-ton Switcher, *57–58*	75	125	___¹
626	B&O GE 44-ton Switcher, *59*	115	305	___¹
627	LV GE 44-ton Switcher, *56–57*	65	105	___¹
628	NP GE 44-ton Switcher, *56–57*	85	125	___¹
629	Burlington GE 44-ton Switcher, *56*	115	340	___¹
633	Santa Fe NW-2 Switcher, *62*	100	185	___¹
634	Santa Fe NW-2 Switcher, *63, 65–66*			
	(A) w/ safety stripes	80	160	___¹
	(B) w/o safety stripes	50	110	___¹
635	UP NW-2 Switcher, *65 u*	65	115	___¹
637	Steam 2-6-4, 2046W/736W Tender, *59–63*			
	(A) 2046W "LIONEL LINES" tender	60	150	___¹
	(B) 736W "PENNSYLVANIA" tender	60	155	___¹
638-2361	Van Camp's Pork & Beans Boxcar, *62 u*	25	39	___¹
645	Union Pacific NW-2 Switcher, *69*	60	115	___¹
646	Steam 4-6-4, 2046W Tdr., *54–58*	140	265	___¹
665	Steam 4-6-4, 2046W/6026W/736W Tender, *54–59, 66*	105	200	___²
670	Pennsylvania Turbine, 6-8-6, *52*		NM	___
671	Steam 6-8-6, *46–49*			
	(A) 671W Tender	115	215	___²
	(B) 2671W Tender	135	265	___²
671R	Steam 6-8-6, 4424W/4671 Tender, *46–49*	130	280	___¹
671RR	Steam 6-8-6, 2046W-50 Tender, *52*	130	200	___¹
671S	Smoke Conversion kit	—	28	___¹

		Good	Exc	Cond/$
674	Steam 2-6-4, *52*		NM	____
675	Steam 2-6-2, 2466W/2466WX/6466WX			
	Tender, *47–49; 2–6–4, 52*			
	(A) 2-6-2, disc drivers	85	165	____[1]
	(B) 2-6-4, spoked drivers	90	180	____[1]
681	Steam Turbine, 6-8-6, 2046W-50/2671W	135	225	____[2]
	Tender, *50–51, 53*			
682	Steam 6-8-6, 2046W-50 Tender, *54–55*	240	385	____[1]
685	Steam 4-6-4, 6026W Tender, *53*	110	215	____[1]
703	Steam 4-6-4, Hudson, *46*		NM	____
703-10	Special Smoke Bulb, *46*	—	23	____[1]
725	Steam 2-8-4, Berkshire, *52*		NM	____
726	Steam 2-8-4 Berkshire, *47–49*			
	(A) 2426W Tender, *46*	290	425	____[2]
	(B) 2426W Tender, *47–49*	270	390	____[2]
726RR	Steam 2-8-4 Berkshire, 2046W Tender, *52*	240	360	____[1]
726S	Smoke Conversion kit	—	600	____[1]
736	Steam 2-8-4, 2671WX/2046W/736W	295	370	____[5]
	Tender, *50–66*			
746	N&W Steam 4-8-4, *57–60*			
	(A) Long stripe Tender	550	1050	____[2]
	(B) Short stripe Tender	470	830	____[2]
760	Curved Track, 16 sec. (O72), *54–57*	19	30	____[1]
773	Steam 4-6-4 Hudson, 2426W Tender, *50*	900	1500	____[2]
773	Steam 4-6-4 Hudson, *64–66*			
	(A) w/ 773W Tender	510	940	____[2]
	(B) w/ 736W Tender	465	760	____[2]
902	Elevated Trestle set, *60*		NRS	____
909	Smoke Fluid, *57–66, 68-69*	8	20	____[1]
919	Artificial Grass, *46–64*	8	15	____[1]
920	Scenic Display set, *57–58*	50	90	____[1]
920-2	Tunnel Portals, pair, *58–59*	25	40	____[1]
920-3	Green Grass, *57*	8	20	____[1]
920-4	Yellow Grass, *57*	8	20	____[1]
920-5	Artificial Rock, *57-58*	8	20	____[1]
920-8	Dyed Lichen, *57-58*	8	20	____[1]
925	Lionel Lubricant, lg. tube, *46–69*	1	5	____[1]
926	Lionel Lubricant, sm. tube, *55*	1	2	____[1]
926-5	Instruction Booklet, *46–48*	1	5	____[1]
927	Lubricating Kit, *50–59*	13	29	____[1]
928	Maint. & Lubricating Kit, *60–63*	26	65	____[1]
943	Ammo Dump, *59–61*	27	55	____[1]
950	U.S. Railroad Map, *58–66*	20	50	____[1]

		Good	Exc	Cond/$
951	Farm set w/ box, *58*	100	200	___¹
952	Figure set w/ box, *58*	100	200	___¹
953	Figure set w/ box, *59–62*	100	200	___¹
954	Swimming Pool/Playground set w/ box, *59*	100	200	___¹
955	Highway set w/ box, *58*	100	200	___¹
956	Stockyard set w/ box, *59*	100	200	___¹
957	Farm Building and Animal set w/ box, *58*	100	200	___¹
958	Vehicle set w/ box, *58*	110	230	___¹
959	Barn set w/ box, *58*	110	230	___¹
960	Barnyard set w/ box, *59–61*	100	200	___¹
961	School set w/ box, *59*	100	200	___¹
962	Turnpike set w/ box, *58*	130	250	___¹
963	Frontier set w/ box, *59–60*	110	230	___¹
963-100	Frontier Set for Halloween General set w/ box, *60*	220	400	___¹
964	Factory Site set w/ box, *59*	110	230	___¹
965	Farm Set, *59*	100	200	___¹
966	Firehouse set w/ box, *58*	100	200	___¹
967	Post Office set w/ box, *58*	100	200	___¹
968	TV Transmitter set w/ box, *58*	100	200	___¹
969	Construction set w/ box, *60*	110	230	___²
970	Ticket Booth, *58–60*	80	150	___¹
971	Lichen Package w/ box, *60–64*	90	190	___¹
972	Landscape Tree Assortment w/ box, *61–64*	180	300	___¹
973	Complete Landscaping set w/ box, *60–64*	210	400	___¹
974	Scenery set w/ box, *58*	500	800	___¹
980	Ranch set w/ box, *60*	100	200	___¹
981	Freight Yard set w/ box, *60*	100	200	___¹
982	Suburban Split Level set w/ box, *60*	100	200	___¹
983	Farm set w/ box, *60–61*	100	200	___¹
984	Railroad set w/ box, *61–62*	100	200	___¹
985	Freight Area set w/ box, *61*	100	200	___¹
986	Farm set w/ box, *62*	100	200	___¹
987	Town set w/ box, *62*	500	800	___¹
988	Railroad Structure set w/ box, *62*	160	300	___¹
1001	Steam 2-4-2, 1001T Tender, *48*			
	(A) Plastic	22	41	___¹
	(B) Die-cast	—	600	___¹
1002	Lionel Gondola, *48–52*			
	(A) Black w/ white lettering	5	9	___¹
	(B) Blue w/ white lettering	6	11	___¹
	(C) Silver w/ black lettering	110	315	___¹
	(D) Yellow w/ black lettering	105	320	___¹

		Good	Exc	Cond/$
	(E) Red w/ white lettering	120	370	___[1]
	(F) Light blue w/ black lettering		NRS	___
X1004	PRR Baby Ruth Boxcar, *48–52*	5	11	___[1]
1005	Sunoco 1-D Tank Car, *48–50*	7	11	___[1]
1007	LL SP-type Caboose, *48–52*	4	9	___[1]
1008	Camtrol Uncoupling Unit (O27), *57–62*	0.55	1	___[1]
1008-50	Camtrol w/ track (O27), *48*	0.25	0.90	___[1]
1010	Transformer, 35 watts, *61–66*	8	19	___[1]
1011	Transformer, 25 watts, *48–49*	8	18	___[1]
1012	Transformer, 35 watts, *50–54*	7	14	___[1]
1013	Curved Track (O27), *45–69*	0.10	0.30	___[1]
1013-17	Steel Pins (O27), *46–60*	—	0.05	___[1]
1013-42	Steel Pins (O27), *61–68*	—	0.50	___[1]
1014	Transformer, 40 watts, *55*	11	22	___[1]
1015	Transformer, 45 watts, *56–60*	8	24	___[1]
1016	Transformer, 35 watts, *59–60*	6	24	___[1]
1018	Straight Track (O27), *45–69*	0.15	0.35	___[1]
1018	1/2 Straight Track (O27), *55–69*	0.15	0.35	___[1]
1019	R.C. Track set (O27), *46–48*	2	7	___[1]
1020	90° Crossing (O27), *55–69*	2.50	6	___[1]
1021	90° Crossing (O27), *45–54*	2	5	___[1]
1022	Man. Switches, pr. (O27), *53–69*	10	19	___[1]
1023	45° Crossing (O27), *56–69*	2	5	___[1]
1024	Man. Switches, pr. (O27), *46–52*	7	14	___[1]
1025	Illuminated Bumper (O27), *46–47*	7	15	___[1]
1025	Transformer, 45 watts, *61–69*	13	24	___[1]
1026	Transformer, 25 watts, *61–64*	5	13	___[1]
1032	Transformer, 75 watts, *48*	25	48	___[1]
1033	Transformer, 90 watts, *48–56*	31	46	___[2]
1034	Transformer, 75 watts, *48–54*	19	38	___[1]
1035	Transformer, 60 watts, *47*	22	41	___[1]
1037	Transformer, 40 watts, *46–47*	10	25	___[1]
1041	Transformer, 60 watts, *45–46*	13	25	___[1]
1042	Transformer, 75 watts, *47–48*	18	49	___[1]
1043	Transformer, *53–58*			
	(A) 50 watts, black, *53–57*	13	24	___[1]
	(B) 60 watts, ivory, *57–58*	55	105	___[1]
1044	Transformer, 90 watts, *57–69*	43	65	___[1]
1045	Operating Watchman, *46–50*	15	47	___[1]
1047	Operating Switchman, *59–61*	50	180	___[1]
1050	Steam 0-4-0, 1050 Tender, *59 u*	75	265	___[1]
1053	Transformer, 60 watts, *56–60*	18	40	___[1]
1055	Texas Special Alco A Unit (adv. cat.), *59–60*	35	70	___[1]

		Good	Exc	Cond/$
1060	Steam 2-4-2, 1050T/1060T Tender (adv. cat.), *60–62*	12	30	___[1]
1061	Steam 0-4-0, 1061T Tender, *64; 2–4–2, 69*			
	(A) Slope-back "LIONEL LINES"	13	33	___[1]
	(B) 1130T "SOUTHERN PACIFIC"	15	41	___[1]
1062	Steam 2-4-2, 1062T Tender, *63–64*			
	(A) 0-4-0 wheel arrangement	12	27	___[1]
	(B) 2-4-2 wheel arrangement	12	27	___[1]
1063	Transformer, 75 watts, *60–64*	16	45	___[1]
1065	Union Pacific Alco A Unit (adv. cat.), *61*	33	70	___[1]
1066	Union Pacific Alco A Unit, *64 u*	50	80	___[1]
1073	Transformer, 60 watts, *61–66*	18	47	___[1]
1101	Steam 2-4-2, 1001T Tender, *48*	20	38	___[1]
1101	Transformer, 25 watts, *48*	8	14	___[1]
1110	Steam 2-4-2, 1001T Tender, *49, 51–52*	15	31	___[1]
1120	Steam 2-4-2, 1001T Tender, *50*	15	31	___[1]
1121	R.C. Switches, pr. (O27), *46–51*	12	27	___[1]
1122	R.C. Switches, pr. (O27), *52–53*	13	27	___[2]
1122E	R.C. Switches, pr. (O27), *53–69*	17	32	___[1]
1122-34	R.C. Switches, pair, *52–53*	14	34	___[1]
1122-500	Gauge Adapter (O27), *57–66*	0.25	0.90	___[1]
1130	Steam 2-4-2, 6066T/1130T Tender, *53–54*			
	(A) Plastic body	20	36	___[1]
	(B) Die-cast body	38	85	___[1]
1615	Steam 0-4-0, 1615T Tender, *55–57*			
	(A) No grab-irons	95	180	___[2]
	(B) Grab-irons on chest/tender	175	320	___[2]
1625	Steam 0-4-0, 1625T Tender, *58*	115	250	___[1]
1640-100	Presidential Kit, *60*	70	220	___[1]
1654	Steam 2-4-2, 1654W Tender, *46–47*	35	70	___[1]
1655	Steam 2-4-2, 6654W Tender, *48–49*	35	70	___[1]
1656	Steam 0-4-0, 6403B Tender, *48–49*	145	355	___[2]
1665	Steam 0-4-0, 2403B Tender, *46*	165	365	___[1]
1666	Steam 2-6-2, 2466W/2466WX Tender, *46–47*	50	110	___[1]
1862	General 4-4-0, 1862T Tender, *59–62*			
	(A) Gray smoke stack	100	205	___[1]
	(B) Black smoke stack	100	205	___[1]
1865	Western & Atlantic Coach, *59–62*	23	46	___[1]
1866	Western & Atlantic Baggage, *59–62*	26	55	___[1]
1872	General 4-4-0, 1872T Tender, *59–62*	85	265	___[1]
1875	Western & Atlantic Coach, *59–62*	155	255	___[1]
1875W	W&A Coach w/ whistle, *59–62*	95	160	___[1]
1876	Western & Atlantic Baggage, *59–62*	33	75	___[1]

		Good	Exc	Cond/$
1877	Flatcar w/ fence and horses, *59–62*	40	60	___[1]
1882	General 4-4-0, 1882T Tender, *60 u*	205	385	___[1]
1885	Western & Atlantic Coach, *60 u*	95	265	___[1]
1887	Flatcar w/ fences and horses, *60 u*	80	135	___[1]
2001	Track Make-up kit (O27), *63*		NRS	___
2002	Track Make-up kit (O27), *63*		NRS	___
2003	Track Make-up kit (O27), *63*		NRS	___
2016	Steam 2-6-4, 6026W Tender, *55–56*	48	120	___[1]
2018	Steam 2-6-4, *56–59, 61*			
	(A) 6026T Tender	40	70	___[1]
	(B) 6026W Tender	60	105	___[1]
	(C) 1130T Tender	43	75	___[1]
2020	Steam 6-8-6, 2020W/6020W Tender, *46–49*	110	170	___[1]
2023	Union Pacific Alco AA Units, *50–51*			
	(A) Yellow body	145	230	___[2]
	(B) Gray nose and side frames		NRS	___
	(C) Silver body	150	290	___[2]
2024	C&O Alco A, *69*	30	65	___[1]
2025	Steam 2-6-2, 2-6-4, with 2466W/6466W	85	140	___[2]
	Tender, *47–49, 52*			
2026	Steam 2-6-2, 2-6-4, *48–49, 51–53*			
	(A) 6466W or 6466WX	60	115	___[2]
	(B) 6466T or 6066T	40	75	___[2]
2028	Pennsylvania GP-7, *55*			
	(A) Gold lettering	165	295	___[1]
	(B) Yellow lettering	140	260	___[1]
	(C) Tan frame	275	540	___[1]
2029	Steam 2-6-4, 234W Tdr., *64–69*			
	(A) 243W "LIONEL LINES" tender	70	115	___[1]
	(B) 243W "PENNSYLVANIA" tender	230	325	___[1]
	(C) (A) w/ "HAGERSTOWN, MAR..."	90	135	___[1]
2031	Rock Island Alco AA Units, *52–54*	135	255	___[1]
2032	Erie Alco AA Units, *52–54*	140	260	___[2]
2033	Union Pacific Alco AA Units, *52–54*	175	270	___[1]
2034	Steam 2-4-2, 6066T Tender, *52*	26	47	___[1]
2035	Steam 2-6-4, 6466W Tender, *50–51*	65	160	___[1]
2036	Steam 2-6-4, 6466W Tender, *50*	65	130	___[1]
2037	Steam 2-6-4, black engine, *54–55, 57–63*			
	(A) w/ 6026T, 1130T	45	80	___[1]
	(B) w/ 6026W, 233W, 234W	65	135	___[1]
2037-500	Steam 2-6-4, pink engine, w/ 1130T-500	360	820	___[1]
	Tender, *57–58*			
2041	Rock Island Alco AA Units, *69*	65	120	___[1]

		Good	Exc	Cond/$
2046	Steam 4-6-4, 2046W Tender, *50–51, 53*	150	230	___²
2055	Steam 4-6-4, 2046W/ 6026W Tender, *53–55*	80	220	___²
2056	Steam 4-6-4, 2046W Tender, *52*	125	225	___²
2065	Steam 4-6-4, 2046W/6026W Tender, *54–56*	120	210	___²
2240	Wabash F-3 AB Units, *56*	470	740	___¹
2242	New Haven F-3 AB Units, *58–59*	530	1050	___¹
2243	Santa Fe F-3 AB Units, *55–57*	245	310	___²
2243C	Santa Fe F-3 B Unit, *55–57*	100	210	___¹
2245	Texas Special F-3 AB Units, *54–55*			
	(A) B Unit w/ portholes, *54*	250	455	___²
	(B) B Unit w/o portholes, *55*	400	720	___²
2257	Lionel SP-type caboose, *47*	7	11	___¹
	(A) Red, no stack	6	11	___¹
	(B) Tuscan, w/ stack	55	200	___¹
	(C) Red, w/ stack	NRS	NRS	___¹
2257	Caboose, red w/ plastic stack	65	85	___¹
2321	Lackawanna Train Master, *54–56*			
	(A) Gray roof	290	420	___⁴
	(B) Maroon roof	390	630	___⁴
2322	Virginian Train Master, *65–66*			
	(A) Unpainted blue stripe	340	610	___²
	(B) Painted blue stripe	400	770	___²
2328	Burlington GP-7, *55–56*	265	395	___³
2329	Virginian Rectifier, *58–59*	335	580	___¹
2330	Pennsylvania GG-1, green, *50*	660	1200	___¹
2331	Virginian Train Master, *55–58*			
	(A) Black stripe/gold lettering, *55*	550	990	___³
	(B) Blue stripe/yellow lettering, *56–58*	345	640	___³
	(C) Blue and yellow, gray mold	680	1200	___³
2332	Pennsylvania GG-1, *47–49*			
	(A) Black	880	1750	___⁴
	(B) Green	325	600	___⁴
2333	Santa Fe F-3 AA Units, *48–49*	275	370	___¹
2333	NYC F-3 AA Units, *48–49*			
	(A) Rubber-stamped lettering	410	780	___¹
	(B) Heat-stamped lettering	285	610	___¹
2337	Wabash GP-7, *58*	125	270	___¹
2338	Milwaukee Road GP-7, *55–56*			
	(A) Orange band around shell	900	1700	___³
	(B) Interrupted orange band	145	245	___³
2339	Wabash GP-7, *57*	200	345	___²
2340	Pennsylvania GG-1, *55*			
	(A) Tuscan	700	1050	___²

		Good	Exc	Cond/$
	(B) Dark green	560	940	___²
2341	Jersey Central Train Master, *56*			
	(A) High gloss orange	1050	2050	___²
	(B) Dull orange	950	1700	___²
2343	Santa Fe F-3 AA Units, *50–52*	190	365	___³
2343C	Santa Fe F-3 B Unit, *50–55*			
	(A) Screen roof vents	95	195	___¹
	(B) Louver roof vents	105	215	___¹
2344	NYC F-3 AA Units, *50–52*	270	640	___³
2344C	NYC F-3 B Unit, *50–55*	130	275	___²
2345	Western Pacific F-3 AA Units, *52*	810	1450	___²
2346	B&M GP-9, *65–66*	175	315	___¹
2347	C&O GP-7, *65 u*	1400	2600	___¹
2348	M&St L GP-9, *58–59*	175	370	___²
2349	Northern Pacific GP-9, *59–60*	215	420	___¹
2350	New Haven EP-5, *56–58*			
	(A) White "N" painted nose	370	680	___²
	(B) White "N" decal nose	210	380	___²
	(C) Orange "N" painted nose	900	1550	___²
	(D) Orange "N" decal nose	510	910	___²
	(E) White "N" orange paint through doors	395	750	___²
2351	Milwaukee Road EP-5, *57–58*	170	400	___¹
2352	Pennsylvania EP-5, *58–59*			
	(A) Tuscan body	225	445	___¹
	(B) Chocolate brown body	220	480	___¹
2353	Santa Fe F-3 AA units, *53–55*	290	480	___³
2354	NYC F-3 AA units, *53–55*	250	485	___²
2355	Western Pacific F-3 AA units, *53*	860	1350	___¹
2356	Southern F-3 AA units, *54–56*	530	880	___¹
2356C	Southern F-3 B Unit, *54–56*	175	330	___¹
2357	Lionel SP-type Caboose, *47–48*			
	(A) Red w/ red stack	140	305	___¹
	(B) Tuscan w/ Tuscan stack	15	27	___¹
2358	Great Northern EP-5, *59–60*	385	670	___¹
2359	Boston & Maine GP-9, *61–62*	170	315	___¹
2360	Penn GG-1, *56–58, 61–63*			
	(A) Tuscan, 5 gold stripes	600	1820	___³
	(B) Dark green, 5 gold stripes	580	1315	___³
	(C) Tuscan, 1 gold stripe, heat-stamped lettering	490	1550	___³
	(D) Tuscan, 1 gold stripe, decaled lettering	455	1440	___³

No.	Description	Good	Exc	Cond/$
2363	Illinois Central F-3 AB Units, *55–56*			
	(A) Black lettering	435	1550	___2
	(B) Brown lettering	435	1400	___2
2365	C&O GP-7, *62–63*	120	235	___1
2367	Wabash F-3 AB Units, *55*	465	1340	___1
2368	B&O F-3 AB Units, *56*	640	2760	___1
2373	CP F-3 AA Units, *57*	1200	2450	___1
2378	Milwaukee Road F-3 AB Units, *56*			
	(A) w/ yellow roof line stripes	1050	2750	___2
	(B) w/o roof line stripes	970	2600	___2
2379	Rio Grande F-3 AB Units, *57–58*	450	1170	___2
2383	Santa Fe F-3 AA Units, *58–66*	220	700	___2
2400	"Maplewood" Pullman, green, *48–49*	65	150	___1
2401	"Hillside" Obs., green, *48–49*	60	130	___1
2402	"Chatham" Pullman, green, *48–49*	65	145	___1
2404	Santa Fe Vista Dome, *64–65*	30	75	___1
2405	Santa Fe Pullman, *64–65*	30	65	___1
2406	Santa Fe Observation, *64–65*	30	60	___1
2408	Santa Fe Vista Dome, *66*	35	75	___1
2409	Santa Fe Pullman, *66*	35	75	___1
2410	Santa Fe Observation, *66*	38	75	___1
2411	Lionel Lines Flatcar, *46–48*			
	(A) w/ pipes, *46*	50	80	___1
	(B) w/ logs, *47–48*	16	28	___1
2412	Santa Fe Vista Dome, *59–63*	31	110	___1
2414	Santa Fe Pullman, *59–63*	27	90	___1
2416	Santa Fe Observation, *59–63*	23	65	___1
2419	DL&W Work Caboose, *46–47*	29	55	___1
2420	DL&W Work Caboose, w/ light, *46–48*	50	100	___1
2421	"Maplewood" Pullman, *50–53*			
	(A) Gray roof	40	75	___1
	(B) Silver roof	40	70	___1
2422	"Chatham" Pullman, *50–53*			
	(A) Gray roof	36	75	___1
	(B) Silver roof	35	70	___1
2423	"Hillside" Observation, *50–53*			
	(A) Gray roof	40	70	___1
	(B) Silver roof	35	65	___1
2429	"Livingston" Pullman, *52–53*			
	(A) Gray roof	44	95	___1
	(B) Aluminum roof, no stripe	55	130	___1
2430	Blue Pullman, *46–47*	25	65	___1
2431	Blue Observation, *46–47*	25	65	___1

		Good	Exc	Cond/$
2432	"Clifton" Vista Dome, *54–58*	34	85	____1
2434	"Newark" Pullman, *54–58*	30	65	____1
2435	"Elizabeth" Pullman, *54–58*	35	70	____1
2436	"Mooseheart" Observation, *57–58*	23	55	____1
2436	"Summit" Observation, *54–56*	25	55	____1
2440	Green Pullman, *46–47*	20	55	____1
2441	Green Observation, *46–47*	20	55	____1
2442	"Clifton", Vista Dome, red stripe, *56*	50	120	____1
2442	Brown Pullman, *46–48*			
	(A) Silver lettering	20	75	____1
	(B) White lettering	25	65	____1
2443	Brown Observation, *46–48*			
	(A) Silver lettering	20	75	____1
	(B) White lettering	25	65	____1
2444	"Newark" Pullman, *56*	37	85	____1
2445	"Elizabeth" Pullman, *56*	80	250	____1
2446	"Summit" Observation, *56*	40	105	____1
2452	Pennsylvania Gondola, *45–47*	9	19	____1
2452X	Pennsylvania Gondola, *46–47*	6	18	____1
X2454	Pennsylvania Boxcar, *46*			
	(A) Brown door	75	160	____1
	(B) Orange door	110	210	____1
X2454	Baby Ruth Boxcar, "PRR" logo, *46–47*	9	26	____1
2456	Lehigh Valley Hopper, *48*	9	29	____1
2457	PRR Caboose, metal, N5, *45–47*			
	(A) Red, white lettering	17	30	____1
	(B) Brown, white lettering	16	34	____1
X2458	Pennsylvania Boxcar, *46–48*	18	50	____1
(2458)	Automobile Boxcar (O), postwar trucks, "2758", *41–42*	38	65	____1
2460	Bucyrus Erie Crane, 12-wheel, *46–50*			
	(A) Gray cab	85	180	____1
	(B) Black cab	35	70	____1
2461	Transformer Car, die-cast, *47–48*			
	(A) Red transformer	42	105	____1
	(B) Black transformer	30	75	____1
2465	Sunoco 2-D Tank Car, *46–48*			
	(A) "GAS/SUNOCO/OILS" in diamond	42	85	____1
	(B) "SUNOCO" in diamond	10	18	____1
	(C) "SUNOCO" goes past diamond	10	18	____1
2472	PRR Caboose, metal, N5, *46–47*	10	21	____1
2481	"Plainfield" Pullman, yellow, *50*	105	270	____1
2482	"Westfield" Pullman, yellow, *50*	105	270	____1

		Good	Exc	Cond/$
2483	"Livingston" Observation, yellow, *50*	95	245	____1
2521	"President McKinley" Obs., *62–66*	65	130	____2
2522	"President Harrison" Vista Dome, *62–66*	80	135	____1
2523	"President Garfield" Pullman, *62–66*	80	155	____1
2530	REA Baggage, *54–60*			
	(A) Large doors	280	500	____3
	(B) Small doors	100	165	____3
2531	"Silver Dawn" Observation, *52–60*	65	120	____2
2532	"Silver Range" Vista Dome, *52–60*	55	110	____2
2533	"Silver Cloud" Pullman, *52–59*	60	105	____1
2534	"Silver Bluff" Pullman, *52–59*	65	125	____1
2541	"Alexander Hamilton" Obs., *55–56**	100	175	____1
2542	"Betsy Ross" Vista Dome, *55–56**	90	205	____1
2543	"William Penn" Pullman, *55–56**	90	155	____1
2544	"Molly Pitcher" Pullman, *55–56**	90	205	____1
2550	B&O RDC Baggage/Mail, *57–58*	200	570	____1
2551	"Banff Park" Observation, *57**	140	295	____1
2552	"Skyline 500" Vista Dome, *57**	125	250	____1
2553	"Blair Manor" Pullman, *57**	220	455	____1
2554	"Craig Manor" Pullman, *57**	170	425	____1
2555	Sunoco 1-D Tank Car, *46–48*	16	42	____1
2559	B&O RDC Passenger, *57–58*	165	340	____2
2560	Lionel Lines Crane, 8-wheel, *46–47*			
	(A) Black boom	22	65	____1
	(B) Brown boom	20	55	____1
	(C) Green boom	22	65	____1
2561	"Vista Valley" Observation, *59–61**	100	260	____1
2562	"Regal Pass" Vista Dome, *59–61**	125	295	____1
2563	"Indian Falls" Pullman, *59–61**	125	295	____1
2625	"Madison" Pullman, *46–47**	100	210	____1
2625	"Manhattan" Pullman, *46–47**	100	215	____1
2625	"Irvington" Pullman, *46–50**			
	(A) No silhouettes	95	175	____1
	(B) w/ silhouettes	115	270	____1
2627	"Madison" Pullman, *48–50**			
	(A) No silhouettes	95	205	____1
	(B) w/ silhouettes	95	235	____1
2628	"Manhattan" Pullman, *48–50**			
	(A) No silhouettes	100	205	____1
	(B) w/ silhouettes	115	250	____1
2671	TCA Tender, *68*	—	55	____1
2855	SUNX 1-D Tank Car, *46–47*			
	(A) Black	65	205	____1

		Good	Exc	Cond/$
	(B) Black, "GAS/OILS" omitted	50	210	___1
	(C) Gray	50	185	___1
2856	B&O Scale Hopper Car, *46–47*		NM	___
2857	NYC Scale Caboose, *46*		NM	___
(3309)	Turbo Missile Launch Car, *63–64*			
	(A) Red body	23	50	___1
	(B) Olive body	100	295	___1
3330	Flatcar w/ Submarine kit, *60–62*	55	105	___1
3330-100	Oper. Submarine kit, *60–61*	50	105	___1
(3349)	Turbo Missile Launch Car, *62–65*			
	(A) Red body	26	47	___2
	(B) Olive drab body	85	320	___2
3356	Operating Horse Car only, *56–60, 64–66*	44	90	___1
3356	Operating Horse Car and Corral set, *56–60, 64–66*	80	125	___1
3356-100	(9) Black Horses, *56–59*	7	23	___1
3356-150	Horse Car Corral, *57–60*	30	75	___1
3357	Hydraulic Maintenance Car, *62–64*	29	75	___1
3359	Lionel Lines Two-bin Dump, *55–58*	22	60	___1
3360	Operating Burro Crane, *56–57*	140	235	___3
3361	Operating Log Dump Car, *55–58*	22	47	___1
3362	Flatcar w/ helium tanks or logs, *61–63*	16	38	___1
3362/3364	Log Dump Car, *65–69*	15	32	___1
3366	Circus Car Corral set, *59–62*	60	105	___1
3366	Circus Car only, *59–62*	170	235	___1
3366-100	(9) White Horses, *59–60*	31	65	___1
3370	W&A Outlaw Car, *61–64*	23	65	___1
3376	Bronx Zoo Car, *60–66, 69*			
	(A) Blue w/ white lettering	20	50	___2
	(B) Green w/ yellow lettering	35	100	___2
	(C) Blue w/ yellow lettering	115	290	___2
3386	Bronx Zoo Car (adv. cat.), *60*	25	65	___1
3409	Helicopter Car (adv. cat.), *61*	45	100	___1
3410	Helicopter Car, *61–63*	40	85	___1
(3413)	Mercury Capsule Car, *62–64*	65	150	___1
3419	Helicopter Car, *59–65*	50	100	___2
3424	Wabash Operating Boxcar, *56–58*	39	85	___3
3424-100	Low Bridge Signal set, *56–58*	13	49	___1
3428	U.S. Mail Oper. Boxcar, *59–60*	45	100	___1
3429	USMC Helicopter Car, *60*	165	350	___1
3434	Poultry Dispatch car, *59–60, 64–66*	55	120	___1

		Good	Exc	Cond/$
3435	Traveling Aquarium Car, *59–62*			
	(A) Gold circle	430	970	___1
	(B) Tank 1, Tank 2	280	770	___1
	(C) Gold lettering	155	305	___1
	(D) Yellow rubber stamp	100	230	___1
3444	Erie Operating Gondola, *57–59*	45	85	___2
3451	Operating Log Dump Car, *46–48*	15	38	___1
3454	PRR Operating Merchandise Car, *46–47*			
	(A) Red lettering		NRS	___
	(B) Blue lettering	65	115	___1
3456	N&W Operating Hopper Car, *50–55*	17	55	___2
3459	LL Operating Dump Car, *46–48*			
	(A) Aluminum bin	100	265	___1
	(B) Black bin	19	48	___1
	(C) Green bin	27	65	___1
3460	Flatcar w/ trailers, *55–57*	25	60	___1
3461	Lionel Operating Log Car, *49–55*			
	(A) Black car	15	37	___1
	(B) Green car	30	60	___1
3462	Automatic Milk Car, *47–48*			___1
	(A) Plain	22	55	___1
	(B) Glossy Eggshell White	—	110	___1
3462P	Milk Car Platform, *47–48*	5	14	___1
X3464	ATSF Operating Boxcar, *49–52*	10	26	___1
X3464	NYC Operating Boxcar, *49–52*	11	23	___1
3469	LL Operating Dump Car, *49–55*	18	43	___1
3470	Target Launcher, *62–64*			
	(A) Dark blue car	30	70	___1
	(B) Light blue car	60	140	___1
3472	Automatic Milk Car, *49–53*	25	65	___2
3474	Western Pacific Boxcar, *52–53*	25	70	___1
3482	Automatic Milk Car, *54–55*			
	(A) "RT34672" number	65	150	___1
	(B) "RT3482" number	22	60	___1
3484	Pennsylvania Operating Boxcar, *53*			
	(A) White lettering	15	45	___1
	(B) Gold lettering	15	45	___1
3484-25	ATSF Operating Boxcar, *54*			
	(A) White lettering	33	90	___1
	(B) Black lettering	38	105	___1
3494-1	NYC Pacemaker Boxcar, *55*	40	80	___1
3494-150	MP Operating Boxcar, *56*	55	110	___1
3494-275	State of Maine Operating Boxcar, *56–58*	50	115	___1

		Good	Exc	Cond/$
3494-550	Monon Operating Boxcar, *57–58*	120	430	____[1]
3494-625	Soo Operating Boxcar, *57–58*	140	470	____[1]
3509	Satellite Car, *61*	25	48	____[1]
(3510)	Satellite Car (adv. cat.), *62*	40	140	____[1]
3512	Fireman and Ladder Car, *59–61*			
	(A) Black rooftop ladder	60	110	____[2]
	(B) Silver rooftop ladder	75	210	____[2]
3519	Satellite Car, *61–64*	31	65	____[1]
3520	Searchlight Car, *52–53*	27	47	____[2]
3530	GM Generator Car, *56–58*			
	(A) Orange generator	65	125	____[3]
	(B) Gray generator	65	135	____[3]
3530-50	Searchlight w/ pole and base, *56–56*	32	65	____[1]
3535	A E C Security Car, *60–61*	35	125	____[1]
3540	Operating Radar Car, *59–60*	50	195	____[1]
3545	Lionel TV Car, *61–62*	55	185	____[1]
3559	Operating Coal Dump Car, *46–48*	14	35	____[1]
3562-1	ATSF Operating Barrel Car, black, *54*			
	(A) Black trough	75	185	____[1]
	(B) Yellow trough	75	180	____[1]
3562-25	ATSF Operating Barrel Car, gray, *54*			
	(A) Red lettering	145	390	____[1]
	(B) Blue lettering	20	55	____[1]
3562-50	ATSF Oper. Barrel Car, yellow, *55–56*			
	(A) Painted	39	85	____[2]
	(B) Unpainted	20	50	____[2]
3562-75	ATSF Operating Barrel Car, orange, *57–58*	35	60	____[1]
3619	Helicopter Boxcar, *62–64*			
	(A) Light yellow	30	90	____[1]
	(B) Dark yellow	40	135	____[1]
3620	Searchlight Car, *54–56*			
	(A) Gray searchlight	25	45	____[2]
	(B) Orange generator/light	55	130	____[2]
3650	Extension Searchlight Car, *56–59*			
	(A) Light gray	41	60	____[2]
	(B) Dark gray	65	140	____[2]
3656	Armour Operating Cattle Car, *49–55*			
	(A) Black letters, Armour sticker	75	190	____[2]
	(B) White letters, Armour sticker	38	70	____[2]
	(C) No "ARMOUR" sticker, black lettering	25	80	____[2]
	(D) White lettering	25	70	____[2]
3656	Stockyard w/ cattle	28	80	____[2]
3662	Automatic Milk Car, *55–60, 64–66*	34	80	____[1]

		Good	Exc	Cond/$
3665	Minuteman Operating Car, *61–64*			
	(A) Medium blue roof	75	155	___2
	(B) Dark blue roof	55	110	___2
3666	Minuteman Boxcar w/ missile, *64 u*	195	540	___1
3672	Bosco Operating Boxcar, *59–60*			
	(A) Unpainted	120	450	___1
	(B) Painted	140	480	___1
3820	Flatcar w/ submarine, *60–62*	70	195	___1
3830	Flatcar w/ submarine, *60–63*	55	105	___1
3854	Operating Merchandise Car, *46–47*	225	650	___1
3927	Lionel Lines Track Cleaner, *56–60*	55	100	___5
3927-50	Track Cleaning Fluid, *57–69*	3	11	___1
3927-75	Track Cleaning Pads, *57–69*	6	22	___1
4357	PRR SP-type Caboose, elec., *48–49*			
	(A) w/ extra roof plank	55	185	___1
	(B) w/o extra roof plank	—	140	___1
4452	PRR Gondola, electronic, *46–49*	100	210	___1
4454	Baby Ruth PRR Boxcar, elec., *46–49*	60	160	___1
4457	PRR N5 Caboose, electronic, *46–47*		170	___1
4681	Steam 6-8-6, electronic, *50*		NM	___
4776-18	(See 2457, 2472)			
5159	Maintenance kit, *63–65*	2	5	___1
5159-50	Maintenance and Lube kit, *66–69*	2	5	___1
5160	Viewing Stand, *63*	50	130	___1
5459	LL Dump Car, electronic, *46–49*	55	160	___1
6002	NYC Gondola, *50*	4	9	___1
X6004	Baby Ruth PRR Boxcar, *50*	4	7	___1
6007	Lionel Lines SP-type Caboose, *50*	3	8	___1
6009	R.C. Uncoupling Track, *53–54*	1	4	___1
6012	Lionel Gondola, *51–56*	2	7	___1
6014	Airex Boxcar, *60 u*	25	49	___1
6014	Bosco PRR Boxcar, *58*			
	(A) White body	35	60	___1
	(B) Red body	4	7	___1
	(C) Orange body	4	7	___1
6014	Chun King Boxcar, *57 u*	60	115	___1
6014	Frisco Boxcar, *57, 63–69*			
	(A) White body	4	8	___1
	(B) Red body	4	7	___1
	(C) White w/ coin slot	25	45	___1
	(D) Orange body	22	40	___1
X6014	Baby Ruth PRR Boxcar, *51–56*			
	(A) White	5	9	___1

		Good	Exc	Cond/$
	(B) Red	10	26	____1
6014-150	Wix Boxcar, *59 u*	80	150	____1
6015	Sunoco 1-D Tank Car, *54–55*			
	(A) Painted tank	39	105	____1
	(B) Unpainted tank	4	8	____1
6017	Lionel Lines SP-type Caboose, *51–62*	2.50	8	____1
6017	Lionel SP-type Caboose, *56*	14	34	____1
6017-50	USMC SP-type Caboose, *58*	24	60	____1
6017-85	LL SP-type Caboose, gray, *58*	19	43	____1
6017-100	B&M SP-type Caboose, *59, 62, 65–66*			
	(A) Purplish blue	255	475	____1
	(B) Medium or light blue	10	41	____1
6017-185	ATSF SP-type Caboose, *59–60*	11	39	____1
6017-200	U.S. Navy SP-type Caboose, *60*	39	85	____1
6017-225	ATSF SP-type Caboose, c. 63 u, *61–62*	15	42	____1
6017-235	ATSF SP-type Caboose, *62*	28	55	____1
6019	RCS Track set (O27), *48–66*	2	7	____1
6024	Nabisco Shredded Wheat Boxcar, *57*	12	25	____1
6024	RCA Whirlpool Boxcar, *57 u*	30	65	____1
6025	Gulf 1-D Tank Car, *56–58*			
	(A) Gray, blue lettering	5	14	____1
	(B) Orange, blue lettering	5	14	____1
	(C) Black, red "GULF" emblem	5	14	____1
6027	Alaska SP-type Caboose, *59*	25	70	____1
6029	Remote Control Uncoupling Track, *55–63*	1	5	____1
6032	Lionel Gondola, black (O27), *52–54*	2	6	____1
X6034	Baby Ruth PRR Boxcar, *53–54*			
	(A) Orange, blue lettering	5	11	____1
	(B) Red, white lettering	5	11	____1
	(C) Orange, black lettering	5	11	____1
6035	Sunoco 1-D Tank Car, *52–53*	3	7	____1
6037	Lionel Lines SP-type Caboose, *52–54*	2	6	____1
6042	Lionel Gondola, *59–61, 62–64 u*	2	5	____1
6044	Airex Boxcar, orange lettering, *59–60 u*			
	(A) Medium blue	6	16	____1
	(B) Teal blue	40	75	____1
	(C) Dark blue/purple	80	250	____1
6044-1X	Nestles/McCall's Boxcar (no lettering), *62–63 u*	450	910	____1
6045	LL 2-D Tank Car (adv. cat.), *59–64*			
	(A) Gray	15	23	____1
	(B) Orange	15	37	____1
6045	Cities Service 2-D Tank, *60 u*	12	35	____1

		Good	Exc	Cond/$
6047	Lionel Lines SP-type Caboose, *62*	2.50	5	___[1]
6050	Lionel Savings Bank Boxcar, *61*	12	26	___[1]
	(A) BLT, *61*	0	29	___[1]
	(B) BUILT	0	225	___[1]
6050	Swift Refrigerator Car, *62–63*	11	21	___[1]
6050	Libby's Boxcar, *63 u*			
	(A) Green stems on tomatoes	18	41	___[1]
	(B) Green stems missing	19	49	___[1]
6057	LL SP-type Caboose, *59–62*	3	9	___[1]
6057-50	LL SP-type Caboose, orange, *62*			
	(A) Unpainted	12	23	___[1]
	(B) Painted	—	275	___[1]
6058	C&O SP-type Caboose, *61*			
	(A) Blue lettering	18	45	___[1]
	(B) Black lettering	18	50	___[1]
6059	M&StL SP-type Caboose, *61–69*			
	(A) Painted, red	13	22	___[1]
	(B) Unpainted, red	4	8	___[1]
	(C) Unpainted, maroon	7	12	___[1]
6062	NYC Gondola, w/ cable reels, *59–62*	10	17	___[1]
6062-50	NYC Gondola, w/ 2 canisters, *69*	5	18	___[1]
(6067)	Caboose (no lett.), SP-type, *62*	3	5	___[1]
6076	ATSF Hopper, *63 u*	10	20	___[1]
6076	LV Hopper, red, black or gray body, *63*			
	(A) Gray body	7	13	___[1]
	(B) Black body	7	13	___[1]
	(C) Red body	7	13	___[1]
	(D) Yellow body	7	13	___[1]
(6076)	Hopper, no lettering, gray or yellow body, *63*			
	(A) Yellow Body	50	90	___[1]
	(B) Gray body	10	18	___[1]
6110	Steam 2-4-2, 6001T Tender, *50–51*	18	34	___[1]
(6111)	Flatcar w/ logs, *55–57*	6	13	___[1]
6112	Lionel Gondola, *56–58*			
	(A) Black body	3	7	___[1]
	(B) Blue body	4	10	___[1]
	(C) White body	11	25	___[1]
6119	DL&W Work Caboose, red, *55–56*	10	26	___[1]
6119-25	DL&W Work Caboose, orange, *56–59*	11	35	___[1]
6119-50	DL&W Caboose, brown, *56*	17	55	___[1]
6119-75	DL&W Caboose, gray, *57*	12	37	___[1]
6119-100	DL&W Work Caboose, red/gray, *57–66, 69*	13	38	___[1]

		Good	Exc	Cond/$
(6119-125)	Rescue Unit Work Caboose (no number), olive drab, *63–64 u*	65	140	___[1]
(6120)	Work Caboose (no lettering), yellow (adv. cat.), *61–62*	7	23	___[1]
(6121)	Flatcar (various colors) w/ pipes, *56–57*	5	14	___[1]
6130	ATSF Work Caboose, *61, 65–69*	12	35	___[1]
6139	R.C. Uncoupling Track (O27), *63*	1	4	___[1]
6142	Lionel Gondola; green, blue or black, *63–66, 69*	2	5	___[1]
6149	Remote Control Uncoupling Track (O27), *64–69*	1	5	___[1]
(6151)	Flatcar (various colors) w/ patrol truck, *58*			
	(A) Yellow car	40	110	___[1]
	(B) Orange car	40	110	___[1]
	(C) Cream car	40	110	___[1]
6162	NYC Gondola, *59–68*			
	(A) Blue body	5	11	___[1]
	(B) Red body	55	165	___[1]
6162-60	Alaska Gondola, *59*	31	75	___[1]
6167	LL SP-type Caboose, red, *63*			
	(A) Unpainted	5	12	___[1]
	(B) Painted	45	225	___[1]
(6167)	Unstamped SP-type Caboose w/o end rails			
	(A) Red body	3	9	___[1]
	(B) Yellow body	10	23	___[1]
	(C) Brown body	15	36	___[1]
	(D) Olive body	130	395	___[1]
6167-85	UP SP-type Caboose, *69*	10	27	___[1]
6175	Flatcar w/ rocket, red or black body, *58–61*			
	(A) Black car	25	65	___[1]
	(B) Red car	25	65	___[1]
6176	LV Hopper, yellow, gray or black body, *64–66, 69*			
	(A) Yellow	3	9	___[1]
	(B) Gray	3	8	___[1]
	(C) Black	3	8	___[1]
(6176)	Hopper (no lettering), *64*			
	(A) Yellow	6	16	___[1]
	(B) Gray	5	14	___[1]
	(C) Olive	30	75	___[1]
6219	C&O Work Caboose, *60*	33	75	___[1]
6220	Santa Fe NW-2 Switcher, *49–50*			
	(A) Large "GM" decal on cab	125	275	___[2]
	(B) Small "GM" decal on cab	125	260	___[2]

		Good	Exc	Cond/$
6250	Seaboard NW-2 Switcher, *54–55*			
	(A) Decals	125	270	____³
	(B) Rubber-stamped	110	255	____³
6257	Lionel SP-type Caboose, *48–56, 63–64*	3	10	____¹
6257-100	Lionel Lines SP-type Caboose	6	15	____¹
6257-25	Lionel SP-type Caboose	3	7	____¹
6257-50	Lionel SP-type Caboose	3	7	____¹
6257X	Lionel SP-type Caboose, *48*	14	34	____¹
6262	Flatcar w/ wheels, *56–57*			
	(A) Black, *56–57*	30	55	____¹
	(B) Red, *56*	170	445	____¹
6264	Flatcar w/ lumber for Fork Lift set, *57–60*			
	(A) No box	22	60	____¹
	(B) Separate-sale box	150	320	____¹
6311	Flatcar w/ three pipes, *55*	17	43	____¹
6315	Gulf 1-D Chemical Tank Car, *56–59, 68–69*			
	(A) Early, painted	38	70	____²
	(B) Late, unpainted	30	55	____²
	(C) Late, unpainted w/ built date	40	75	____²
6315	Lionel Lines 1-D Tank Car, *63–66*	17	37	____¹
6342	NYC Gondola, *56–58, 64–66*	13	35	____¹
6343	Barrel Ramp Car, *61–62*	15	35	____¹
6346	Alcoa Quad Hopper, *56*	22	55	____¹
6352	PFE Reefer from 352 Ice Depot, *55–57*			
	(A) No box	55	130	____¹
	(B) Separate-sale box	650	1700	____¹
6356	NYC Stock Car, 2 level, *54–55*	15	38	____¹
6357	Lionel SP-type Caboose, *48–61*	8	24	____¹
6357-50	ATSF SP-type Caboose, *60*	325	820	____¹
6361	Flatcar w/ timber, *60–61, 64–69*	29	70	____²
6362	Truck Car w/ 3 trucks, *55–56*			
	(A) Shiny orange	20	50	____¹
	(B) Dull orange	80	130	____¹
6376	LL Circus Stock Car, *56–57*	34	75	____²
(6401)	Flatcar, no load, gray, *60*	2	7	____¹
(6402)	Flatcar w/ reels or boat, *62, 64–66, 69*			
	(A) w/ reels	6	14	____¹
	(B) w/ boat	25	60	____¹
6404	Black Flatcar w/ brown auto, *60*			
	(A) w/ red auto	—	180	____¹
	(B) w/ yellow auto	—	520	____¹
	(C) w/ brown auto	—	930	____¹
	(D) w/ green auto	—	930	____¹

		Good	Exc	Cond/\$
6405	Maroon Flatcar w/ trailer, *61*	15	41	___¹
(6406)	Flatcar w/ yellow auto, *61*			
	(A) Maroon w/ red auto	35	75	___¹
	(B) Maroon w/ yellow auto	70	255	___¹
	(C) Gray w/ dark brown car	—	315	___¹
(6407)	Flatcar w/ rocket, *63*	125	440	___¹
(6408)	Flatcar w/ pipes, *63*	13	26	___¹
(6409)	Flatcar w/ pipes, *63*	13	27	___¹
6411	Flatcar w/ logs, *48–50*	15	30	___¹
6413	Mercury Project Car, *62–63*			
	(A) Powder blue car	75	130	___¹
	(B) Aquamarine car	95	150	___¹
6414	Evans Auto Loader w/ 4 cars, *55–66*			
	(A) Early premium cars w/ windows, chrome bumpers and rubber tires; red, yellow, blue and white	44	110	___⁴
	(B) 4 cheap cars, w/o trim, 2 red, 2 yellow	300	540	___⁴
	(C) 4 red cars w/ gray bumpers	50	160	___⁴
	(D) 4 yellow cars w/ gray bumpers	150	365	___⁴
	(E) Dark yellow, gray bumpers		NRS	___
	(F) Dark brown, chrome bumpers		NRS	___
	(G) 4 brown cars w/ gray bumpers	315	710	___⁴
	(H) Medium green, chrome bumpers		NRS	___
	(I) 4 green cars w/ gray bumpers	405	890	___⁴
6415	Sunoco 3-D Tank Car, *53–55, 64–66, 69*	11	34	___¹
6416	Boat Loader Car, *61–63*	95	240	___¹
6417	PRR Porthole Caboose, *53–57*			
	(A) w/ "NEW YORK ZONE"	10	36	___²
	(B) w/o "NEW YORK ZONE"	105	230	___²
6417-3	(See 6417-25)			
6417-25	Lionel Lines N5C Caboose, *54*	15	40	___¹
6417-50	LV porthole Caboose, *54*			
	(A) Tuscan	375	960	___¹
	(B) Gray	50	125	___¹
6417-51	(See 6417-50)			
6417-53	(See 6417-25)			
6418	(See 214)			
6418	Flatcar w/ steel girders, *55–57*	50	105	___²
6419	DL&W Work Caboose, early frame, *48–50, 52–57*	18	43	___²
6419-25	DL&W Work Caboose, *54–55*	15	37	___¹
6419-50	DL&W Work Caboose, late frame, *56–57*	17	50	___¹
6419-57	(See 6419-100)			

		Good	Exc	Cond/$
6419-75	DL&W Work Caboose, late frame, *56–57*	15	45	___¹
6419-100	N&W Work Caboose, *57–58*	50	115	___¹
6420	DL&W Work Caboose, w/ light, *48–50*	33	75	___¹
6424	Flatcar w/ two autos, *56–59*	26	47	___²
6425	Gulf 3-D Tank Car, *56–58*	17	48	___¹
6427	Lionel Lines Porthole Caboose, *54–60*	13	38	___¹
6427-60	Virginian Porthole Caboose, *58*	140	410	___¹
6427-500	PRR Porthole Caboose, Girls', *57–58**	145	415	___¹
6428	U.S. Mail Boxcar, *60–61, 65–66*	19	37	___¹
6429	DL&W Work Caboose, AAR trucks, *63*	130	330	___¹
6430	Flat. w/ Cooper-Jarrett vans, *56–58*			
	(A) Gray vans	22	60	___¹
	(B) White vans	20	55	___¹
6431	Flatcar w/ vans, *66*	90	245	___¹
6434	Poultry Dispatch, *58–59*	40	75	___¹
6436-1	LV Quad Hopper, black, *55*	15	38	___¹
6436-25	LV Quad Hopper, maroon, *55–57*	18	32	___¹
6436-57	(See 6436-500)			
6436-110	LV Quad Hopper, red, *63–68*			
	(A) w/o cover, no built date			
	(B) w/ cover and "NEW 3-55"			
	(C) w/o cover and "NEW 3-55"			
6436-500	LV Girls' Hopper, lilac, "643657", *57–58**	75	235	___¹
6436-1969	TCA Quad Hopper, *69*	55	85	___¹
6437	PRR Porthole Caboose, *61–68*	16	31	___¹
6440	Flatcar with vans, *61–63*	26	90	___¹
6440	Green Pullman, *48–49*	22	46	___¹
6441	Green Observation, *48–49*	22	46	___¹
6442	Brown Pullman, *49*	33	70	___¹
6443	Brown Observation, *49*	33	60	___¹
6445	Fort Knox Gold Reserve, *61–63*	70	125	___¹
(6446)	N&W Quad Hopper "546446", black or gray, *54–55*	21	50	___¹
6446-25	N&W Quad Hopper "644625", black or gray, *55–57*			
	(A) Black, white lettering	17	65	___¹
	(B) Gray, black lettering	17	65	___¹
6446-60	See 6436-110(B)			
6447	PRR Porthole Caboose, *63*	140	405	___¹
6448	Target Car, *61–64*			
	(A) Red, white lettering	17	35	___¹
	(B) White, red lettering	17	35	___¹
6452	Pennsylvania Gondola, black, *48–49*	6	17	___¹
X6454	Baby Ruth PRR Boxcar, *48*	65	220	___¹

		Good	Exc	Cond/$
X6454	NYC Boxcar, *48*			
	(A) Brown body	18	55	____[1]
	(B) Orange body	50	160	____[1]
	(C) Tan body	16	30	____[1]
X6454	Santa Fe Boxcar, *48*	15	36	____[1]
X6454	SP Boxcar, *49–52*	15	40	____[1]
X6454	Erie Boxcar, *49–52*	22	55	____[1]
X6454	PRR Boxcar, *49–52*	25	65	____[1]
6456	Lehigh Valley Short Hopper, *48–55*			
	(A) Black	8	15	____[2]
	(B) Maroon	6	14	____[2]
	(C) Gray	15	36	____[2]
	(D) Enamel red, yellow lettering	50	130	____[2]
	(E) Enamel red, white lettering	225	510	____[2]
	(F) Enamel gray, maroon letter		NRS	____
6457	Lionel SP-type Caboose, *49–52*	17	36	____[2]
6460	Bucyrus Erie black cab Crane, 8-wheel, *52–54*			
	(A) Black cab	17	49	____[2]
	(B) Red cab	29	80	____[2]
6460-25	Bucyrus Erie red cab Crane, 8-wheel, w/ box, *54*	42	90	____[1]
6461	Transformer Car, *49–50*	28	80	____[1]
6462	Pennsylvania Gondola, black, *49*	—	60	____
6462	NYC Gondola, *49–57*			
	(A) Black	9	12	____[2]
	(B) Green	8	19	____[2]
	(C) Red	5	15	____[2]
6462-500	NYC Girls' Gondola, pink, *57–58**	65	160	____[1]
6463	Rocket Fuel 2-D Tank, *62–63*	11	48	____[1]
6464-1	WP Boxcar, *53–54*			
	(A) Blue lettering	35	65	____[3]
	(B) Red lettering	450	1150	____[3]
	(C) Orange, silver lettering		NRS	____
6464-25	GN Boxcar, *53–54*	43	85	____[3]
6464-50	M&StL Boxcar, *53–56*	43	70	____[2]
6464-75	RI Boxcar, *53–54, 69*	42	80	____[3]
6464-100	WP Boxcar, *54–55*			
	(A) Silver body, yellow feather	60	115	____[1]
	(B) Orange body, blue feather	355	810	____[1]
	(C) Orange, blue feather, "1954"		NRS	____
	(D) (C) w/ "6464-100"		NRS	____
6464-125	NYC Boxcar, *54–56*	42	115	____[1]
6464-150	MP Boxcar, *54–55, 57*	39	110	____[2]

6464-175 Rock Island Boxcar, *54–55*
    (A) Blue lettering | 50 | 90 | ___1
    (B) Black lettering | 450 | 950 | ___1

	Good	Exc	Cond/$
6464-175 Rock Island Boxcar, *54–55*			
(A) Blue lettering	50	90	___1
(B) Black lettering	450	950	___1
6464-200 Pennsylvania Boxcar, *54–55, 69*	85	145	___1
6464-225 SP Boxcar, *54–56*	55	120	___2
6464-250 WP Boxcar, *66*	105	205	___2
6464-275 State of Maine Boxcar, *55, 57–59*			
(A) Striped doors	48	85	___2
(B) Solid doors	55	135	___2
6464-300 Rutland Boxcar, *55–56*			
(A) Rubber-stamped	40	100	___2
(B) Split door	310	850	___2
(C) Solid shield	850	2250	___2
(D) Heat-stamped	50	135	___2
6464-325 B&O Sentinel Boxcar, *56*	320	640	___1
6464-350 MKT Katy Boxcar, *56*	125	245	___1
6464-375 Central of Georgia Boxcar, *56–57, 66*			
(A) Unpainted, maroon body	45	110	___2
(B) Painted, red body	800	1550	___2
6464-400 B&O Time-saver Boxcar, *56–57, 69*			
(A) Lettered "BLT 5-54"	40	110	___2
(B) Lettered "BLT 2-56"	95	230	___2
6464-425 New Haven Boxcar, *56–58*	32	65	___2
6464-450 Great Northern Boxcar, *56–57, 66*	65	105	___2
6464-475 B&M Boxcar, *57–60, 65–66, 68*	38	80	___2
6464-500 Timken Boxcar, yellow and white, charcoal lettering (Also see 6464-500 in MPC) 57-58, *69*	65	130	___1
6464-510 NYC Pacemaker Boxcar, *57–58*	345	640	___1
6464-515 MKT Boxcar, *57–58*	300	610	___1
6464-525 M&StL Boxcar, *57–58, 64–66*			
(A) Red, white lettering	30	60	___2
(B) Maroon, white lettering	—	530	___2
6464-650 D&RGW Boxcar, *57–58, 66*			
(A) Unpainted yellow body	50	115	___2
(B) (A) w/o black stripe	150	195	___2
(C) Painted yellow body and roof	500	900	___2
6464-700 Santa Fe Boxcar, *61, 66*	55	115	___1
6464-725 New Haven Boxcar, *62–66, 68*			
(A) Orange body	30	55	___1
(B) Black body	70	205	___1
6464-825 Alaska Boxcar, *59–60*	135	350	___2
6464-900 NYC Boxcar, *60–66*	50	120	___2

		Good	Exc	Cond/$
6464-1965	TCA Pittsburgh Boxcar, *65*	—	205	___¹
6464-1970	(See MPC)			
6464-1971	(See MPC)			
6465	Sunoco 2-D Tank Car, *48–56*	5	16	___¹
6465	Cities Service 2-D Tank, *60–62*	14	26	___¹
6465	Gulf 2-D Tank Car, *58*			
	(A) Black tank	25	60	___¹
	(B) Gray tank	10	23	___¹
6465	LL 2-D Tank Car, *59, 63–64*			
	(A) Black tank	10	26	___¹
	(B) Orange tank	5	14	___¹
6467	Bulkhead Flatcar, *56*	22	60	___¹
6468	B&O Auto Boxcar, *53–55*			
	(A) Tuscan	140	290	___¹
	(B) Blue	20	45	___¹
6468-25	NH Auto Boxcar, *56–58*			
	(A) Black "N" over white "H"	41	155	___¹
	(B) White "N" over black "H"	215	470	___¹
(6469)	Lionel Liquefied Gases Car, *63*	65	155	___¹
6470	Explosives Boxcar, *59–60*	14	37	___¹
6472	Refrigerator Car, *50–53*	19	39	___¹
6473	Horse Transport Car, *62–69*	9	24	___¹
6475	Heinz 57 Vat Car, post-factory alteration, *65–66*	50	105	___¹
6475	Libby's Crushed Pineapple Vat Car, *63 u*	22	65	___¹
6475	Pickles Vat Car, *60–62*	22	45	___¹
6476	LV Hopper, red, black, and gray body, *57–69*			
	(A) Red body	4	9	___¹
	(B) Gray body	4	9	___¹
	(C) Black body	4	10	___¹
6476-1	LV Hopper, gray, TTOS, *69*	25	70	___¹
6476-135	LV Hopper, yellow, *64–66, 68*	6	11	___¹
6476-160	LV Hopper, black, *69*	7	16	___¹
6476-185	LV Hopper, yellow, *69*	6	14	___¹
6477	Bulkhead Car w/ pipes, *57–58*	23	65	___¹
6480	Explosives Boxcar, red (adv. cat.), *61*	27	48	___¹
6482	Refrigerator Car, *57*	30	50	___¹
(6500)	Flatcar w/ Bonanza plane, *62, 65*			
	(A) Plane w/ red top and wings	365	730	___²
	(B) Plane w/ white top and wings	290	570	___²
(6501)	Flatcar w/ jet boat, *62–63*	70	130	___¹
(6502)	Flatcar w/ bridge girder, *62*	20	45	___¹
6511	Flatcar w/ pipes, *53–56*	18	40	___²
(6512)	Cherry Picker Car, *62–63*	32	90	___¹

		Good	Exc	Cond/$
6517	LL Bay Window Caboose, *55–59*			
	(A) Underscored	30	70	___2
	(B) Not underscored	20	60	___2
6517-75	Erie B/W Caboose, *66*	185	445	___1
6517-1966	TCA B/W Caboose, *66*	90	190	___1
6518	Transformer Car, *56–58*	55	110	___1
6519	Allis-Chalmers Flatcar, *58–61*			
	(A) Dark/medium orange base	35	70	___1
	(B) Dull light orange base	40	100	___1
6520	Searchlight Car, *49–51*			
	(A) Tan diesel generator	200	450	___2
	(B) Green diesel generator	160	315	___2
	(C) Maroon or orange diesel gen.	25	55	___2
	(D) Orange generator, gray light	25	50	___2
6530	Fire Fighting Car, red, *60–61*			
	(A) Red, white lettering	40	70	___1
	(B) Black, white lettering	—	415	___1
6536	M&St L Quad Hopper, *58–59, 63*	20	45	___1
6544	Missile Firing Car, *60–64*			
	(A) White-lettered console	45	100	___1
	(B) Black-lettered console	175	390	___1
6555	Sunoco 1-D Tank Car, *49–50*	17	40	___1
6556	MKT Stock Car, *58*	75	280	___1
6557	Lionel SP-type Caboose, smoke, *58–59*	90	275	___2
6560	Bucyrus Erie Crane w/ stack, 8-wheel, *55–58, 68–69*			
	(A) Reddish-orange or black cab, early construction	65	160	___2
	(B) Gray cab	40	75	___2
	(C) Red cab	23	45	___2
	(D) Dark blue (Hagerstown)	40	85	___2
6560-25	Bucyrus Erie Crane, 8-whl., *56*	45	90	___1
6561	Reel Car, *53–56*			
	(A) Orange reels	20	55	___1
	(B) Gray reels	25	60	___1
6562	NYC Gondola w/ canisters, *56–58*			
	(A) Gray body, 1956	15	44	___1
	(B) Red body, 1956, 1958	15	38	___1
	(C) Black body, 1957	15	38	___1
6572	REA Refrig. Car, *58–59, 63*	55	125	___1
6630	IRBM Rocket Launcher (adv. cat.), *61*	30	85	___1
6636	Alaska Quad Hopper, *59–60*	17	47	___1

		Good	Exc	Cond/$
6640	USMC Rocket Launcher, *60*	75	175	____[1]
6646	Lionel Lines Stock Car, *57*	16	45	____[1]
6650	IRBM Rocket Launcher, *59–63*	25	55	____[1]
6650-80	Missile, *60*	3	9	____[1]
6651	USMC Cannon Car, *64 u*	65	190	____[1]
6656	Lionel Lines Stock Car, *49–55*			
	(A) With brown "ARMOUR" decal	55	105	____[2]
	(B) Without decal	9	23	____[2]
6657	Rio Grande SP-type Caboose, *57–58*	55	165	____[1]
6660	Flatcar w/ crane, *58*	30	70	____[1]
6670	Flatcar w/ crane, *59–60*	20	65	____[1]
6672	Santa Fe Refrigerator Car, *54–56*			
	(A) Blue lettering, 2 lines	25	60	____[1]
	(B) Black lettering, 2 lines	22	65	____[1]
	(C) Blue lettering, 3 lines	75	250	____[1]
6736	Detroit & Mack. Quad Hopper, *60–62*	17	40	____[1]
6800	Flatcar w/ airplane, *57–60*			
	(A) Yellow plane w/ black top	75	175	____[2]
	(B) Black plane w/ yellow top	75	160	____[2]
6801	Flatcar w/ boat, *57–60*			
	(A) Boat with blue hull	45	100	____[1]
	(B) Brownish-yellow boat hull	45	100	____[1]
	(C) Boat with white hull	45	85	____[1]
6802	Flatcar w/ bridge, *58–59*	15	27	____[1]
6803	Flatcar w/ tank and truck, *58–59*	70	160	____[1]
6804	Flatcar w/ USMC trucks, *58–59*	80	200	____[1]
6805	Atomic Disposal Flatcar, *58–59*	48	150	____[1]
6806	Flatcar w/ USMC trucks, *58–59*	80	185	____[1]
6807	Lionel Flatcar w/ boat, *58–59*	60	120	____[1]
6808	Flatcar w/ USMC trucks, *58–59*	110	250	____[1]
6809	Flatcar w/ USMC trucks, *58–59*	95	190	____[1]
6810	Flatcar w/ trailer, *58*	23	50	____[1]
6812	Track Maintenance Car, *59*			
	(A) Dark yellow-gold superstructure	18	80	____[1]
	(B) Black base and gray top	18	80	____[1]
	(C) Gray base, black top	18	80	____[1]
	(D) Cream base and top	19	85	____[1]
	(E) Light yellow base and top	18	80	____[1]
6814	Lionel Rescue Caboose, *59–61*	30	100	____[1]
6816	Flatcar w/ Allis-Chalmers tractor dozer, *59–60*			
	(A) Red car	210	425	____[1]
	(B) Black car	485	1440	____[1]

		Good	Exc	Cond/$
6816-100	Allis-Chalmers Tractor Dozer, *59–60*			
	(A) No box	75	200	___ [1]
	(B) Separate-sale box	1050	2400	___ [1]
6817	Flatcar w/ Allis-Chalmers motor scraper, *59–60*			
	(A) Red car	210	430	___ [1]
	(B) Black car	370	1900	___ [1]
6817-100	Allis-Chalmers Motor Scraper, *59–60*			
	(A) No box	105	250	___ [1]
	(B) Separate-sale box	1150	2600	___ [1]
6818	Transformer Car, *58*	25	50	___ [1]
6819	Flatcar w/ helicopter, *59–60*	21	60	___ [1]
6820	Flatcar w/ missile transport helicopter, *60–61*			
	(A) Light blue-painted flatcar	80	205	___ [1]
	(B) Darker blue flatcar	50	135	___ [1]
6821	Flatcar w/ crates, *59–60*	21	33	___ [1]
6822	Searchlight Car, *61–69*			
	(A) Black base, gray light	20	42	___ [2]
	(B) Gray base, black light	20	44	___ [2]
6823	Flatcar w/ IRBM missiles, *59–60*	21	55	___ [1]
6824	USMC Work Caboose, *60*	70	185	___ [1]
6825	Flatcar w/ bridge, *59–62*	22	41	___ [1]
6826	Flatcar w/ trees, *59–60*	50	95	___ [1]
6827	Flatcar w/ steam shovel, *60–63*	70	145	___ [1]
6827-100	Harnischfeger Tractor Shovel, *60*			
	(A) No box	55	110	___ [1]
	(B) Separate-sale box	105	185	___ [1]
6828	Flatcar w/ crane, *60–63, 66*	100	200	___ [1]
6828-100	Harnischfeger Construction Crane, *60*			
	(A) No box	55	135	___ [1]
	(B) Separate-sale box	115	170	___ [1]
6830	Flatcar w/ submarine, *60–61*	50	90	___ [1]
6844	Flatcar w/ missiles, *59–60*			
	(A) Black plastic flatcar	20	75	___ [1]
	(B) Red plastic flatcar	300	590	___ [1]
63132	(See 3464)			
64173	(See 6427 LL)			
65400	(See 2454 or 6454)			
81000	(See 6417 PRR)			
96743	(See 6454)			
159000	(See 3464)			
336155	(See 3361)			
477618	(See 2457 or 2472)			
536417	(See 6417 PRR)			

		Good	Exc	Cond/$
546446	(See 6446)			
576419	(See 6419-100)			
576427	(See 6427-500)			
641751	(See 6417-50)			
A	Transformer, 90 watts, *47–48*	25	70	___1
CTC	Lockon (O and O27), *47–69*	—	0.65	___1
ECU-1	Electronic Control Unit, *46*	22	65	___1
KW	Transformer, 190 watts, *50–65*	100	130	___4
LTC	Lockon (O and O27), *50–69*	—	3	___1
LW	Transformer, 125 watts, *55–56*	95	105	___3
OC	Curved Track (O), *45–61*	—	1.50	___1
OC1/2	Half Sec. Curve Track (O), *45–66*	—	1.50	___1
OCS	Curved Insulated Track (O), *46–50*		NRS	___
OS	Straight Track (O), *45–61*	—	1.50	___1
OSS	Straight Insulated Track, *46–50*		NRS	___
OTC	Lockon Track (O and O27)	—	3	___1
Q	Transformer, 75 watts, *46*	20	60	___1
R	Transformer, 110 watts, *46–47*	30	65	___1
RW	Transformer, 110 watts, *48–54*	42	70	___1
RCS	Remote Control Track (O), *45–48*	6	10	___1
SP	Smoke Pellets, bottle, *48–69*	6	18	___1
SW	Transformer, 130 watts, *61–66*	55	90	___1
TW	Transformer, 175 watts, *53–60*	80	120	___1
TOC	Curved Track (O), *62–66, 68–69*	—	1.50	___1
TOC1/2	Half Sec. Str. Trk. (O), *62–6(*	—	1.50	___1
TOS	Straight Track (O), *62–69*	—	1.50	___1
UCS	Remote Control Track (O), *45–69*	8	17	___1
UTC	Lockon (O, O27, Standard), *45*	—	1.50	___1
V	Transformer, 150 watts, *46–47*	85	150	___1
VW	Transformer, 150 watts, *48–49*	70	140	___1
Z	Transformer, 250 watts, *45–47*	100	180	___1
ZW	Transformer, 250 watts, *48–49*	115	215	___1
ZW	Transformer, 275 watts, *50–66*	155	240	___5

No Number SP-type Caboose, (see 6067, 6167)
No Number Work Caboose, (see 6119-125, 6120)
No Number Flatcar (see 6401, 6402, 6406)
No Number Gondola (see 6142)
No Number Hopper (see 6176)
No Number Turbo Missile Car (see 3309, 3349)
No Number Rolling Stock (see 3413, 3510, 6111, 6121,
            6151, 6407, 6408, 6409, 6469, 6500, 6501,
            6502, 6512)

Section 3
MODERN ERA 1970–2004
MPC/LTI/LLC

		Exc	New	Cond/$
3	(See 8104, 8630, 8701)			
[4]	Midwest TCA C&NW F-3 A Unit, shell only, *77 u*		NRS	___
4	(See 18008, 18013)			
T-4	(See 12923)			
[00005]	Midwest TCA Covered Quad Hopper, *78 u*	—	50	___ 1
6	(See 18023)			
[10]	METCA Jersey Central F-3 A Unit, shell only, *71 u*		NRS	___
12	(See 16137, 52029)			
14	(See 52032)			
27	(See 18841)			
29	(See 52039)			
36	(See 19042)			
40	(See 11737)			
52	(See 18555)			
65-00637	(See 18927)			
74	(See 19718)			
79C95204C	Sears Santa Fe Diesel set, *71 u*	150	165	___ 1
79C9715C	Sears 4-unit set, *75 u*	50	65	___ 1
79C9717C	Sears 7-unit set, *75 u*	150	165	___ 1
79N95223C	Sears 6-unit set, *74 u*	150	165	___ 1
79N9552C	Sears 6-unit set, *72 u*	150	165	___ 1
79N9553C	Sears 6-unit Diesel set, *72 u*	150	165	___ 1
79N96178C	Sears 4-unit set, *74 u*	50	65	___ 1
79N97082C	Sears set, *70 u*		NRS	___
79N97101C	Sears 5-unit set, *75 u*	150	165	___ 1
79N98765C	Sears Logging Empire set, *78 u*	100	115	___ 1
91	(See 18558)			
102	(See 19538)			
109	(See 11809)			
0121	(See 19717)			
125	(See 19724)			
150	(See 18553)			
154	(See 18223)			
155	(See 18224)			
190	(See 17899)			
197	(See 18843)			
200	(See 18117/18118)			
200A	(See 18121)			

		Exc	New	Cond/$
200B	(See 18122)			
D200	(See 18512)			
D202	(See 18506)			
D203	(See 18506)			
211	(See 19136)			
C217	(See 19715)			
D250	(See 18512)			
254	(See 18920)			
260	(See 19133)			
300	(See 17307, 18934/18935)			
C300	(See 19719)			
301	(See 16807, 17308)			
302	(See 17309)			
[303]	LOTS Stauffer Chemical 1-D Tank Car, *85 u*	85	195	____[1]
303	(See 17310)			
304	(See 18934/18935)			
342	(See 11903)			
342B	(See 11903)			
343	(See 11903)			
351C	(See 11724)			
366A	(See 11724)			
370B	(See 11724)			
371	(See 18907)			
371B	(See 18108)			
400	(See 18505)			
401	(See 18505)			
425	(See 19135)			
469	(See 19132)			
483	(See 18306)			
484	(See 8587)			
484	(See 18310)			
485	(See 18310)			
490	(See 18043)			
491	(See 7203)			
494	(See 19140)			
495	(See 19141)			
501	(See 17213)			
504	(See 18504)			
507	(See 19128)			
(0511)	TCA St. Louis Baggage Car "1981", *81 u*	50	60	____[1]
0512	Toy Fair Reefer, *81 u*	75	95	____[1]
537	(See 19143)			
538	(See 19142)			

		Exc	New	Cond/$
539	(See 16539)			
550	(See 8378)			
(550C)	Curved Track 31" (O), *70*	0.85	1.50	___¹
(550S)	Straight Track (O), *70*	0.85	1.50	___¹
576	(See 19108)			
577	(See 9562)			
577	(See 19139)			
578	(See 9563)			
579	(See 9564)			
580	(See 9565)			
581	(See 9566)			
582	(See 9567)			
582	(See 19144)			
600	(See 18824)			
601	(See 19111)			
611	(See 8100)			
612	(See 18040)			
618	(See 18042)			
619	(See 18041)			
634	Santa Fe NW-2, *70 u*	47	85	___¹
638	(See 18638)			
639	(See 18639)			
659	(See 8101)			
665E	Johnny Cash "Blue Train" 4-6-4, *71 u*		NRS	___
672	(See 8610)			
680	(See 51229)			
681	(See 51240)			
684	(See 51233)			
685	(See 51245)			
700	(See 18046)			
721	(See 18554)			
725A	(See 11734)			
725B	(See 11734)			
736A	(See 11734)			
779	(See 8215)			
0780	LRRC Boxcar, *82 u*	60	70	___¹
0781	LRRC Flatcar w/ trailers, *83 u*	65	75	___¹
0782	LRRC 1-D Tank Car, *85 u*	43	55	___¹
783	(See 8406)			
0784	LRRC Covered Quad Hopper, *84 u*	55	65	___¹
784	(See 8606)			
785	(See 18002)			
788	(See 19818)			

		Exc	New	Cond/$
789	(See 19134)			
858	(See 18116)			
859	(See 18116)			
863	(See 18309)			
868	(See 18842)			
901	(See 19532)			
907	(See 16566, 18024)			
914	(See 17893)			
1017	(See 18921)			
[1018-1979]	TCA Mortgage Burning Hi-cube Boxcar, *79 u*	32	37	___[1]
1041	(See 16538)			
(1050)	New Englander set, *80–81*	155	185	___[1]
(1051)	T&P Diesel set, *80*		NM	___
(1052)	Chesapeake Flyer set, *80*	140	150	___[1]
(1053)	The James Gang set, *80- ??*	175	220	___[1]
(1070)	The Royal Limited set, *80*	310	355	___[1]
(1071)	Mid Atlantic Limited set, *80*	285	295	___[1]
(1072)	Cross Country Express set, *80–81*	270	350	___[1]
(1076)	Lionel Clock, *76–77 u*	500	575	___[1]
(1081)	Wabash Cannonball set, *70–72*	105	120	___[1]
(1082)	Yard Boss set, *70*	120	165	___[1]
(1083)	Pacemaker set, *70*	105	120	___[1]
(1084)	Grand Trunk & Western set, *70*	120	140	___[1]
(1085)	Santa Fe Express Diesel Freight set, *70*	175	190	___[1]
(1086)	The Mountaineer set, *70*		NM	___
(1087)	Midnight Express set, *70*		NM	___
(1091)	Sears Special set, *70 u*	150	165	___[1]
(1092)	79N97081C Sears set, *70 u*	150	165	___[1]
(1092)	79C97105C Sears 6-unit set, *71 u*	150	165	___[1]
(1100)	Happy Huff n' Puff, *74–75 u*	50	60	___[1]
1115	(See 19040)			
1116	(See 19041)			
(1150)	L.A.S.E.R. Train set, *81–82*	165	185	___[1]
(1151)	Union Pacific Thunder Freight set, *81–82*	150	175	___[1]
(1153)	JC Penney Thunderball Freight set, *81 u*	165	180	___[1]
(1154)	Reading Yard King set, *81–82*	180	200	___[1]
(1155)	Cannonball Freight set, *82*	75	85	___[1]
(1157)	Lionel Leisure Wabash Cannonball set, *81 u*		NRS	___
(1158)	Maple Leaf Limited set, *81*	350	410	___[1]
(1159)	Toys "R" Us Midnight Flyer set, *81 u*	130	140	___[1]
(1160)	Great Lakes Limited set, *81*	305	325	___[1]
(T-1171)	Canadian National Steam Loco set, *71 u*	240	275	___[1]
(T-1172)	Yardmaster set, *71 u*	NRS	200	___[1]

		Exc	New	Cond/$
(T-1173)	Grand Trunk & Western set, *71–73 u*	175	195	___1
(T-1174)	Canadian National set, *71–73 u*	265	300	___1
(1182)	The Yardmaster set, *71–72*	85	105	___1
(1183)	The Silver Star set, *71–72*	65	80	___1
(1184)	The Allegheny set, *71*	120	150	___1
(1186)	Cross Country Express set, *71–72*	210	260	___1
(1187)	Illinois Central set (SSS), *71*	400	485	___1
(1190)	Sears Special #1 set, *71 u*	85	100	___1
1192	(See 19120)			
(1195)	JC Penney Special set, *71 u*	150	165	___1
(1198)	Unnamed set, *71 u*	—	175	___1
(1199)	Ford-Autolite Allegheny set, *71 u*	175	195	___1
(1200)	Gravel Gus, *75 u*	75	100	___1
1200	(See 19116)			
1201	(See 18022)			
[1203]	NETCA B&M NW-2, shell only, *72 u*	—	65	___1
1212	(See 19118)			
[1223]	LOTS Seattle & North Coast Hi-cube Boxcar, *86 u*	150	200	___1
1240	(See 19117)			
(1250)	New York Central set (SSS), *72*	350	420	___1
(1252)	Heavy Iron set, *82–83*	95	135	___1
(1253)	Quicksilver Express set, *82–83*	230	285	___1
(1254)	Black Cave Flyer set, *82*	75	105	___1
(1260)	Continental Limited set, *82*	285	350	___1
(1261)	49N95211 Sears Black Cave Flyer set, *82 u*	165	195	___1
(1262)	Toys "R" Us Heavy Iron set, *82 u*	150	165	___1
(1263)	XU671-0701A JC Penney Overland Freight set, *82 u*	150	165	___1
(1264)	Nibco Express set, *82 u*	200	225	___1
(1265)	Tappan Special set, *82 u*	130	155	___1
(T-1272)	Yardmaster set, *72–73 u*	150	165	___1
(T-1273)	Silver Star set, *72–73 u*	90	115	___1
(1280)	Kickapoo Valley & Northern set, *72*	60	75	___1
(1284)	Allegheny set, *72*	140	165	___1
(1285)	Santa Fe Twin Diesel set, *72*	95	140	___1
(1287)	Pioneer Dockside Switcher set, *72*	100	95	___1
[1287]	Midwest TCA C&NW Reefer, *84 u*		NRS	___
1289	(See 17875)			
(1290)	Sears set, *72 u*	150	165	___1
(1291)	Sears set, *72 u*	150	165	___1
(1300)	Gravel Gus Junior, *75 u*	70	90	___1
1322	(See 19119)			

		Exc	New	Cond/$
(1350)	Canadian Pacific set (SSS), *73*	570	770	____[1]
(1351)	Baltimore & Ohio set, *83–84*	205	245	____[1]
(1352)	Rocky Mountain Freight set, *83–84*	75	95	____[1]
(1353)	Southern Streak set, *83–85*	75	95	____[1]
(1354)	Northern Freight Flyer set, *83–85*	250	305	____[1]
(1355)	Commando Assault Train set, *83–84*	175	265	____[1]
(1359)	Train Display Case for set 1355, *83 u*	75	95	____[1]
(1361)	Gold Coast Limited set, *83*	580	600	____[1]
(1362)	Lionel Leisure BN Express set, *83 u*	200	300	____[1]
(1380)	US Steel Industrial Switcher set, *73–75*	60	75	____[1]
(1381)	Cannonball set, *73–75*	70	75	____[1]
(1382)	Yardmaster set, *73–74*	100	120	____[1]
(1383)	Santa Fe Freight set, *73–75*	100	125	____[1]
(1384)	Southern Express set, *73–76*	75	120	____[1]
(1385)	Blue Streak Freight set, *73–74*	100	120	____[1]
(1386)	Rock Island Express set, *73–74*	120	140	____[1]
(1387)	Milwaukee Road Special set, *73*	185	280	____[1]
(1388)	Golden State Arrow set, *73–75*	215	240	____[1]
(1390)	Sears 7-unit set, *73 u*	150	165	____[1]
1390	(See 18044)			
(1392)	79C95224C Sears 8-unit set, *73 u*	150	165	____[1]
(1393)	79C95223C Sears 6-unit set, *73 u*	150	165	____[1]
(1395)	JC Penney set, *73 u*	150	165	____[1]
(1400)	Happy Huff n' Puff Junior, *75 u*	130	140	____[1]
(1402)	Chessie System set, *84–85*	135	160	____[1]
(1403)	Redwood Valley Express set, *84–85*	170	205	____[1]
1403	(See 19145)			
(1450)	D&RGW set (SSS), *74*	380	470	____[1]
(1451)	Erie-Lackawanna Limited set, *84*	540	600	____[1]
1458	(See 52031)			
(1460)	Grand National set, *74*	265	305	____[1]
(1461)	Black Diamond set, *74 u, 75*	100	120	____[1]
(1463)	Coca-Cola Special set, *74 u, 75*	190	235	____[1]
(1487)	Broadway Limited set, *74–75*	225	285	____[1]
(1489)	Santa Fe Double Diesel set, *74–76*	140	165	____[1]
(1492)	79N96185C Sears 7-unit set, *74 u*	150	165	____[1]
(1493)	79N96185C Sears 7-unit set, *74 u*	150	165	____[1]
(1499)	JC Penney Great Express set, *74 u*	150	165	____[1]
(1501)	Midland Freight set, *85–86*	75	95	____[1]
1501	(See 18003)			
(1502)	Yard Chief set, *85–86*	200	225	____[1]
(1506)	Sears Chessie System set, *85 u*	165	195	____[1]
(1512)	JC Penney Midland Freight set, *85 u*	90	115	____[1]

		Exc	New	Cond/$
1538	(See 18838)			
(1549)	Toys "R" Us Heavy Iron set, *85–89 u*	200	240	___1
(1552)	Burlington Northern Limited set, *85*	610	690	___1
1552	(See 52007)			
(1560)	North American Express set, *75*	225	280	___1
(1562)	Fast Freight Flyer set, *85 u*	120	140	___1
(1577)	Liberty Special set, *75 u*	160	190	___1
(1579)	Milwaukee Road set (SSS), *75*	370	470	___1
(1581)	Thunderball Freight set, *75–76*	85	95	___1
(1582)	Yard Chief set, *75–76*	115	155	___1
(1584)	Norfolk & Western "Spirit of America" set, *75*	200	215	___1
(1585)	75th Anniversary Special set, *75–77*	205	240	___1
(1586)	Chesapeake Flyer set, *75–77*	160	190	___1
(1587)	Capitol Limited set, *75*	255	280	___1
(1594)	Sears set, *75 u*		NRS	___
(1595)	79C9716C Sears 6-unit set, *75 u*	150	165	___1
(1602)	Nickel Plate Special set, *86–91*	120	125	___1
(1606)	Sears Nickel Plate Special set, *86 u*	165	195	___1
(1608)	American Express General set, *86 u*	185	280	___1
(1615)	Cannonball Express set, *86–90*	65	75	___1
1623	(See 19146)			
(1632)	Santa Fe Work Train set (SSS), *86*	195	225	___1
(1652)	B&O Freight set, *86*	165	190	___1
(1658)	Town House TV and Appliances set, *86 u*	80	95	___1
(1660)	Yard Boss set, *76*	95	110	___1
(1661)	Rock Island Line set, *76–77*	95	120	___1
(1662)	Black River Freight set, *76–78*	75	95	___1
(1663)	Amtrak Lake Shore Limited set, *76–77*	215	270	___1
(1664)	Illinois Central Freight set, *76–77*	265	355	___1
(1665)	NYC Empire State Express set, *76*	315	450	___1
(1672)	Northern Pacific set (SSS), *76*	240	310	___1
(1685)	True Value Freight Flyer set, *86–87 u*	60	75	___1
(1686)	Kay Bee Toys Freight Flyer set, *86 u*	150	165	___1
(1687)	Freight Flyer set, *87–90*	39	47	___1
(1693)	Toys "R" Us Rock Island Line set, *76 u*	110	130	___1
(1694)	Toys "R" Us Black River Freight set, *76 u*	110	130	___1
(1696)	Sears set, *76 u*	110	130	___1
(1698)	True Value Rock Island Line set, *76 u*	110	130	___1
1750	(See 52035)			
1754	(See 52037)			
(1760)	Trains n' Truckin' Steel Hauler set, *77–78*	90	95	___1
(1761)	Trains n' Truckin' Cargo King set, *77–78*	85	150	___1
(1762)	Wabash Cannonball set, *77*	135	190	___1

		Exc	New	Cond/$
(1764)	Heartland Express set, *77*	185	215	____[1]
(1765)	Rocky Mountain Special set, *77*	205	265	____[1]
(1766)	B&O Budd Car set (SSS), *77*	285	315	____[1]
1776	(See 8559, 8665, 9170)			
1776	Seaboard U36B, *74–76*	120	170	____[1]
(1790)	Lionel Leisure Steel Hauler set, *77 u*	150	200	____[1]
(1791)	Toys "R" Us Steel Hauler set, *77 u*	130	175	____[1]
(1792)	True Value Rock IslandLine set, *77 u*	100	135	____[1]
(1793)	Toys "R" Us Black River Freight set, *77 u*	120	155	____[1]
(1796)	JC Penney Cargo Master set, *77 u*	—	200	____[1]
1803	(See 19147)			
1815	(See 18815)			
1818	(See 18931)			
1821	(See 18840)			
(1860)	Workin' on the Railroad Timberline set, *78*	60	75	____[1]
(1862)	Workin' on the Railroad Logging Empire set, *78*	75	95	____[1]
(1864)	Santa Fe Double Diesel set, *78–79*	155	190	____[1]
(1865)	Chesapeake Flyer set, *78–79*	140	165	____[1]
(1866)	Great Plains Express set, *78–79*	195	270	____[1]
(1867)	Milwaukee Road Limited set, *78*	245	295	____[1]
(1868)	M&StL set (SSS), *78*	220	255	____[1]
(1892)	JC Penney Logging Empire set, *78 u*	95	125	____[1]
(1893)	Toys "R" Us Logging Empire set, *78 u*	175	225	____[1]
1900	(See 18502)			
1905-95	(See 16953)			
1921	(See 52047)			
1947	(See 18830)			
1952	(See 19960)			
(1960)	Midnight Flyer set, *79–81*	55	75	____[1]
1960	(See 18943)			
(1962)	Wabash Cannonball set, *79*	90	105	____[1]
(1963)	Black River Freight set, *79–81*	75	85	____[1]
(1964)	Radio Control Express set, *79 u*		NM	____
(1965)	Smokey Mountain Line set, *79*	65	85	____[1]
(1970)	Southern Pacific Limited set, *79 u*	375	415	____[1]
1970	(See 8615)			
(1971)	Quaker City Limited Set, *1979*	380	415	____[1]
[1971-1976] Rocky Mountain TCA Reefer, *76 u*			NRS	____
1973	(See 9123)			
1973	TCA Bicentennial Observation Car (O27), *76 u*	34	50	____[1]
1974	TCA Bicentennial Passenger Car (O27), *76 u*	34	50	____[1]
1975	TCA Bicentennial Passenger Car (O27), *76 u*	34	50	____[1]
1976	TCA Seaboard U36B, *76 u*	140	185	____[1]

Exc New Cond/$

		Exc	New	Cond/$
[1976]	Southern TCA Florida East Coast F-3 ABA, shells only, *76 u*		NRS	___
[1979]	IETCA Boxcar, *79 u*	—	15	___1
1980	(See 8068, 9544)			
[1980]	IETCA SP-type Caboose, *80 u*	—	14	___1
[1980]	Atlantic TCA Flatcar w/ trailers, *80 u*	28	34	___1
1981	(See 0511)			
[1981]	IETCA Quad Hopper, *81 u*	—	14	___1
[1981]	LCOL Boxcar, *81 u*	—	23	___1
1982	(See 7205)			
[1982]	IETCA 3-D Tank Car, *82 u*	—	14	___1
1983	(See 7206)			
[1983]	IETCA Reefer, *83 u*	—	14	___1
[1983]	TTOS Phoenix 3-D Tank Car, *83 u*	—	100	___1
[1983]	Great Lakes TCA Churchill Downs Boxcar, *83 u*		NRS	___
[1983]	Great Lakes TCA Churchill Downs Reefer, *83 u*		NRS	___
1984	(See 7212)			
[1984]	TTOS Sacramento Northern Boxcar, *84 u*	65	85	___1
[1984-30X]	Ft. Pitt TCA Heinz Ketchup Boxcar, *84 u*		NRS	___
[1985]	TTOS Snowbird Covered Quad Hopper, *85 u*	42	55	___1
[1986]	IETCA Bunk Car, *86 u*	—	14	___1
[1986]	Southern TCA Bunk Car, *86 u*	—	30	___1
[1986]	LCOL Work Caboose, shell only, *86 u*	—	14	___1
1987	(See 16205, 16310, 16311, 16507, 18605)			
[1988]	Midwest TCA IC Boxcar, *88 u*		NRS	___
1989	(See 16110, 17879, 18614)	—	20	___1
(1990)	Mystery Glow Midnight Flyer set, *79 u*	75	90	___1
1990	(See 17883, 18090, 19708)			
(1991)	JC Penney Wabash Cannonball Deluxe Express set, *79 u*	150	165	___1
1992	(See 18818)			
(1993)	Toys "R" Us Midnight Flyer set, *79 u*	110	130	___1
1993	(See 16655, 18713, 19927)			
1993X	(See 52008)			
1994	(See 52043, 52050)	—	300	___1
1995	(See 19934, 19935, 52062)			
1996	(See (52079, 52085), *99 u*	—	300	___1
(1999)	LCCA Ft. Worth & Weston Boxcar, *99 u*	—	50	___
2000	(See 18710, 18711, 18712, 19131)			
2100	(See 18006)			
2101	(See 18011, 18557)			
2110	Graduated Trestle set (22), *70–88*	9	13	___1
2111	Elevated Trestle set (10), *70–88*	8	11	___1

		Exc	New	Cond/$
(2113)	Tunnel Portals (2), *84–87*	11	17	___[1]
(2115)	Dwarf Signal, *84–87*	12	13	___[1]
(2117)	Block Target Signal, *84–87*	20	25	___[1]
(2122)	Extension Bridge w/ rock piers, *76–87*	24	34	___[1]
2125	Whistling Freight Shed, *71*	36	43	___[1]
2126	Whistling Freight Shed, *76–87*	25	26	___[1]
2127	Diesel Horn Shed, *76–87*	25	30	___[1]
(2128)	Operating Switchman, *83–86*	25	28	___[1]
2129	Illuminated Freight Station, *83–86*	26	29	___[1]
(2133)	Lighted Freight Station, *72–78, 80–84*	33	42	___[1]
2140	Automatic Banjo Signal, *70–84*	17	21	___[1]
(2145)	Automatic Gateman, *72–84*	36	55	___[1]
(2151)	Operating Semaphore, *78–82*	15	19	___[1]
(2152)	Automatic Crossing Gate, *70–84*	21	25	___[1]
2154	Automatic Highway Flasher, *70–87*	19	24	___[1]
2156	Illuminated Station Platform, *70–71*	26	34	___[1]
(2162)	Automatic Crossing Gate and Signal "262", *70–87, 94, 96–98*	20	34	___[1]
(2163)	Block Target Signal, *70–78*	13	17	___[1]
(2170)	Street Lamps (3), *70–87*	14	19	___[1]
(2171)	Gooseneck Street Lamps (2), *80–81, 83–84*	15	18	___[1]
(2175)	Sandy Andy Gravel Loader kit, *76–79*	31	50	___[1]
(2180)	Road Signs (16) "307", *77–98*	—	6	___[1]
(2181)	Telephone Pole set "150", *77–98*	—	5	___[1]
2184	(See 17218)			
(2195)	Floodlight Tower, *70–71*	38	50	___[1]
(2199)	Microwave Tower, *72–75*	30	39	___[1]
(2214)	Girder Bridge, *70–71, 72 u, 73–87*	5	9	___[1]
2256	Station Platform, *73–81*	15	19	___[1]
[2256]	TCA Station Platform, *75 u*	22	30	___[1]
(2260)	Illuminated Bumper, *70–71, 72 u, 73*	23	35	___[1]
(2280)	Non-Illuminated Bumpers (3), *73–84*	2.50	4	___[1]
2282	Die-cast Bumpers (2), *83 u*	17	18	___[1]
2283	(See 52039)			
(2283)	Die-cast illuminated bumpers "260", *84–99*	19	20	___[1]
(2290)	Illuminated Bumpers (2), *75 u, 76–86*	9	10	___[1]
(2292)	Station Platform, *85–87*	5	9	___[1]
(2300)	Operating Oil Drum Loader, *83–87*	100	120	___[1]
(2301)	Operating Sawmill, *80–84*	70	75	___[2]
2302	Union Pacific Manual Gantry Crane, *80–82*	24	31	___[1]
2303	Santa Fe Manual Gantry Crane, *80–81, 83 u*	17	21	___[1]
2305	Getty Operating Oil Derrick, *81–84*	105	115	___[2]

		Exc	New	Cond/$
(2306)	Operating Ice Station w/ 6700 PFE Ice Car, *82–83*	120	155	___ 2
(2307)	Lighted Billboard, *82–86*	17	21	___ 1
2308	Animated Newsstand, *82–83*	115	140	___ 1
(2309)	Mechanical Crossing Gate, *82–92*	4	7	___ 1
(2310)	Mechanical Crossing Gate, *73–77*	2.50	4	___ 1
(2311)	Mechanical Semaphore, *82–92*	4	7	___ 1
(2312)	Mechanical Semaphore, *73–77*	2.50	4	___ 1
(2313)	Floodlight Tower, *75–86*	22	27	___ 1
(2314)	Searchlight Tower, *75–84*	22	27	___ 1
(2315)	Operating Coaling Station, *83–84*	95	125	___ 1
2316	N&W Operating Gantry Crane, *83–84*	95	120	___ 1
2317	Operating Drawbridge, *75 u, 76–81*	100	125	___ 1
(2318)	Operating Control Tower, *83–86*	65	75	___ 1
2319	Illuminated Watchtower, *75–78, 80*	27	30	___ 1
2320	Flagpole kit, *83–87*	10	14	___ 1
2321	Operating Sawmill, *84, 86–87*	115	135	___ 1
2323	Operating Freight Station, *84–87*	65	75	___ 1
2324	Operating Switch Tower, *84–87*	65	70	___ 1
(2346)	LCAC TH&B Gondola, *99 u*	—	45	___ 1
(2354)	LCAC TH&B Gondola, *99 u*	—	45	___ 1
(2390)	Lionel Mirror, *82 u*	55	85	___ 1
2400	(See 18305)			
2401	(See 18304)			
2402	(See 18304)			
2403	(See 18305)			
2487	(See 18833)			
2494	Rotary Beacon, *72–74*	37	44	___ 1
2504	(See 19150)			
2601	(See 52023)			
2626	(See 18016)			
(2709)	Rico Station kit, *81–98*	—	32	___ 1
2710	Billboards (5), *70–84*	4	7	___ 1
(2714)	Tunnel, *75 u, 76–77*	36	43	___ 1
(2716)	Short Extension Bridge, *88–98*	3	8	___ 1
(2717)	Short Extension Bridge, *77–87*	2.50	4	___ 1
(2718)	Barrel Platform kit, *77–84*	3	5	___ 1
(2719)	Watchman's Shanty kit, *77–87*	2.50	4	___ 1
(2720)	Lumber Shed kit, *77–84, 87*	3	5	___ 1
(2721)	Operating Log Mill kit, *78*	2.50	4	___ 1
(2722)	Barrel Loader kit, *78*	2.50	4	___ 1
(2729)	Water Tower kit, *85*		NM	___
(2783)	Freight Station kit, *84*	6	10	___ 1

		Exc	New	Cond/$
(2784)	Freight Platform kit, *81–90*	5	8	___¹
(2785)	Engine House kit, *73–77*	27	34	___¹
(2786)	Freight Platform kit, *73–77*	4	6	___¹
(2787)	Freight Station kit, *73–77, 83*	6	9	___¹
(2788)	Coal Station kit, *75 u, 76–77*	18	30	___¹
(2789)	Water Tower kit, *75–77, 80*	17	21	___¹
(2791)	Cross Country set, *70–71*	22	30	___¹
(2792)	Whistle Stop set, *70–71*	24	34	___¹
(2792)	Layout Starter Pak, *80–84*	9	21	___¹
(2793)	Alamo Junction set, *70–71*	22	30	___¹
(2796)	Grain Elevator kit, *76 u, 77*	50	55	___¹
(2797)	Rico Station kit, *76–77*	23	34	___¹
2848	(See 12848)			
(2900)	Lockon, *70–98*	—	1.50	___¹
(2901)	Track Clips (12) (O27), *71–98*	—	6	___¹
2902	(See 12902)			
2903	(See 18630)			
(2905)	Lockon and Wire, *74–00*	—	3	___¹
(2909)	Smoke Fluid, *70–98*	—	4	___¹
2910	OTC Contactor, *84–86, 88*	4	7	___¹
(2911)	Smoke Pellets, *70–73*	10	12	___¹
2925	Lubricant, *70–71, 72 u, 73–75*	—	1.50	___¹
(2927)	Maintenance kit, *70, 78–98*	—	11	___¹
2928	Oil, *71*	—	1.50	___¹
2930	(See 12930)			
2951	Track Layout Book, *70–86*	0.85	1.50	___¹
2952	Train and Accessory Manual, *70–74*	0.85	1.50	___¹
2953	Train and Accessory Manual, *75–86*	0.85	1.50	___¹
2956	(See 19721)			
(2960)	Lionel 75th Anniversary Book, *75 u, 76*	9	17	___¹
(2980)	Magnetic Conversion Coupler, *70–71*	0.85	1.50	___¹
(2985)	The Lionel Train Book, *86–98*	—	11	___¹
3000	(See 18009, 33000)			
3004	(See 33004)			
3005	(See 33005)			
3010	(See 23010)			
3011	(See 23011)			
3100	Great Northern 4-8-4 (FARR #3), *81*	375	415	___²
3158	(See 18034)			
3285	(See 16805)			
3400	(See 19109)			
3500	(See 19110)			
[3764]	LOTS Kahn Boxcar, *81 u*	65	75	___¹

		Exc	New	Cond/$
3768	(See 18028)			
4000	(See 18812, 18825)			
4002	(See 18211)			
4004	(See 18218)			
4023	(See 52030)			
04039	(See 16908)			
04040	(See 16939)			
4044	Transformer, 45-watt, *70–71*	2.50	4	___1
4045	Safety Transformer, *70–71*	2.50	3	___1
4050	Safety Transformer, *72–79*	2.50	3	___1
4060	(See 18831)			
4060	Power Master Transformer, *80–93*	—	13	___1
4065	DC Hobby Transformer, *81–83*	2.50	3	___1
4090	Power Master Transformer, *70–84*	47	65	___1
4100	(See 18030)			
4124	(See 18514)			
4125	Transformer, 25-watt, *72*	2.50	3	___1
4136	(See 18819)			
4150	Trainmaster Transformer, *72–73, 75–77*	4	10	___1
4250	Trainmaster Transformer, *74*	5	10	___1
4410	(See 18007)			
4449	(See 8307)			
4501	(See 8309)			
4501	(See 18018)			
4574	(See 18306)			
4600	(See 18816)			
4651	Trainmaster Transformer, *78–79*	1.50	2.50	___1
4690	MW Transformer, *86–89*	65	80	___1
4851	DC Transformer, *85–91, 94–96*	5	10	___1
4866	(See 18308)			
4870	DC Hobby Transformer and Throttle Controller, *77–78*	2.50	3	___1
4907	(See 18313)			
4935	(See 8150)			
(5012)	Curved Track 27", card of 4 (O27), *70–96*	—	17	___1
(5013)	Curved Track 27" (O27), *70–78*	—	0.45	___1
(5014)	Half-Curved Track 27" (O27), *70–98*	—	0.70	___1
(5016)	36" Straight Track (O27), *87–88*	1.50	2.50	___1
(5017)	Straight Track, card of 4 (O27), *70–96*		CP	___
5017	(See 51230)	—	38	___1
(5018)	Straight Track (O27), *70–78*	0.45	0.65	___1
(5019)	Half-Straight Track (O27), *70–98*	—	0.70	___1
5020	(See 51234)			

		Exc	New	Cond/$
(5020)	90° Crossover (O27), *70–98*	—	7	___1
(5021)	Left Manual Switch 27" (O27), *70–98*	—	15	___1
(5022)	Right Manual Switch 27" (O27), *70–98*	—	15	___1
(5023)	45° Crossover (O27), *70–98*	—	6	___1
(5024)	35" Straight Track (O27), *88–98*	—	2.50	___1
(5025)	Manumatic Uncoupler, *71–72*	0.85	1.50	___1
(5027)	Pair Manual Switches 27" (O27), *74–84*	13	21	___1
(5030)	Track Expander set (O27), *71–84*	18	26	___1
(5031)	Ford-Autolite Layout Expander set, *71 u*	50	65	___1
(5033)	Curved Track 27" (O27), *79–98*	—	0.85	___1
(5038)	Straight Track (O27), *79–98*	—	0.85	___1
(5041)	Insulator Pins (12) (O27), *70–98*	—	1.50	___1
(5042)	Steel Pins (12) (O27), *70–98*	—	1.50	___1
(5044)	Curved Track Ballast 42" (O27), *88*		NM	___
(5045)	Curved Track Ballast 54" (O27), *87–88*	0.85	1.50	___1
(5046)	Curved Track Ballast 27" (O27), *87–88*	0.85	1.50	___1
(5047)	Straight Track Ballast (O27), *87–88*	0.85	1.50	___1
(5049)	Curved Track 42" (O27), *88–98*	—	1.50	___1
(5090)	Three Pair Manual Switches 27" (O27), *78–84*	55	70	___1
5100	(See 18001)			
(5113)	Curved Track 54" (O27), *79–98*	—	1.50	___1
(5121)	Left Remote Switch 27" (O27), *70–98*	—	22	___1
(5122)	Right Remote Switch 27" (O27), *70–98*	20	22	___1
(5125)	Pair Remote Switches 27" (O27), *71–83*	20	30	___1
5132	Right Remote Switch 31" (O), *80–94*	22	30	___1
5133	Left Remote Switch 31" (O), *80–94*	22	30	___1
(5149)	Remote Uncoupling Section (O27), *70–98*	—	7	___1
(5165)	Right Remote Switch 72" (O), *87–98*	20	65	___1
(5166)	Left Remote Switch 72" (O), *87–98*	20	75	___1
(5167)	Right Remote Switch 42" (O27), *88–98*	—	37	___1
(5168)	Left Remote Switch 42" (O27), *88–98*	—	37	___1
(5193)	Three Pair Remote Switches 27" (O27), *78–83*	80	95	___1
5300	(See 18636)			
5340	(See 18005, 18012)			
5366	(See 52078)			
5450	(See 18026, 18027, 18029)			
5484	(See 8476)			
5500	(See 18216)			
(5500)	Straight Track 10" (O), *71–98*	—	1.50	___1
(5501)	Curved Track 31" (O), *71–98*	—	1.50	___1
(5502)	Remote Uncoupling Section (O), *71–72*	7	9	___1
(5504)	Half-Curved Track 31" (O), *83–98*	—	0.85	___1
(5505)	Half-Straight Track (O), *83–98*	—	0.85	___1

		Exc	New	Cond/$
5512	(See 18221)			
5517	(See 18222)			
5520	90° Crossover (O), *71–72*	6	9	___¹
(5522)	36" 540, *87–88*	3	3	___¹
(5523)	40" Straight Track (O), *88–98*	—	4	___¹
(5530)	Remote Uncoupling Section (O), *81–98*	—	19	___¹
(5540)	90° Crossover (O), *81–98*	—	10	___¹
(5543)	Insulator Pins (12) (O), *70–98*	—	1.50	___¹
(5545)	45° Crossover (O), *83–98*	—	9	___¹
(5551)	Steel Pins (12) (O), *70–98*	—	1.50	___¹
(5554)	Curved Track 54" (O), *90–98*	—	2.50	___¹
(5560)	Curved Track Ballast 72" (O), *87–88*	0.85	1.50	___¹
(5561)	Curved Track Ballast 31" (O), *87–88*	0.85	1.50	___¹
(5562)	Straight Track Ballast (O), *87–88*	0.85	1.50	___¹
(5572)	Curved Track 72" (O), *79–98*	—	3	___¹
5600	Curved Track (TT), *73–74*	0.85	1.50	___¹
5601	Curved Track, card of 4 (TT), *73–74*	6	10	___¹
5602	Curved Track Ballast, card of 4 (TT), *73–74*	5	9	___¹
5605	Straight Track (TT), *73–74*	0.85	1.50	___¹
5606	Straight Track, card of 4 (TT), *73–74*	5	9	___¹
5607	Straight Track Ballast, card of 4 (TT), *73–74*	5	9	___¹
5620	Left Manual Switch (TT), *73–74*	4	13	___¹
5625	Left Remote Switch (TT), *73–74*	9	17	___¹
5630	Right Manual Switch (TT), *73–74*	4	13	___¹
5635	Right Remote Switch (TT), *73–74*	9	17	___¹
5640	Left Switch Ballast, card of 2 (TT), *73–74*	5	9	___¹
5650	Right Switch Ballast, card of 2 (TT), *73–74*	5	9	___¹
5655	Lockon (TT), *73–74*	0.85	1.50	___¹
5658	(See 16559)			
5660	Terminal Track w/ lockon (TT), *74*	1.50	3	___¹
5700	Oppenheimer Reefer, *81*	35	45	___¹
[5700]	Ozark TCA Oppenheimer Reefer, *81 u*	49	95	___¹
5701	Dairymen's League Reefer, *81*	27	30	___¹
5702	National Dairy Despatch Reefer, *81*	24	34	___¹
5703	North American Despatch Reefer, *81*	26	32	___¹
5704	Budweiser Reefer, *81–82*	55	80	___¹
5705	Ball Glass Jars Reefer, *81–82*	30	36	___¹
5706	Lindsay Brothers Reefer, *81–82*	29	33	___¹
5707	American Refrigerator Reefer, *81–82*	24	25	___¹
5708	Armour Reefer, *82–83*	17	22	___¹
5709	REA Reefer, *82–83*	25	29	___²
5710	Canadian Pacific Reefer, *82–83*	17	19	___¹
[5710]	NETCA CP Reefer, *82 u*	33	39	___¹

		Exc	New	Cond/$
[5710]	LCAC CP Reefer, *83 u*	—	250	___1
5711	Commercial Express Reefer, *82–83*	17	20	___1
5712	Lionel Lines Reefer, *82 u*	170	200	___2
5713	Cotton Belt Reefer, *83–84*	21	25	___1
5714	Michigan Central Reefer, *83–84*	17	25	___1
[5714]	LCAC Michigan Central Reefer, *85 u*	120	150	___1
5715	Santa Fe Reefer, *83–84*	23	33	___1
5716	Central Vermont Reefer, *83–84*	23	27	___1
[5716]	NETCA Central Vermont Reefer, *83 u*	25	30	___1
5717	Santa Fe Bunk Car, *83*	26	34	___2
5718	(See 9849)			
5719	Canadian National Reefer, *84*	15	16	___1
5720	Great Northern Reefer, *84*	80	90	___1
5721	Soo Line Reefer, *84*	23	26	___1
5722	NKP Reefer, *84*	16	18	___1
5724	PRR Bunk Car, *84*	26	29	___1
[5724]	LCOL PRR Bunk Car, *84 u*	30	39	___1
5726	Southern Bunk Car, *84 u*	27	33	___1
5727	US Marines Bunk Car, *84–85*	28	33	___1
5728	Canadian Pacific Bunk Car, *86*	23	29	___1
5730	Strasburg RR Reefer, *85–86*	23	33	___1
5731	L&N Reefer, *85–86*	17	21	___1
[5731]	TCA Museum L&N Reefer, *90 u*	95	95	___1
5732	Jersey Central Reefer, *85–86*	23	23	___1
5733	Lionel Lines Bunk Car, *86 u*	27	34	___1
5734	TCA REA Reefer, *85 u*	65	90	___2
5735	NYC Bunk Car, *85–86*	36	39	___1
5739	B&O Tool Car, *86*	36	41	___1
5745	Santa Fe Bunk Car (SSS), *86*	40	47	___1
5760	Santa Fe Tool Car (SSS), *86*	35	41	___1
5800	(See 18836)			
5808	(See 18826)			
5900	AC/DC Converter, *79–83*	3	5	___1
6001	(See 18107)			
6002	(See 18107)			
6003	(See 17611)			
6005	(See 18821)			
6006	(See 18210)			
6007	(See 18217)			
[6014-900]	LCCA Frisco Boxcar (O27), *75–76 u*	19	30	___1
6061	(See 16061)			
6062	(See 16062)			
6063	(See 16063)			

		Exc	New	Cond/$
6064	(See 16064)			
6065	(See 16065)			
6066	(See 16066)			
6067	(See 16067)			
6068	(See 16068)			
6069	(See 16069)			
6070	(See 16070)			
6071	(See 16071)			
6072	(See 16072)			
6073	(See 16073)			
6074	(See 16074)			
6076	LV Hopper (O27), *70 u*	17	21	___¹
6076	TTOS Santa Fé Hopper (O27), *70 u*	—	85	___¹
6080	(See 16080)			
6081	(See 16081)			
6082	(See 16082)			
6083	(See 16083)			
6084	(See 16084)			
6086	(See 16086)			
6087	(See 16087)			
6088	(See 16088)			
6089	(See 16089)			
6090	(See 16090)			
6100	Ontario Northland Covered Quad Hopper, *81–82*	36	40	___¹
[6100]	LCAC Ontario Northland Covered Quad Hopper, *82 u*	—	250	___¹
6101	Burlington Northern Covered Quad Hopper, *81–82*	23	34	___¹
[6101]	Atlantic TCA Burlington Northern Covered Quad Hopper, *82 u*	21	34	___¹
6102	GN Covered Quad Hopper (FARR #3), *81*	33	37	___¹
6103	Canadian National Covered Quad Hopper, *81*	32	40	___¹
6104	Southern Quad Hopper w/ coal load (FARR #4), *83*	70	85	___¹
6105	Reading Operating Hopper, *82*	39	45	___¹
6106	N&W Covered Quad Hopper, *82*	27	35	___¹
6107	Shell Covered Quad Hopper, *82*	22	26	___¹
6108	(See 16108)			
6109	C&O Operating Hopper, *83*	31	45	___¹
6110	Missouri Pacific Covered Quad Hopper, *83–84*	16	25	___¹
6111	L&N Covered Quad Hopper, *83–84*	13	20	___¹
[6111]	Southern TCA L&N Covered Quad Hopper, *83 u*	20	22	___¹

		Exc	New	Cond/$
[6111]	LOTS L&N Covered Quad Hopper, *83 u*	37	42	___[1]
6112	LCCA Commonwealth Edison Quad Hopper w/ coal load, *83 u*	45	60	___[1]
6113	Illinois Central Hopper (O27), *83–85*	11	17	___[1]
6114	C&NW Covered Quad Hopper, *83*	85	95	___[1]
6115	Southern Hopper (O27), *83–86*	15	19	___[1]
6116	Soo Line Ore Car, *84*	31	41	___[1]
6117	Erie Operating Hopper, *84*	36	38	___[1]
6118	Erie Covered Quad Hopper, *84*	37	40	___[1]
6122	Penn Central Ore Car, *84*	28	32	___[1]
6123	PRR Covered Quad Hopper (FARR #5), *84–85*	50	75	___[1]
6124	D&H Covered Quad Hopper, *84*	22	33	___[1]
[6124]	NETCA D&H Covered Quad Hopper, *84 u*	25	30	___[1]
6126	Canadian National Ore Car, *86*	26	30	___[1]
6127	(See 5735)			
6127	Northern Pacific Ore Car, *86*	21	26	___[1]
6131	Illinois Terminal Covered Quad Hopper, *85–86*	20	24	___[1]
6134	Burlington Northern 2-bay ACF Hopper (Std. O), *86 u*	110	130	___[2]
6135	C&NW 2-bay ACF Hopper (Std. O), *86 u*	95	105	___[2]
6137	NKP Hopper (O27), *86–91*	13	17	___[1]
6138	B&O Quad Hopper w/ coal load, *86*	24	28	___[1]
6150	Santa Fe Hopper (O27), *85–86, 92 u*	10	15	___[1]
6177	Reading Hopper (O27), *86–90*	13	17	___[1]
6200	FEC Gondola w/ canisters, *81–82*	14	24	___[1]
6200	(See 8404)			
6200	(See 18010)			
6201	Union Pacific Animated Gondola, *82–83*	21	29	___[1]
6202	WM Gondola w/ coal load, *82*	34	36	___[1]
(6203)	Black Cave Gondola (O27), *82*	2.50	4	___[1]
6205	CP Gondola w/ canisters, *83*	23	28	___[1]
6206	C&IM Gondola w/ canisters, *83–85*	18	26	___[1]
6207	Southern Gondola w/ canisters (O27), *83–85*	6	8	___[1]
6208	Chessie System Gondola w/ canisters, *83 u*	23	26	___[1]
6209	NYC Gondola w/ coal load (Std. O), *84–85*	40	44	___[1]
6210	Erie-Lackawanna Gondola w/ canisters, *84*	23	30	___[1]
6211	C&O Gondola w/ canisters, *84–85*	—	10	___[1]
[6211]	LOTS C&O Gondola w/ canisters, *86 u*	55	80	___[1]
6214	Lionel Lines Gondola w/ canisters, *84 u*	37	44	___[1]
6226	(See 16226)			
6230	Erie-Lackawanna Reefer (Std. O), *86 u*	105	125	___[1]
6231	Railgon Gondola w/ coal load (Std. O), *86 u*	85	85	___[1]
6232	Illinois Central Boxcar (Std. O), *86 u*	80	90	___[1]

		Exc	New	Cond/$
6233	Canadian Pacific Flatcar w/ stakes (Std. O), *86 u*	65	80	____¹
6234	Burlington Northern Boxcar (Std. O), *85*	41	55	____¹
6235	Burlington Northern Boxcar (Std. O), *85*	37	50	____¹
6236	Burlington Northern Boxcar (Std. O), *85*	37	50	____¹
6237	Burlington Northern Boxcar (Std. O), *85*	38	55	____¹
6238	Burlington Northern Boxcar (Std. O), *85*	37	50	____¹
6239	Burlington Northern Boxcar (Std. O), *86 u*	43	55	____¹
6251	NYC Coal Dump Car, *85*	18	28	____¹
6254	NKP Gondola w/ canisters, *86–91*	9	10	____¹
6258	Santa Fe Gondola w/ canisters (O27), *85–86, 92 u*	—	3	____¹
X6260	NYC Gondola w/ canisters, *85–86*	13	15	____¹
6272	Santa Fe Gondola w/ cable reels (SSS), *86*	20	25	____¹
6300	Corn Products 3-D Tank Car, *81–82*	20	26	____¹
6301	Gulf 1-D Tank Car, *81*	22	29	____¹
6302	Quaker State 3-D Tank Car, *81*	43	48	____¹
6304	GN 1-D Tank Car (FARR #3), *81*	44	55	____¹
6305	British Columbia 1-D Tank Car, *81*	44	65	____¹
6306	Southern 1-D Tank Car (FARR #4), *83*	49	55	____¹
6307	PRR 1-D Tank Car (FARR #5), *84–85*	70	85	____¹
6308	Alaska 1-D Tank Car (O27), *82–83*	27	35	____¹
6310	Shell 2-D Tank Car (O27), *83–84*	19	24	____¹
6312	C&O 2-D Tank Car (O27), *84–85*	18	26	____¹
6313	Lionel Lines 1-D Tank Car, *84 u*	43	50	____¹
6314	B&O 3-D Tank Car, *86*	39	47	____¹
6315	TCA Pittsburgh 1-D Tank Car, *72 u*	65	70	____¹
6317	Gulf 2-D Tank Car (O27), *84–85*	19	23	____¹
6323	LCCA Virginia Chemicals 1-D Tank Car, *86 u*	47	65	____¹
6325	(See 6579)			
6336	(See 16336)			
6357	Frisco 1-D Tank Car, *83*	49	60	____¹
6401	Virginian B/W Caboose, *81*	32	40	____¹
[6401]	Sacramento-Sierra TCA Virginian B/W Caboose, *84 u*	—	35	____¹
6403	Amtrak Vista Dome Car (O27), *76–77*	30	31	____¹
6404	Amtrak Passenger Car (O27), *76–77*	24	31	____¹
6405	Amtrak Passenger Car (O27), *76–77*	24	31	____¹
6406	Amtrak Observation Car (O27), *76–77*	22	29	____¹
6408	(See 16408)			
6410	Amtrak Passenger Car (O27), *77*	21	34	____¹
6411	Amtrak Passenger Car (O27), *77*	22	32	____¹
6412	Amtrak Vista Dome Car (O27), *77*	20	29	____¹

		Exc	New	Cond/$
6420	Reading Transfer Caboose, *81–82*	14	19	___¹
6421	Joshua L. Cowen B/W Caboose, *82*	36	42	___¹
6422	DM&IR B/W Caboose, *81*	32	42	___¹
6425	Erie-Lackawanna B/W Caboose, *83–84*	35	43	___¹
6426	Reading Transfer Caboose, *82–83*	13	21	___¹
6427	Burlington Northern Transfer Caboose, *83–84*	12	21	___¹
6428	C&NW Transfer Caboose, *83–85*	22	25	___¹
6430	Santa Fe SP-type Caboose, *83–89*	4	7	___¹
6431	Southern B/W Caboose (FARR #4), *83*	42	55	___¹
6432	Union Pacific SP-type Caboose, *81–82*	9	10	___¹
6433	Canadian Pacific B/W Caboose, *81*	65	75	___¹
6435	US Transfer Caboose, *83–84*	9	17	___¹
6438	GN B/W Caboose (FARR #3), *81*	38	47	___¹
6439	Reading B/W Caboose, *84–85*	19	26	___¹
6441	Alaska B/W Caboose, *82–83*	42	47	___¹
6446-25	N&W Covered Quad Hopper, *70 u*	135	175	___¹
6449	Wendy's N5C Caboose, *81–82*	49	60	___¹
6464	(See 19248, 19249, 19250, 19258, 19269, 19275)			
6464-095	(See 52051)			
6464-100	(See 19259, 19260)			
6464-125	(See 19267, 52063)			
6464-150	(See 19268, 52064)			
6464-225	(See 19274)			
6464-275	(See 19273)			
6464-500	Timken Boxcar, *70 u*	150	195	___¹
6464-555	(See 52081)			
6464-1895	(See 52058)			
6464-1970	TCA Chicago Boxcar, *70 u*	105	135	___¹
6464-1971	TCA Disneyland Boxcar, *71 u*	245	275	___¹
6464-1972	(See 52086)			
6464-1993	(See 52009)			
6464-1995	(See 52057)			
6464-1996	(See 52087)			
6464-2003	Maddox Retirement Boxcar, *02*			
(6476-135)	Lehigh Valley Hopper "25000" (O27), *70–71 u*	6	11	___¹
(6478)	Black Cave SP-type Caboose, *82*	5	9	___¹
6482	Nibco Express SP-type Caboose, *82 u*	26	34	___¹
6483	LCCA Jersey Central SP-type Caboose, *82 u*	26	34	___¹
6485	Chessie System SP-type Caboose, *84–85*	6	10	___¹
6486	Southern SP-type Caboose, *83–85*	5	7	___¹
6490	NKP N5C Caboose, *84 u*		NRS	___
6491	Erie-Lackawanna Transfer Caboose, *85–86*	9	17	___¹

Exc New Cond/$

		Exc	New	Cond/$
6493	L&C B/W Caboose, *86–87*	16	25	___¹
6494	Santa Fe Bobber Caboose, *85–86*	7	9	___¹
6496	Santa Fe Work Caboose (SSS), *86*	24	34	___¹
(6504)	L.A.S.E.R. Flatcar w/ helicopter (O27), *81–82*	18	26	___¹
(6505)	L.A.S.E.R. Radar Car, *81–82*	17	25	___¹
(6506)	L.A.S.E.R. Security Car, *81–82*	18	26	___¹
(6507)	L.A.S.E.R. Flatcar w/ cruise missile, *81–82*	21	30	___¹
6508	Canadian Pacific Crane Car, *81*	65	85	___¹
6508	(See 16508)			
[6508]	LCOL Canadian Pacific Crane Car, *83 u*	—	40	___¹
(6509)	Depressed Flatcar w/ girders, *81*	60	70	___¹
6510	Union Pacific Crane Car, *82*	65	70	___¹
6515	Union Pacific Flatcar (O27), *83–84, 86*	5	9	___¹
6521	NYC Flatcar w/ stakes (Std. O), *84–85*	38	46	___¹
6522	C&NW Searchlight Car, *83–85*	27	30	___¹
6524	Erie Crane Car, *84*	60	65	___¹
6526	US Marines Searchlight Car, *84–85*	27	30	___¹
6528	(See 16528)			
6529	NYC Searchlight Car, *85–86*	21	27	___¹
6531	Express Mail Flatcar w/ trailers, *85–86*	28	38	___¹
6560	Bucyrus Erie Crane Car, *71*	115	130	___¹
(6561)	Flatcar w/ cruise missile (O27), *83–84*	13	26	___¹
(6562)	Flatcar w/ fences (O27), *83–84*	13	21	___¹
(6564)	Flatcar w/ two USM.C. tanks (O27), *83–84*	13	21	___¹
(6567)	LCCA ICG Crane Car "100408", *85 u*	55	65	___²
(6573)	Redwood Valley Express Flatcar w/ dump bin (O27), *84–85*	7	13	___¹
(6574)	Redwood Valley Express Flatcar w/ crane (O27), *84–85*	7	13	___¹
(6575)	Redwood Valley Express Flatcar w/ fences (O27), *84–85*	7	13	___¹
6576	Santa Fe Flatcar w/ crane (O27), *85–86, 92 u*	7	10	___¹
6579	NYC Crane Car, *85–86*	40	49	___¹
6582	TTOS Portland Flatcar w/ wood load, *86 u*	65	85	___¹
6585	PRR Flatcar w/ fences (O27), *86–90*	5	9	___¹
6587	W&ARR Flatcar w/ horses, *86 u*	18	26	___¹
6593	Santa Fe Crane Car (SSS), *86*	41	48	___¹
6602	(See 16053)			
6603	(See 16054)			
6609	(See 16079)			
6616	(See 16052, 16077)			
6620	(See 16050, 16075)			
6630	(See 16051, 16076)			

		Exc	New	Cond/$
6670	(See 9378)			
6700	PFE Ice Car (See 2306), *82–83*		NRS	___
6900	N&W E/V Caboose, *82*	65	75	___1
6901	Ontario Northland E/V Caboose, *82 u*	38	49	___2
6903	Santa Fe E/V Caboose, *83*	105	125	___2
6904	Union Pacific E/V Caboose, *83*	120	140	___1
6905	NKP E/V Caboose, *83 u*	45	55	___1
6906	Erie-Lackawanna E/V Caboose, *84*	75	90	___1
6907	NYC Woodside Caboose (Std. O), *86 u*	80	90	___2
6908	PRR N5C Caboose (FARR #5), *84–85*	60	65	___1
6910	NYC E/V Caboose, *84 u*	50	55	___2
(6912)	Redwood Valley Express SP-type Caboose, *84–85*	9	16	___1
6913	Burlington Northern E/V Caboose, *85*	70	90	___1
6916	NYC Work Caboose, *85–86*	16	22	___1
6917	Jersey Central E/V Caboose, *86*	50	60	___1
6918	B&O SP-type Caboose, *86*	10	15	___1
6919	Nickel Plate Road SP-type Caboose, *86–91*	5	9	___1
6920	B&A Woodside Caboose (Std. O), *86 u*	70	80	___2
6921	PRR SP-type Caboose, *86–90*	5	9	___1
6926	TCA New Orleans E/V Caboose, *86 u*	33	50	___1
7000	(See 51301)			
7200	Quicksilver Passenger Car (O27), *82–83*	26	34	___1
7200	(See 19415)			
7201	Quicksilver Passenger Car (O27), *82–83*	26	34	___1
7202	Quicksilver Observation Car (O27), *82–83*	26	34	___1
(7203)	N&W Dining Car "491", *82 u*	180	285	___1
(7204)	Southern Pacific Dining Car, *82 u*	255	335	___1
(7205)	TCA Denver Combination Car "1982", *82 u*	37	50	___1
(7206)	TCA Louisville Passenger Car "1983", *83 u*	40	55	___1
7207	NYC Dining Car, *83 u*	110	160	___1
(7208)	PRR Dining Car, *83 u*	105	115	___2
7210	Union Pacific Dining Car, *84*	85	110	___1
(7211)	Southern Pacific Vista Dome Car, *83 u*	210	250	___1
(7212)	TCA Pittsburgh Passenger Car "1984", *84 u*	41	50	___1
7215	B&O Passenger Car, *83–84*	43	50	___1
7216	B&O Passenger Car, *83–84*	43	50	___1
7217	B&O Baggage Car, *83–84*	43	50	___1
7220	Illinois Central Baggage Car, *85, 87*	105	135	___1
7221	Illinois Central Combination Car, *85, 87*	85	105	___1
7222	Illinois Central Passenger Car, *85, 87*	85	105	___1
7223	Illinois Central Passenger Car, *85, 87*	85	105	___1
7224	Illinois Central Dining Car, *85, 87*	75	90	___1

7225	Illinois Central Observation Car, *85, 87*	95	115	___¹
7227	Wabash Dining Car (FF #1), *86–87*	90	100	___¹
7228	Wabash Baggage Car (FF #1), *86–87*	90	100	___¹
7229	Wabash Combination Car (FF #1), *86–87*	90	100	___¹
7230	Wabash Passenger Car (FF #1), *86–87*	90	100	___¹
7231	Wabash Passenger Car (FF #1), *86–87*	90	100	___¹
7232	Wabash Observation Car (FF #1), *86–87*	75	85	___¹
7241	W&ARR Passenger Car, *86 u*	43	50	___¹
7242	W&ARR Baggage Car, *86 u*	43	50	___¹
7301	Norfolk & Western Stock Car, *82*	37	38	___¹
7302	Texas & Pacific Stock Car (O27), *83–84*	12	15	___¹
7303	Erie Stock Car, *84*	45	55	___¹
7304	Southern Stock Car (FARR #4), *83 u*	46	50	___¹
7309	Southern Stock Car (O27), *85–86*	12	16	___¹
7312	W&ARR Stock Car (O27), *86 u*	25	30	___¹
7401	Chessie System Stock Car (O27), *84–85*	13	17	___¹
7403	LCCA LNAC Boxcar, *84 u*	23	33	___¹
7404	Jersey Central Boxcar, *86*	35	45	___¹
7420	(See 18513)			
(7500)	Lionel 75th Anniversary U36B, *75–77*	115	135	___¹
7500	(See 18214)			
7501	Lionel 75th Anniversary Boxcar, *75–77*	21	28	___¹
7502	Lionel 75th Anniversary Reefer, *75–77*	23	32	___¹
7503	Lionel 75th Anniversary Reefer, *75–77*	26	37	___¹
7504	Lionel 75th Anniversary Covered Quad Hopper, *75–77*	23	33	___¹
7505	Lionel 75th Anniversary Boxcar, *75–77*	26	37	___¹
7506	Lionel 75th Anniversary Boxcar, *75–77*	20	27	___¹
7507	Lionel 75th Anniversary Reefer, *75–77*	26	37	___¹
7508	Lionel 75th Anniversary N5C Caboose, *75–77*	22	27	___¹
7509	Kentucky Fried Chicken Reefer, *81–82*	32	36	___¹
7510	Red Lobster Reefer, *81–82*	30	34	___¹
7511	Pizza Hut Reefer, *81–82*	33	38	___¹
7512	Arthur Treacher's Reefer, *82*	26	31	___¹
7513	Bonanza Reefer, *82*	26	31	___¹
7514	Taco Bell Reefer, *82*	40	55	___¹
7515	Denver Mint Car, *81*	60	65	___¹
7517	Philadelphia Mint Car, *82*	45	49	___¹
7518	Carson City Mint Car, *83*	42	49	___¹
[7518]	IETCA Carson City Mint Car, *84 u*	—	43	___¹
7519	Toy Fair Reefer, *82 u*	55	65	___¹
7520	Nibco Express Boxcar, *82 u*	265	440	___¹
7521	Toy Fair Reefer, *83 u*	60	75	___¹

		Exc	New	Cond/$
7522	New Orleans Mint Car, *84 u*	36	43	____2
[7522]	Lone Star TCA New Orleans Mint Car w/ coin, *86 u*	—	320	____1
7523	Toy Fair Reefer, *84 u*	65	65	____1
7524	Toy Fair Reefer, *85 u*	85	100	____1
7525	Toy Fair Boxcar, *86 u*	80	90	____1
7530	Dahlonega Mint Car, *86 u*	46	60	____1
7600	Frisco "Spirit of '76" N5C Caboose, *74–76*	30	39	____1
[7600]	Midwest TCA Frisco "Spirit of '76" N5C Caboose "00003", *76 u*	—	35	____1
7601	Delaware Boxcar, *74–76*	19	22	____1
7602	Pennsylvania Boxcar, *74–76*	23	27	____1
7603	New Jersey Boxcar, *74–76*	25	27	____1
7604	Georgia Boxcar, *74 u, 75–76*	25	26	____1
7605	Connecticut Boxcar, *74 u, 75–76*	25	30	____1
7606	Massachusetts Boxcar, *74 u, 75–76*	26	31	____1
7607	Maryland Boxcar, *74 u, 75–76*	26	40	____1
7608	South Carolina Boxcar, *75 u, 76*	26	40	____1
7609	New Hampshire Boxcar, *75 u, 76*	49	60	____1
7610	Virginia Boxcar, *75 u, 76*	155	200	____1
7611	New York Boxcar, *75 u, 76*	60	85	____1
7612	North Carolina Boxcar, *75 u, 76*	35	55	____1
7613	Rhode Island Boxcar, *75 u, 76*	35	55	____1
7613	(See 17613)			
7643	(See 18215)			
[7679]	VTC Boxcar, *79 u*	—	17	____1
[7681]	VTC N5C Caboose, *81 u*	—	23	____1
[7682]	VTC Covered Quad Hopper, *82 u*	—	26	____1
[7683]	VTC Virginia Fruit Express Reefer, *83 u*	—	26	____1
[7684]	VTC Vitraco Oil 3-D Tank Car, *84 u*	—	26	____1
[7685]	VTC Boxcar, *85 u*	—	27	____1
[7686]	VTC GP-7, *86 u*	—	100	____1
[7692-1]	VTC Baggage Car (O27), *92 u*	35	45	____1
[7692-2]	VTC Combination Car (O27), *92 u*	35	45	____1
[7692-3]	VTC Dining Car (O27), *92 u*	35	45	____1
[7692-4]	VTC Passenger Car (O27), *92 u*	35	45	____1
[7692-5]	VTC Vista Dome Car (O27), *92 u*	35	45	____1
[7692-6]	VTC Passenger Car (O27), *92 u*	35	45	____1
[7692-7]	VTC Observation Car (O27), *92 u*	35	45	____1
7694	(See 52060)			
7700	Uncle Sam Boxcar, *75 u*	43	47	____2
7701	Camel Boxcar, *76–77*	36	50	____1
7702	Prince Albert Boxcar, *76–77*	36	50	____1

7703	Beechnut Boxcar, *76–77*	19	28	___¹
7704	Toy Fair Boxcar, *76 u*	115	125	___¹
7705	Canadian Toy Fair Boxcar, *76 u*	130	145	___¹
7706	Sir Walter Raleigh Boxcar, *77–78*	36	50	___¹
7707	White Owl Boxcar, *77–78*	36	50	___¹
7708	Winston Boxcar, *77–78*	40	55	___¹
7709	Salem Boxcar, *78*	36	50	___¹
7710	Mail Pouch Boxcar, *78*	45	60	___¹
7711	El Producto Boxcar, *78*	45	60	___¹
7712	Santa Fe Boxcar (FARR #1), *79*	25	29	___¹
[7780]	TCA Museum Boxcar, *80 u*	—	26	___¹
[7781]	TCA Hafner Boxcar, *81 u*	—	26	___¹
[7782]	TCA Carlisle & Finch Boxcar, *82 u*	—	26	___¹
[7783]	TCA Ives Boxcar, *83 u*	—	26	___¹
[7784]	TCA Voltamp Boxcar, *84 u*	—	23	___¹
[7785]	TCA Hoge Boxcar, *85 u*	—	23	___¹
7800	Pepsi Boxcar, *76 u, 77*	50	55	___¹
7801	A&W Boxcar, *76 u, 77*	36	50	___¹
7802	Canada Dry Boxcar, *76 u, 77*	36	50	___¹
7803	Trains n' Truckin' Boxcar, *77 u*	22	29	___¹
7805	(See 16078)			
7806	Season's Greetings Boxcar, *76 u*	70	95	___¹
7807	Toy Fair Boxcar, *77 u*	70	95	___¹
7808	Northern Pacific Stock Car, *77*	43	50	___¹
7809	Vernors Boxcar, *77 u, 78*	40	55	___¹
7810	Orange Crush Boxcar, *77 u, 78*	40	55	___¹
7811	Dr Pepper Boxcar, *77 u, 78*	40	55	___¹
7812	TCA Houston Stock Car, *77 u*	15	24	___¹
7813	Season's Greetings Boxcar, *77 u*	65	90	___¹
7814	Season's Greetings Boxcar, *78 u*	70	95	___¹
7815	Toy Fair Boxcar, *78 u*	65	85	___¹
7816	Toy Fair Boxcar, *79 u*	70	95	___¹
7817	Toy Fair Boxcar, *80 u*	105	120	___¹
7890	(See 17303)			
7900	D&RGW Operating Cowboy Car (O27), *82–83*	22	26	___¹
7901	Lionel Lines Cop and Hobo Car (O27), *82–83*	27	31	___¹
7902	Santa Fe Boxcar (O27), *82–85*	5	9	___¹
7903	Rock Island Boxcar (O27), *83*	7	11	___¹
7904	San Diego Zoo Giraffe Car (O27), *83–84*	44	55	___¹
(7905)	Black Cave Boxcar (O27), *82*	6	9	___¹
7908	Tappan Boxcar (O27), *82 u*	39	55	___¹
7909	L&N Boxcar (O27), *83–84*	40	49	___¹
7910	Chessie System Boxcar (O27), *84–85*	20	25	___¹

		Exc	New	Cond/$
7912	Toys "R" Us Giraffe Car (O27), *82–84 u*	70	80	1
7913	Turtleback Zoo Giraffe Car (O27), *85–86*	39	45	1
7914	Toys "R" Us Giraffe Car (O27), *85–89 u*	70	90	1
7920	Sears Centennial Boxcar (O27), *85–86 u*	39	44	1
7925	Erie-Lackawanna Boxcar (O27), *86–90*	10	18	1
7926	NKP Boxcar (O27), *86–91*	8	10	1
7930	True Value Boxcar (O27), *86–87 u*	34	50	1
7931	Town House TV and Appliances Boxcar (O27), *86 u*	31	39	1
7932	Kay Bee Toys Boxcar (O27), *86–87 u*	40	49	1
8001	NKP 2-6-4, *80 u*	55	65	1
8002	Union Pacific 2-8-4 (FARR #2), *80*	400	500	3
8003	Chessie System 2-8-4, *80*	375	475	3
8004	Rock Island 4-4-0, *80–82*	165	190	2
8004	(See 18004)			
8005	Santa Fe 4-4-0, *80–82*	65	75	1
8006	ACL 4-6-4, *80 u*	420	500	1
8007	NYNH&H 2-6-4, *80–81*	65	75	1
8008	Chessie System 4-4-2, *80*	65	75	1
8010	Santa Fe NW-2, *70, 71 u*	65	65	1
8014	(See 18014)			
8020	Santa Fe Alco A Unit, *70–72, 74–76*	65	85	1
8020	Santa Fe Alco A Unit Dummy, *70*	45	60	1
8021	Santa Fe Alco B Unit, *71–72, 74–76*	45	65	1
8022	Santa Fe Alco A Unit, *71 u*	80	105	1
8025	CN Alco A Unit, *71–73 u*	85	105	1
8025	CN Alco A Unit Dummy, *71–73 u*	45	65	1
8030	Illinois Central GP-9, *70–72*	90	95	2
8031	Canadian National GP-7, *71–73 u*	85	155	1
8031	Illinois Central GP-9 Dummy, *70*		NM	
8040	NKP 2-4-2, *70–72*	26	34	1
8040	Canadian National 2-4-2, *71 u*	43	85	1
8041	NYC 2-4-2, *70*	55	65	1
8041	PRR 2-4-2, *71 u*	55	65	1
8042	GTW 2-4-2, *70, 71–73 u*	26	34	1
8043	NKP 2-4-2, *70 u*	45	65	1
8050	D&H U36C, *80*	105	220	1
8051	D&H U36C Dummy, *80*	95	115	1
[8051]	NETCA Hood's Milk Boxcar, *86 u*	44	65	1
8054/8055	Burlington F-3 AA set, *80*	360	385	1
8056	C&NW FM Trainmaster, *80*	220	255	3
8057	Burlington NW-2, *80*	115	140	1
8059	Pennsylvania F-3 B Unit, *80 u*	305	375	1

		Exc	New	Cond/$
8060	Pennsylvania F-3 B Unit, *80 u*	335	420	___[1]
8061	Chessie System U36C, *80*	150	180	___[1]
8062	Great Northern 4-6-4, *70*		NM	___
8062	Burlington F-3 B Unit, *80 u*	205	245	___[1]
8063	Seaboard SD-9, *80*	95	120	___[1]
8064	Florida East Coast GP-9, *80*	145	195	___[1]
8065	Florida East Coast GP-9 Dummy, *80*	95	120	___[1]
8066	TP&W GP-20, *80–81, 83 u*	70	90	___[1]
8067	Texas & Pacific Alco A Unit, *80*		NM	___
(8068)	LCCA Rock Island GP-20 "1980", *80 u*	80	105	___[1]
8071	Virginian SD-18, *80 u*	150	180	___[1]
8072	Virginian SD-18 Dummy, *80 u*	75	110	___[1]
(8100)	Norfolk & Western 4-8-4 "611", *81*	630	650	___[3]
8100	(See 11711)			
(8101)	Chicago & Alton 4-6-4 "659", *81*	375	455	___[2]
8101	(See 11711)			
8102	Union Pacific 4-4-2, *81–82*	49	65	___[1]
8102	(See 11711)			
[8103]	LCAC Toronto, Hamilton & Buffalo Boxcar, *81 u*		NRS	___
8103	(See 18103)			
(8104)	Union Pacific 4-4-0 "3", *81 u*	190	250	___[1]
8111	DT&I NW-2, *71–74*	50	65	___[1]
8119	(See 18119/18120)			
8120	(See 18119/18120)			
8124	(See 51300)			
8140	Southern 2-4-0, *71 u*	22	30	___[1]
8141	PRR 2-4-2, *71–72*	36	43	___[1]
8142	C&O 4-4-2, *71–72*	55	55	___[1]
(8150)	PRR GG-1 "4935", *81*	355	420	___[1]
8151	Burlington SD-28, *81*	125	150	___[1]
8152	Canadian Pacific SD-24, *81*	155	165	___[1]
8153	Reading NW-2, *81–82*	120	140	___[1]
8154	Alaska NW-2, *81–82*	110	150	___[1]
8155	Monon U36B, *81–82*	110	135	___[1]
8156	Monon U36B Dummy, *81–82*	65	65	___[1]
8157	Santa Fe FM Trainmaster, *81*	285	280	___[3]
8158	DM&IR GP-35, *81–82*	80	135	___[1]
8159	DM&IR GP-35 Dummy, *81–82*	65	75	___[1]
8160	Burger King GP-20, *81–82*	105	135	___[1]
8161	L.A.S.E.R. Diesel Switcher, *81–82*	23	55	___[1]
8162	Ontario Northland SD-18, *81 u*	130	155	___[1]
8163	Ontario Northland SD-18 Dummy, *81 u*	85	105	___[1]
8164	Pennsylvania F-3 B Unit, *81 u*	360	460	___[1]

		Exc	New	Cond/$
8182	Nibco Express NW-2, *82 u*	90	130	___1
(8190)	Diesel Horn kit, *81 u*	—	31	___1
8200	"Kickapoo" Dockside 0-4-0T, *72*	30	39	___1
8200	(See 18200)			
8201	(See 18201)			
8203	PRR 2-4-2, *72, 74 u, 75*	26	34	___1
8203	(See 18203)			
8204	C&O 4-4-2, *72*	55	60	___1
[8204]	LCAC Algoma Central Boxcar, *82 u*	—	150	___1
8204	(See 18204)			
8206	NYC 4-6-4, *72–75*	140	155	___1
8206	(See 18206)			
8209	"Pioneer" Dockside 0-4-0T w/ tender, *72*	45	65	___1
8209	"Pioneer" Dockside 0-4-0T w/o tender, *73–76*	42	55	___1
8209	(See 18209)			
8210	Joshua L. Cowen 4-6-4, *82*	380	410	___2
8212	Black Cave 0-4-0, *82*	30	49	___1
8212	(See 18212)			
8213	D&RGW 2-4-2, *82–83, 84–91 u*	55	60	___1
8214	Pennsylvania 2-4-2, *82–83*	55	65	___1
(8215)	Nickel Plate Road 2-8-4 "779", *82 u*	315	370	___2
8223	(See 18835)			
8250	Santa Fe GP-9, *72, 74–75*	95	110	___1
(8251-50)	Horn/Whistle Controller, *72–74*	1.50	2.50	___1
8252	D&H Alco A Unit, *72*	75	110	___1
8253	D&H Alco B Unit, *72*	50	70	___1
8254	Illinois Central GP-9 Dummy, *72*	65	75	___1
8255	Santa Fe GP-9 Dummy, *72*	65	75	___1
8258	Canadian National GP-7 Dummy, *72–73 u*	65	85	___1
8260/8262	Southern Pacific F-3 AA set, *82*	490	520	___1
8261	Southern Pacific F-3 B Unit, *82 u*	570	680	___1
8263	Santa Fe GP-7, *82*	65	80	___1
8264	CP Vulcan Switcher w/ snowplow, *82*	115	120	___2
8265	Santa Fe SD-40, *82*	225	245	___2
8266	Norfolk & Western SD-24, *82*	150	225	___1
8268	Quicksilver Alco A Unit, *82–83*	95	120	___1
8269	Quicksilver Alco A Unit Dummy, *82–83*	55	65	___1
8272	Pennsylvania EP-5, *82 u*	225	290	___1
8300	Santa Fe 2-4-0, *73–74*	19	21	___1
8300	(See 18300)			
8301	(See 18301)			
8302	Southern 2-4-0, *73–76*	29	30	___1
8302	(See 18302)			

		Exc	New	Cond/$
8303	Jersey Central 2-4-2, *73–74*	47	49	___¹
8303	(See 18303)			
8304	Rock Island 4-4-2, *73–75*	85	105	___¹
8304	Pennsylvania 4-4-2, *74–75*	75	105	___¹
8304	B&O 4-4-2, *75*	75	105	___¹
8304	C&O 4-4-2, *75–77*	75	105	___¹
8305	Milwaukee Road 4-4-2, *73*	95	120	___¹
(8307)	Southern Pacific 4-8-4 "4449", *83*	740	860	___³
8308	Jersey Central 2-4-2, *73–74 u*	36	43	___¹
(8309)	Southern 2-8-2 "4501" (FARR #4), *83*	415	530	___¹
8310	Nickel Plate Road 2-4-0, *73 u*	26	50	___¹
8310	Santa Fe 2-4-0, *74–75 u*	26	34	___¹
8310	Jersey Central 2-4-0, *74–75 u*	26	50	___¹
8311	Southern 0-4-0, *73 u*	26	34	___¹
8311	(See 18311)			
8313	Santa Fe 0-4-0, *83–84*	13	17	___¹
8314	Southern 2-4-0, *83–85*	17	21	___¹
8315	B&O 4-4-0, *83–84*	85	120	___¹
8341	ACL SP-type Caboose, *86 u, 87–90*	6	8	___¹
8350	US Steel Diesel Switcher, *73–75*	18	26	___¹
8351	Santa Fe Alco A Unit, *73–75*	55	60	___¹
8352	Santa Fe GP-20, *73–75*	60	95	___¹
8353	Grand Trunk GP-7, *73–75*	70	105	___¹
8354	Erie NW-2, *73, 75*	90	105	___¹
8355	Santa Fe GP-20 Dummy, *73–74*	75	105	___¹
8356	Grand Trunk GP-7 Dummy, *73–75*	65	75	___¹
8357	PRR GP-9, *73–75*	110	125	___¹
8358	PRR GP-9 Dummy, *73–75*	55	100	___¹
(8359)	Chessie System GP-7 "GM50", *73*	105	105	___²
8360	Long Island GP-20, *73–74*	70	105	___¹
8361	Western Pacific Alco A Unit, *73–75*	55	75	___¹
8362	Western Pacific Alco B Unit, *73–75*	45	65	___¹
8363	B&O F-3 A Unit, *73–75*	285	290	___¹
8364	B&O F-3 A Unit Dummy, *73–75*	125	160	___¹
8365/8366	CP F-3 AA set (SSS), *73*	385	510	___¹
8367	Long Island GP-20 Dummy, *73–75*	80	100	___¹
8368	Alaska Vulcan Switcher, *83*	95	125	___²
8369	Erie-Lackawanna GP-20, *83–85*	125	140	___¹
8370/8372	NYC F-3 AA set, *83*	330	435	___¹
8371	NYC F-3 B Unit, *83*	105	150	___¹
8374	Burlington Northern NW-2, *83–85*	105	110	___¹
8375	C&NW GP-7, *83–85*	135	165	___¹
8376	Union Pacific SD-40, *83*	180	205	___¹

		Exc	New	Cond/$
8377	US Diesel Switcher, *83–84*	55	65	___¹
(8378)	Wabash FM Trainmaster "550", *83 u*	810	940	___¹
8379	PRR Fire Car, *83 u*	105	120	___²
8380	Lionel Lines SD-28, *83 u*	175	220	___²
[8389]	NLOE Long Island Boxcar, *89 u*		NRS	___
[8390]	NLOE Long Island Covered Quad Hopper, *90 u*	70	100	___¹
[8391A]	NLOE Long Island Bunk Car, *91 u*		NRS	___
[8391B]	NLOE Long Island Tool Car, *91 u*		NRS	___
8392	NLOE Long Island 1-D Tank Car, *92 u*	70	90	___¹
8393	(See 52019, 52020)			
8394	(See 52026)			
8395	(See 52061)			
8396	(See 52076)			
8400	(See 18400)			
8402	Reading 4-4-2, *84–85*	47	55	___¹
8403	Chessie System 4-4-2, *84–85*	55	65	___¹
(8404)	PRR 6-8-6 "6200" (FARR #5), *84–85*	320	405	___³
8404	(See 18404)			
(8406)	NYC 4-6-4 "783", *84*	520	710	___³
8410	Redwood Valley Express 4-4-0, *84–85*	34	50	___¹
8419	(See 18419)	—	125	___¹
8446	(See 18832)			
8452	Erie Alco A Unit, *74–75*	75	95	___¹
8453	Erie Alco B Unit, *74–75*	55	75	___¹
8454	D&RGW GP-7, *74–75*	80	110	___¹
8455	D&RGW GP-7 Dummy, *74–75*	50	85	___¹
8458	Erie-Lackawanna SD-40, *84*	270	290	___²
8459	D&RGW Vulcan Rotary Snowplow, *84*	155	180	___²
8459	(See 18202)			
8460	MKT NW-2, *74–75*	45	65	___¹
8463	Chessie System GP-20, *74 u*	110	125	___¹
8464/8465	D&RGW F-3 AA set (SSS), *74*	235	320	___¹
8466	Amtrak F-3 A Unit, *74–76*	200	245	___¹
8467	Amtrak F-3 A Unit Dummy, *74–76*	95	105	___¹
8468	B&O F-3 B Unit, *74–75*	110	120	___¹
8469	CP F-3 B Unit (SSS), *74*	105	140	___¹
8470	Chessie System U36B, *74*	95	130	___¹
8471	Pennsylvania NW-2, *74–76*	190	180	___¹
8473	Coca-Cola NW-2, *74 u, 75*	95	120	___¹
8474	D&RGW F-3 B Unit (SSS), *74*	100	130	___¹
8475	Amtrak F-3 B Unit, *74*	95	120	___¹
(8476)	TCA 4-6-4 "5484", *85 u*	320	325	___¹
8477	NYC GP-9, *84 u*	190	215	___³

		Exc	New	Cond/$
8480/8482	Union Pacific F-3 AA set, *84*	280	365	___¹
8481	Union Pacific F-3 B Unit, *84*	180	185	___¹
8485	US Marines NW-2, *84–85*	120	155	___¹
8490	(See 8690)			
8500	Pennsylvania 2-4-0, *75–76*	17	21	___¹
8500	(See 18500, 18550)			
8501	(See 18219, 18501)			
8502	Santa Fe 2-4-0, *75*	17	21	___¹
8502	(See 18220)			
8503	(See 18503)			
8506	PRR 0-4-0, *75–77*	105	115	___¹
8507	Santa Fe 2-4-0, *75 u*	22	26	___¹
[8507]/[8508]	LCAC CN F-3 AA set, shells only, *85 u*		NRS	___
8512	Santa Fe 0-4-0T, *85–86*	22	30	___¹
8516	NYC 0-4-0, *85–86*	105	130	___¹
8550	Jersey Central GP-9, *75–76*	105	135	___¹
8551	Pennsylvania EP-5, *75–76*	150	155	___²
8552/8553/8554	Southern Pacific Alco ABA set, *75–76*	200	245	___¹
8555/8557	Milwaukee Road F-3 AA set (SSS), *75*	290	370	___¹
8556	Chessie System NW-2, *75–76*	155	190	___²
8558	Milwaukee Road EP-5, *76–77*	170	210	___¹
(8559)	N&W GP-9 "1776", *75*	115	145	___¹
8560	Chessie System U36B Dummy, *75*	65	100	___¹
8561	Jersey Central GP-9 Dummy, *75–76*	70	95	___¹
8562	Missouri Pacific GP-20, *75–76*	135	130	___¹
8563	Rock Island Alco A Unit, *75–76 u*	70	95	___¹
8564	Union Pacific U36B, *75*	105	145	___¹
8565	Missouri Pacific GP-20 Dummy, *75–76*	55	70	___¹
8566	Southern F-3 A Unit, *75–77*	250	340	___¹
8567	Southern F-3 A Unit Dummy, *75–77*	115	155	___¹
8568	Preamble Express F-3 A Unit, *75 u*	80	105	___¹
8569	Soo Line NW-2, *75–77*	60	65	___¹
8570	Liberty Special Alco A Unit, *75 u*	75	90	___¹
8571	Frisco U36B, *75–76*	75	95	___¹
8572	Frisco U36B Dummy, *75–76*	55	55	___¹
8573	Union Pacific U36B Dummy, *75 u*	140	165	___¹
8575	Milwaukee Road F-3 B Unit (SSS), *75*	95	150	___¹
8576	Penn Central GP-7, *75 u, 76–77*	90	105	___¹
8578	NYC Ballast Tamper, *85, 87*	115	125	___¹
8580/8582	Illinois Central F-3 AA set, *85, 87*	380	425	___¹
8581	Illinois Central F-3 B Unit, *85, 87*	135	160	___¹
8585	Burlington Northern SD-40, *85*	400	425	___¹
8586	(See 18208)			

		Exc	New	Cond/$
(8587)	Wabash GP-9 "484", *85 u*	240	270	___[1]
8600	NYC 4-6-4, *76*	175	195	___[1]
8600	(See 18600)			
8601	Rock Island 0-4-0, *76–77*	17	21	___[1]
8601	(See 18601)			
8602	D&RGW 2-4-0, *76–78*	22	26	___[1]
8602	(See 18602)			
8603	C&O 4-6-4, *76–77*	135	190	___[1]
8604	Jersey Central 2-4-2, *76 u*	39	44	___[1]
8604	(See 18604)			
(8606)	B&A 4-6-4 "784", *86 u*	890	1000	___[5]
8606	(See 18606)			
8607	(See 18607)			
8608	(See 18608)			
8609	(See 18609)			
8610	(See 18610)			
(8610)	Wabash 4-6-2 "672" (FF #1), *86–87*	520	660	___[1]
8611	(See 18611)			
8612	(See 18612)			
8613	(See 18613)			
(8615)	L&N 2-8-4 "1970", *86 u*	630	740	___[1]
8615	(See 18615)			
8616	Santa Fe 4-4-2, *86*	60	65	___[1]
8616	(See 18616)			
8617	Nickel Plate Road 4-4-2, *86–91*	60	65	___[1]
8618	(See 18618)			
8620	(See 18620)			
8621	(See 18621)			
8622	(See 18622)			
8623	(See 18623)			
8625	(See 18625, 18635)			
8625	Pennsylvania 2-4-0, *86–90*	21	34	___[1]
8626	(See 18626)			
8627	(See 18627)			
8628	(See 18628)			
(8630)	W&ARR 4-4-0 "3", *86 u*	110	130	___[1]
8632	(See 18632)			
8633	(See 18627, 18633, 18637)			
8635	Santa Fe 0-4-0 (SSS), *86*	85	100	___[1]
8640	(See 18640)			
8641	(See 18641)			
8642	(See 18642)			
8650	Burlington Northern U36B, *76–77*	110	150	___[1]

		Exc	New	Cond/$
8651	Burlington Northern U36B Dummy, *76–77*	75	95	___¹
8652	Santa Fe F-3 A Unit, *76–77*	295	380	___¹
8653	Santa Fe F-3 A Unit Dummy, *76–77*	150	170	___¹
8654	Boston & Maine GP-9, *76–77*	125	160	___¹
8655	Boston & Maine GP-9 Dummy, *76–77*	90	110	___¹
8656	Canadian National Alco A Unit, *76*	150	195	___¹
8657	Canadian National Alco B Unit, *76*	60	75	___¹
8658	Canadian National Alco A Unit Dummy, *76*	85	170	___¹
8659	Virginian Rectifier, *76–77*	135	165	___²
8660	CP Rail NW-2, *76–77*	100	135	___¹
8661	Southern F-3 B Unit (SSS), *76*	130	135	___¹
8662	B&O GP-7, *86*	120	130	___¹
8664	Amtrak Alco A Unit, *76–77*	85	120	___¹
8665	BAR "Jeremiah O'Brien" GP-9 "1776", *76 u*	70	115	___¹
8666	Northern Pacific GP-9 (SSS), *76*	125	175	___¹
8667	Amtrak Alco B Unit, *76–77*	60	80	___¹
8668	Northern Pacific GP-9 Dummy (SSS), *76*	100	130	___¹
8669	Illinois Central Gulf U36B, *76–77*	90	110	___¹
8670	Chessie System Diesel Switcher, *76*	30	55	___¹
8679	Northern Pacific GP-20, *86*	100	120	___¹
8687	Jersey Central FM Trainmaster, *86*	280	340	___²
8688	(See 18213)			
8689	(See 18207)			
8690	Lionel Lines Trolley, *86*	105	115	___¹
8699	(See 18307)			
8700	(See 18700)			
(8701)	W&ARR 4-4-0 "3", *77–79*	220	235	___¹
8702	Southern 4-6-4, *77–78*	335	315	___²
8702	(See 18702)			
8703	Wabash 2-4-2, *77*	22	30	___¹
8704	(See 18704)			
8705	(See 18705)			
8706	(See 18706)			
8707	(See 18707)			
8716	(See 18716)			
8750	Rock Island GP-7, *77–78*	110	125	___¹
8751	Rock Island GP-7 Dummy, *77–78*	45	70	___¹
8753	Pennsylvania GG-1, *77 u*	380	415	___²
8754	New Haven Rectifier, *77–78*	135	160	___¹
8755	Santa Fe U36B, *77–78*	130	150	___¹
8756	Santa Fe U36B Dummy, *77–78*	75	95	___¹
8757	Conrail GP-9, *76 u, 77–78*	95	140	___¹
8758	Southern GP-7 Dummy, *77 u, 78*	75	95	___¹

		Exc	New	Cond/$
8759	Erie-Lackawanna GP-9, *77–79*	110	155	___¹
8760	Erie-Lackawanna GP-9 Dummy, *77–79*	95	115	___¹
8761	GTW NW-2, *77–78*	95	130	___¹
8762	Great Northern EP-5, *77–78*	180	190	___¹
8763	Norfolk & Western GP-9, *76 u, 77–78*	95	120	___¹
8764	B&O Budd RDC Passenger (SSS), *77*	115	140	___¹
8765	B&O Budd RDC Baggage Dummy (SSS), *77*	60	80	___¹
8766	B&O Budd RDC Baggage (SSS), *77*	265	265	___¹
8767	B&O Budd RDC Passenger Dummy (SSS), *77*	85	105	___¹
8768	B&O Budd RDC Passenger Dummy (SSS), *77*	85	105	___¹
8769	Republic Steel Diesel Switcher, *77–78*	22	39	___¹
8770	EMD NW-2, *77–78*	80	65	___¹
8771	Great Northern U36B, *77*	100	125	___¹
8772	GM&O GP-20, *77*	85	95	___¹
8773	Mickey Mouse U36B, *77–78*	385	530	___²
8774	Southern GP-7, *77 u, 78*	110	135	___¹
8775	Lehigh Valley GP-9, *77 u, 78*	85	105	___¹
8776	C&NW GP-20, *77 u, 78*	105	135	___¹
8777	Santa Fe F-3 B Unit (SSS), *77*	135	145	___¹
8778	Lehigh Valley GP-9 Dummy, *77 u, 78*	80	95	___¹
8779	C&NW GP-20 Dummy, *77 u, 78*	110	135	___¹
8800	Lionel Lines 4-4-2, *78–81*	75	105	___¹
8800	(See 18800)			
8801	Blue Comet 4-6-4, *78–80*	395	560	___²
8801	(See 18801)			
8802	(See 18802)			
8803	Santa Fe 0-4-0, *78*	14	24	___¹
8803	(See 18803)			
8804	(See 18804)			
8805	(See 18805, 18890)			
8806	(See 18806)			
8807	(See 18807)			
8808	(See 18808)			
8809	(See 18551)			
8810	(See 18810)			
8811	(See 18811)			
8813	(See 18552)			
8814	(See 18814)			
8820	(See 18820)			
8827	(See 18827)			
8834	(See 18834)			
8837	(See 18837)			
8850	Penn Central GG-1, *78 u, 79*	330	400	___²

		Exc	New	Cond/$
8851/8852	New Haven F-3 AA set, *78 u, 79*	280	375	___¹
8854	CP Rail GP-9, *78–79*	100	140	___¹
8855	Milwaukee Road SD-18, *78*	130	120	___¹
8857	Northern Pacific U36B, *78–80*	105	135	___¹
8858	Northern Pacific U36B Dummy, *78–80*	55	85	___¹
8859	Conrail Rectifier, *78–82*	120	160	___¹
8860	Rock Island NW-2, *78–79*	85	105	___¹
8861	Santa Fe Alco A Unit, *78–79*	65	85	___¹
8862	Santa Fe Alco B Unit, *78–79*	36	43	___¹
8864	New Haven F-3 B Unit, *78*	85	105	___¹
8866	M&St L GP-9 (SSS), *78*	90	125	___¹
8867	M&St L GP-9 Dummy (SSS), *78*	65	95	___¹
8868	Amtrak Budd RDC Baggage, *78, 80*	135	175	___¹
8869	Amtrak Budd RDC Passenger Dummy, *78, 80*	75	95	___¹
8870	Amtrak Budd RDC Passenger Dummy, *78, 80*	75	100	___¹
8871	Amtrak Budd RDC Baggage Dummy, *78, 80*	75	95	___¹
8872	Santa Fe SD-18, *78 u, 79*	110	155	___¹
8873	Santa Fe SD-18 Dummy, *78 u, 79*	65	95	___¹
8900	Santa Fe 4-6-4 (FARR #1), *79*	310	335	___²
8900	(See 18900)			
8901	(See 18901/18902)			
8902	(See 18901/18902)			
8902	ACL 2-4-0, *79–82, 86 u, 87–90*	13	17	___¹
8903	D&RGW 2-4-2, *79–81*	17	21	___¹
8903	(See 18903/18904)			
8904	Wabash 2-4-2, *79, 81 u*	30	34	___¹
8904	(See 18903/18904)			
8905	"Smokey Mountain" Dockside 0-4-0T, *79*	9	17	___¹
8906	(See 18906)			
8908	(See 18908/18909)			
8909	(See 18908/18909)			
8910	(See 18910)			
8911	(See 18911)			
8912	(See 18912)			
[8912]	LCAC Canada Southern Operating Hopper, *89 u*	—	95	___¹
8913	(See 18913)			
8915	(See 18915)			
8916	(See 18916)			
8918	(See 18918)			
8919	(See 18919)			
8922	(See 18922)			
8923	(See 18923)			
8924	(See 18924)			

No.	Description	Exc	New	Cond/$
8925	(See 18925)			
8926	(See 18926)			
8932	(See 18932)			
8933	(See 18933)			
8936	(See 18936)			
8937	(See 18937)			
8950	Virginian FM Trainmaster, *79*	265	300	___[3]
8951	Southern Pacific FM Trainmaster, *79*	320	370	___[3]
8952/8953	PRR F-3 AA set, *79*	—	520	___[1]
8955	Southern U36B, *79*	120	170	___[1]
8956	Southern U36B Dummy, *79*	75	105	___[1]
8957	Burlington Northern GP-20, *79*	120	150	___[1]
[8957]	Detroit-Toledo TCA Burlington Northern GP-20, *80 u*		NRS	___
8958	Burlington Northern GP-20 Dummy, *79*	95	105	___[1]
[8958]	Detroit-Toledo TCA Burlington Northern GP-20 Dummy, *80 u*		NRS	___
8960	Southern Pacific U36C, *79 u*	95	125	___[1]
8961	Southern Pacific U36C Dummy, *79 u*	65	75	___[1]
8962	Reading U36B, *79*	110	120	___[1]
8970/8971	PRR F-3 AA set, *79 u, 80*	405	495	___[1]
8977	(See 18000)			
8999	Lone Star Aquarium Car, *99*			
9001	Conrail Boxcar (027), *86–87 u, 88–90*	5	10	___[1]
9010	GN Hopper (027), *70–71*	6	8	___[1]
9011	GN Hopper (027), *70 u, 75–76, 78–83*	6	9	___[1]
9011	(See 19011)			
9012	TA&G Hopper (027), *71–72*	7	8	___[1]
9013	Canadian National Hopper (027), *72–76*	4	8	___[1]
9014	Trailer Train Flatcar (027), *78–79*		NM	___
9015	Reading Hopper (027), *73–75*	17	21	___[1]
9015	(See 19015)			
9016	Chessie System Hopper (027), *75–79, 87–88, 89 u*	4	6	___[1]
[9016]	LCCA Chessie System Hopper (027), *79–80 u*	16	20	___[1]
9016	(See 19016)			
9017	Wabash Gondola w/ canisters (027), *78–82*	3	5	___[1]
9017	(See 19017)			
9018	DT&I Hopper (027), *78–79, 81–82*	4	7	___[1]
9018	(See 19018)			
(9019)	Unlettered Flatcar (027), *78*	2.50	3	___[1]
9019	(See 19019)			
9020	Union Pacific Flatcar (027), *70–78*	3	5	___[1]

		Exc	New	Cond/$
9021	Santa Fe Work Caboose, *70–71, 73–75*	9	13	___¹
9022	Santa Fe Bulkhead Flatcar (O27), *70–72, 75–79*	7	13	___¹
9023	MKT Bulkhead Flatcar (O27), *73–74*	7	10	___¹
9023	(See 19023)			
9024	C&O Flatcar (O27), *73–75*	3	6	___¹
9024	(See 19024)			
9025	DT&I Work Caboose, *71–74, 77–78*	7	9	___¹
9025	(See 19025)			
9026	Republic Steel Flatcar (O27), *75–82*	5	7	___¹
9026	(See 19026)			
9027	Soo Line Work Caboose, *75–76*	7	9	___¹
9027	(See 19027)			
(9030)	"Kickapoo" Gondola (O27), *72, 79*	5	9	___¹
9031	(See 19031)			
9031	NKP Gondola w/ canisters (O27), *73–75, 82–83, 84–91 u*	4	7	___¹
9032	Southern Pacific Gondola w/ canisters (O27), *75–78*	3	3	___¹
9032	(See 19032)			
9033	(See 19033)			
9033	PC Gondola w/ canisters (O27), *76–78, 82, 86 u, 87–90, 92 u*	3	3	___¹
9034	Lionel Leisure Hopper (O27), *77 u*	27	34	___¹
9035	Conrail Boxcar (O27), *78–82*	5	9	___¹
9036	Mobilgas 1-D Tank Car (O27), *78–82*	7	13	___¹
[9036]	LCCA Mobilgas 1-D Tank Car (O27), *78–79 u*	20	22	___¹
9037	Conrail Boxcar (O27), *78 u, 80*	6	9	___¹
9038	Chessie System Hopper (O27), *78 u, 80*	15	19	___¹
9039	Mobilgas 1-D Tank Car (O27), *78 u, 80*	10	15	___¹
9040	General Mills Wheaties Boxcar (O27), *70–72*	8	11	___¹
9041	Hershey's Boxcar (O27), *70–71, 73–76*	15	25	___¹
9042	Ford-Autolite Boxcar (O27), *71 u, 72, 74–76*	11	18	___¹
9043	Erie-Lackawanna Boxcar (O27), *73–75*	13	20	___¹
9044	D&RGW Boxcar (O27), *75–76*	5	8	___¹
9045	Toys "R" Us Boxcar (O27), *75 u*	36	43	___¹
9046	True Value Boxcar (O27), *76 u*	26	34	___¹
9047	Toys "R" Us Boxcar (O27), *76 u*	40	43	___¹
9047	(See 19047)			
9048	Toys "R" Us Boxcar (O27), *76 u*	33	41	___¹
9048	(See 19048)			
(9049)	Toys "R" Us Boxcar (O27), *78 u*		NRS	___
9049	(See 19049)			
9050	Sunoco 1-D Tank Car (O27), *70–71*	17	23	___¹

		Exc	New	Cond/$
9050	(See 19050)			
9051	Firestone 1-D Tank Car (O27), *74–75, 78*	15	19	___¹
9052	Toys "R" Us Boxcar (O27), *77 u*	26	34	___¹
9053	True Value Boxcar (O27), *77 u*	28	40	___¹
9054	JC Penney Boxcar (O27), *77 u*	14	19	___¹
9055	Republic Steel Gondola w/ canisters, *78 u*	9	10	___¹
9057	CP Rail SP-type Caboose, *78–79*	10	15	___¹
9058	Lionel Lines SP-type Caboose, *78–79, 83*	5	7	___¹
9059	Lionel Lines SP-type Caboose, *79 u, 81 u*	7	9	___¹
9060	Nickel Plate Road SP-type Caboose, *70–72*	5	7	___¹
9061	Santa Fe SP-type Caboose, *70–76*	5	8	___¹
9062	Penn Central SP-type Caboose, *70–72, 74–76*	6	9	___¹
9063	GTW SP-type Caboose, *70, 71–73 u*	14	19	___¹
9064	C&O SP-type Caboose, *71–72, 75–77*	7	10	___¹
9065	Canadian National SP-type Caboose, *71–73 u*	19	24	___¹
9066	Southern SP-type Caboose, *73–76*	7	9	___¹
(9067)	Kickapoo Valley Bobber Caboose, *72*	6	9	___¹
9068	Reading Bobber Caboose, *73–76*	5	7	___¹
[9068]	Gateway TCA Reading Bobber Caboose, *76 u*	—	20	___¹
9069	Jersey Central SP-type Caboose, *73–74, 75–76 u*	5	8	___¹
9070	Rock Island SP-type Caboose, *73–74*	11	17	___¹
9071	Santa Fe Bobber Caboose, *74 u, 77–78*	7	9	___¹
9073	Coca-Cola SP-type Caboose, *74 u, 75*	15	19	___¹
9075	Rock Island SP-type Caboose, *75–76 u*	13	17	___¹
9076	"We The People" SP-type Caboose, *75 u*	19	28	___¹
9077	D&RGW SP-type Caboose, *76–83, 84–91 u*	6	8	___¹
9078	Rock Island Bobber Caboose, *76–77*	5	7	___¹
9079	GTW Hopper (O27), *77*	21	30	___¹
9080	Wabash SP-type Caboose, *77*	9	10	___¹
9085	Santa Fe Work Caboose, *79–82*	4	5	___¹
9090	General Mills Mini-Max Car, *71*	24	28	___¹
9100	(See 18205, 19100)			
9101	(See 19101)			
9102	(See 19102)			
9103	(See 19103)			
9104	(See 19104)			
9105	(See 19105)			
9106	Miller Vat Car, *84–85*	31	46	___¹
9106	(See 19106)			
9107	Dr Pepper Vat Car, *86–87*	24	33	___¹
9110	B&O Quad Hopper, *71*	25	30	___¹
9111	N&W Quad Hopper, *72–75*	17	22	___¹

		Exc	New	Cond/$
9112	D&RGW Covered Quad Hopper, *73–75*	20	24	___¹
9113	Norfolk & Western Quad Hopper (SSS), *73*	27	32	___¹
[9113]	Three Rivers TCA N&W Quad Hopper, *76 u*	27	30	___¹
9114	Morton Salt Covered Quad Hopper, *74–76*	18	23	___¹
9115	Planter's Covered Quad Hopper, *74–76*	21	24	___¹
9116	Domino Sugar Covered Quad Hopper, *74–76*	19	25	___¹
9117	Alaska Covered Quad Hopper (SSS), *74–76*	24	29	___¹
9118	LCCA Corning Covered Quad Hopper, *74 u*	65	85	___¹
9119	Detroit & Mackinac Covered Quad Hopper (SSS), *75*	25	30	___¹
[9119]	Detroit-Toledo TCA Detroit & Mackinac Covered Quad Hopper, *77 u*	20	27	___¹
[9119]	North Texas TCA Detroit & Mackinac Covered Quad Hopper, *78 u*	22	30	___¹
9120	Northern Pacific Flatcar w/ trailers, *70–71*	28	33	___¹
9121	L&N Flatcar w/ bulldozer and scraper, *71–79*	50	65	___¹
9121	(See 19121)			
9122	Northern Pacific Flatcar w/ trailers, *72–75*	26	33	___¹
9123	C&O Auto Carrier (3-tier), *72 u, 73–74*	20	30	___¹
(9123)	TCA Dearborn Auto Carrier "1973" (3-tier), *73 u*	25	33	___¹
9124	P&LE Flatcar w/ log load, *73–74*	18	25	___¹
9125	Norfolk & Western Auto Carrier (2-tier), *73–77*	23	28	___¹
9126	C&O Auto Carrier (3-tier), *73–75*	23	34	___¹
9128	Heinz Vat Car, *74–76*	21	31	___¹
9129	N&W Auto Carrier (3-tier), *75–76*	22	26	___¹
9129	(See 19129)			
9130	B&O Quad Hopper, *70*	19	20	___¹
9131	D&RGW Gondola w/ canisters, *73–77*	5	8	___¹
9132	Libby's Vat Car (SSS), *75–77*	16	23	___¹
9133	Burlington Northern Flatcar w/ trailers, *76–77, 80*	21	29	___¹
9134	Virginian Covered Quad Hopper, *76–77*	28	28	___¹
9135	N&W Covered Quad Hopper, *70 u, 71, 75*	17	22	___¹
9136	Republic Steel Gondola w/ canisters, *72–76, 79*	9	11	___¹
9138	Sunoco 3-D Tank Car (SSS), *78*	35	40	___¹
9139	PC Auto Carrier (3-tier), *76–77*	23	32	___¹
9140	Burlington Gondola w/ canisters, *70, 73–82, 87–89*	7	9	___¹
9141	Burlington Northern Gondola w/ canisters, *70–72*	8	10	___¹
9142	Republic Steel Gondola w/ canisters, *71*	7	9	___¹

		Exc	New	Cond/$
[9142]	LCCA Republic Steel Gondola w/ canisters, 77–78 u	14	19	____[1]
9143	Canadian National Gondola w/ canisters, 71–73 u	30	34	____[1]
9144	D&RGW Gondola w/ canisters (SSS), 74–76	9	13	____[1]
9145	ICG Auto Carrier (3-tier), 77–80	18	25	____[1]
9146	Mogen David Vat Car, 77–81	21	26	____[1]
9146	(See 19821)			
9147	Texaco 1-D Tank Car, 77–78	35	47	____[1]
9148	Du Pont 3-D Tank Car, 77–81	20	24	____[1]
9149	CP Rail Flatcar w/ trailers, 77–78	23	37	____[1]
9150	Gulf 1-D Tank Car, 70 u, 71	19	24	____[1]
9151	Shell 1-D Tank Car, 72	30	34	____[1]
9152	Shell 1-D Tank Car, 73–76	29	35	____[1]
9153	Chevron 1-D Tank Car, 74–76	29	33	____[1]
9154	Borden 1-D Tank Car, 75–76	33	47	____[1]
9155	LCCA Monsanto 1-D Tank Car, 75 u	45	55	____[1]
9156	Mobilgas 1-D Tank Car, 76–77	26	37	____[1]
9157	C&O Flatcar w/ crane, 76–78, 81–82	34	40	____[1]
9158	PC Flatcar w/ shovel, 76–77, 80	32	39	____[1]
9159	Sunoco 1-D Tank Car, 76	35	50	____[1]
9160	Illinois Central N5C Caboose, 70–72	17	27	____[1]
9161	CN N5C Caboose, 72–74	18	34	____[1]
9162	PRR N5C Caboose, 72–76	28	30	____[1]
9163	Santa Fe N5C Caboose, 73–76	17	24	____[1]
9165	Canadian Pacific N5C Caboose (SSS), 73	21	30	____[1]
9166	D&RGW SP-type Caboose (SSS), 74–75	19	24	____[1]
9167	Chessie System N5C Caboose, 74–76	24	31	____[1]
9168	Union Pacific N5C Caboose, 75–77	22	25	____[1]
9169	Milwaukee Road SP-type Caboose (SSS), 75	23	29	____[1]
(9170)	N&W N5C Caboose "1776", 75	27	30	____[1]
9171	Missouri Pacific SP-type Caboose, 75 u, 76–77	21	24	____[1]
9172	Penn Central SP-type Caboose, 75 u, 76–77	22	30	____[1]
9173	Jersey Central SP-type Caboose, 75 u, 76–77	21	31	____[1]
9174	NYC P&E B/W Caboose, 76	65	75	____[1]
9175	Virginian N5C Caboose, 76–77	26	28	____[1]
9176	BAR N5C Caboose, 76 u	18	30	____[1]
9177	Northern Pacific B/W Caboose (SSS), 76	30	43	____[1]
9178	ICG SP-type Caboose, 76–77	21	27	____[1]
9179	Chessie System Bobber Caboose, 76	5	9	____[1]
9180	Rock Island N5C Caboose, 77–78	15	30	____[1]
9181	B&M N5C Caboose, 76 u, 77	29	38	____[1]
[9181]	NETCA B&M N5C Caboose, 77 u	22	30	____[1]

		Exc	New	Cond/$
9182	N&W N5C Caboose, *76 u, 77–80*	24	32	___¹
9183	Mickey Mouse N5C Caboose, *77–78*	35	55	___¹
9184	Erie B/W Caboose, *77–78*	24	31	___²
[9184]	North Texas TCA Erie B/W Caboose, *77 u*	19	24	___¹
[9184]	LCOL Erie B/W Caboose, *82 u*	17	21	___¹
9185	GTW N5C Caboose, *77*	21	29	___¹
9186	Conrail N5C Caboose, *76 u, 77–78*	27	35	___¹
[9186]	Atlantic TCA Conrail N5C Caboose, *79 u*	22	30	___¹
9187	GM&O SP-type Caboose, *77*	15	26	___¹
9188	GN N5C Caboose, *77*	26	32	___¹
9189	Gulf 1-D Tank Car, *77*	43	50	___¹
9193	Budweiser Vat Car, *83–84*	90	145	___¹
[9193]	Atlantic TCA Budweiser Vat Car, *84 u*	80	110	___¹
9200	Illinois Central Boxcar, *70–71*	18	24	___¹
9201	Penn Central Boxcar, *70*	16	24	___¹
9202	Santa Fe Boxcar, *70*	39	37	___¹
9203	Union Pacific Boxcar, *70*	27	27	___¹
9204	Northern Pacific Boxcar, *70*	27	26	___¹
9205	Norfolk & Western Boxcar, *70*	23	28	___¹
9206	Great Northern Boxcar, *70–71*	20	20	___¹
9207	Soo Line Boxcar, *71*	17	25	___¹
9208	CP Rail Boxcar, *71*	20	22	___¹
9209	Burlington Northern Boxcar, *71–72*	16	21	___¹
9210	B&O DD Boxcar, *71*	19	23	___¹
9211	Penn Central Boxcar, *71*	19	31	___¹
9212	LCCA SCL Flatcar w/ trailers, *76 u*	21	25	___¹
9213	M&StL Covered Quad Hopper (SSS), *78*	19	27	___¹
9214	Northern Pacific Boxcar, *71–72*	18	24	___¹
9215	Norfolk & Western Boxcar, *71*	20	27	___¹
9215	(See 52004)			
9216	Great Northern Auto Carrier (3-tier), *78*	26	40	___¹
9217	Soo Line Operating Boxcar, *82–84*	24	29	___¹
9218	Monon Operating Boxcar, *81*	28	33	___¹
9219	Missouri Pacific Operating Boxcar, *83*	23	28	___¹
9220	Borden Milk Car, *83–86*	115	150	___¹
9221	Poultry Dispatch Operating Chicken Car, *83–85*	43	47	___¹
9222	L&N Flatcar w/ trailers, *83–84*	29	44	___¹
9223	Reading Operating Boxcar, *84*	28	34	___¹
9224	Churchill Downs Operating Horse Car, *84–86*	105	125	___¹
9225	Conrail Operating Barrel Car, *84*	55	75	___¹
9226	Delaware & Hudson Flatcar w/ trailers, *84–85*	32	44	___¹
9228	Canadian Pacific Operating Boxcar, *86*	22	34	___¹
9229	Express Mail Operating Boxcar, *85–86*	27	37	___²

		Exc	New	Cond/$
9230	Monon Boxcar (SSS), *71, 72 u*	15	21	___[1]
9231	Reading B/W Caboose, *79*	27	36	___[1]
9232	Allis-Chalmers Condenser Car, *80–81, 83 u*	46	55	___[1]
9233	Depressed Flatcar w/ transformer, *80*	65	70	___[1]
9234	Lionel Radioactive Waste Car, *80*	55	85	___[1]
9235	Union Pacific Derrick Car, *83–84*	16	22	___[1]
9236	C&NW Derrick Car, *83–85*	22	30	___[1]
9237	UPS Operating Boxcar, *84*		NM	___
9238	Northern Pacific Log Dump Car, *84*	15	22	___[1]
9239	Lionel Lines N5C Caboose, *83 u*	47	55	___[1]
9240	NYC Operating Hopper, *86*	32	40	___[1]
9240	NYC Hopper (O27), *87 u*	17	24	___[1]
9241	PRR Log Dump Car, *85–86*	17	19	___[1]
9245	Illinois Central Derrick Car, *85*		NM	___
9247	(See 6529)			
9250	WaterPoxy 3-D Tank Car, *70–71*	26	31	___[1]
X9259	LCCA Southern B/W Caboose, *77 u*	36	41	___[1]
9260	Reynolds Aluminum Covered Quad Hopper, *75–76*	19	23	___[1]
9261	Sun-maid Raisins Covered Quad Hopper, *75 u, 76*	17	25	___[1]
9262	Ralston Purina Covered Quad Hopper, *75 u, 76*	47	60	___[2]
9263	PRR Covered Quad Hopper, *75 u, 76–77*	30	41	___[1]
9264	Illinois Central Covered Quad Hopper, *75 u, 76–77*	34	38	___[1]
[9264]	Midwest TCA Museum Express Illinois Central Covered Quad Hopper, *78 u*	22	26	___[1]
9265	Chessie System Covered Quad Hopper, *75 u, 76–77*	24	27	___[1]
9266	Southern "Big John" Covered Quad Hopper, *76*	49	65	___[1]
9267	Alcoa Covered Quad Hopper (SSS), *76*	24	32	___[1]
9268	Northern Pacific B/W Caboose, *77 u*	32	42	___[1]
9269	Milwaukee Road B/W Caboose, *78*	35	48	___[1]
9270	Northern Pacific N5C Caboose, *78*	11	21	___[1]
9271	M&StL B/W Caboose (SSS), *78–79*	19	38	___[1]
9272	New Haven B/W Caboose, *78–80*	20	34	___[1]
[9272]	METCA New Haven B/W Caboose, *79 u*	21	25	___[1]
[9272]	Detroit-Toledo TCA New Haven B/W Caboose, *79 u*	19	22	___[1]
9273	Southern B/W Caboose, *78 u*	39	50	___[1]
9274	Santa Fe B/W Caboose, *78 u*	50	55	___[1]
9276	Peabody Quad Hopper, *78*	24	33	___[1]
9277	Cities Service 1-D Tank Car, *78*	47	55	___[1]

		Exc	New	Cond/$
9278	Life Savers 1-D Tank Car, *78–79*	100	165	___2
9279	Magnolia 3-D Tank Car, *78, 79 u*	20	26	___1
9280	Santa Fe Operating Stock Car (O27), *77–81*	20	24	___1
9281	Santa Fe Auto Carrier (3-tier), *78–80*	23	29	___1
9282	Great Northern Flatcar w/ trailers, *78–79, 81–82*	29	37	___1
9283	Union Pacific Gondola w/ canisters, *77*	15	21	___1
9284	Santa Fe Gondola w/ canisters, *77*	19	27	___1
9285	ICG Flatcar w/ trailers, *77*	43	50	___1
9286	B&LE Covered Quad Hopper, *77*	18	30	___1
9287	Southern N5C Caboose, *77 u, 78*	16	26	___1
[9287]	Southern TCA Southern N5C Caboose, *77 u*	15	21	___1
9288	Lehigh Valley N5C Caboose, *77 u, 78, 80*	35	45	___1
9288	(See 18844)			
9289	C&NW N5C Caboose, *77 u, 78, 80*	27	39	___1
[9289]	Midwest TCA Museum Express C&NW N5C Caboose, *80 u*	36	43	___1
9290	Union Pacific Operating Barrel Car, *83*	75	85	___1
9300	PC Log Dump Car, *70–75, 77*	14	18	___1
9301	US Mail Operating Boxcar, *73–84*	27	35	___1
[9301]	Sacramento-Sierra TCA US Mail Operating Boxcar, *76 u*	26	38	___1
9302	L&N Searchlight Car, *72 u, 73–78*	21	24	___1
9303	Union Pacific Log Dump Car, *74–78, 80*	11	19	___1
9304	C&O Coal Dump Car, *74–78*	10	20	___1
9305	Santa Fe Operating Cowboy Car (O27), *80–82*	16	23	___1
9306	Santa Fe Flatcar w/ horses, *80–82*	18	26	___1
9307	Erie Animated Gondola, *80–84*	50	65	___1
9308	Aquarium Car, *81–84*	175	185	___2
9309	TP&W B/W Caboose, *80–81, 83 u*	21	29	___1
9310	Santa Fe Log Dump Car, *78 u, 79–83*	11	22	___1
9311	Union Pacific Coal Dump Car, *78 u, 79–82*	11	22	___1
9312	Conrail Searchlight Car, *78 u, 79–83*	15	22	___1
9312	(See 18905)			
9313	Gulf 3-D Tank Car, *79 u*	47	55	___1
9315	Southern Pacific Gondola w/ canisters, *79 u*	22	32	___1
9316	Southern Pacific B/W Caboose, *79 u*	60	70	___2
9317	Santa Fe B/W Caboose, *79*	30	44	___1
9319	TCA Silver Jubilee Mint Car, *79 u*	145	170	___2
9320	Fort Knox Mint Car, *79 u*	175	225	___1
9321	Santa Fe 1-D Tank Car (FARR #1), *79*	28	36	___1
9322	Santa Fe Covered Quad Hopper (FARR #1), *79*	50	60	___1
9323	Santa Fe B/W Caboose (FARR #1), *79*	39	48	___1

		Exc	New	Cond/$
9324	Tootsie Roll 1-D Tank Car, *79–81*	55	80	___[1]
9325	(See 9363, 9364)			
9325	Norfolk & Western Flatcar w/ fences, *79–81 u*	6	10	___[1]
9326	Burlington Northern B/W Caboose, *79–80*	31	40	___[1]
[9326]	TTOS Burlington Northern B/W Caboose, *82 u*	—	22	___[1]
9327	Bakelite 3-D Tank Car, *80*	22	30	___[1]
9328	Chessie System B/W Caboose, *80*	37	47	___[1]
9329	Chessie System Crane Car, *80*	55	65	___[1]
(9330)	"Kickapoo" Dump Car, *72, 79*	3	7	___[1]
9331	Union 76 1-D Tank Car, *79*	50	60	___[1]
9332	Reading Crane Car, *79*	48	70	___[1]
9333	Southern Pacific Flatcar w/ trailers, *79–80*	31	41	___[1]
9334	Humble 1-D Tank Car, *79*	21	26	___[1]
9335	B&O Log Dump Car, *86*	16	22	___[1]
9336	CP Rail Gondola w/ canisters, *79*	24	34	___[1]
9338	Penn Power Quad Hopper, *79*	70	95	___[1]
9339	Great Northern Boxcar (O27), *79–83, 85 u, 86*	7	10	___[1]
9340	Illinois Central Gondola w/ canisters (O27), *79–81, 82 u, 83*	5	9	___[1]
9341	ACL SP-type Caboose, *79–82, 86 u, 87–90*	6	8	___[1]
9344	Citgo 3-D Tank Car, *80*	44	42	___[1]
9345	Reading Searchlight Car, *84–85*	19	22	___[1]
9346	Wabash SP-type Caboose, *79*	6	10	___[1]
9347	TTOS Niagara Falls 3-D Tank Car, *79 u*	38	46	___[1]
9348	Santa Fe Crane Car (FARR #1), *79 u*	60	70	___[1]
9349	San Francisco Mint Car, *80*	75	100	___[2]
9351	PRR Auto Carrier (3-tier), *80*	20	36	___[1]
9352	Trailer Train Flatcar w/ C&NW trailers, *80*	35	65	___[1]
9353	Crystal Line 3-D Tank Car, *80*	18	26	___[1]
9354	Pennzoil 1-D Tank Car, *80, 81 u*	50	65	___[1]
9355	Delaware & Hudson B/W Caboose, *80*	34	41	___[1]
[9355]	TTOS D&H B/W Caboose, *82 u*		NRS	___
9356	Life Savers Stik-O-Pep 1-D Tank Car, *80 u*		NM	___
9357	Smokey Mountain Bobber Caboose, *79*	8	10	___[1]
9358	LCCA Sands of Iowa Covered Quad Hopper, *80 u*	22	28	___[1]
9359	National Basketball Association Boxcar (O27), *79–80 u*	19	24	___[1]
9360	National Hockey League Boxcar (O27), *79–80 u*	21	26	___[1]
9361	C&NW B/W Caboose, *80*	55	65	___[1]
[9361]	TTOS C&NW B/W Caboose, *82 u*	—	50	___[1]
9362	Major League Baseball Boxcar (O27), *79–80 u*	17	21	___[1]
(9363)	N&W Flatcar w/ dump bin "9325" (O27), *79*	4	7	___[1]

		Exc	New	Cond/$
(9364)	N&W Flatcar w/ crane "9325" (O27), *79*	7	9	___¹
9365	Toys "R" Us Boxcar (O27), *79 u*	36	43	___¹
9366	Union Pacific Covered Quad Hopper (FARR #2), *80*	24	27	___¹
9367	Union Pacific 1-D Tank Car (FARR #2), *80*	28	40	___¹
9368	Union Pacific B/W Caboose (FARR #2), *80*	33	42	___¹
9369	Sinclair 1-D Tank Car, *80*	55	75	___¹
9370	Seaboard Gondola w/ canisters, *80*	20	25	___¹
9371	Atlantic Sugar Covered Quad Hopper, *80*	25	34	___¹
9372	Seaboard B/W Caboose, *80*	30	40	___¹
9373	Getty 1-D Tank Car, *80–81, 83 u*	36	44	___¹
9374	Reading Covered Quad Hopper, *80–81, 83 u*	41	45	___¹
9375	Union Pacific Flatcar w/ fences (O27), *80*		NM	___
9376	Texas & Pacific SP-type Caboose, *80*		NM	___
9376	Soo Line Boxcar (O27), *81 u*	40	50	___¹
9377	Missouri Pacific Boxcar (O27), *80*		NM	___
9378	Lionel Derrick Car, *80–82*	20	24	___¹
9379	Santa Fe Gondola w/ canisters, *80–81, 83 u*	22	30	___¹
9380	NYNH&H SP-type Caboose, *80–81*	9	10	___¹
9381	Chessie System SP-type Caboose, *80*	7	9	___¹
9382	Florida East Coast B/W Caboose, *80*	39	55	___¹
[9382]	TTOS Florida East Coast B/W Caboose, *82 u*	—	80	___¹
9383	UP Flatcar w/ trailers (FARR #2), *80 u*	35	42	___¹
9384	Great Northern Operating Hopper, *81*	55	65	___¹
9385	Alaska Gondola w/ canisters, *81*	33	41	___¹
9386	Pure Oil 1-D Tank Car, *81*	55	60	___¹
9387	Burlington B/W Caboose, *81*	42	55	___¹
9388	Toys "R" Us Boxcar (O27), *81 u*	38	45	___¹
9389	Lionel Radioactive Waste Car, *81–82*	60	75	___¹
9398	PRR Coal Dump Car, *83–84*	22	27	___¹
9399	C&NW Coal Dump Car, *83–85*	17	22	___¹
9400	Conrail Boxcar, *78*	16	22	___¹
[9400]	NETCA Conrail Boxcar, *78 u*	23	27	___¹
9401	Great Northern Boxcar, *78*	16	20	___¹
[9401]	Detroit-Toledo TCA GN Boxcar, *78 u*	—	23	___¹
9402	Susquehanna Boxcar, *78*	29	31	___¹
9403	Seaboard Coast Line Boxcar, *78*	16	22	___¹
[9403]	Southern TCA SCL Boxcar, *78 u*	—	18	___¹
9404	NKP Boxcar, *78*	19	22	___¹
9405	Chattahoochee Boxcar, *78*	16	21	___¹
[9405]	Southern TCA Chattahoochee Boxcar, *79 u*	—	21	___¹
9405	(See 19716)			
9406	D&RGW Boxcar, *78–79*	17	21	___¹

		Exc	New	Cond/$
9407	Union Pacific Stock Car, *78*	33	36	___¹
9408	Lionel Lines Circus Stock Car (SSS), *78*	28	36	___¹
9411	Lackawanna "Phoebe Snow" Boxcar, *78*	45	55	___¹
9412	RF&P Boxcar, *79*	21	30	___¹
[9412]	WB&A TCA RF&P Boxcar, *79 u*	—	26	___¹
9413	Napierville Junction Boxcar, *79*	14	19	___¹
[9413]	LCAC Napierville Junction Boxcar, *80 u*		NRS	___
9414	Cotton Belt Boxcar, *79*	17	21	___¹
[9414]	Sacramento-Sierra TCA Cotton Belt Boxcar, *80 u*	—	35	___¹
[9414]	LOTS Cotton Belt Boxcar, *80 u*	39	55	___¹
9415	Providence & Worcester Boxcar, *79*	15	22	___¹
[9415]	NETCA Providence & Worcester Boxcar, *79 u*	28	34	___¹
9416	MD&W Boxcar, *79, 81*	11	15	___¹
9417	CP Rail Boxcar, *79*	38	50	___¹
9418	FARR Boxcar, *79 u*	42	50	___¹
9419	Union Pacific Boxcar (FARR #2), *80*	23	32	___¹
9420	B&O "Sentinel" Boxcar, *80*	33	39	___¹
9421	Maine Central Boxcar, *80*	12	20	___¹
9422	EJ&E Boxcar, *80*	13	21	___¹
9423	NYNH&H Boxcar, *80*	15	24	___¹
[9423]	NETCA NYNH&H Boxcar, *80 u*	25	30	___¹
9424	TP&W Boxcar, *80*	17	21	___¹
9425	British Columbia DD Boxcar, *80*	23	27	___¹
9426	Chesapeake & Ohio Boxcar, *80*	20	32	___¹
9427	Bay Line Boxcar, *80–81*	14	18	___¹
[9427]	Sacramento-Sierra TCA Bay Line Boxcar, *81 u*	—	30	___¹
9428	TP&W Boxcar, *80–81, 83 u*	24	23	___¹
9429	"The Early Years" Boxcar, *80*	29	40	___¹
9430	"The Standard Gauge Years" Boxcar, *80*	21	24	___¹
9431	"The Prewar Years" Boxcar, *80*	20	25	___¹
9432	"The Postwar Years" Boxcar, *80*	65	75	___¹
9433	"The Golden Years" Boxcar, *80*	60	75	___¹
9434	"Joshua Lionel Cowen—The Man" Boxcar, *80 u*	33	42	___¹
9435	LCCA Central of Georgia Boxcar, *81 u*	24	30	___¹
9436	Burlington Boxcar, *81*	35	43	___¹
9437	Northern Pacific Stock Car, *81*	25	40	___¹
9438	Ontario Northland Boxcar, *81*	27	38	___¹
9439	Ashley Drew & Northern Boxcar, *81*	11	20	___¹
9440	Reading Boxcar, *81*	50	65	___¹
9441	Pennsylvania Boxcar, *81*	44	60	___¹
9442	Canadian Pacific Boxcar, *81*	14	22	___¹

		Exc	New	Cond/$
9443	Florida East Coast Boxcar, *81*	17	19	___¹
[9443]	Southern TCA Florida East Coast Boxcar, *81 u*	—	23	___¹
9444	Louisiana Midland Boxcar, *81*	16	21	___¹
[9444]	Sacramento-Sierra TCA Louisiana Midland Boxcar, *82 u*	—	35	___¹
9445	Vermont Northern Boxcar, *81*	15	19	___¹
[9445]	NETCA Vermont Northern Boxcar, *81 u*	29	34	___¹
9446	Sabine River & Northern Boxcar, *81*	15	21	___¹
9447	Pullman Standard Boxcar, *81*	17	22	___¹
9448	Santa Fe Stock Car, *81–82*	34	40	___¹
9449	Great Northern Boxcar (FARR #3), *81*	33	39	___¹
9450	Great Northern Stock Car (FARR #3), *81 u*	65	70	___¹
9451	Southern Boxcar (FARR #4), *83*	33	37	___¹
9452	Western Pacific Boxcar, *82–83*	13	18	___¹
[9452]	Sacramento-Sierra TCA WP Boxcar, *83 u*	—	35	___¹
9453	MPA Boxcar, *82–83*	13	18	___¹
9454	New Hope & Ivyland Boxcar, *82–83*	18	25	___¹
9455	Milwaukee Road Boxcar, *82–83*	13	17	___¹
9456	PRR DD Boxcar (FARR #5), *84–85*	28	35	___¹
9460	LCCA D&TS DD Boxcar, *82 u*	26	32	___¹
9461	Norfolk & Southern Boxcar, *82*	29	49	___¹
9462	Southern Pacific Boxcar, *83–84*	18	23	___¹
9463	Texas & Pacific Boxcar, *83–84*	15	19	___¹
9464	NC&StL Boxcar, *83–84*	14	19	___¹
9465	Santa Fe Boxcar, *83–84*	14	21	___¹
9466	Wanamaker Boxcar, *82 u*	60	70	___¹
[9466]	Atlantic TCA Wanamaker Boxcar, *83 u*	105	135	___¹
9467	Tennessee World's Fair Boxcar, *82 u*	30	37	___¹
9468	Union Pacific DD Boxcar, *83*	35	38	___¹
9469	NYC "Pacemaker" Boxcar (Std. O), *84–85*	55	65	___²
9470	Chicago Beltline Boxcar, *84*	15	20	___¹
9471	Atlantic Coast Line Boxcar, *84*	14	19	___¹
[9471]	Southern TCA Atlantic Coast Line Boxcar, *84 u*	—	23	___¹
9472	Detroit & Mackinac Boxcar, *84*	23	27	___¹
9473	Lehigh Valley Boxcar, *84*	22	26	___¹
9474	Erie-Lackawanna Boxcar, *84*	29	35	___¹
9475	D&H "I Love NY" Boxcar, *84 u*	24	35	___¹
[9475]	LCOL D&H "I Love New York" Boxcar, *85 u*	—	30	___¹
9476	PRR Boxcar (FARR #5), *84–85*	38	41	___¹
9480	MN&S Boxcar, *85–86*	17	21	___¹
9481	Seaboard System Boxcar, *85–86*	15	18	___¹
9482	Norfolk & Southern Boxcar, *85–86*	16	22	___¹
[9482]	Southern TCA Norfolk & Southern Boxcar, *85 u*	—	23	___¹

		Exc	New	Cond/$
9483	Manufacturers Railway Boxcar, *85–86*	17	23	___ [1]
9484	Lionel 85th Anniversary Boxcar, *85*	20	24	___ [2]
9486	GTW "I Love Michigan" Boxcar, *86*	22	33	___ [1]
9486	Artrain GTW "I Love Michigan" Boxcar, *87 u*	—	305	___ [1]
9490	Christmas Boxcar for Lionel Employees, *85 u*	—	1750	___ [1]
9491	Christmas Boxcar, *86 u*	33	47	___ [1]
9492	Lionel Lines Boxcar, *86*	29	34	___ [1]
9500	Milwaukee Road Passenger Car, *73*	34	65	___ [1]
9501	Milwaukee Road Passenger Car, *73 u, 74–76*	30	39	___ [1]
9502	Milwaukee Road Observation Car, *73*	30	48	___ [1]
9503	Milwaukee Road Passenger Car, *73*	30	48	___ [1]
9504	Milwaukee Road Passenger Car, *73 u, 74–76*	30	38	___ [1]
9505	Milwaukee Road Passenger Car, *73 u, 74–76*	30	38	___ [1]
9506	Milwaukee Road Combination Car, *74 u, 75–76*	29	39	___ [1]
9507	PRR Passenger Car, *74–75*	37	55	___ [1]
9508	PRR Passenger Car, *74–75*	34	50	___ [1]
9509	PRR Observation Car, *74–75*	42	60	___ [1]
9510	PRR Combination Car, *74 u, 75–76*	31	42	___ [1]
9511	Milwaukee Road Passenger Car, *74 u*	27	50	___ [1]
9512	TTOS Summerdale Junction Passenger Car, *74 u*	44	55	___ [1]
9513	PRR Passenger Car, *75–76*	27	44	___ [1]
9514	PRR Passenger Car, *75–76*	23	36	___ [1]
9515	PRR Passenger Car, *75–76*	21	34	___ [1]
9516	B&O Passenger Car, *76*	27	42	___ [1]
9517	B&O Passenger Car, *75*	45	65	___ [1]
9517	(See 52005)			
9518	B&O Observation Car, *75*	45	65	___ [1]
9519	B&O Combination Car, *75*	55	85	___ [1]
9520	TTOS Phoenix Combination Car, *75 u*	26	29	___ [1]
9521	PRR Baggage Car, *75 u, 76*	70	85	___ [1]
9522	Milwaukee Road Baggage Car, *75 u, 76*	65	80	___ [1]
9523	B&O Baggage Car, *75 u, 76*	65	70	___ [1]
9524	B&O Passenger Car, *76*	27	37	___ [1]
9525	B&O Passenger Car, *76*	30	43	___ [1]
9526	TTOS Snowbird Observation Car, *76 u*	36	42	___ [1]
(9527)	Milwaukee Road Campaign Observation Car, *76 u*	45	65	___ [1]
(9528)	PRR Campaign Observation Car, *76 u*	55	75	___ [1]
(9529)	B&O Campaign Observation Car, *76 u*	49	80	___ [1]
9530	Southern Baggage Car, *77–78*	50	70	___ [1]
9531	Southern Combination Car, *77–78*	36	50	___ [1]
9532	Southern Passenger Car, *77–78*	39	55	___ [1]

		Exc	New	Cond/$
9533	Southern Passenger Car, *77–78*	34	48	____[1]
9534	Southern Observation Car, *77–78*	36	55	____[1]
9535	TTOS Columbus Baggage Car, *77 u*	33	43	____[1]
9536	Blue Comet Baggage Car, *78–80*	34	47	____[1]
9537	Blue Comet Combination Car, *78–80*	35	50	____[1]
9538	Blue Comet Passenger Car, *78–80*	35	47	____[1]
9539	Blue Comet Passenger Car, *78–80*	36	50	____[1]
9540	Blue Comet Observation Car, *78–80*	32	47	____[1]
9541	Santa Fe Baggage Car, *80–82*	21	30	____[1]
(9544)	TCA Chicago Observation Car "1980", *80 u*	—	50	____[1]
9545	Union Pacific Baggage Car, *84*	105	155	____[1]
9546	Union Pacific Combination Car, *84*	85	105	____[1]
9547	Union Pacific Observation Car, *84*	85	105	____[1]
(9548)	Union Pacific "Placid Bay" Passenger Car, *84*	85	105	____[1]
(9549)	Union Pacific "Ocean Sunset" Passenger Car, *84*	85	105	____[1]
9551	W&ARR Baggage Car, *77 u, 78–80*	46	60	____[1]
9552	W&ARR Passenger Car, *77 u, 78–80*	46	60	____[1]
9553	W&ARR Flatcar w/ horses, *77 u, 78–80*	34	42	____[1]
(9554)	Chicago & Alton Baggage Car, *81*	50	75	____[1]
(9555)	Chicago & Alton Combination Car, *81*	50	75	____[1]
(9556)	Chicago & Alton "Wilson" Passenger Car, *81*	50	75	____[1]
(9557)	Chicago & Alton "Webster Groves" Passenger Car, *81*	50	75	____[1]
(9558)	Chicago & Alton Observation Car, *81*	50	75	____[1]
9559	Rock Island Baggage Car, *81–82*	37	55	____[1]
9560	Rock Island Passenger Car, *81–82*	39	60	____[1]
9561	Rock Island Passenger Car, *81–82*	37	55	____[1]
(9562)	Norfolk & Western Baggage Car "577", *81*	75	115	____[1]
(9563)	Norfolk & Western Combination Car "578", *81*	80	105	____[1]
(9564)	Norfolk & Western Passenger Car "579", *81*	90	100	____[1]
(9565)	Norfolk & Western Passenger Car "580", *81*	85	100	____[1]
(9566)	Norfolk & Western Observation Car "581", *81*	100	110	____[1]
(9567)	Norfolk & Western Vista Dome Car "582", *81 u*	205	320	____[1]
9569	PRR Combination Car, *81 u*	115	170	____[1]
9570	PRR Baggage Car, *79*	85	115	____[1]
9571	PRR Passenger Car, *79*	125	145	____[1]
9572	PRR Passenger Car, *79*	110	125	____[1]
9573	PRR Vista Dome Car, *79*	95	120	____[1]
9574	PRR Observation Car, *79*	85	100	____[1]
9575	PRR Passenger Car, *79–80 u*	100	135	____[1]
9576	Burlington Baggage Car, *80*	105	130	____[1]
9577	Burlington Passenger Car, *80*	95	105	____[1]

		Exc	New	Cond/$
9578	Burlington Passenger Car, *80*	105	110	____[1]
9579	Burlington Vista Dome Car, *80*	95	110	____[1]
9580	Burlington Observation Car, *80*	95	110	____[1]
9581	Chessie System Baggage Car, *80*	47	55	____[1]
9582	Chessie System Combination Car, *80*	47	55	____[1]
9583	Chessie System Passenger Car, *80*	40	47	____[1]
9584	Chessie System Passenger Car, *80*	34	40	____[1]
9585	Chessie System Observation Car, *80*	55	65	____[1]
9586	Chessie System Dining Car, *86 u*	85	90	____[1]
9588	Burlington Vista Dome Car, *80 u*	110	120	____[1]
(9589)	Southern Pacific Baggage Car, *82–83*	100	120	____[1]
(9590)	Southern Pacific Combination Car, *82–83*	100	120	____[1]
(9591)	Southern Pacific "Pullman" Passenger Car, *82–83*	90	105	____[1]
(9592)	Southern Pacific "Chair" Passenger Car, *82–83*	90	105	____[1]
(9593)	Southern Pacific Observation Car, *82–83*	100	115	____[1]
9594	NYC Baggage Car, *83–84*	110	135	____[1]
9595	NYC Combination Car, *83–84*	90	105	____[1]
(9596)	NYC "Wayne County" Passenger Car, *83–84*	80	95	____[1]
(9597)	NYC "Hudson River" Passenger Car, *83–84*	70	85	____[1]
(9598)	NYC Observation Car, *83–84*	85	100	____[1]
(9599)	Chicago & Alton Dining Car, *86 u*	75	85	____[1]
9600	Chessie System Hi-cube Boxcar, *75 u, 76–77*	21	30	____[1]
9601	ICG Hi-cube Boxcar, *75 u, 76–77*	22	24	____[1]
[9601]	Gateway TCA ICG Hi-cube Boxcar, *77 u*	—	21	____[1]
9602	Santa Fe Hi-cube Boxcar, *75 u, 76–77*	19	20	____[1]
9603	Penn Central Hi-cube Boxcar, *76–77*	21	23	____[1]
9604	Norfolk & Western Hi-cube Boxcar, *76–77*	21	23	____[1]
9605	NH Hi-cube Boxcar, *76–77*	19	25	____[1]
9606	Union Pacific Hi-cube Boxcar, *76 u, 77*	21	23	____[1]
9607	Southern Pacific Hi-cube Boxcar, *76 u, 77*	21	23	____[1]
9608	Burlington Northern Hi-cube Boxcar, *76 u, 77*	21	23	____[1]
9610	Frisco Hi-cube Boxcar, *77*	28	39	____[1]
9611	TCA Boston Hi-cube Boxcar, *78 u*	26	31	____[1]
9620	NHL Wales Boxcar, *80*	24	31	____[1]
9621	NHL Campbell Boxcar, *80*	21	26	____[1]
9622	NBA Western Boxcar, *80*	24	31	____[1]
9623	NBA Eastern Boxcar, *80*	24	31	____[1]
9624	National League Baseball Boxcar, *80*	21	26	____[1]
9625	American League Baseball Boxcar, *80*	21	27	____[1]
9626	Santa Fe Hi-cube Boxcar, *82–84*	12	16	____[1]
9627	Union Pacific Hi-cube Boxcar, *82–83*	18	25	____[1]
9628	Burlington Northern Hi-cube Boxcar, *82–84*	13	17	____[1]

		Exc	New	Cond/$
9629	Chessie System Hi-cube Boxcar, *83–84*	23	34	___¹
9660	Mickey Mouse Hi-cube Boxcar, *77–78*	36	46	___¹
9661	Goofy Hi-cube Boxcar, *77–78*	48	55	___¹
9662	Donald Duck Hi-cube Boxcar, *77–78*	41	45	___¹
9663	Dumbo Hi-cube Boxcar, *77 u, 78*	35	60	___¹
9664	Cinderella Hi-cube Boxcar, *77 u, 78*	50	75	___¹
9665	Peter Pan Hi-cube Boxcar, *77 u, 78*	48	75	___¹
9666	Pinocchio Hi-cube Boxcar, *78*	120	175	___²
9667	Snow White Hi-cube Boxcar, *78*	325	440	___¹
9668	Pluto Hi-cube Boxcar, *78*	125	160	___¹
9669	Bambi Hi-cube Boxcar, *78 u*	60	100	___¹
9670	Alice In Wonderland Hi-cube Boxcar, *78 u*	55	90	___¹
9671	Fantasia Hi-cube Boxcar, *78 u*	50	90	___¹
9672	Mickey Mouse 50th Anniversary Hi-cube Boxcar, *78 u*	370	460	___¹
9678	TTOS Hollywood Hi-cube Boxcar, *78 u*	21	24	___¹
9695	(See 52077)			
9700	Southern Boxcar, *72–73*	24	31	___¹
9700-1976	(See 9779)			
9701	B&O DD Boxcar, *72*	14	19	___¹
9701	TCA B&O DD Boxcar, *72 u*	50	65	___¹
[9701]	LCCA B&O DD Boxcar, *72 u*	—	170	___¹
9702	Soo Line Boxcar, *72–73*	14	19	___¹
9703	CP Rail Boxcar, *72*	34	44	___¹
9704	Norfolk & Western Boxcar, *72*	12	20	___¹
9705	D&RGW Boxcar, *72*	15	23	___¹
[9705]	Sacramento-Sierra TCA D&RGW Boxcar, *75 u*	—	38	___¹
9706	C&O Boxcar, *72*	17	19	___¹
9706	(See 19706)			
9707	MKT Stock Car, *72–75*	17	24	___¹
9708	US Mail Boxcar, *72–75*	19	24	___¹
9708	US Mail Toy Fair Boxcar, *73 u*	75	85	___¹
9709	BAR "State of Maine" Boxcar (SSS), *72–74*	34	38	___¹
9710	Rutland Boxcar (SSS), *72–74*	22	26	___¹
9711	Southern Boxcar, *74–75*	15	22	___¹
9712	B&O DD Boxcar, *73–74*	27	30	___¹
9713	CP Rail Boxcar, *73–74*	21	26	___¹
9713	CP Rail Season's Greetings Boxcar, *74 u*	95	120	___¹
9714	D&RGW Boxcar, *73–74*	20	24	___¹
9715	C&O Boxcar, *73–74*	17	22	___¹
9716	Penn Central Boxcar, *73–74*	19	24	___¹
9717	Union Pacific Boxcar, *73–74*	24	29	___¹
9718	Canadian National Boxcar, *73–74*	19	24	___¹

		Exc	New	Cond/$
[9718]	LCAC Canadian National Boxcar, *79 u*		NRS	___
9719	New Haven DD Boxcar, *73 u*	25	35	___¹
9723	Western Pacific Boxcar (SSS), *73–74*	26	28	___¹
9723	Western Pacific Toy Fair Boxcar, *74 u*	75	85	___¹
[9723]	Sacramento-Sierra TCA WP Boxcar, *73 u*	—	29	___¹
9724	Missouri Pacific Boxcar (SSS), *73–74*	24	28	___¹
9725	MKT Stock Car (SSS), *73–75*	17	21	___¹
[9725]	Midwest TCA Stock Car "00002", *75 u*		NRS	___
9726	Erie-Lackawanna Boxcar (SSS), *78*	25	30	___¹
[9726]	Sacramento-Sierra TCA Erie-Lack. Boxcar, *79 u*	—	31	___¹
9727	LCCA TA&G Boxcar, *73 u*	115	125	___¹
9728	LCCA Union Pacific Stock Car, *78 u*	24	27	___²
9729	CP Rail Boxcar, *78*	45	32	___¹
9730	CP Rail Boxcar, *74–75*	22	26	___¹
[9730]	Detroit-Toledo TCA CP Rail Boxcar, *76 u*	—	27	___¹
[9730]	Sacramento-Sierra TCA CP Rail Boxcar, *77 u*	—	30	___¹
[9730]	Western Michigan TCA CP Rail Boxcar, *74 u*	—	25	___¹
9731	Milwaukee Road Boxcar, *74–75*	14	19	___¹
9732	Southern Pacific Boxcar, *79 u*	30	40	___¹
9733	LCCA Airco Boxcar w/ tank, *79 u*	42	55	___¹
9734	Bangor & Aroostook Boxcar, *79*	31	41	___¹
9735	Grand Trunk Boxcar, *74–75*	14	19	___¹
9737	Central Vermont Boxcar, *74–76*	18	23	___¹
9738	Illinois Terminal Boxcar, *82*	55	70	___¹
9739	D&RGW Boxcar (SSS), *74–76*	17	22	___¹
[9739]	North Texas TCA D&RGW Boxcar, *76 u*	—	20	___¹
[9739]	LCCA D&RGW Boxcar, *78 u*	—	150	___¹
9740	Chessie System Boxcar, *74–75*	13	17	___¹
[9740]	Great Lakes TCA Chessie System Boxcar, *76 u*	—	23	___¹
[9740]	WB&A TCA Chessie System Boxcar, *76 u*	—	23	___¹
9742	M&StL Boxcar, *73 u*	22	26	___¹
9742	M&StL Season's Greetings Boxcar, *73 u*	85	105	___¹
9743	Sprite Boxcar, *74 u, 75*	15	21	___¹
9744	Tab Boxcar, *74 u, 75*	15	21	___¹
9745	Fanta Boxcar, *74 u, 75*	15	24	___¹
9747	Chessie System DD Boxcar, *75–76*	27	28	___¹
9748	CP Rail Boxcar, *75–76*	15	20	___¹
9749	Penn Central Boxcar, *75–76*	14	18	___¹
9750	DT&I Boxcar, *75–76*	16	25	___¹
9751	Frisco Boxcar, *75–76*	15	19	___¹
9752	L&N Boxcar, *75–76*	17	22	___¹
9753	Maine Central Boxcar, *75–76*	16	22	___¹

		Exc	New	Cond/$
[9753]	NETCA Maine Central Boxcar, *75 u*	24	34	___1
9754	NYC "Pacemaker" Boxcar (SSS), *75–77*	22	34	___2
[9754]	METCA NYC "Pacemaker" Boxcar, *76 u*	—	27	___1
9755	Union Pacific Boxcar, *75–76*	22	28	___1
9757	Central of Georgia Boxcar, *74 u*	21	25	___1
9758	Alaska Boxcar (SSS), *75–77*	30	38	___1
9759	Paul Revere Boxcar, *75 u*	36	43	___1
9760	Liberty Bell Boxcar, *75 u*	40	49	___1
9761	George Washington Boxcar, *75 u*	36	43	___1
(9762)	Toy Fair Boxcar, *75 u*	115	150	___1
9763	D&RGW Stock Car, *76–77*	18	23	___1
9764	GTW DD Boxcar, *76–77*	28	35	___1
9767	Railbox Boxcar, *76–77*	20	23	___1
[9767]	Gateway TCA Railbox Boxcar, *78 u*	—	20	___1
9768	B&M Boxcar, *76–77*	22	35	___1
[9768]	NETCA B&M Boxcar, *76 u*	28	34	___1
9769	B&LE Boxcar, *76–77*	19	24	___1
9770	Northern Pacific Boxcar, *76–77*	17	22	___1
9771	Norfolk & Western Boxcar, *76–77*	16	21	___1
[9771]	TCA Museum N&W Boxcar, *77 u*	24	31	___1
[9771]	WB&A TCA N&W Boxcar, *78 u*	—	30	___1
[9771]	LCCA N&W Boxcar, *77 u*		NRS	___
9772	Great Northern Boxcar, *76*	55	75	___1
9773	NYC Stock Car, *76*	31	38	___1
9774	TCA Orlando Southern Belle Boxcar, *75 u*	30	39	___1
9775	M&StL Boxcar (SSS), *76*	21	24	___1
9776	Southern Pacific "Overnight" Boxcar (SSS), *76*	40	46	___1
9777	Virginian Boxcar, *76–77*	22	25	___1
9778	Season's Greetings Boxcar, *75 u*	165	185	___1
(9779)	TCA Philadelphia Boxcar "9700-1976", *76 u*	27	33	___1
9780	Johnny Cash Boxcar, *76 u*	29	42	___1
9781	Delaware & Hudson Boxcar, *77–78*	17	20	___1
9782	Rock Island Boxcar, *77–78*	17	21	___1
9783	B&O "Time-Saver" Boxcar, *77–78*	27	30	___1
[9783]	WB&A TCA B&O "Time-Saver" Boxcar, *77 u*	—	30	___1
9784	Santa Fe Boxcar, *77–78*	19	25	___1
9785	Conrail Boxcar, *78*			
9785	Conrail Boxcar, *77–78*	17	21	___1
[9785]	Midwest TCA Museum Express Conrail Boxcar, *77 u*		NRS	___
[9785]	NETCA Conrail Boxcar, *78 u*	22	26	___1
[9785]	Sacramento-Sierra TCA Conrail Boxcar, *78 u*	—	27	___1
9786	C&NW Boxcar, *77–79*	18	26	___1

		Exc	New	Cond/$
[9786]	Midwest TCA Museum Express C&NW Boxcar, *79 u*		NRS	___
9787	Jersey Central Boxcar, *77–79*	17	25	___ [1]
9788	Lehigh Valley Boxcar, *77–79*	18	25	___ [1]
[9788]	Atlantic TCA Lehigh Valley Boxcar, *78 u*	19	24	___ [1]
9789	Pickens Boxcar, *77*	25	33	___ [1]
9790	(See 19243)			
9791	(See 19244)			
9801	B&O "Sentinel" Boxcar (Std. O), *73–75*	27	41	___ [3]
9802	Miller High Life Reefer (Std. O), *73–75*	33	38	___ [1]
9803	Johnson Wax Boxcar (Std. O), *73–75*	30	36	___ [3]
9805	Grand Trunk Reefer (Std. O), *73–75*	30	34	___ [2]
9806	Rock Island Boxcar (Std. O), *74–75*	38	44	___ [2]
9807	Stroh's Beer Reefer (Std. O), *74–76*	55	80	___ [1]
9808	Union Pacific Boxcar (Std. O), *75–76*	50	70	___ [2]
9809	Clark Reefer (Std. O), *75–76*	34	37	___ [1]
9811	Pacific Fruit Express Reefer (FARR #2), *80*	25	32	___ [1]
9812	Arm & Hammer Reefer, *80*	18	23	___ [1]
9813	Ruffles Reefer, *80*	24	31	___ [1]
9814	Perrier Reefer, *80*	25	33	___ [1]
9815	NYC "Early Bird" Reefer (Std. O), *84–85*	50	55	___ [2]
9816	Brach's Candy Reefer, *80*	21	26	___ [1]
9817	Bazooka Gum Reefer, *80*	22	27	___ [1]
9818	Western Maryland Reefer, *80*	22	29	___ [1]
9819	Western Fruit Express Reefer (FARR #3), *81*	33	44	___ [1]
9820	Wabash Gondola w/ coal load (Std. O), *73–74*	32	40	___ [1]
9821	Southern Pacific Gondola w/ coal load (Std. O), *73–75*	39	42	___ [1]
9822	Grand Trunk Gondola w/ coal load (Std. O), *74–75*	30	32	___ [1]
9823	Santa Fe Flatcar w/ crates (Std. O), *75–76*	60	70	___ [1]
9824	NYC Gondola w/ coal load (Std. O), *75–76*	39	55	___ [1]
9825	Schaefer Reefer (Std. O), *76–77*	50	70	___ [2]
9826	P&LE Boxcar (Std. O), *76–77*	55	60	___ [2]
9827	Cutty Sark Reefer, *84*	21	25	___ [1]
9828	J&B Reefer, *84*	23	27	___ [1]
9829	Dewar's White Label Reefer, *84*	21	23	___ [1]
9830	Johnnie Walker Red Label Reefer, *84*	21	25	___ [1]
9831	Pepsi Cola Reefer, *82*	45	60	___ [1]
9832	Cheerios Reefer, *82*	100	125	___ [1]
9833	Vlasic Pickles Reefer, *82*	23	29	___ [1]
9834	Southern Comfort Reefer, *83–84*	25	30	___ [1]
9835	Jim Beam Reefer, *83–84*	22	27	___ [1]

		Exc	New	Cond/$
9836	Old Grand-Dad Reefer, *83–84*	22	27	___[1]
9837	Wild Turkey Reefer, *83–84*	30	50	___[1]
9840	Fleischmann's Gin Reefer, *85*	22	26	___[1]
9841	Calvert Gin Reefer, *85*	23	28	___[1]
9842	Seagram's Gin Reefer, *85*	24	28	___[1]
9843	Tanqueray Gin Reefer, *85*	24	28	___[1]
9844	Sambuca Reefer, *86*	25	31	___[1]
9845	Baileys Irish Cream Reefer, *86*	30	50	___[1]
9846	Seagram's Vodka Reefer, *86*	22	27	___[1]
9847	Wolfschmidt Vodka Reefer, *86*	23	27	___[1]
9849	Lionel Lines Reefer, *83 u*	42	49	___[1]
9850	Budweiser Reefer, *72 u, 73–75*	37	45	___[1]
9851	Schlitz Reefer, *72 u, 73–75*	21	28	___[1]
9852	Miller Reefer, *72 u, 73–77*	21	25	___[1]
9853	Cracker Jack Reefer, caramel, *72 u, 73–75*			
	(A) Caramel color body.	27	30	___[1]
	(B) White body, black logo border.	21	26	___[1]
9854	Baby Ruth Reefer, *72 u, 73–76*	19	25	___[1]
9855	Swift Reefer, *72 u, 73–77*	27	32	___[1]
9856	Old Milwaukee Reefer, *75–76*	25	29	___[1]
9858	Butterfinger Reefer, *73 u, 74–76*	22	27	___[1]
9859	Pabst Reefer, *73 u, 74–75*	25	30	___[1]
9860	Gold Medal Reefer, *73 u, 74–76*	19	24	___[1]
9861	Tropicana Reefer, *75–77*	23	31	___[1]
9862	Hamm's Reefer, *75–76*	22	27	___[1]
9863	REA Reefer (SSS), *74–76*	26	30	___[1]
9864	TCA Seattle Reefer, *74 u*	31	34	___[1]
9866	Coors Reefer, *76–77*	36	47	___[1]
9867	Hershey's Reefer, *76–77*	44	55	___[1]
9868	TTOS Oklahoma City Reefer, *80 u*	36	44	___[1]
9869	Santa Fe Reefer (SSS), *76*	27	32	___[1]
9870	Old Dutch Cleanser Reefer, *77–78, 80*	18	25	___[1]
9871	Carling Black Label Reefer, *77–78, 80*	27	31	___[1]
9872	Pacific Fruit Express Reefer, *77–79*	22	26	___[1]
[9872]	Midwest TCA PFE Reefer, *79 u*		NRS	___
9873	Ralston Purina Reefer, *78*	26	33	___[1]
9874	Miller Lite Beer Reefer, *78–79*	31	45	___[2]
9875	A&P Reefer, *78–79*	20	28	___[1]
9876	Central Vermont Reefer, *78*	27	31	___[1]
9877	Gerber Reefer, *79–80*	55	65	___[1]
9878	Good and Plenty Reefer, *79*	21	27	___[1]
9879	Hills Bros. Reefer, *79–80*	21	27	___[1]
9879	Kraft Reefer, *79 u*		NM	___

		Exc	New	Cond/$
9880	Santa Fe Reefer (FARR #1), *79*	37	41	___¹
9881	Rath Packing Reefer, *79 u*	38	41	___²
9882	NYC "Early Bird" Reefer, *79*	26	31	___¹
9883	Nabisco Oreo Reefer, *79*	70	75	___¹
[9883]	TTOS Phoenix Reefer, *83 u*	—	50	___¹
9884	Fritos Reefer, *81–82*	23	30	___¹
9885	Lipton Tea Reefer, *81–82*	24	31	___¹
9886	Mounds Reefer, *81–82*	20	25	___¹
9887	Fruit Growers Express Reefer (FARR #4), *83*	29	38	___¹
9888	Green Bay & Western Reefer, *83*	55	60	___¹
10001	(See 19251)			
10009	(See 17008)			
10131	(See 16541)			
(11006)	Lionel Lion Set, *03 u*		CP	___
(11700)	Conrail Limited set, *87*	400	465	___¹
(11701)	Rail Blazer set, *87–88*	—	55	___¹
(11702)	Black Diamond set, *87*	170	230	___¹
(11703)	Iron Horse Freight set, *88–91*	100	105	___¹
(11704)	Southern Freight Runner set (SSS), *87*	230	305	___¹
(11705)	Chessie System Unit Train set, *88*	405	415	___¹
(11706)	Dry Gulch Line set (SSS), *88*	180	245	___¹
(11707)	Silver Spike set, *88–89*	190	220	___¹
(11708)	Midnight Shift set, *88 u, 89*	60	75	___¹
(11710)	CP Rail Freight set, *89*	345	435	___¹
(11711)	Santa Fe F-3 ABA set "8100", "8101", "8102", *91*	450	550	___⁵
(11712)	Great Lakes Express set (SSS), *90*	275	295	___¹
(11713)	Santa Fe Dash 8-40B set, *90*	370	445	___¹
(11714)	Badlands Express set, *90–91*	49	60	___¹
(11715)	Lionel 90th Anniversary set, *90*	240	290	___¹
(11716)	Lionelville Circus Special set, *90–91*	195	245	___²
(11717)	CSX Freight set, *90*	190	250	___¹
(11718)	Norfolk Southern Dash 8-40C Unit Train set, *92*	530	620	___¹
(11719)	Coastal Freight set (SSS), *91*	200	260	___¹
(11720)	Santa Fe Special set, *91*	49	60	___¹
(11721)	Mickey's World Tour Train set, *91, 92 u*	105	135	___¹
(11722)	Girl's Train set, *91*	610	810	___¹
(11723)	Amtrak Maintenance Train set, *91, 92 u*	215	250	___¹
(11724)	Great Northern F-3 ABA set "366A", "370B", "351C", *92*	750	880	___³
(11726)	Erie-Lackawanna Freight set, *91 u*	235	285	___¹
(11727)	Coastal Limited set, *92*	80	100	___¹

		Exc	New	Cond/$
(11728)	High Plains Runner set, *92*	120	130	___[1]
(11729)	L&N Express set, *92*		NM	___
11730	Evergreen Intermodal Container (See 12805)			
11731	Maersk Intermodal Container (See 12805)			
11732	American President Lines Intermodal Container (See 12805)			
(11733)	Feather River set (SSS), *92*	270	310	___[1]
(11734)	Erie Alco ABA set "725A", "725B", "736A" (FF #7), *93*	295	360	___[1]
(11735)	NYC Flyer Freight set "1735WS", *93–99*	125	140	___[1]
(11736)	Union Pacific Express set, *93–95*	110	130	___[1]
(11737)	TCA F-3 ABA set "40", *93 u*	600	790	___[1]
(11738)	Soo Line set (SSS), *93*	240	270	___[1]
(11739)	Super Chief set, *93–94*	120	135	___[1]
(11740)	Conrail Consolidated set, *93*	235	255	___[1]
(11741)	Northwest Express set, *93*	115	135	___[1]
(11742)	Coastal Limited set, *93 u*	80	100	___[1]
(11743)	Chesapeake & Ohio Freight set, *94*	230	280	___[1]
(11744)	NYC Passenger/Freight set (SSS), *94*	300	340	___[1]
(11745)	US Navy set, *94–95*	175	200	___[1]
(11746)	Seaboard Freight set, *94, 95 u*	80	100	___[1]
(11747)	Lionel Lines Steam set, *95*	260	280	___[1]
(11748)	Amtrak Alco Passenger set, *95–96*	115	145	___[1]
(11749)	Western Maryland set (SSS), *95*	240	255	___[1]
(11750)	McDonald's Nickel Plate Special set, *87 u*	135	145	___[1]
(11751)	49C95171C Sears Pennsylvania Passenger set, *87 u*	120	155	___[1]
(11752)	JC Penney Timber Master set, *87 u*	75	115	___[1]
(11753)	Kay Bee Toys Rail Blazer set, *87 u*	80	100	___[1]
(11754)	Key America set, *87 u*	150	165	___[1]
(11755)	Timber Master set, *87 u*	150	165	___[1]
(11756)	Hawthorne Freight Flyer set, *87–88 u*	65	85	___[1]
(11757)	Chrysler Mopar Express set, *88 u*	235	255	___[1]
(11758)	The Desert King set (SSS), *89*	175	220	___[1]
(11759)	JC Penney Silver Spike set, *88 u*	175	250	___[1]
(11761)	JC Penney Iron Horse Freight set, *88 u*	120	125	___[1]
(11762)	True Value Cannonball Express set, *89 u*	85	130	___[1]
(11763)	United Model Freight Hauler set, *88 u*	135	145	___[1]
(11764)	49N95178 Sears Iron Horse Freight set, *88 u*	155	190	___[1]
(11765)	Spiegel Silver Spike set, *88 u*	175	250	___[1]
(11767)	Shoprite Freight Flyer set, *88 u*	85	130	___[1]
(11769)	JC Penney Midnight Shift set, *89 u*	100	175	___[1]

		Exc	New	Cond/$
(11770)	49GY95280 Sears Circus set, *89 u*	185	220	____¹
(11771)	K-Mart Microracers set, *89 u*	70	95	____¹
(11772)	Macy's Freight Flyer set, *89 u*	150	190	____¹
(11773)	49GY95281 Sears NYC Passenger set, *89 u*	175	200	____¹
(11774)	Ace Hardware Cannonball Express set, *89 u*	145	175	____¹
(11775)	Anheuser-Busch set, *89–92 u*	175	215	____¹
(11776)	Pace Iron Horse Freight set, *89 u*	115	135	____¹
(11777)	49N95265 Sears Lionelville Circus Special set, *90 u*	175	190	____¹
(11778)	49N95264 Sears Badlands Express set, *90 u*	49	60	____¹
(11779)	49N95267 Sears CSX Freight set, *90 u*	190	230	____¹
(11780)	49N95266 Sears Northern Pacific Passenger set, *90 u*	155	190	____¹
(11781)	True Value Cannonball Express set, *90 u*	75	115	____¹
(11783)	Toys "R" Us Heavy Iron set, *90–91 u*	155	190	____¹
(11784)	Pace Iron Horse Freight set, *90 u*	115	135	____¹
(11785)	Costco Union Pacific Express set, *90 u*	175	200	____¹
(11789)	Sears Illinois Central Passenger set, *91 u*	155	175	____¹
(11793)	Santa Fe set w/ mailer, *91 u*	49	60	____¹
(11794)	Mickey's World Tour set w/ mailer, *91 u*	80	100	____¹
(11796)	Union Pacific Express set, *91 u*	145	155	____¹
(11797)	Sears Coastal Limited set w/ mailer, *92 u*	80	100	____¹
(11800)	Toys "R" Us Heavy Iron Thunder Limited set, *92–93 u*	185	215	____¹
(11803)	Mall Promotion Nickel Plate Special set, *92 u*	135	145	____¹
(11804)	K-Mart Coastal Limited set, *92 u*	80	100	____¹
(11809)	Lionel Village Trolley Company set "1809" (O), *95–97*	50	70	____¹
(11810)	Budweiser Modern Era set, *93–94 u*	165	180	____¹
(11811)	United Auto Workers set, *93 u*	170	550	____¹
(11812)	Mall Promotion Coastal Limited set, *93 u*	95	115	____¹
(11813)	Crayola Activity Train set, *94 u, 95*	55	80	____¹
(11814)	Ford Limited Edition set, *94 u*	170	200	____¹
(11818)	Chrysler Mopar set, *94 u*	170	190	____¹
(11819)	Georgia Power set, *95 u*	450	600	____¹
(11820)	Red Wing Shoes NYC Flyer set, *95 u*	195	250	____¹
(11821)	Sears Zenith set, *95 u*	—	750	____¹
(11822)	Chevrolet set, *96 u*	235	265	____¹
(11825)	Bloomingdale's set, *96 u*	—	300	____¹
(11826)	Zenith/Sears Freight set, *95–96 u*	—	650	____¹
(11827)	Sears set, *96 u*	—	575	____¹
(11828)	NJ Transit Passenger set, *96 u*	—	235	____¹
(11833)	NJ Transit GP-38 Passenger Set, *97*	230	245	____¹

		Exc	New	Cond/$
(11837)	UP GP-9 Unit Train set, *97*	—	650	___2
(11838)	AT&SF Warhorse Hudson Freight set, *97*	—	680	___2
(11839)	SP&S 4-6-2 Steam Freight set, *97*	—	280	___1
(11841)	Bloomingdales set, *97 u*	—	250	___1
(11843)	Boston & Maine GP-9 A-B-A Diesel Locomotive set, *98*	—	570	___1
(11844)	Union Pacific Die-Cast Ore Cars 4-pack, *98*	—	195	___1
(11846)	Kal Kan Pet Care Train set, *01u*	—	900	___1
(11849)	1998 Lionel Centennial Series Reefer Cars 4-pack, *98*	—	130	___1
(11850)	Rice-A-Roni Trolley set, *02u*		NRS	___
(11851)	PFE Reefer 6-pack (Std. O), *02*	—	270	___1
(11863)	Southern Pacific GP-9 "2383", *98*	—	220	___1
(11864)	New York Central GP-9 "2383", *98*	—	270	___1
(11865)	Alaska GP-7 "1802", *98–99*	—	95	___1
(11900)	SF Special Freight set "1900WS" (O), *96–01*	—	130	___1
(11903)	Atlantic Coast Line F-3 ABA set "342", "342B", "343", *96*	—	670	___3
(11905)	US Coast Guard set, *96*	—	155	___1
(11906)	Factory Selection Special set, *95 u*	—	85	___1
(11909)	N&W J 4-8-4 Warhorse set, *96*	—	630	___2
(11910)	Lionel Lines set (O27), *96*	—	130	___1
(11912)	"57" Switcher Service Exclusive, *96*	—	445	___3
(11913)	SP GP-9 Freight set, *97*	—	435	___1
(11914)	NYC GP-9 Freight set, *97*	—	365	___1
(11918)	Conrail SD-20 Service Exclusive "X1144" (SSS), *97*	—	330	___2
(11919)	Lionel Docksider set "1919" (O), *97*	—	70	___1
(11920)	Port of Lionel City Dive Team set "1920", *97*	—	185	___1
(11921)	Lionel Lines Freight set "1113WS", *97*	—	130	___1
(11929)	AT&SF Warbonnet Pass. set "1929W", *97–99*	—	165	___1
(11930)	Warbonnet Pass. 2-pack "2404-05", *97–99*	—	85	___1
(11931)	Chessie Flyer Freight set "1931S" (O), *97–99*	—	165	___1
(11933)	Dodge Motorsports Freight set, *96 u*	—	240	___1
(11934)	Virginian Rectifier Freight set, *97–99*	—	305	___2
(11935)	Lionel NYC Flyer Freight set, *97*	—	155	___1
(11936)	Little League Baseball Steam set, *97*	180	195	___1
(11939)	SP&S 4-6-2 Steam Freight set, *97*	—	220	___1
(11940)	Southern Pacific SD40 Warhorse Coal set, *98*	—	570	___1
(11944)	Lionel Lines 4-4-2 Steam Freight set, *98*	—	175	___1
(11956)	UP GP-9 "2380", "2381" (Powered and Dummy), *97*	—	360	___1
(11957)	Mobil Oil Steam Special set, *97*	—	575	___1

		Exc	New	Cond/$
(11971)	D&H 4-4-2 Steam Freight set, *98*	—	135	___[1]
(11972)	ARR GP-7 Train set, *98–99*	—	155	___[1]
(11974)	Station Accessory set, *98*	—	22	___[1]
(11975)	Freight Accessory Pack, *98*	—	25	___[1]
(11977)	NP 4-pack Freight Cars, *98*	—	185	___[1]
(11979)	N&W 4-4-2 Steam Freight set, *98*	—	75	___[1]
(11981)	1998 Holiday Trolley set, *98*	—	75	___[1]
(11983)	Farmrail Agricultural set, *99*	—	375	___[1]
(11984)	Corvette GP-7 set, *99*	—	405	___[1]
(11988)	NYC Firecar "18444" & Instruction Car "19853" set, *99*	—	155	___[1]
12000	(See 52000)			
(12014)	Straight Track 10" (FasTrack), *03*		CP	___
(12015)	Curved Track O-36 (FasTrack), *03*		CP	___
(12016)	Terminal Track 10" (FasTrack), *03*		CP	___
(12017)	Left Manual Switch O-36 (FasTrack), *03*		CP	___
(12018)	Right Manual Switch O-36 (FasTrack), *03*		CP	___
(12019)	90° Crossover (FasTrack), *03*		CP	___
(12020)	Uncoupling Track 5" (FasTrack), *03*		CP	___
(12022)	Half Curved Track O-36 (FasTrack), *03*		CP	___
(12023)	Quarter Curved Track O-36 (FasTrack), *03*		CP	___
(12024)	Half Straight Track (FasTrack), *03*		CP	___
(12025)	Straight Track 4½" (FasTrack), *03*		CP	___
(12026)	Straight Track 1¾" (FasTrack), *03*		CP	___
(12027)	Insulated Track 5" (FasTrack), *03*		CP	___
(12028)	Inner Passing Loop Track Pack (FasTrack), *03*		CP	___
(12029)	Accessory Activator Pack (FasTrack), *03*		CP	___
(12030)	Figure 8 Track Pack (FasTrack), *03*		CP	___
(12031)	Outer Passing Loop Track Pack (FasTrack), *03*		CP	___
(12032)	Straight Track 10" 4-pack (FasTrack), *03*		CP	___
(12033)	Curved Track O-36 4-pack (FasTrack), *03*		CP	___
12046	(See 52046)			
12700	Erie Magnetic Gantry Crane, *87*	140	165	___[1]
(12701)	Operating Fueling Station, *87*	65	80	___[1]
(12702)	Control Tower, *87*	70	85	___[1]
(12703)	Icing Station, *88–89*	70	75	___[2]
(12704)	Dwarf Signal, *88–93*	9	11	___[1]
(12705)	Lumber Shed kit "832K", *88–99*		CP	___
(12706)	Barrel Loader Building kit, *87–99*		CP	___
(12707)	Billboards (3), *87–99*	—	4	___[1]
(12708)	Street Lamps (3), *88–93*	6	9	___[1]
(12709)	Banjo Signal "140", *87–91, 95–00*	—	33	___[1]
(12710)	Engine House kit, *87–91*	21	25	___[1]

		Exc	New	Cond/$
(12711)	Water Tower kit, *87–99*	—	13	___¹
(12712)	Automatic Ore Loader, *87–88*	17	21	___¹
(12713)	Automatic Gateman "145", *87–88, 94–00*	—	40	___¹
(12714)	Crossing Gate "252", *87–91, 93–03*	—	26	___¹
(12715)	Illuminated Bumpers "261", *87–03*	—	3	___¹
(12716)	Searchlight Tower, *87–89, 91–92*	19	22	___¹
(12717)	Non-Illuminated Bumpers (3), *87–03*		CP	___
(12718)	Barrel Shed kit, *87–99*	—	10	___¹
(12719)	Animated Refreshment Stand, *88–89*	70	80	___¹
12720	Rotary Beacon, *88–89*	40	45	___¹
(12721)	Illuminated Extension Bridge w/ rock piers, *89*	26	38	___¹
(12722)	Roadside Diner w/ smoke, *88–89*	18	25	___¹
(12723)	Microwave Tower, *88–91, 94–95*	19	25	___¹
(12724)	Double Signal Bridge, *88–90*	46	60	___¹
12725	Lionel Tractor and Trailer, *88–89*	18	21	___¹
(12726)	Grain Elevator kit, *88–91, 94–99*	—	40	___¹
(12727)	Operating Semaphore "159", *89–99*	—	24	___¹
(12728)	Illuminated Freight Station, *89*	29	38	___¹
(12729)	Mail Pick-up set, *88–91, 95*	13	18	___¹
(12730)	Girder Bridge "314", *88–03*	—	11	___¹
(12731)	Station Platform "158", *88–00*	—	9	___¹
(12732)	Coal Bag "206", *88–03*		CP	___
(12733)	Watchman Shanty kit, *88–99*	—	5	___¹
(12734)	Passenger/Freight Station, *89–99*	—	16	___¹
(12735)	Diesel Horn Shed, *88–91*	19	24	___¹
(12736)	Coaling Station kit, *88–91*	21	27	___¹
(12737)	Whistling Freight Shed "118", *88–99*	—	27	___¹
(12739)	Lionel Gas Company Tractor and Tanker, *89*	20	25	___¹
(12740)	Genuine Wood Logs (3), *88–92, 94–95, 97–99*		CP	___
12741	Union Pacific Intermodal Crane, *89*	170	190	___¹
(12742)	Gooseneck Lamps "58", *89–00*	—	30	___¹
(12743)	Track Clips (12) (O), *89–03*		CP	___
(12744)	Rock Piers (2) "920-5", *89–92, 94–03*	—	10	___¹
(12745)	Barrel Pack (6), *89–03*		CP	___
(12746)	Operating/Uncoupling Track (O27), *89–03*	—	7	___¹
(12748)	Illuminated Passenger Platform "157", *89–99*	—	18	___¹
(12749)	Rotary Radar Antenna, *89–92, 95*	32	36	___¹
(12750)	Crane kit, *89–91*	8	10	___¹
(12751)	Shovel kit, *89–91*	8	10	___¹
(12752)	History of Lionel Trains video (VHS), *89–92, 94*	19	21	___¹
(12753)	Ore Load (2), *89–91, 95*	1.50	2.50	___¹
(12754)	Graduated Trestle set (22) "110", *89–03*	—	15	___¹

Exc New Cond/$

		Exc	New	Cond/$
(12755)	Elevated Trestle set (10) "111", 89–03	—	15	___¹
(12756)	The Making of the Scale Hudson video (VHS), 91–94	20	22	___¹
(12759)	Floodlight Tower "195", 90–00	—	25	___¹
(12760)	Automatic Highway Flasher, 90–91	26	30	___¹
(12761)	Animated Billboard, 90–91, 93, 95	19	22	___¹
(12762)	Freight Station w/ train control and sounds, 90–91		NM	___
(12763)	Single Signal Bridge, 90–91, 93	25	28	___¹
(12765)	Die-cast Auto Assortment (6), 90		NM	___
(12767)	Steam Clean and Wheel Grind Shop, 92–93, 95	265	300	___¹
(12768)	Burning Switch Tower, 90, 93	95	110	___¹
(12770)	Arch-Under Bridge "332", 90–03	—	25	___¹
(12771)	Mom's Roadside Diner w/ smoke, 90–91	34	50	___¹
(12772)	Truss Bridge w/ Flasher and Piers "318", 90–03		CP	___
(12773)	Freight Platform kit, 90–98	—	38	___¹
(12774)	Lumber Loader kit, 90–99	—	20	___¹
12777	Chevron Tractor and Tanker, 90–91	10	15	___¹
12778	Conrail Tractor and Trailer, 90	10	15	___¹
12779	Lionelville Grain Company Tractor and Trailer, 90	11	17	___¹
(12780)	RS-1 50-watt Transformer, 90–93	110	150	___¹
12781	N&W Intermodal Crane, 90–91	180	210	___¹
(12782)	Lift Bridge, 91–92	620	760	___¹
12783	Monon Tractor and Trailer, 91	11	17	___¹
(12784)	Intermodal Containers (3), 91	11	15	___¹
12785	Lionel Gravel Company Tractor and Trailer, 91	10	15	___¹
12786	Lionel Steel Company Tractor and Trailer, 91	10	14	___¹
12787	Family Lines Intermodal Container (See 12784)			
12788	UP Intermodal Container (See 12784)			
12789	B&M Intermodal Container (See 12784)			
(12790)	ZW-II Transformer, 91		NM	___
(12791)	Animated Passenger Station, 91	75	80	___¹
(12794)	Lionel Tractor, 91	8	12	___¹
(12795)	Lionel Cable Reels (2) "40-15", 91–98	3	5	___¹
(12797)	Crossing Gate and Signal, 91		NM	___
(12798)	Forklift Loader Station, 92–95	46	55	___²
(12800)	Scale Hudson Replacement Pilot Truck, 91 u	13	17	___¹
(12802)	"Chat & Chew" Roadside Diner w/ smoke and lights, 92–95	37	40	___¹
(12804)	Highway Lights "72", 92–99, 02–03	10	14	___¹

		Exc	New	Cond/$
(12805)	Intermodal Containers (3), *92*	9	12	___[1]
12806	Lionel Lumber Company Tractor and Trailer, *92*	8	11	___[1]
(12807)	Little Caesars Tractor and Trailer, *92*	9	13	___[1]
12808	Mobil Tractor and Tanker, *92*	8	11	___[1]
(12809)	Animated Billboard, *92–93*	22	26	___[1]
(12810)	American Flyer Tractor and Trailer "DX26925", *94*	12	16	___[1]
12811	Alka Seltzer Tractor and Trailer, *92*	12	19	___[1]
(12812)	Illuminated Freight Station "133", *93–00*	—	31	___[1]
(12818)	Animated Freight Station, *92, 94–95*	55	65	___[1]
12819	Inland Steel Tractor and Trailer, *92*	10	15	___[1]
(12821)	Lionel Catalog video (VHS), *92*	13	17	___[1]
(12826)	Intermodal Containers (3), *93*	10	15	___[1]
(12827)	CSX Intermodal Container "610584" (See 12826)			
(12828)	NYC Intermodal Container (See 12826)			
(12829)	Great Northern Container (See 12826)			
12831	Rotary Beacon, *93–95*	25	28	___[1]
(12832)	Block Target Signal "253", *93–98*	—	25	___[1]
(12833)	RoadRailer Tractor and Trailer, *93*	10	14	___[1]
12834	Pennsylvania Magnetic Gantry Crane, *93*	150	200	___[1]
(12835)	Operating Fueling Station, *93*	65	75	___[1]
12836	Santa Fe Quantum Tractor and Trailer, *93*	8	12	___[1]
(12837)	Humble Oil Tractor and Tanker, *93*	10	15	___[1]
(12838)	Crate Load (2), *93–97*	—	3	___[1]
(12839)	Grade Crossing (2), *93–03*	—	5	___[1]
(12897)	Engine House kit, *96–98*	—	25	___[1]
(12840)	Insulated Straight Track (O), *93–03*		CP	___
(12841)	Insulated Straight Track (O27), *93–03*		CP	___
(12842)	Dunkin' Donuts Tractor and Trailer, *92 u*	32	35	___[1]
(12843)	Die-cast Metal Sprung Trucks (2), *93–99*		CP	___
(12844)	Coil Covers (2) (O), *93–98*	—	3	___[1]
(12847)	Animated Ice Depot "352", *94–99*	—	75	___[1]
(12848)	Lionel Oil Company Oil Derrick "2848", *94*	65	80	___[2]
(12849)	Lionel Controller w/ wall pack, *94, 95 u*		CP	___
(12852)	Die-cast Intermodal Trailer Frame, *94–01*	—	4	___[1]
(12853)	Coil Covers (2) (Std. O), *94–98*	—	7	___[1]
(12854)	US Navy Tractor and Tanker, *94–95*	—	34	___[1]
(12855)	Intermodal Containers (3), *94–95*	9	13	___[1]
12856	CP Rail Intermodal Container (See 12855)			
12857	Frisco Intermodal Container (See 12855)			
12858	Vermont Railways Intermodal Container (See 12855)			
(12860)	Lionel Visitor's Center Tractor and Trailer, *94 u*	12	16	___[1]
(12861)	Lionel Leasing Company Tractor, *94*	4	8	___[1]

		Exc	New	Cond/$
(12862)	Oil Drum Loader, *94–95*	80	95	___1
(12864)	Little Caesars Tractor and Trailer, *94*	8	12	___1
(12865)	Wisk Tractor and Trailer, *94*	8	12	___1
(12866)	TMCC 135-watt PowerHouse Power Supply, *94 u, 95–03*	—	42	___1
(12867)	TMCC 135 PowerMaster Power Distribution Center, *94 u, 95–03*	—	42	___1
(12868)	TMCC CAB-1 Remote Controller, *94 u, 95–03*		CP	___
(12869)	Marathon Oil Tractor and Tanker, *94*	16	22	___1
(12873)	Operating Sawmill "464", *95–97*	—	70	___1
(12874)	Classic Street Lamps "71", *94–00*	—	13	___1
(12875)	Lionel Railroader Club Tractor and Trailer, *94 u*	15	22	___1
(12877)	Operating Fueling Station, *95*	70	75	___1
(12878)	Control Tower, *95*	55	65	___1
(12880)	Power Station Transformer, *96*		NM	___
(12881)	Chrysler Mopar Tractor and Trailer, *94 u*	32	37	___1
(12882)	Lighted Billboard, *95*	9	13	___1
(12883)	Dwarf Signal "148", *95–03*	—	25	___1
(12884)	Truck Loading Dock kit, *95–98*	—	14	___1
(12885)	40-watt Control System, *94 u, 95–03*	—	26	___1
(12886)	Floodlight Tower "395", *95–98*	—	32	___1
(12887)	Lionel Conductor Display, *95*		NM	___
(12888)	Railroad Crossing Flasher "154", *95–03*	—	38	___1
(12889)	Operating Windmill "453", *95–98*	—	45	___1
(12890)	Big Red Control Button, *94 u, 95–00*	—	45	___1
(12891)	Lionel Lines Refrigerator Tractor and Trailer, *95*	13	15	___1
(12892)	Automatic Flagman "1045", *92–98*	—	26	___1
(12893)	TMCC PowerMaster Power Adapter Cable, *94 u, 95–03*		CP	___
(12894)	Signal Bridge "452", *95–01*	—	35	___1
(12895)	Double-track Signal Bridge "450", *95–00*	—	44	___1
(12896)	Tunnel Portals (2) "920-2", *95–03*	—	5	___1
(12898)	Flagpole "89", *95–97*	—	8	___1
(12899)	Searchlight Tower "496", *95–98*	—	25	___1
(12900)	Crane kit "6828-100", *95–98*	—	7	___1
(12901)	Shovel kit "6827-100", *95–98*	—	7	___1
(12902)	Marathon Oil Derrick "2902", *94 u, 95*	200	250	___1
(12903)	Diesel Horn Shed "114", *95–98*	—	29	___1
(12904)	Coaling Station kit, *95–98*	—	17	___1
(12905)	Factory kit, *95–98*	—	20	___1
(12906)	Maintenance Shed kit, *95–98*	—	20	___1
(12907)	Intermodal Containers (3), *95*	8	12	___1
(12908)	Western Pacific Intermodal Container (See 12907)			

(12909)	Northern Pacific Intermodal Container "33621" (See 12907)			
(12910)	CP Rail Intermodal Container "680441" (See 12907)			
(12911)	TMCC Command Base, *95–03*	—	45	___1
(12912)	Oil Pumping Station "457", *95–98*	—	65	___1
(12914)	SC-1 Switch and Accessory Controller, *95–98*	—	35	___1
(12915)	Log Loader "164", *96*	—	160	___2
(12916)	Water Tower "138", *96–97*	—	65	___1
(12917)	Animated Switch Tower "445", *96–98*	—	22	___1
(12921)	LRRC Illuminated Station Platform, *95 u*	24	29	___1
12922	NYC Operating Gantry Crane w/ coil covers, *96*	90	105	___1
(12923)	Red Wing Shoes Tractor and Trailer "T-4", *95 u*	31	34	___1
(12925)	Curved Track Section 42" (O), *96–03*		CP	___
(12926)	Globe Street Lamps "64", *96–03*	—	10	___1
(12927)	Yard Light "65", *96–03*		CP	___
(12929)	Rail-truck Loading Dock, *96*	—	37	___1
(12930)	Lionelville Oil Company Oil Derrick "2930", *95 u, 96*	75	95	___1
(12931)	Electrical Substation, *96*	—	22	___1
(12932)	Laimbeer Packaging Tractor & Trailer set, *96*	—	12	___1
(12936)	SP Intermodal Crane "292", *97*	—	200	___1
(12937)	NS Intermodal Crane "292", *97*	—	200	___1
(12938)	PS PowerStation—PowerHouse set, *97–00*	—	150	___1
(12939)	PG PowerGrid—PowerHouse set, *97*		NM	___
(12943)	Illuminated Station Platform, *97–00*	—	24	___1
(12944)	Sunoco Oil Derrick "455", *97*	—	95	___1
(12945)	Sunoco Pumping Oil Station "457", *97*	—	80	___1
(12948)	Bascule Bridge "313", *97*	—	285	___2
(12949)	Billboard set "310", *97–00*	—	7	___1
(12951)	Airplane Hangar kit "837K", *97–98*	—	21	___1
(12952)	Big L Diner kit "838K", *97*	—	22	___1
(12953)	Linex Gas Tall Oil Tank "840K", *97*	—	9	___1
(12954)	Linex Gas Wide Oil Tank "839K", *97*	—	10	___1
(12955)	Road Runner & Wile E. Coyote Ambush Shack "145", *97*	—	75	___1
(12958)	Industrial Water Tower "193", *97–98*	—	50	___1
(12960)	Rotary Radar Antenna "197", *97*	—	23	___1
(12961)	Lionel News Stand w/ diesel horn "114", *97*	—	30	___1
(12962)	LL Passenger Service Train Whistle "118", *97–99*	—	26	___1
(12964)	Donald Duck Radar Antenna "197", *97*	—	60	___1
(12965)	Goofy Rotary Beacon "494", *97*	—	55	___1
(12966)	Lionel Rotary Aircraft Beacon "494", *97–00*	—	37	___1

(12968)	Girder Bridge Building kit "841K", *97*	—	22	___¹
(12969)	TMCC Command set, *97–03*	—	80	___¹
(12974)	Blinking-light Billboard "410", *97–00*		CP	___
(12975)	"Steiner" Victorian Building kit "842K", *97–98*	—	31	___¹
(12976)	"Dobson" Victorian Building kit "843K", *97–98*	—	35	___¹
(12977)	"Kindler" Victorian Building kit "844K", *97–98*	—	35	___¹
(12982)	Culvert Loader, *98–00*	—	190	___¹
(12983)	Culvert Unloader (Conventional), *99*	—	215	___¹
(12987)	Intermodal 3-pack, *98*	—	15	___¹
(12989)	Lionel Logo Tractor-Trailer, *98*	—	14	___¹
(12991)	Linex Gas Tractor-Tanker, *98*	—	15	___¹
(14000)	Operating Forklift Platform (#264), *00*	—	185	___¹
(14001)	Operating Belt Lumber Loader (#364), *00*	—	105	___¹
(14002)	ZW Amp/Volt Meter (for new ZW's), *00–03*	—	80	___¹
(14003)	80-watt Transformer/Controller, *00–03*	—	70	___¹
(14004)	Operating Coal Loader (#397), *00*	—	185	___¹
(14005)	Operating Coal Ramp (#456), *00*	—	165	___¹
(14018)	ElectroCoupler Kit for Command Upgradeable GP9s, *00*	—	20	___¹
(14062)	O31 Remote Switch (LH), *01–03*		CP	___
(14063)	O31 Remote Switch (RH), *01–03*		CP	___
(14065)	463 Nuclear Reactor, *00*	—	175	___¹
(14071)	#70 Yard Light, *00–03*	—	24	___¹
(14072)	Haunted House, *01*	—	150	___¹
(14073)	Video: History of Lionel, The First 90 Years, *00*		CP	___
(14075)	Video: A Century of Lionel, 1900-1969, *00*		CP	___
(14076)	Video: A Century of Lionel, 1970-2000, *00*		CP	___
(14077)	ZW Amp/Volt Meter (for older ZW's), *00–03*		CP	___
(14078)	Die-Cast Sprung Trucks, *00–03*		CP	___
(14079)	Operating North Pole Pylon, *01*	—	90	___¹
(14080)	Hobo Hotel, *01*	—	47	___¹
(14081)	Shell Oil Derrick, *01*	—	170	___¹
(14082)	Pedestrian Walkover w/ speed sensor, *01–03*		CP	___
(14083)	Pedestrian Walkover, *01–03*		CP	___
(14084)	Lionel Heliport, *01*	—	60	___¹
(14085)	Newsstand, *01*	—	85	___¹
(14086)	#38 Water Tower, *00*	—	100	___¹
(14087)	Lionel Lighthouse, *01*	—	125	___¹
(14090)	Banjo Signal, *01–03*	—	33	___¹
(14091)	Automatic Gateman, *01–03*		CP	___
(14092)	Floodlight Tower, *01–03*	—	26	___¹
(14093)	Single Signal Bridge, *01–03*	—	36	___¹
(14094)	Double Signal Bridge, *01–03*	—	44	___¹

(14095)	Illuminated Station Platform, *01–03*		CP	___
(14096)	Station Platform, *01–03*		CP	___
(14097)	Rotary Aircraft Beacon, *01–03*	—	46	___¹
(14098)	Auto Crossing Gate, *01–03*	—	55	___¹
(14099)	Block Target Signal, *01–03*	—	21	___¹
(14100)	Blinking Light Billboard, *01–03*		CP	___
(14101)	Red Baron Pylon, *01*	—	100	___¹
(14102)	175 Rocket Launcher, *01*	—	250	___¹
(14104)	Burning Switch Tower, *00*	—	80	___¹
(14105)	Lionel "505" Aquarium, *01*	—	205	___¹
(14106)	#356 Operating Freight Station, *00*	—	70	___¹
(14107)	Lionel Postwar Coaling Station, "497", *01–03*	—	95	___¹
(14109)	Carousel, *01*	—	275	___¹
(14110)	Operating Ferris Wheel, *02*	—	150	___¹
(14110)	Ferris Wheel, *01*	—	150	___¹
(14111)	1531R Controller, *00–03*		CP	___
(14112)	Lighted Lockon, *01–03*		CP	___
(14113)	Engine Transfer Table, *01*	—	175	___¹
(14114)	Engine Transfer Table Extension, *01*	—	60	___¹
(14116)	PRR Die-cast Girder Bridge, *01*	—	20	___¹
(14117)	NYC Die-cast Girder Bridge, *01*	—	20	___¹
(14119)	Gooseneck Lamps, Green, *01–03*	—	22	___¹
(14121)	Classic Billboard set (3), *01–03*		CP	___
14124	ZW Controller w/ two 135W packs, *01*	—	300	___¹
(14125)	Christmas Tree w/400E Train set, *00*	—	50	___¹
(14133)	Madison Hobby Shop, *01*	—	315	___¹
(14134)	Triple Action Magnetic Crane, *01*	—	230	___¹
(14135)	Die-cast NS Black Girder Bridge, *02*		CP	___
(14137)	Generic Die-cast Girder Bridge, *01–03*	—	18	___¹
(14142)	Industrial Smokestack, *02–03*		CP	___
(14143)	Industrial Tank, *02–03*		CP	___
(14145)	Operating Lumberjacks, *02–03*	—	70	___¹
(14147)	Die-cast Old Style Clock Tower, *02–03*	—	43	___¹
(14148)	Operating Billboard Signmen, *02–03*	—	70	___¹
(14149)	Scale-sized Banjo Signal, *02–03*		CP	___
(14151)	Die-cast Dwarf Signal, *02–03*	—	28	___¹
(14152)	Passenger Station "133", *02*	—	37	___¹
(14153)	Lion Oil Derrick, *02–03*		CP	___
(14154)	Water Tower "193", *01–02*	—	50	___¹
(14155)	Floodlight Tower "395", *02–03*		CP	___
(14156)	Lion Oil Diesel Fueling Station "415", *02–03*		CP	___
(14157)	Coal Loader "397", *01–03*	—	135	___¹
(14158)	Icing Station "352", *01–02*	—	75	___¹

		Exc	New	Cond/$
(14159)	Animated Billboard, 02–03		CP	
(14160)	Frank's Hotdog Stand, 03		CP	
(14161)	Smoking Hobo Shack, 02	—	55	___[1]
(14162)	Missile Launching Platform "470", 02–03	—	50	___[1]
(14163)	Industrial Power Station "840", 02–03	—	500	___[1]
(14164)	Lionelville Bandstand, 02	—	140	___[1]
(14167)	Operating Lift Bridge "213", 02	—	295	___[1]
(14168)	Operating Harry's Barber Shop, 02	—	110	___[1]
(14170)	Amusement Park Swing Ride, 03		CP	
(14171)	Pirate Ship Ride, 02–03		CP	
(14172)	NYC Railroad Tugboat, 02	—	165	___[1]
(14173)	Drawbridge, 02–03		CP	
(14175)	Santa Fe Die-cast Girder Bridge, 01–03		CP	
(14176)	Norfolk Southern Die-cast Girder Bridge, blue, 03		CP	
(14176)	Norfolk Southern Die-cast Girder Bridge, 02	—	18	___[1]
(14178)	TMCC Direct Lockon, 02–03		CP	
(14179)	TMCC Track Power Controller "400", 02–03	—	130	___[1]
(14180)	B&O Railroad Tugboat, 02–03	—	155	___[1]
(14181)	TMCC Action Recorder Controller, 02–03	—	60	___[1]
(14182)	TMCC Accessory Switch Controller, 02–03	—	55	___[1]
(14183)	TMCC Accessory Motor Controller, 02–03	—	60	___[1]
(14184)	TMCC Block Power Controller, 02–03	—	55	___[1]
(14185)	TMCC Operating Track Controller, 02–03	—	49	___[1]
(14186)	TMCC Accessory Voltage Controller, 02–03	—	90	___[1]
(14187)	TMCC How-To Video, 02–03	—	11	___[1]
(14189)	TMCC Track Power Controller "300", 02–03	—	90	___[1]
(14191)	TMCC Command Base Cable (6 feet), 02–03	—	6	___[1]
(14192)	TMCC 3-wire Command Base Cable, 02–03	—	8	___[1]
(14193)	TMCC Controller to Controller Cable (1 foot), 02–03		CP	
(14194)	TMCC TPC Cable set, 02–03	—	9	___[1]
(14195)	TMCC Command Base Cable (20 feet), 02–03	—	8	___[1]
(14196)	TMCC Controller to Controller Cable (6 feet), 02–03	—	4	___[1]
(14197)	TMCC Controller to Controller Cable (20 feet), 02–03	—	6	___[1]
(14198)	CW-80 80-watt Transformer, 03		CP	
(14199)	Playground Swings, 03		CP	
(14500)	KCS F3 AA "2388" Passenger set, 01	—	710	___[1]
(14512)	EMD F3 ABA "291", CC, 01	—	445	___[1]
(14517)	Santa Fe Powered B Unit, "2343C", 01	—	305	___[1]
(14518)	CP F3 B Unit w/ RailSounds "2373C", CC, 01	—	260	___[1]
(14520)	Texas Special B Unit w/ Railsounds, 01	—	340	___[1]

		Exc	New	Cond/$
(14521)	Rock Island E-6 AA, *01*	—	530	___ 1
(14524)	Atlantic Coast Line E-6 AA, *01*	—	700	___ 1
(14532)	Lionel Century Club PRR Sharknose AA "9744", CC, *00 u*	—	600	___ 1
(14539)	Santa Fe F3 B Unit, *03*		CP	___
(14540)	D&RGW F3 B Unit w/ RailSounds, CC, *01*	—	250	___ 1
(14541)	C&O F3 B Unit w/ RailSounds, CC, *01*	—	250	___ 1
(14542)	KCS F3 B Unit w/ RailSounds "2388C", CC, *01*	—	350	___ 1
(14543)	SP F3 B Unit w/ RailSounds, CC, *01*	—	250	___ 1
(14544)	Southern EMD E6 AA Diesels, CC, *02*	—	520	___ 1
(14547)	Burlington EMD E5 AA Diesels, CC, *02*	—	540	___ 1
(14555)	NYC F3 B Unit, *03*		CP	___
(14557)	WP F3 B Unit (non-powered), *03*		CP	___
(14558)	B&O F3 B Unit (non-powered), *03*		CP	___
(14559)	D&RG F-3 AA, *01*	—	720	___ 1
(14560)	NP F3 B Unit (Freight) "2390B", *02*	—	175	___ 1
(14561)	NP F3 B Unit (Passenger) "2390B", *02*	—	180	___ 1
(14562)	Milwaukee Road F3 B Unit "75C", *02*	—	180	___ 1
(14563)	Erie Lackawanna F3 B Unit "7094", *02*	—	175	___ 1
(14564)	CP F3 B Unit "237C", CC, *02*	—	265	___ 1
(14565)	B&O F3 A-A set, *03*		CP	___
(14568)	WP F3 A-A set, *03*		CP	___
(14571)	Santa Fe PA A-A set "51-51", CC, *03*		CP	___
(14574)	D&H PA A-A set "18-19", CC, *03*		CP	___
(14584)	Wabash F3 A Unit (non-powered), *03*		CP	___
(14586)	D&H PB Unit, *03*		CP	___
(14587)	Santa Fe PB Unit, *03*		CP	___
(14536)	Santa Fe F3 A-A set w/ RailSounds, CC, *03*		CP	___
(14552)	NYC F3 A-A set w/ RailSounds, CC, *03*		CP	___
15000	D&RGW Waffleside Boxcar, *95*	17	19	___ 1
15001	Seaboard Waffleside Boxcar, *95*	15	19	___ 1
(15002)	Chesapeake & Ohio Waffleside Boxcar, *96*	20	25	___ 1
(15003)	Green Bay & Western Waffleside Boxcar, *96*	18	22	___ 1
(15004)	Bloomingdales Boxcar, *97 u*	—	40	___ 1
(15005)	"I Love NY" Boxcar, *97 u*	—	65	___ 1
(15008)	CP Rail Boxcar		NRS	___
15013	L&N Waffleside "102402" Boxcar, *00*	—	29	___ 1
15014	Seaboard Waffleside "125925" Boxcar, *00*	—	25	___ 1
(15015)	C&NW Waffleside Boxcar "161013", *03*		CP	___
(15100)	Amtrak Passenger Car, *95–97*	—	34	___ 1
15101	Reading Baggage Car (O27), *96*	—	23	___ 1
15102	Reading Combination Car (O27), *96*	—	23	___ 1
15103	Reading Passenger Car (O27), *96*	—	23	___ 1

		Exc	New	Cond/$
15104	Reading Vista Dome Car (O27), *96*	—	26	___1
15105	Reading Full Vista Dome Car (O27), *96*	—	26	___1
15106	Reading Observation Car (O27), *96*	—	23	___1
(15107)	Amtrak Vista Dome Car, *96*	—	33	___1
(15108)	Northern Pacific Vista Dome Car, *96*	—	34	___1
(15109)	AT&SF Combine Car "2407", *97*	—	35	___1
(15110)	AT&SF Vista Dome Car "2404", *97*	—	35	___1
(15111)	AT&SF Observation Car "2406", *97*	—	35	___1
(15112)	AT&SF Coach Albuquerque, "2405", *97*	—	34	___1
(15113)	AT&SF Vista Dome Culebra, "2404", *97*	—	34	___1
(15114)	NJ Transit Coach "5610", *96 u*	—	45	___1
(15115)	NJ Transit Coach "5611", *96 u*	—	45	___1
(15116)	NJ Transit Coach "5612", *96 u*	—	45	___1
(15117)	Annie Passenger Coach, surprised face, *97*	—	23	___1
(15118)	Clarabel Passenger Coach, smiling face, *97*	—	23	___1
(15122)	NJ Transit Passenger Coach "5613", *97u*	—	45	___1
(15123)	NJ Transit Passenger Coach "5614", *97u*	—	45	___1
(15124)	NJ Transit Passenger Coach "5615", *97u*	—	45	___1
(15125)	Amtrak Observation Car, *97u*	—	50	___1
(15126)	Stars & Stripes General Coach "Abraham Lincoln", *99*	—	60	___1
(15127)	Stars & Stripes General Coach "Ulyssesl S. Grant", *99*	—	60	___1
15128	Pride of Richmond General Coach "Robert E. Lee", *99*	—	60	___1
15129	Pride of Richmond General Coach "Jefferson Davis", *99*	—	60	___1
(15136)	Custom Series Short Observation (blue), *99*	—	40	___1
(15136)	Custom Series Short Passenger Observation Car, *99*	—	40	___1
(15137)	Custom Series Short Observation, red, *99*	—	40	___1
(15138)	Pratt's Hollow Baggage Car, *98*	NRS		___
(15139)	Pratt's Hollow Vista Dome, *98*	NRS		___
(15140)	Pratt's Hollow Coach, *98*	NRS		___
(15141)	Pratt's Hollow Observation, *98*	NRS		___
(15142)	US Army "Baby" Heavyweight Coach, *00*	—	50	___1
(15143)	US Army "Baby" Heavyweight Coach, *00*	—	50	___1
(15153)	Pullman Baby Madison Set 4-pack, *01*	—	190	___1
(15163)	T&P "Baby" Heavyweight Coach, *01*	—	30	___1
(15169)	C&O Streamliner Passenger Car 4-pack, *03*	CP		___
(15170)	L&N Streamliner Passenger Car 4-pack, *03*	CP		___
(15300)	NYC Superliner Aluminum Passenger Car 4-pack, *02*	—	360	___1

		Exc	New	Cond/$
(15301)	NYC Superliner Passenger Car "Manhattan", *02*		CP	___
(15302)	NYC Superliner Passenger Car "Queens", *02*		CP	___
(15304)	NYC Superliner Passenger Car "Staten Island", *02*		CP	___
(15305)	NYC Superliner Passenger Car "Brooklyn", *02*		CP	___
(15311)	CB&Q California Zephyr Aluminum Passenger Car 4-pack, *03*		CP	___
(15312)	Santa Fe Super Chief Aluminum Passenger Car 4-pack, *03*		CP	___
(15314)	Amtrak Superliner 2-pack, *03*		CP	___
(15315)	Santa Fe Superliner 2-pack, *03*		CP	___
(15316)	NYC Superliner 2-pack, *03*		CP	___
(15317)	Southern "The Southerner" Aluminum Passenger Car 4-pack, *03*		CP	___
(15319)	Santa Fe Superliner Aluminum Passenger Car 2-pack, *03*		CP	___
(15326)	NYC 20th Century Limited Aluminum Passenger Car 6-pack, *02*	—	470	___[1]
(15333)	N&W Powhatan Arrow Aluminum Passenger Car 6-pack, *02*	—	465	___[1]
(15340)	Pennsylvania South Wind Aluminum Passenger Car 6-pack, *02*	—	465	___[1]
(15384)	N&W Powhattan Arrow StationSounds Diner, *03*		CP	___
(15385)	Pennsylvania South Wind StationSounds Diner, *03*		CP	___
(15394)	Amtrak Streamliner Passenger Car 4-pack, *03*		CP	___
(15395)	Alaska Streamliner Passenger Car 4-pack, *03*		CP	___
(15396)	Amtrak Superliner Diner w/ StationSounds, *03*		CP	___
(15397)	Santa Fe Superliner Diner w/ StationSounds, *03*		CP	___
(15398)	NYC Superliner Diner w/ StationSounds, *03*		CP	___
(15405)	50th Anniversary Heavyweight Diner "Hillside" w/ StationSounds, *02*	—	195	___[1]
(15406)	Blue Comet Heavyweight Diner "Giacobini" w/ StationSounds, *02*	—	215	___[1]
(15504)	Alton Limited StationSounds Diner, *03*		CP	___
(15507)	Phantom III Passenger Car 4-pack, *02*	—	245	___[1]
(15512)	Phantom II Passenger Car 4-pack, *02*	—	250	___[1]
(15517)	Southern Crescent Limited Heavyweight Passenger Car 2-pack, *03*		CP	___
(15520)	Southern Crescent Limited Heavyweight Diner w/ StationSounds, *03*		CP	___
15791	(See 17889)			
15906	RailSounds Trigger Button, *90–95*	—	12	___[1]
16000	PRR Vista Dome Car (O27), *87–88*	30	44	___[1]
16001	PRR Passenger Car (O27), *87–88*	30	36	___[1]

Exc New Cond/$

		Exc	New	Cond/$
16002	PRR Passenger Car (O27), *87–88*	24	29	___1
16003	PRR Observation Car (O27), *87–88*	24	29	___1
16009	PRR Combination Car (O27), *88*	36	38	___1
16010	Virginia & Truckee Passenger Car (SSS), *88*	36	43	___1
16011	Virginia & Truckee Passenger Car (SSS), *88*	36	43	___1
16012	Virginia & Truckee Baggage Car (SSS), *88*	36	43	___1
16013	Amtrak Combination Car (O27), *88–89*	21	34	___1
16014	Amtrak Vista Dome Car (O27), *88–89*	21	34	___1
16015	Amtrak Observation Car (O27), *88–89*	21	34	___1
16016	NYC Baggage Car (O27), *89*	30	44	___1
16017	NYC Combination Car (O27), *89*	21	29	___1
16018	NYC Passenger Car (O27), *89*	21	29	___1
16019	NYC Vista Dome Car (O27), *89*	21	29	___1
16020	NYC Passenger Car (O27), *89*	23	33	___1
16021	(See 17210)	—	40	___1
16021	NYC Observation Car (O27), *89*	21	29	___1
16022	(See 17211)			
16022	Pennsylvania Baggage Car (O27), *89*	27	38	___1
16023	(See 17212)			
16023	Amtrak Passenger Car (O27), *89*	21	30	___1
16024	NP Dining Car (O27), *92*	39	44	___1
16027	LL Combination Car (O27) (SSS), *90*	39	48	___1
16028	LL Passenger Car (O27) (SSS), *90*	35	42	___1
16029	LL Passenger Car (O27) (SSS), *90*	35	42	___1
16030	LL Observation Car (O27) (SSS), *90*	35	42	___1
16031	Pennsylvania Dining Car (O27), *90*	35	39	___1
16033	Amtrak Baggage Car (O27), *90*	28	38	___1
16034	NP Baggage Car (O27), *90–91*	21	30	___1
16035	NP Combination Car (O27), *90–91*	18	26	___1
16036	NP Passenger Car (O27), *90–91*	21	30	___1
16037	NP Vista Dome Car (O27), *90–91*	18	26	___1
16038	NP Passenger Car (O27), *90–91*	17	25	___1
16039	NP Observation Car (O27), *90–91*	18	26	___1
16040	Southern Pacific Baggage Car, *90–91*	22	30	___1
16041	NYC Dining Car (O27), *91*	40	50	___1
16042	Illinois Central Baggage Car (O27), *91*	24	34	___1
16043	Illinois Central Combination Car (O27), *91*	22	30	___1
16044	Illinois Central Passenger Car (O27), *91*	24	34	___1
16045	Illinois Central Vista Dome Car (O27), *91*	22	30	___1
16046	Illinois Central Passenger Car (O27), *91*	24	34	___1
16047	Illinois Central Observation Car (O27), *91*	24	34	___1
16048	Amtrak Dining Car (O27), *91–92*	33	40	___1
16049	Illinois Central Dining Car (O27), *92*	24	33	___1

		Exc	New	Cond/$
(16050)	C&NW Baggage Car "6620", *93*	44	55	___¹
(16051)	C&NW Combination Car "6630", *93*	40	50	___¹
(16052)	C&NW Passenger Car "6616", *93*	34	42	___¹
(16053)	C&NW Passenger Car "6602", *93*	37	46	___¹
(16054)	C&NW Observation Car "6603", *93*	38	47	___¹
16055	Santa Fe Passenger Car (O27), *93–94*	27	35	___¹
16056	Santa Fe Vista Dome Car (O27), *93–94*	28	37	___¹
16057	Santa Fe Passenger Car (O27), *93–94*	30	40	___¹
16058	Santa Fe Combination Car (O27), *93–94*	27	35	___¹
16059	Santa Fe Vista Dome Car (O27), *93–94*	26	34	___¹
16060	Santa Fe Observation Car (O27), *93–94*	25	31	___¹
(16061)	N&W Baggage Car "6061", *94*	50	65	___¹
(16062)	N&W Combination Car "6062", *94*	44	55	___¹
(16063)	N&W Passenger Car "6063", *94*	37	46	___¹
(16064)	N&W Passenger Car "6064", *94*	37	46	___¹
(16065)	N&W Observation Car "6065", *94*	40	50	___¹
(16066)	NYC Combination Car "6066" (SSS), *94*	44	55	___¹
(16067)	NYC Passenger Car "6067" (SSS), *94*	38	47	___¹
(16068)	UP Baggage Car "6068" (O27), *94*	36	43	___¹
(16069)	UP Combination Car "6069" (O27), *94*	36	43	___¹
(16070)	UP Passenger Car "6070" (O27), *94*	36	43	___¹
(16071)	UP Dining Car "6071" (O27), *94*	36	46	___¹
(16072)	UP Vista Dome Car "6072" (O27), *94*	36	43	___¹
(16073)	UP Passenger Car "6073" (O27), *94*	36	42	___¹
(16074)	UP Observation Car "6074" (O27), *94*	36	43	___¹
(16075)	Missouri Pacific Baggage Car "6620", *95*	36	44	___¹
(16076)	Missouri Pacific Combination Car "6630", *95*	34	41	___¹
(16077)	Missouri Pacific Passenger Car "6616", *95*	34	41	___¹
(16078)	Missouri Pacific Passenger Car "7805", *95*	34	39	___¹
(16079)	Missouri Pacific Observation Car "6609", *95*	34	41	___¹
(16080)	New Haven Baggage Car "6080" (O27), *95*	39	48	___¹
(16081)	New Haven Combination Car "6081" (O27), *95*	28	37	___¹
(16082)	New Haven Passenger Car "6082" (O27), *95*	28	37	___¹
(16083)	New Haven Vista Dome Car "6083" (O27), *95*	30	39	___¹
(16084)	New Haven Full Vista Dome Car "6084" (O27), *95*	33	39	___¹
(16086)	New Haven Observation Car "6086" (O27), *95*	31	40	___¹
(16087)	NYC Baggage Car "6087" (SSS), *95*	44	55	___¹
(16088)	NYC Passenger Car "6088" (SSS), *95*	36	43	___¹
(16089)	NYC Dining Car "6089" (SSS), *95*	36	43	___¹
(16090)	NYC Observation Car "6090" (SSS), *95*	40	48	___¹
(16091)	NYC Passenger Cars, set of 4 (SSS), *95*	135	160	___¹
16092	Santa Fe Full Vista Dome Car (O27), *95*	30	38	___¹

		Exc	New	Cond/$
16093	Illinois Central Full Vista Dome Car (O27), *95*	29	38	___[1]
16094	Pennsylvania Full Vista Dome Car (O27), *95*	30	39	___[1]
16095	Amtrak Combination Car (O27), *95*	19	23	___[1]
16096	Amtrak Vista Dome Car (O27), *95*	19	23	___[1]
16097	Amtrak Observation Car (O27), *95*	19	23	___[1]
(16098)	Amtrak Passenger Car, *95–97*	18	29	___[1]
(16099)	Amtrak Vista Dome Car, *95–97*	18	29	___[1]
16102	Southern 3-D Tank Car (SSS), *87*	23	30	___[1]
16103	Lehigh Valley 2-D Tank Car (O27), *88*	19	22	___[1]
16104	Santa Fe 2-D Tank Car (O27), *89*	19	23	___[1]
16105	D&RGW 3-D Tank Car (SSS), *89*	48	65	___[1]
(16106)	Mopar Express 3-D Tank Car, *88 u*	70	120	___[1]
16107	Sunoco 2-D Tank Car (O27), *90*	18	22	___[1]
(16108)	Racing Fuel 1-D Tank Car "6108" (O27), *89 u, 92 u*	9	13	___[1]
16109	B&O 1-D Tank Car (SSS), *91*	29	34	___[1]
(16110)	Circus Animals Operating Stock Car "1989" (O27), *89 u*	24	34	___[1]
16111	Alaska 1-D Tank Car (O27), *90–91*	19	24	___[1]
16112	Dow Chemical 3-D Tank Car, *90*	21	28	___[1]
16113	Diamond Shamrock 2-D Tank Car (O27), *91*	22	27	___[1]
16114	Hooker Chemicals 1-D Tank Car (O27), *91*	13	17	___[1]
16115	MKT 3-D Tank Car, *92*	20	25	___[1]
16116	US Army 1-D Tank Car, *91 u*	44	55	___[1]
16119	MKT 2-D Tank Car (O27), *92, 93 u*	14	19	___[1]
16121	C&NW Stock Car (SSS), *92*	65	75	___[1]
16123	Union Pacific 3-D Tank Car, *93–95*	16	22	___[1]
16124	Penn Salt 3-D Tank Car, *93*	19	24	___[1]
16125	Virginian Stock Car, *93*	20	25	___[1]
16126	Jefferson Lake 3-D Tank Car, *93*	24	28	___[1]
16127	Mobil 1-D Tank Car, *93*	25	30	___[1]
16128	Alaska 1-D Tank Car, *94*	21	25	___[1]
16129	Alaska 1-D Tank Car (O27), *93 u, 94*	23	30	___[1]
16130	SP Stock Car (O27), *93 u, 94*	9	11	___[1]
16131	T&P Reefer, *94*	19	24	___[1]
16132	Deep Rock 3-D Tank Car, *94*	25	30	___[1]
16133	Santa Fe Reefer, *94*	23	29	___[1]
16134	Reading Reefer, *94*	17	21	___[1]
16135	C&O Stock Car, *94*	23	27	___[1]
16136	B&O 1-D Tank Car, *94*	28	32	___[1]
16137	Ford 1-D Tank Car "12", *94 u*	34	39	___[1]
16138	Goodyear 1-D Tank Car, *95*	28	34	___[1]
16140	Domino Sug, *95*	25	30	___[1]

		Exc	New	Cond/$
16141	Erie Stock Car, *95*	24	28	___¹
16142	Santa Fe 1-D Tank Car, *95*	29	33	___¹
16143	Reading Reefer, *95*	18	21	___¹
16144	San Angelo 3-D Tank Car, *95*	23	27	___¹
16146	Dairy Despatch Reefer, *95*	17	22	___¹
(16147)	Clearly Canadian 1-D Tank Car (O27), *94 u*	70	85	___¹
16149	Zep Chemical 1-D Tank Car (O27), *95 u*	60	75	___¹
(16150)	Sunoco 1-D Tank Car "6315", *97*	—	29	___¹
(16152)	Sunoco 3-D Tank Car "6415", *97*	—	23	___¹
(16153)	AEC Reactor Fluid "6315-1" 1-D Tank Car, *97*	—	100	___¹
(16154)	AEC Reactor Fluid "6315-2" 1-D Tank Car, *97*	—	100	___¹
(16155)	AEC Reactor Fluid "6315-3" 1-D Tank Car, *97*	—	100	___¹
(16157)	Gatorade Little League Baseball 1-D Tank Car "6315", *97u*	—	45	___¹
(16160)	Atomic Energy Commission Tank Car w/ Reactor Fluid "6515", *98*	—	47	___¹
(16162)	Hooker 1-D Tank Car "6315-1", *97*	—	50	___¹
(16163)	Hooker 1-D Tank Car "6315-2", *97*	—	50	___¹
(16164)	Hooker 1-D Tank Car "6315-3", *97*	—	50	___¹
(16165)	Mobilfuel 3-D Tank Car "6415", *97u*	—	50	___¹
(16171)	Alaska 1-D Tank Car "6171", *98–99*	—	30	___¹
(16173)	Harold the Helicopter Flatcar, *98*	—	42	___¹
(16175)	NJ Transit Ore Car "9125" Port Morris, *98*	—	45	___¹
(16176)	NJ Transit Ore Car "9126" Raritan Yard, *98u*	—	45	___¹
(16177)	NJ Transit Ore Car "9127" Gladstone Yard, *98u*	—	45	___¹
(16178)	NJ Transit Ore Car "9128" Bay Head Yard, *98u*	—	45	___¹
(16179)	NJ Transit Ore Car "9129" Dover Yard, *98u*	—	45	___¹
(16180)	Tabasco 1-D Tank Car, *98*	50	65	___¹
(16181)	Biohazard Tank Car w/ Lights, *98*	—	60	___¹
(16182)	Gatorade 1-D Tank Car "6315", *98u*	—	50	___¹
(16187)	Linex 3-D Tank Car "6425", *99*	—	30	___¹
(16188)	Kodak 1-D Tank Car "6515", *99*	75	90	___¹
(16196)	Lava Lite 1-D Tank Car "9968", *99*		NM	___
(16199)	UP 1-D Tank Car "6035", *99–00*	—	29	___¹
16200	Rock Island Boxcar (O27), *87–88*	7	10	___¹
16201	Wabash Boxcar (O27), *88–91*	7	10	___¹
16203	Key America Boxcar (O27), *87 u*	45	65	___¹
16204	Hawthorne Boxcar (O27), *87 u*	50	85	___¹
(16205)	Mopar Express Boxcar "1987" (O27), *87–88 u*	47	55	___¹
16206	D&RGW Boxcar (SSS), *89*	38	43	___¹
16207	True Value Boxcar (O27), *88 u*	32	47	___¹
16208	PRR Auto Carrier w/ autos (3-tier), *89*	30	49	___¹
16209	Disney Magic Boxcar (O27), *88 u*	80	100	___¹

		Exc	New	Cond/$
16211	Hawthorne Boxcar (O27), *88 u*	45	65	___¹
16213	Shoprite Boxcar (O27), *88 u*	55	80	___¹
16214	D&RGW Auto Carrier, *90*	29	40	___¹
16215	Conrail Auto Carrier, *90*	28	40	___¹
16217	Burlington Northern Auto Carrier, *92*	29	40	___¹
16219	True Value Boxcar (O27), *89 u*	48	65	___¹
(16220)	Ace Hardware Boxcar (O27), *89 u*	50	70	___¹
(16221)	Macy's Boxcar (O27), *89 u*	50	70	___¹
16222	Great Northern Boxcar (O27), *90–91*	8	15	___¹
(16223)	Budweiser Reefer, *89–92 u*	47	55	___¹
16224	True Value "Lawn Chief" Boxcar (O27), *90 u*	45	60	___¹
16225	Budweiser Vat Car, *90–91 u*	120	140	___¹
(16226)	Union Pacific Boxcar "6226" (O27), *90–91 u*	15	19	___¹
16227	Santa Fe Boxcar (O27), *91*	13	17	___¹
16228	Union Pacific Auto Carrier, *92*	28	33	___¹
16229	Erie-Lackawanna Auto Carrier, *91 u*	45	55	___¹
16232	Chessie System Boxcar, *92, 93 u, 94, 95 u*	25	30	___¹
16233	MKT DD Boxcar, *92*	20	29	___¹
16234	ACY Boxcar (SSS), *92*	34	41	___¹
16235	Railway Express Agency Reefer, *92*	25	31	___¹
16236	NYC "Pacemaker" Boxcar, *92 u*	29	32	___¹
16237	Railway Express Agency Boxcar, *92 u*	31	34	___¹
16238	NYNH&H Boxcar, *93–95*	—	3	___¹
16239	Union Pacific Boxcar, *93–95*	15	20	___¹
16241	Toys "R" Us Boxcar, *92–93 u*	39	45	___¹
16242	Grand Trunk Auto Carrier, *93*	35	40	___¹
16243	Conrail Boxcar, *93*	26	34	___¹
16244	Duluth, South Shore & Atlantic Boxcar, *93*	19	23	___¹
16245	(See 52068)			
16245	Contadina Boxcar, *93*	15	19	___¹
16247	(See 52046)			
16247	ACL Boxcar, *94*	17	21	___¹
16248	Budweiser Boxcar, *93–94 u*	32	40	___¹
16249	United Auto Workers Boxcar, *93 u*	—	50	___¹
16250	Santa Fe Boxcar (O27), *93 u, 94*	8	10	___¹
16251	Columbus & Greenville Boxcar, *94*	12	13	___¹
(16252)	US Navy Boxcar "6106888", *94–95*	—	30	___¹
16253	Santa Fe Auto Carrier, *94*	32	38	___¹
16255	Wabash DD Boxcar, *95*	21	27	___¹
16256	Ford DD Boxcar, *94 u*	30	34	___¹
(16257)	Crayola Boxcar, *94 u, 95*	15	20	___¹
16258	Lehigh Valley Boxcar, *95*	18	23	___¹
16259	Chrysler Mopar Boxcar, *907u*	29	34	___¹

		Exc	New	Cond/$
16260	Chrysler Mopar Auto Carrier, *96 u*	47	55	___[1]
16261	Union Pacific DD Boxcar, *95*	26	29	___[1]
(16263)	AT&SF Boxcar, *96–99*	—	25	___[1]
16264	Red Wing Shoes Boxcar, *95*	23	28	___[1]
16265	Georgia Power "Atlanta '96" Boxcar, *95 u*	150	180	___[1]
16266	Crayola Boxcar, *95*	17	23	___[1]
16267	Sears/Zenith Boxcar, *95–96 u*	—	40	___[1]
16268	GM/AC Delco Boxcar, *95 u*	—	45	___[1]
(16270)	Dept. 56 Boxcar "9746", *96 u*	—	60	___[1]
(16272)	1997 Christmas Boxcar "9700", *97*	—	33	___[1]
(16274)	Marvin the Martian Boxcar "9700", *97*	—	35	___[1]
16275	Eastwood Radio Flyer Boxcar "16275", *96*			
(16279)	Dodge Motorsports Boxcar, *96 u*	105	125	___[1]
(16284)	Galveston Wharves Boxcar "9700", *98*	—	28	___[1]
(16285)	Savannah State Docks Boxcar "9700", *98*	—	26	___[1]
(16291)	1998 Christmas Boxcar, *98*	—	43	___[1]
(16292)	Lionel Christmas Employee Boxcar "9700", *98*	280	325	___[1]
(16293)	JC Penney Boxcar, *97*	—	100	___[1]
(16294)	Pedigree Boxcar, *97*	105	125	___[1]
(16295)	Kal Kan Boxcar, *97*	105	125	___[1]
(16296)	Whiskas Boxcar, *97*	105	125	___[1]
(16297)	Sheba Boxcar, *97*	105	125	___[1]
(16298)	Mobil Boxcar "9700", *97*	—	45	___[1]
16300	Rock Island Flatcar w/ fences (O27), *87–88*	8	10	___[1]
16301	Lionel Barrel Ramp Car, *87*	14	19	___[1]
16303	PRR Flatcar w/ trailers, *87*	25	32	___[1]
16304	Rock Island Gondola w/ cable reels (O27), *87–88*	5	9	___[1]
16305	Lehigh Valley Ore Car, *87*	85	135	___[1]
16306	Santa Fe Barrel Ramp Car, *88*	11	14	___[1]
16307	NKP Flatcar w/ trailers, *88*	33	39	___[1]
16308	Burlington Northern Flatcar w/ trailer, *88–89*	24	30	___[1]
16309	Wabash Gondola w/ canisters, *88–91*	9	13	___[1]
(16310)	Mopar Express Gondola w/ canisters "1987", *87–88 u*	30	34	___[1]
(16311)	Mopar Express Flatcar w/ trailers "1987", *87–88 u*	85	125	___[1]
(15313)	D&H Aluminum Passenger Car 4-pack, *03*		CP	___
16313	PRR Gondola w/ cable reels (O27), *88 u, 89*	9	10	___[1]
16314	Wabash Flatcar w/ trailers, *89*	27	31	___[1]
16315	PRR Flatcar w/ fences (O27), *88 u, 89*	7	9	___[1]
16317	PRR Barrel Ramp Car, *89*	17	21	___[1]

		Exc	New	Cond/$
(16318)	Lionel Lines Superliner Aluminum Passenger Car 2-pack, *03*		CP	___
16318	Lionel Lines Depressed Flatcar w/ cable reels, *89*	21	25	___ [1]
16320	Great Northern Barrel Ramp Car, *90*	12	16	___ [1]
16321/16322	Sealand TTUX Flatcar set w/ trailers, *90*	65	85	___ [1]
16323	Lionel Lines Flatcar w/ trailers, *90*	22	26	___ [1]
16324	PRR Depressed Flatcar w/ cable reels, *90*	17	21	___ [1]
16325	Microracers Exhibition Ramp Car, *89 u*	20	27	___ [1]
16326	Santa Fe Depressed Flatcar w/ cable reels, *91*	18	23	___ [1]
(16327)	"The Big Top" Circus Gondola w/ canisters, *89 u*	19	24	___ [1]
16328	NKP Gondola w/ cable reels, *90–91*	17	23	___ [1]
16329	SP Flatcar w/ horses (O27), *90–91*	19	24	___ [1]
16330	MKT Flatcar w/ trailers, *91*	25	30	___ [1]
16331	Southern Barrel Ramp Car, *91*		NM	___
16332	Lionel Lines Depressed Flatcar w/ transformer, *91*	29	34	___ [1]
16333	Frisco Bulkhead Flatcar w/ wood load, *91*	20	24	___ [1]
(16334)	C&NW TTUX Flatcar set w/ trailers "16337" and "16338", *91*	55	55	___ [2]
16335	NYC "Pacemaker" Flatcar w/ trailer (SSS), *91*	50	70	___ [1]
(16336)	UP Gondola w/ canisters "6336", *90–91 u*	17	21	___ [1]
16337/16338	C&NW TTUX Flatcars w/ trailers (See 16334)			
16339	Mickey's World Tour Gondola w/ canisters (O27), *91, 92 u*	17	21	___ [1]
16340	Amtrak Flatcar w/ stakes, *91*		NM	___
16341	NYC Depressed Flatcar w/ transformer, *92*	25	29	___ [1]
16342	CSX Gondola w/ coil covers, *92*	18	21	___ [1]
16343	Burlington Gondola w/ coil covers, *92*	20	23	___ [1]
16345/16346	SP TTUX Flatcar set w/ trailers, *92*	55	65	___ [1]
16347	Ontario Northland Bulkhead Flatcar w/ pulp load, *92*	28	31	___ [1]
16348	Lionel-Erie Liquefied Gas Car, *92*	31	33	___ [1]
16349	Allis Chalmers Condenser Car, *92*	27	33	___ [1]
16350	CP Rail Bulkhead Flatcar w/ wood load, *91 u*	20	25	___ [1]
16351	Lionel Flatcar w/ USN. submarine, *92*	38	49	___ [2]
16352	US Military Flatcar w/ cruise missile, *92*	32	45	___ [1]
16353	B&M Gondola w/ coil covers, *91 u*	30	34	___ [1]
16355	Burlington Gondola, *92, 93 u, 94–95*	9	14	___ [1]
16356	MKT Depressed Flatcar w/ cable reels, *92*	17	21	___ [1]
16357	L&N Flatcar w/ trailer, *92*	26	33	___ [2]

		Exc	New	Cond/$
16358	L&N Gondola w/ coil covers, *92*	19	23	___¹
16359	Pacific Coast Gondola w/ coil covers (SSS), *92*	33	38	___¹
(16360)	N&W Maxi-Stack Flatcar set w/ containers "16361" and "16362", *93*	47	55	___²
16361/16362	N&W Maxi-Stack Flatcars w/ containers (See 16360)			
(16363)	Southern TTUX Flatcar set w/ trailers "16364" and "16365", *93*	47	55	___¹
16364/16365	Southern TTUX Flatcars w/ trailers (See 16363)			
16367	Clinchfield Gondola w/ coil covers, *93*	18	21	___¹
16368	MKT Liquid Oxygen Car, *93*	24	26	___¹
16369	Amtrak Flatcar w/ wheel load, *92 u*	19	28	___¹
16370	Amtrak Flatcar w/ rail load, *92 u*	19	28	___¹
16371	BN I-Beam Flatcar w/ load, *92 u*	27	32	___²
16372	Southern I-Beam Flatcar w/ load, *92 u*	20	25	___²
16373	Erie-Lackawanna Flatcar w/ stakes, *93*	19	23	___¹
16374	D&RGW Flatcar w/ trailer, *93*	24	29	___¹
16375	NYC Bulkhead Flatcar, *93–95*	22	26	___¹
16376	UP Flatcar w/ trailer, *93–95*	32	38	___¹
16378	Toys "R" Us Flatcar w/ trailer, *92–93 u*	65	100	___¹
16379	NP Bulkhead Flatcar w/ pulp load, *93*	16	23	___¹
16380	(See 52084)			
16380	UP I-Beam Flatcar w/ load, *93*	29	32	___¹
16381	CSX I-Beam Flatcar w/ load, *93*	21	25	___¹
16382	Kansas City Southern Bulkhead Flatcar, *93*	14	18	___¹
(15383)	NYC 20th Century Limited StationSounds Diner, *03*		CP	___
16383	Conrail Flatcar w/ trailer, *93*	47	55	___¹
16384	Soo Line Gondola w/ cable reels, *93*	14	19	___¹
16385	Soo Line Ore Car, *93*	55	65	___¹
16386	SP Flatcar w/ wood load, *94*	17	21	___¹
16387	Kansas City Southern Gondola w/ coil covers, *94*	15	19	___¹
16388	LV Gondola w/ canisters, *94*	18	22	___¹
16389	PRR Flatcar w/ wheel load, *94*	25	30	___¹
16390	Lionel Flatcar w/ water tank, *94*	25	32	___¹
16391	Lionel Lines Gondola, *93 u*	—	15	___¹
16392	Wabash Gondola w/ canisters (O27), *93 u, 94*	7	9	___¹
16393	Wisconsin Central Bulkhead Flatcar, *94*	13	17	___¹
16394	Central Vermont Bulkhead Flatcar, *94*	20	30	___¹
16395	CP Flatcar w/ rail load, *94*	18	23	___¹

Exc New Cond/$

		Exc	New	Cond/$
16396	Alaska Bulkhead Flatcar, *94*	15	19	____¹
16397	Milwaukee Road I-Beam Flatcar w/ load, *94*	38	43	____¹
16398	C&O Flatcar w/ trailer, *94*	70	75	____¹
16399	Western Pacific I-Beam Flatcar w/ load, *94*	29	33	____¹
16400	PRR Hopper (O27), *88 u, 89*	15	18	____¹
16402	Southern Quad Hopper w/ coal load (SSS), *87*	33	47	____¹
16406	CSX Quad Hopper w/ coal load, *90*	32	37	____¹
16407	B&M Covered Quad Hopper (SSS), *91*	30	40	____¹
(16408)	Union Pacific Hopper "6408" (O27), *90–91 u*	17	21	____¹
16410	MKT Hopper (O27), *92, 93 u*	19	24	____¹
16411	L&N Quad Hopper w/ coal load, *92*	28	32	____¹
16412	C&NW Covered Quad Hopper, *94*	14	19	____¹
16413	(See 52059)			
16413	Clinchfield Quad Hopper w/ coal load, *94*	16	22	____¹
16414	CCC&St L Hopper (O27), *94*	14	19	____¹
16416	D&RGW Covered Quad Hopper, *95*	18	23	____¹
16417	Wabash Quad Hopper w/ coal load, *95*	19	23	____¹
16418	C&NW Hopper w/ coal load (O27), *95*	16	22	____¹
(16419)	Tennessee Central Hopper, *96*	—	17	____¹
16420	Western Maryland Quad Hopper w/ coal load (SSS), *95*	27	30	____¹
16421	Western Maryland Quad Hopper w/ coal load (SSS), *95*	30	33	____¹
16422	Western Maryland Quad Hopper w/ coal load (SSS), *95*	—	31	____¹
16423	Western Maryland Quad Hopper w/ coal load (SSS), *95*	—	31	____¹
16424	Western Maryland Covered Quad Hopper (SSS), *95*	30	34	____¹
16425	Western Maryland Covered Quad Hopper (SSS), *95*	26	29	____¹
16426	Western Maryland Covered Quad Hopper (SSS), *95*	24	27	____¹
16427	Western Maryland Covered Quad Hopper (SSS), *95*	27	30	____¹
(16429)	Western Maryland Quad Hoppers w/ coal loads (2) (See 16422)	—	70	____¹
(16430)	Georgia Power Quad Hopper w/ coal load "82947", *95 u*	—	90	____¹
(16431)	Lionel Corporation 2-bay Hopper "6456-1", *96*	—	25	____¹
(16432)	Lionel Corporation 2-bay Hopper "6456-2", *96*	—	18	____¹
(16433)	Lionel Corporation 2-bay Hopper "6456-3", *96*	—	19	____¹
(16434)	LV 2-bay Hopper "6456", "TLDX", *97*	—	22	____¹

		Exc	New	Cond/$
(16435)	Virginian 2-bay Hopper "6456-1", *97*	—	30	___¹
(16436)	N&W 2-bay Hopper "6456-2", *97*	—	30	___¹
(16437)	C&O 2-bay Hopper "6456-3", *97*	—	30	___¹
(16438)	Frisco 4-bay Covered Hopper "87538", *98*	—	30	___¹
(16439)	Southern 4-bay Covered Hopper "87538", *98*	—	31	___¹
(16440)	Alaska 2-bay Hopper "7100", *98–99*	—	35	___¹
(16441)	New York Central 4-bay Hopper "6446", *99*	—	25	___¹
(16442)	Bethlehem Gondola "6462" (SSS), *99*	—	35	___¹
(16443)	GN 2-bay 6476 "172364", *99–00*	—	20	___¹
(16444)	CNJ 2-bay Hopper "643", *00*	—	20	___¹
(16445)	Frisco 2-bay Hopper "93108", *00*	—	20	___¹
(16446)	Burlington 2-bay Hopper, *00*	—	20	___¹
(16447)	PRR Tuscan 2-bay Hopper, *00u*	—	30	___¹
(16448)	PRR Gray 2-bay Hopper, *00u*	—	30	___¹
(16449)	PRR Black 2-bay Hopper, *00u*		CP	___
(16450)	PRR Green 2-bay Hopper, *00u*		CP	___
(16451)	Lionel Mines 2-bay Hopper, *00u*	—	50	___¹
(16453)	SP 2-bay "460604" Hopper, *01*	—	15	___¹
(16454)	Bethlehem Steel "41025" Hopper, *01*	—	35	___¹
(16455)	Pioneer Seed 2-bay Hopper, *00u*	—	50	___¹
(16456)	B&O 2-bay Hopper, *01*	—	20	___¹
(16459)	LV 2-bay Hopper "51102", *01*	—	20	___¹
(16460)	Reading 2-bay Hopper "79636", *02*	—	19	___¹
(16463)	Rio Grande Icebreaker Tunnel Car "18936", *02*	—	32	___¹
(16464)	NYC Icebreaker Tunnel Car "X3200", *02*	—	32	___¹
(16465)	WP 2-bay Hopper "100340", *03*		CP	___
(16466)	Pennsylvania Icebreaker Tunnel Car "16466", *03*		CP	___
(16467)	Naughty and Nice Hopper 2-pack, *02*	—	60	___¹
(16469)	B&O Hopper "435351", *02*	—	19	___¹
(16470)	Naughty and Nice Ore Car 2-pack, *03*		CP	___
(16473)	Rock Island Ore Car "99122", *03*		CP	___
16500	Rock Island Bobber Caboose, *87–88*	9	13	___¹
16501	Lehigh Valley SP-type Caboose, *87*	19	24	___¹
16503	NYC Transfer Caboose, *87*	16	22	___¹
16504	Southern N5C Caboose (SSS), *87*	17	30	___¹
16505	Wabash SP-type Caboose, *88–91*	10	15	___¹
16506	Santa Fe B/W Caboose, *88*	25	29	___¹
(16507)	Mopar Express SP-type Caboose "1987", *87–88 u*	40	49	___¹
(16508)	Lionel Lines SP-type Caboose "6508", *89 u*	13	17	___¹
16509	D&RGW SP-type Caboose (SSS), *89*	19	24	___¹
16510	New Haven B/W Caboose, *89*	25	30	___¹
16511	PRR Bobber Caboose, *88 u, 89*	9	13	___¹

		Exc	New	Cond/$
16513	Union Pacific SP-type Caboose, *89*	14	21	___¹
16515	Lionel Lines RailScope SP-type Caboose, *89*	22	26	___¹
16516	Lehigh Valley SP-type Caboose, *90*	15	26	___¹
16517	Atlantic Coast Line B/W Caboose, *90*	21	25	___¹
16518	Chessie System B/W Caboose, *90*	39	48	___¹
16519	Rock Island Transfer Caboose, *90*	13	17	___¹
(16520)	"Welcome To The Show" Circus SP-type Caboose, *89 u*	13	21	___¹
16521	PRR SP-type Caboose, *90–91*	8	11	___¹
16522	"Chills & Thrills" Circus N5C Caboose, *90–91*	10	15	___¹
16523	Alaska SP-type Caboose, *91*	26	34	___¹
(16524)	Anheuser-Busch SP-type Caboose, *89–92 u*	30	39	___¹
16525	D&H B/W Caboose (SSS), *91*	27	35	___¹
16526	Kansas City Southern SP-type Caboose, *91*	17	21	___¹
16527	Western Pacific Work Caboose, *92*		NM	___
(16528)	Union Pacific SP-type Caboose "6528", *90–91 u*	17	21	___¹
(16529)	Santa Fe SP-type Caboose "16829", *91*	9	13	___¹
(16530)	Mickey's World Tour SP-type Caboose "16830", *91, 92 u*	13	17	___¹
16531	Texas &Pacific SP-type Caboose, *92*	18	23	___¹
16533	C&NW B/W Caboose, *92*	26	36	___¹
16534	Delaware & Hudson SP-type Caboose, *92*	15	19	___¹
16535	Erie-Lackawanna B/W Caboose, *91 u*	30	38	___¹
16536	Chessie System SP-type Caboose, *92, 93 u, 94, 95 u*	30	23	___¹
16537	MKT SP-type Caboose, *92, 93 u*	17	21	___¹
(16538)	L&N B/W Caboose "1041", *92 u*	29	33	___¹
16538	L&N/Family Lines Steelside Caboose w/ smoke (Std. O), *92*		NM	___
(16539)	WP Steelside Caboose w/ smoke "539" (Std. O) (SSS), *92*	60	65	___¹
(16541)	Montana Rail Link E/V Caboose w/ smoke "10131", *93*	55	65	___¹
(16543)	NYC SP-type Caboose, *93–95*	—	20	___¹
16544	(See 16564)			
16544	Union Pacific SP-type Caboose, *93–95*	22	26	___¹
16546	Clinchfield SP-type Caboose, *93*	22	26	___¹
16547	Happy Holidays SP-type Caboose, *93–95*	38	44	___¹
16548	Conrail SP-type Caboose, *93*	22	30	___¹
16549	Soo Line Work Caboose, *93*	18	26	___¹
16550	US Navy Searchlight Caboose, *94–95*	17	21	___¹
16551	Budweiser SP-type Caboose, *93–94 u*	24	29	___¹

		Exc	New	Cond/$
16552	Frisco Searchlight Caboose, *94*	30	34	___1
16553	United Auto Workers SP-type Caboose, *93 u*	—	40	___1
(16554)	GT E/V Caboose w/ smoke "79052", *94*	40	47	___1
16555	C&O SP-type Caboose, *94*	22	26	___1
16556	(See 16909)			
16557	Ford SP-type Caboose, *94 u*	19	24	___1
(16558)	Crayola SP-type Caboose, *94 u, 95*	17	21	___1
(16559)	Seaboard CC Caboose "5658", *95*	26	28	___1
16560	Chrysler Mopar Caboose, *94 u*	22	24	___1
(16561)	Union Pacific CC Caboose "25766", *95*	27	31	___1
16562	Reading CC Caboose, *95*	29	33	___1
(16563)	Lionel Lines SP-type Caboose, *95*	22	26	___1
16564	Western Maryland CC Caboose (SSS), *95*	30	34	___1
16565	Milwaukee Road B/W Caboose, *95*	55	65	___1
(16566)	US Army SP-type Caboose "907", *95*	—	23	___1
(16568)	AT&SF SP-type Caboose, *96–99*	—	23	___1
16570	NdeM E/V Caboose, *96*		NM	___
(16571)	Georgia Power SP-type Caboose "52789", *95 u*	—	60	___1
(16575)	Sears Zenith, SP-type Caboose, *95*	—	38	___1
(16577)	US Coast Guard Work Caboose, *96*	—	26	___1
16578	Lionel Lines SP-type Caboose, *95 u*	—	20	___1
(16579)	GM/AC Delco, SP-type Caboose, *95*	—	35	___1
(16580)	Lionel SP-type Caboose, *96–99*	—	11	___1
(16581)	Union Pacific Illuminated Caboose, *96*	—	33	___1
(16585)	LL Illuminated Caboose "6257", *97*		NM	___
(16586)	SP Illuminated Caboose "6357", *97*	—	29	___1
(16590)	Dodge Motorsports SP-type Caboose, "6950", *96*	—	40	___1
(16591)	Little League Baseball SP-type Caboose "6397", *97*	—	30	___1
(16593)	Lionel Belt Line Caboose "6257", *98*	—	33	___1
(16594)	Lionel Caboose "6357", *98*	—	35	___1
16600	Illinois Central Coal Dump Car, *88*	13	21	___1
16601	Canadian National Searchlight Car, *88*	19	24	___1
16602	Erie-Lackawanna Coal Dump Car, *87*	16	26	___1
16603	Detroit Zoo Giraffe Car (O27), *87*	40	49	___1
16604	NYC Log Dump Car, *87*	14	24	___1
16605	Bronx Zoo Giraffe Car (O27), *88*	39	44	___1
16606	Southern Searchlight Car, *87*	13	21	___1
[16606]	Southern TCA Southern Searchlight Car, *88 u*	17	24	___1
(16607)	Southern Coal Dump Car "16707" (SSS), *87*	18	26	___1
16608	Lehigh Valley Searchlight Car, *87*	22	30	___1
16609	Lehigh Valley Derrick Car, *87*	22	30	___1

		Exc	New	Cond/$
16610	Lionel Track Maintenance Car, *87–88*	14	24	___[1]
16611	Santa Fe Log Dump Car, *88*	13	21	___[1]
16612	Soo Line Log Dump Car, *89*	14	24	___[1]
16613	MKT Coal Dump Car, *89*	13	21	___[1]
16614	Reading Cop and Hobo Car (O27), *89*	27	29	___[1]
16615	Lionel Lines Extension Searchlight Car, *89*	20	28	___[1]
16616	D&RGW Searchlight Car (SSS), *89*	22	30	___[1]
16617	C&NW Boxcar w/ ETD, *89*	21	32	___[1]
16618	Santa Fe Track Maintenance Car, *89*	13	21	___[1]
16619	Wabash Coal Dump Car, *90*	14	24	___[1]
16620	C&O Track Maintenance Car, *90–91*	16	22	___[1]
16621	Alaska Log Dump Car, *90*	19	24	___[1]
16622	CSX Boxcar w/ ETD, *90–91*	21	30	___[1]
16623	MKT DD Boxcar w/ ETD, *91*	16	23	___[1]
16624	NH Cop and Hobo Car (O27), *90–91*	23	31	___[1]
16625	NYC Extension Searchlight Car, *90*	18	24	___[1]
16626	CSX Searchlight Car, *90*	18	26	___[1]
16627	CSX Log Dump Car, *90*	19	23	___[1]
16628	"Laughter" Circus Animated Gondola, *90–91*	36	43	___[1]
16629	"Animal Car" Circus Elephant Car (O27), *90–91*	38	50	___[1]
16630	SP Operating Cowboy Car (O27), *90–91*	22	26	___[1]
16631	RI Boxcar w/ Steam RailSounds, *90*	110	120	___[1]
16632	BN Boxcar w/ Diesel RailSounds, *90*	90	95	___[1]
16633	Great Northern Cop and Hobo Car (O27), *91*		NM	___
16634	WM Coal Dump Car, *91*	22	27	___[1]
16635	CP Rail Track Maintenance Car, *91*		NM	___
16636	D&RGW Log Dump Car, *91*	15	19	___[1]
16637	WP Extension Searchlight Car, *91*	27	30	___[1]
16638	Lionelville Circus Operating Animal Car (O27), *91*	60	65	___[1]
16639	B&O Boxcar w/ Steam RailSounds, *91*	100	110	___[1]
16640	Rutland Boxcar w/ Diesel RailSounds, *91*	100	105	___[1]
16641	Toys "R" Us Giraffe Car (O27), *90–91 u*	45	65	___[1]
16642	Mickey's World Tour Goofy Car (O27), *91, 92 u*	38	47	___[1]
16643	Amtrak Coal Dump Car, *91*		NM	___
16644	Amtrak Crane Car, *91, 92 u*	39	46	___[1]
16645	Amtrak Searchlight Caboose, *91, 92 u*	27	30	___[1]
16646	Railbox Boxcar w/ ETD, *92*		NM	___
16649	Railway Express Agency Boxcar w/ Steam (O27), *91, 92 u*	115	145	___[1]
16650	NYC "Pacemaker" Boxcar w/ Diesel RailSounds, *92*	110	145	___[1]

		Exc	New	Cond/$
16651	Circus Operating Clown Car (O27), *92*	33	38	___²
16652	Lionel Radar Car, *92*	25	30	___²
16653	Western Pacific Crane Car (SSS), *92*	48	65	___¹
16654	(See 17214)			
(16655)	Steam Tender w/ RailSounds "1993", *93*	115	140	___¹
16656	Burlington Log Dump Car, *92 u*	17	21	___¹
16657	Lehigh Valley Coal Dump Car, *92 u*	19	25	___¹
16658	Erie-Lackawanna Crane Car, *93*	47	55	___¹
16659	Union Pacific Searchlight Car, *93–95*	17	21	___¹
16660	Lionel Fire Car w/ ladders, *93–94*	30	32	___²
16661	Lionel Flatcar w/ boat, *93*	20	24	___³
16662	Looney Tunes Operating Bugs Bunny and Yosemite Sam Car (O27), *93–94*	30	31	___¹
16663	Missouri Pacific Searchlight Car, *93*	19	22	___¹
16664	L&N Coal Dump Car, *93*	22	25	___¹
16665	Maine Central Log Dump Car, *93*	25	30	___¹
16666	Lionel Toxic Waste Car, *93–94*	32	42	___¹
16667	Conrail Searchlight Car, *93*	27	30	___¹
16668	Ontario Northland Log Dump Car, *93*	21	25	___¹
16669	Soo Line Searchlight Car, *93*	17	21	___¹
16670	Lionel TV Car, *93–94*	21	25	___²
(16673)	Lionel Lines Tender w/ whistle, *94–97*	—	34	___¹
16674	Pinkerton Animated Gondola, *94*	32	37	___¹
16675	Great Northern Log Dump Car, *94*	22	26	___¹
16676	Burlington Coal Dump Car, *94*	23	28	___¹
16677	NATO Flatcar w/ Royal Navy submarine, *94*	30	34	___²
16678	Rock Island Searchlight Car, *94*	25	27	___¹
16679	US Mail Operating Boxcar, *94*	45	50	___¹
16680	Lionel Cherry Picker Car, *94*	23	26	___¹
16681	Aquarium Car, *95*	55	60	___³
16682	Lionelville Farms Operating Stock Car (O27), *94*	23	27	___¹
16683	Los Angeles Zoo Elephant Car (O27), *94*	24	29	___¹
16684	US Navy Crane Car, *94–95*	35	40	___¹
16685	Erie Extension Searchlight Car, *95*	30	34	___¹
16686	Mickey Mouse and Big Bad Pete Animated Boxcar, *95*	35	39	___¹
16687	US Mail Operating Boxcar, *94*	36	46	___¹
16688	Lionel Fire Car w/ ladders, *94*	42	55	___¹
16689	Lionel Toxic Waste Car, *94*	31	35	___¹
16690	Looney Tunes Operating Bugs Bunny and Yosemite Sam Car (O27), *94*	32	35	___¹
16701	Southern Tool Car (SSS), *87*	43	55	___¹
16702	Amtrak Bunk Car, *91, 92 u*	25	27	___¹

		Exc	New	Cond/$
16703	NYC Tool Car, *92*	23	30	___[1]
16704	Lionel TV Car, *94*	28	31	___[1]
16705	Chesapeake & Ohio Cop and Hobo Car, *95*	33	37	___[1]
16706	Animal Transport Service Giraffe Car, *95*	25	28	___[1]
16707	(See 16607)			
16708	C&NW Track Maintenance Car, *95*	29	35	___[1]
16709	New York Central Derrick Car, *95*	29	34	___[1]
16710	US Army Operating Missile Car, *95*	34	36	___[2]
16711	Pennsylvania Searchlight Car, *95*	27	31	___[1]
16712	Pinkerton Animated Gondola, *95*	30	34	___[1]
16713	Great Northern Log Dump Car, *95*		NM	___
16714	Burlington Coal Dump Car, *95*		NM	___
(16715)	AT&SF Log Dump Car, *96–99*	—	25	___
16717	Jersey Central Crane Car, *96*	—	36	___[1]
16718	USM.C. Missile Launching Flatcar, *96*	39	38	___[1]
(16719)	Exploding Boxcar, *96*	—	32	___[1]
(16720)	Lionel Lines Searchlight Car "3650", *96–97*	—	45	___[1]
(16724)	Mickey and Friends Submarine Car, *96*	—	38	___[1]
(16725)	Rhino Transport Car, *97*	—	26	___[1]
(16726)	US Army Fire Ladder Car, *96*	—	48	___[1]
(16734)	USC.G Searchlight Car, *96*	—	30	___[1]
(16735)	USC.G Flatcar w/ Radar, *96*	—	35	___[1]
16736	USC.G. Derrick Car, *96*	—	34	___[1]
(16737)	Warner Bros. Road Runner & Wile E. Coyote ACME Gondola "3444", *96*	—	40	___[1]
(16738)	Warner Bros. Pepe Le Pew & Penelope Boxcar "3370", *96*	—	38	___[1]
(16739)	Warner Bros. Foghorn Leghorn Poultry Car "6434", *96*	—	42	___[1]
(16740)	Lionel Corporation Mail Car "3428", *96*	—	44	___[1]
(16741)	Union Pacific Illuminated Bunk Car, *97*	—	28	___[1]
(16742)	Trout Ranch Aquarium Car "3435", *96*	—	50	___[2]
(16744)	Port of Lionel City Searchlight Car, *97*	—	30	___[1]
(16745)	Port of Lionel City Flatcar w/ Radar, *97*	—	30	___[1]
(16746)	Port of Lionel City Derrick Car, *97*	—	30	___[1]
(16747)	Breyer Animated Horsecar "6473", *97*	—	33	___[1]
(16748)	US Forest Service Log-Dump Car "3361", *97*	—	34	___[1]
(16749)	Midget Mines Ore-Dump Car "3479", *97*	—	36	___[1]
(16750)	Lionel City Aquarium Car "3436", *97*	—	33	___[1]
(16751)	WLNL Channel 7-AIREX Sports TV Car "3545", *97*	—	32	___[1]
(16752)	Warner Bros. Marvin the Martian Missile-Launching Flatcar "6655", *97*	75	90	___[1]

		Exc	New	Cond/$
(16754)	Warner Bros. Porky Pig and Instant Martians "6805", *97*	95	110	___[1]
(16755)	Warner Bros. Daffy Duck Animated Balloon Car "3470", *97*	75	90	___[1]
(16757)	Johnny Lightning Auto Carrier "3435", *96u*	—	70	___[1]
(16760)	Pluto and Cats Animated Gondola "3444", *97*	—	46	___[1]
(16765)	Bureau of Land Management Log Car "3351", *98*	—	33	___[1]
(16766)	Bureau of Land Management Ore Car "3479", *98*	—	31	___[1]
(16767)	New York Central Ice Docks Ice Car "6352", *98*	—	47	___[1]
(16776)	Lionel Holiday Railsounds Boxcar, *98*	—	105	___[1]
(16777)	Lionel Cola Animated Car & Platform, *98*	—	110	___[1]
(16782)	Bethlehem Ore Dumpcar "3479", *99*	—	95	___[1]
(16783)	Westside Lumber Log Dumpcar "3351", *99*	—	32	___[1]
(16784)	Pratt's Hollow Seed Dumpcar "3479", *99*	—	45	___[1]
(16785)	Happy Holidays Music Reefer "5700", *99*	—	145	___[1]
(16789)	Easter Operating Boxcar "9700", *99*	—	43	___[1]
(16790)	UP Crowsounds Stock Car "3356", *99*	—	100	___[1]
(16791)	NY City Lights Boxcar "9700", *99*	—	42	___[1]
(16792)	Constellation Boxcar "9600", *99*	—	49	___[1]
(16793)	Animated Glow-in-the-Dark Alien Boxcar "9700", *99*	—	37	___[1]
(16794)	Wicked Witch Halloween Boxcar "9700", *99*	—	35	___[1]
(16795)	Elf Chasing Rudolph Gondola "6462", *99*	—	60	___[1]
(16796)	Snowman Loading Ice Car "6352", *99*	—	55	___[1]
16800	Lionel Railroader Club Ore Car, *86 u*	60	65	___[1]
16801	Lionel Railroader Club Bunk Car, *88 u*	28	42	___[1]
16802	Lionel Railroader Club Tool Car, *89 u*	27	33	___[1]
16803	Lionel Railroader Club Searchlight Car, *90 u*	26	30	___[2]
16804	Lionel Railroader Club B/W Caboose, *91 u*	27	38	___[1]
(16805)	Budweiser Malt Nutrine Reefer "3285", *91–92 u*	70	85	___[1]
16806	Toys "R" Us Boxcar, *92 u*	27	31	___[2]
(16807)	H.J. Heinz Reefer "301", *93*	24	28	___[1]
16808	Toys "R" Us Boxcar, *93 u*	37	43	___[1]
16811	Rutland Box Car TCA, *96*			
(16812)	LOTS Grand Trunk 2-bay Hopper, *96 u*	—	60	___[1]
(16813)	LOTS Pa. Power and Light Hopper (Std. O), *97 u*	—	90	___[1]
(16817)	Ambassador 1-D Tank Car "1999", *00 u*	—	70	___[1]
(16818)	Engineer Award Tank Car, *00u*		CP	___
(16819)	JLC Award Tank Car, *00u*		CP	___
(16820)	Ambassador Thank You Boxcar "2000", *00 u*	290	325	___[1]
16829	(See 16529)			

		Exc	New	Cond/$
16830	(See 16530)			
(16901)	Lionel Catalog video (VHS), *91 u*	17	21	___¹
16903	CP Bulkhead Flatcar w/ pulp load (SSS), *94*	22	25	___¹
(16904)	NYC "Pacemaker" TTUX Flatcar set w/ trailers "16905" and "16906", *94*	60	65	___²
16905/16906	NYC "Pacemaker" TTUX Flatcars w/ trailers (See 16904)			
16907	Lionel Flatcar w/ farm tractors, *94*	29	36	___¹
(16908)	US Navy Flatcar "04039" w/ submarine "930", *94–95*	43	50	___¹
(16909)	US Navy Gondola w/ canisters "16556", *94–95*	16	22	___¹
16910	Missouri Pacific Flatcar w/ trailer, *94*	23	28	___¹
16911	NETCA B&M Flatcar w/ trailer "1985", *95*	—	120	___¹
16911	B&M Flatcar w/ trailer, *94*	25	30	___¹
(16912)	CN Maxi-Stack Flatcar set w/ containers "640000" and "640001", *94*	60	65	___¹
(16913)/(16914)	CN Maxi-Stack Flatcars w/ containers "640000" and "640001" (See 16912)			
16915	Lionel Lines Gondola (O27), *93–94 u*	6	9	___¹
16916	Ford Flatcar w/ trailer, *94 u*	40	47	___¹
(16917)	Crayola Gondola w/ crayons, *94 u, 95*	8	9	___¹
(16918)	Budweiser Flatcar w/ trailer, *94*		NM	___
16919	Chrysler Mopar Gondola w/ coil covers, *94 u*	28	33	___¹
(16919)	Chrysler Mopar Gondola w/ coil covers, *94–96*	36	42	___¹
16920	Lionel Flatcar w/ construction block helicopter, *95*		NM	___
16922	Chesapeake &Ohio Flatcar w/ trailer, *95*	24	29	___¹
16923	Lionel Intermodal Service Flatcar w/ wheelchocks, *95*	21	27	___¹
(16924)	Lionel Corporation Trailer-on-Flatcar "6424", *96*	—	29	___¹
16925	New York Central Flatcar w/ trailer, *95*	65	90	___¹
16926	Frisco Flatcar w/ trailers, *95*	22	28	___¹
16927	New York Central Flatcar w/ gondola, *95*	18	23	___¹
16928	Soo Line Flatcar w/ dump bin (O27), *95*	14	19	___¹
16929	BCRail Gondola w/ cable reels, *95*	19	23	___¹
16930	Santa Fe Flatcar w/ wheel load, *95*	20	25	___¹
16932	Erie Flatcar w/ rail load, *95*	18	23	___¹
16933	Lionel Lines Flatcar w/ automobiles, *95*	22	23	___²
16934	Pennsylvania Flatcar w/ Ertl road grader, *95*	31	45	___²
16935	UP Depressed Flatcar w/ Ertl bulldozer, *95*	28	45	___²
(16936)	Sealand Maxi-Stack Flatcar set w/ containers "16937" and "16938", *95*	70	80	___¹

16937/16938 Sealand Maxi-Stack Flatcars w/ containers
(See 16936)

		Exc	New	Cond/$
(16939)	USNavy Flatcar w/ boat "04040", *95*	22	27	___1
(16940)	AT&SF Flatcar w/ trailer, *96–99*	—	40	___1
(16941)	AT&SF Flatcar w/ autos, *96–99*	—	25	___1
16943	Jersey Central Gondola, *96*	—	16	___1
(16944)	Georgia Power Depressed Flatcar *u* w/ transformer "31438", *95*	—	50	___1
(16945)	Georgia Power Depressed Flatcar w/ cable reels "31950", *95 u*	—	50	___1
(16946)	C&O F9 Well Car "3840", *96*	—	32	___2
(16951)	Southern I-Beam Flatcar w/ load "9823", *97*	—	33	___1
16952	USNavy Flatcar w/ Ertl helicopter, *96*	—	30	___2
(16953)	NYCFlatcar w/ Red Wing Shoes trailer "1905-95", *95 u*	33	38	___1
(16954)	NYC Flatcar w/ Ertl Scraper "6424", *96*	—	32	___1
(16955)	AT&SF Flatcar w/ Ertl Challenger, *96*	—	34	___1
(16956)	Zenith Flatcar w/Trailer, *95 u*	—	115	___1
(16957)	Lionel Depressed-Center Flatcar w/ Ertl Case 4WD tractor "6461", *96*	—	29	___1
(16958)	Lionel Flatcar w/ Ertl New Holland loader, *96*	—	29	___1
(16960)	USC.G Flatcar w/ boat, *96*	—	35	___1
(16961)	GM/AC Delco Flatcar w/ trailer, *95*	—	70	___1
(16963)	Lionel Corporation Flatcar "6411", *96–97*	—	33	___1
(16964)	Lionel Corporation Gondola "6462", *97*	—	19	___1
(16965)	Lionel Scout Flatcar w/ stakes "6424", *96–97*	—	20	___1
(16967)	Lionel Depressed-Center Flatcar w/ transformer "6461", *96*	—	29	___1
(16968)	Lionel Aviation Depressed-center Flatcar w/ General Hospital LifeFlight Ertl helicopter "6461", *96*	—	29	___2
(16969)	Flatcar w/ Beechcraft Bonanza "6411", *96*	—	30	___2
(16970)	LA County Flatcar w/ motorized LA County Lifeguard Powerboat "6424", *96*	—	22	___1
(16971)	Port of Lionel City Flatcar w/ boat, *97*	—	35	___1
(16972)	P&LE Gondola "6462", *97*	—	22	___1
(16975)	Lionel Double-stack set "6480", 2 well cars, *97*	—	70	___1
(16978)	MILW Flatcar "6424" w/ P&H shovel kit, *97*	—	39	___1
(16980)	Warner Bros. Speedy Gonzales Missile Flatcar "6823", *97*	—	34	___1
(16982)	BC Rail Bulkhead Flatcar w/ wood load "9823", *97*	—	33	___1
(16983)	PRR F9 Well Car w/ cable reels "6983", *97*	—	37	___1

		Exc	New	Cond/$
(16985)	Ford Eastwood Flatcar w/ Vans, *97 u*	—	47	___1
(16986)	Sears Zenith Flatcar w/ Bulkheads, *96 u*	—	45	___1
(16987)	Musco Lighting Flatcar w/ Bulkheads, *97 u*	—	35	___1
(16997)	Lionel Lines Recovery Crane Car, *99*	—	45	___1
17000	(See 17107)			
17002	Conrail 2-bay ACF Hopper (Std. O), *87*	60	65	___1
17003	Du Pont 2-bay ACF Hopper (Std. O), *90*	50	60	___1
17004	MKT 2-bay ACF Hopper (Std. O), *91*	24	27	___1
17005	Cargill 2-bay ACF Hopper (Std. O), *92*	31	41	___1
17006	Soo Line 2-bay ACF Hopper (Std. O) (SSS), *93*	46	55	___1
(17007)	GN 2-bay ACF Hopper "173872" (Std. O), *94*	29	35	___1
(17008)	D&RGW 2-bay ACF Hopper "10009" (Std. O), *95*	—	28	___1
(17009)	New York Central 2-bay ACF Hopper, *96*	—	32	___1
(17010)	Government du Canada ACF 2-bay Covered Hopper "7000", *98*	—	32	___1
(17011)	NP ACF 2-bay Covered Hoppers "75052", *98*	—	44	___1
(17012)	Government du Canada ACF 2-bay Covered Hopper "7001", *98*	—	41	___1
(17013)	NYC Graffiti 2-bay Coverd Hopper "7000", *99*	—	50	___1
(17014)	Graffiti 2-bay Covered Hopper (Std O), *99*	—	39	___1
(17015)	Corning 2-bay Hopper "90409" (Std. O), *01*	—	40	___1
(17016)	C&NW 2-bay Hopper "96644" (Std. O), *01*	—	40	___1
(17016)	C&NW 2-bay "96644" Hopper, *01*	—	60	___1
(17017)	Chessie System 2-bay Hopper "605527" (Std. O), *02*	—	32	___1
(17018)	Nickel Plate Road Offset Hopper "33074", *02*	—	43	___1
(17019)	Santa Fe Offset Hopper "78299", *02*	—	43	___1
(17020)	Frisco Offset Hopper "92092", *02*	—	43	___1
(17021)	NYC Offset Hopper "867999", *02*	—	43	___1
(17022)	Burlington 2-bay ACF Hopper "183925" (Std. O), *03*		CP	___
(17024)	Reading Offset Hopper "81089" (Std. O), *03*		CP	___
(17025)	C&O Offset Hopper "300027" (Std. O), *03*		CP	___
(17026)	D&H Offset Hopper "7215" (Std. O), *03*		CP	___
(17027)	IC Offset Hopper "92142" (Std. O), *03*		CP	___
(17028)	GE PS-2 2-bay Covered Hopper "326" (Std. O), *03*		CP	___
(17029)	CNJ PS-2 2-bay Covered Hopper "803" (Std. O), *03*		CP	___
(17030)	Milwaukee Road PS-2 2-bay Covered Hopper "99708" (Std. O), *03*		CP	___
(17031)	SP PS-2 2-bay Covered Hopper "401306" (Std. O), *03*		CP	___
17100	Chessie System 3-bay ACF Hopper (Std. O), *88*	38	65	___1

		Exc	New	Cond/$
17101	Chessie System 3-bay ACF Hopper (Std. O), *88*	36	43	___¹
17102	Chessie System 3-bay ACF Hopper (Std. O), *88*	32	37	___¹
17103	Chessie System 3-bay ACF Hopper (Std. O), *88*	27	30	___¹
17104	Chessie System 3-bay ACF Hopper (Std. O), *88*	38	46	___¹
17105	Chessie System 3-bay ACF Hopper (Std. O), *95*	39	46	___¹
17107	Sclair 3-bay ACF Hopper (Std. O), *89*	70	80	___¹
17108	Santa Fe 3-bay ACF Hopper (Std. O), *90*	50	55	___¹
17109	N&W 3-bay ACF Hopper (Std. O), *91*	23	35	___¹
17110	Union Pacific Hopper w/ coal load (Std. O), *91*	23	29	___²
17111	Reading Hopper w/ coal load (Std. O), *91*	26	34	___¹
17112	Erie-Lack. 3-bay ACF Hopper (Std. O), *92*	23	34	___¹
17113	LV Hopper w/ coal load (Std. O), *92–93*	27	33	___¹
17114	Peabody Hopper w/ coal load (Std. O), *92–93*	40	47	___¹
(17118)	Archer Daniels Midland 3-bay ACF Hopper "60029" (Std. O), *93*	32	40	___¹
(17120)	CSX Hopper w/ coal load "295110" (Std. O), *94*	33	42	___¹
(17121)	ICG Hopper w/ coal load "72867" (Std. O), *94*	26	33	___¹
(17122)	RI 3-bay ACF Hopper "800200" (Std. O), *94*	32	39	___¹
(17123)	Cargill Covered Grain Hopper "844304" (Std. O), *95*	29	40	___¹
(17124)	Archer Daniels Midland 3-bay ACF Hopper "50224" (Std. O), *95*	26	33	___¹
(17125)	Goodyear 3-bay ACF Hopper (Std. O), *95*		NM	___
(17127)	Delaware & Hudson 3-bay Hopper, *96*	—	37	___¹
(17128)	Chesapeake & Ohio 3-bay hopper, *96*	—	35	___¹
(17129)	WM 3-bay hopper w/ coal load "9300" (Std O), *97*	—	35	___¹
(17132)	PRR 3-bay SCF Hopper "260815", *98*	—	46	___¹
(17133)	BNSF ACE 3-bay Covered Hopper "403698", *98*	—	38	___¹
(17134)	BNSF 3-bay Covered Hopper "403698" (Std. O), *01*	—	38	___¹
(17135)	BNSF ACF 3-bay Covered Hopper With ETD, *98*	—	38	___¹
(17137)	Cargill 3-bay Covered Hopper "1219" (Std. O), *99*	—	45	___¹
(17138)	Farmers Elevator 3-bay Covered Hopper (Std. O), *99*	—	45	___¹
(17139)	Grain 3-bay Hopper "BLMR 1025", *99–00*	—	44	___¹
(17140)	Virginian 3-bay Hopper "5260-5265" (6-pack), *99*	—	190	___¹
(17143)	Gondola w/ parts load (SSS), 00 (6-pack), *99*	—	25	___¹
(17147)	C&O 3-bay Hopper "156330-156335" (6-pack), *99*	—	190	___¹

		Exc	New	Cond/$
(17154)	Alberta Cylindrical Hopper "628373" (Std. O), _01_	—	35	____[1]
(17155)	Shell Cylindrical Hopper "385206" (Std. O), _01_	—	35	____[1]
(17155)	Shell "3627" Cyl Hopper, _01_	—	40	____[1]
(17156)	ACF Pressureaide 3-bay Hopper "59267" (Std. O), _01_	—	30	____[1]
(17157)	Wonder Bread "56670" 3-bay Hopper, _01_	—	40	____[1]
(17158)	Conrail Coal Hopper "487739" (Std. O), _01_	—	42	____[1]
(17159)	N&W Coal Hopper "1776" (Std. O), _01_	—	45	____[1]
(17170)	General Mills 3-bay Covered Hopper (Std. O), _00u_	—	65	____[1]
17171	Lionel Lion Cylindrical Hopper (Std. O), _01_	—	39	____[1]
(17172)	CP Rail Cylindrical Hopper "385206" (Std. O), _02_	—	37	____[1]
17173	Government of Canada Cylindrical Hopper "111031" (Std. O), _02_	—	33	____[1]
(17174)	GN 3-bay Hopper "171250" (Std. O), _02_	—	33	____[1]
(17175)	IC PS-2CD 4427 Covered Hopper "57031" (Std. O), _02_	—	40	____[1]
(17176)	Cargill PS-2CD 4427 Covered Hopper "2514" (Std. O), _02_	—	40	____[1]
(17177)	PS-2CD 4427 Demonstrator Covered Hopper 2500 (Std. O), _02_	—	40	____[1]
(17178)	Santa Fe PS-2CD 4427 Covered Hopper 304774 (Std. O), _02_	—	40	____[1]
(17179)	Indianapolis Power & Light Coal Hopper "10074", Std. O, _02_	—	40	____[1]
(17180)	Rock Island Coal Hopper "700665", Std. O, _02_	—	40	____[1]
(17181)	NYC 4-bay ACF Centerflow Hopper "892138" (Std. O), _03_		CP	____
(17182)	Sigco, Hybrids 4-bay ACF Centerflow Hopper "1100" (Std. O), _03_		CP	____
(17183)	C&O Hopper "156341" (Std. O), _01_	—	30	____[1]
(17184)	Virginian Hopper "5271" (Std. O), _01_	—	30	____[1]
(17185)	LLCX Bathtub Gondola "877900" (Std. O), _01_	—	36	____[1]
(17186)	Cannonaide 4-bay ACF Centerflow Hopper "96169" (Std. O), _03_		CP	____
(17187)	Rio Grande 4-bay ACF Centerflow Hopper "15521" (Std. O), _03_		CP	____
(17188)	Govt. of Canada 3-bay Cylindrical Hopper "106068" (Std. O), _03_		CP	____
(17189)	Saskatchewan Grain 3-bay Cylindrical Hopper "1625338" (Std. O), _03_		CP	____

		Exc	New	Cond/$
(17190)	Soo/CP 3-bay ACF Hopper "119303" (Std. 0), *03*		CP	___
(17191)	BN PS-2CD 4427 Hopper "450669" (Std. 0), *03*		CP	___
(17192)	Lehigh Valley PS-2CD 4427 Hopper "51118" (Std. 0), *03*		CP	___
(17193)	Chessie System/WM PS-2CD 4427 Hopper "4673" (Std. 0), *03*		CP	___
(17194)	MKT PS-2CD 4427 Hopper "1122" (Std. 0), *03*		CP	___
17200	Canadian Pacific Boxcar (Std. 0), *89*	37	38	___[1]
17201	Conrail Boxcar (Std. 0), *87*	39	45	___[1]
17202	Santa Fe Boxcar w/ Diesel RailSounds (Std. 0), *90*	85	90	___[1]
17203	Cotton Belt DD Boxcar (Std. 0), *91*	33	36	___[1]
17204	Missouri Pacific DD Boxcar (Std. 0), *91*	28	30	___[2]
17207	C&IM DD Boxcar (Std. 0), *92*	32	36	___[1]
17208	Union Pacific DD Boxcar (Std. 0), *92*	30	32	___[1]
(17209)	B&O DD Boxcar "296000" (Std. 0), *93*	38	44	___[1]
(17210)	Chicago & Illinois Midland Boxcar "16021" (Std. 0), *92 u*	30	39	___[1]
(17211)	Chicago & Illinois Midland Boxcar "16022" (Std. 0), *92 u*	30	39	___[1]
(17212)	Chicago & Illinois Midland Boxcar "16023" (Std. 0), *92 u*	24	31	___[1]
(17213)	Susquehanna Boxcar "501" (Std. 0), *93*	31	34	___[1]
17214	Railbox Boxcar w/ Diesel RailSounds (Std. 0), *93*	95	105	___[1]
(17216)	PRR DD Boxcar "60155" (Std. 0), *94*	40	44	___[1]
(17217)	New Haven "State of Maine" Boxcar "45003" (Std. 0), *95*	28	36	___[1]
(17218)	BAR "State of Maine" Boxcar "2184" (Std. 0), *95*	25	33	___[1]
17219	Tazmanian Devil 40th Birthday Boxcar (Std. 0), *95*	32	38	___[1]
17220	Pennsylvania Boxcar (Std. 0), *96*	—	38	___[1]
17221	NYC Boxcar (Std. 0), *96*	—	38	___[1]
17222	Western Pacific Boxcar (Std. 0), *96*	—	38	___[1]
(17223)	Milwaukee Road DD Boxcar, *96*	—	36	___[1]
(17224)	Central of Georgia Boxcar "9464-197" (Std 0), *97*	—	34	___[1]
(17225)	Penn Central Boxcar "9464-297" (Std 0), *97*	—	34	___[1]
(17226)	Milwaukee Road Boxcar "9464-397" (Std 0), *97*	—	34	___[1]
(17227)	UP DD Boxcar "9200" (Std 0), *97*	—	36	___[1]

		Exc	New	Cond/$
(17231)	Wisconsin Central Double-door Boxcar w/ auto frames "9200", *98*	—	40	___[1]
(17232)	Southern Pacific/Union Pacific Merger DD Boxcar "9200", *98*	—	41	___[1]
(17233)	Western Pacific box car "9464-198", *98*	—	27	___[1]
17234	LCCA/LOTS Port Huron & Detroit Boxcar "9464-298", *99*	—	60	___[1]
(17234)	Port Huron & Detroit Boxcar "9464-298", *98*	—	36	___[1]
(17235)	Boston & Maine Boxcar "9464-398", *98*	—	40	___[1]
(17239)	AT&SF Texas Chief Boxcar "9464-1", *97*	—	50	___[1]
(17240)	AT&SF Super Chief Boxcar "9464-2", *97*	—	50	___[1]
(17241)	AT&SF El Capitan Boxcar "9464-3", *97*	—	50	___[1]
(17242)	AT&SF Grand Canyon Boxcar "9464-4", *97*	—	65	___[1]
(17243)	NP Boxcar "8722", *98*	—	48	___[1]
(17244)	Santa Fe Chief Boxcar, *98*	—	39	___[1]
(17245)	C&O Boxcar w/ Chessie Kitten, *98*	—	46	___[1]
(17246)	NYC Pacemaker Rolling Stock 4-pack, *98*	—	190	___[1]
(17247)	NYC 9464 Boxcar "174940", *98*	—	160	___[1]
(17248)	NYC 9464 Boxcar "174945", *98*	—	135	___[1]
(17249)	NYC 9464 Boxcar "174949", *98*	—	135	___[1]
(17250)	UP Boxcar "507406" (Std. O), *99*	—	45	___[1]
(17251)	BNSF Modern Boxcar "103277", *99*	—	37	___[1]
(17252)	NS Modern Boxcar "564824" (Std O), *99*	—	39	___[1]
(17253)	CSX Modern Boxcar "141756" (Std O), *99*	—	39	___[1]
(17254)	Union Pacific Modern Boxcar "551967" (Std O), *99*	—	44	___[1]
(17255)	Chevy Modern DD Boxcar "9200" (Std O), *99*	—	43	___[1]
(17257)	Atlantic Coast Line Boxcar "9464", *99*	—	39	___[1]
(17258)	D&H Boxcar "9464", *99*	—	42	___[1]
(17259)	MKT Boxcar "9464, *99*	—	44	___[1]
(17260)	CP Rail "286138" Boxcar, silver, *00*	—	45	___[1]
(17261)	CP Rail "85154" Boxcar, green, *00*	—	45	___[1]
(17262)	CP Rail "56776" Boxcar, red, *00*	—	48	___[1]
(17263)	NYC Boxcar "45725" (Std O), *00*	—	35	___[1]
(17264)	C&O Boxcar "6054" (Std O), *00*	—	40	___[1]
(17265)	US Army Boxcar, (Std O), *00*	—	39	___[1]
(17266)	Monon Boxcar "911" (Std O), *00*	—	43	___[1]
(17268)	C&O Boxcar 9464, *01*	—	44	___[1]
(17269)	Western Maryland 9464 Boxcar, *01*	—	44	___[1]
(17270)	B&O TimeSaver 9464 Boxcar, *01*	—	42	___[1]
(17271)	The Rock Modern Boxcar "300324" (Std. O), *01*	—	37	___[1]
(17272)	Railbox Modern Boxcar "15150" (Std. O), *01*	—	30	___[1]
(17273)	DT&I DD Boxcar, *01*	—	42	___[1]

		Exc	New	Cond/$
(17274)	Soo Line DD Boxcar, *01*	—	42	___¹
(17275)	NYC PS-1 Boxcar "175008" (Std. O), *02*	—	42	___¹
(17276)	SSW (Cotton Belt) PS-1 Boxcar "75000" (Std. O), *02*	—	41	___¹
(17277)	Rio Grande PS-1 Boxcar "69676" (Std. O), *02*	—	42	___¹
(17278)	WP PS-1 Boxcar "1953" (Std. O), *02*	—	41	___¹
(17279)	Ontario Northland Modern Boxcar "7428" (Std. O), *02*	—	38	___¹
(17280)	Santa Fe DD Boxcar w/ automobile frames 600194 (Std. O), *02*	—	45	___¹
(17285)	CSX Big Blue Modern Boxcar "151296" (Std. O), *03*		CP	___
(17287)	BAR Modern Boxcar "5976" (Std. O), *03*		CP	___
(17288)	NYC PS-1 Boxcar "175012" (Std. O), *03*		CP	___
(17289)	GN PS-1 Boxcar "18485" (Std. O), *03*		CP	___
(17290)	Seaboard PS-1 Boxcar "24452" (Std. O), *03*		CP	___
(17291)	Rock Island PS-1 Boxcar "21110" (Std. O), *03*		CP	___
17300	Canadian Pacific Reefer (Std. O), *89*	31	36	___²
17301	Conrail Reefer (Std. O), *87*	32	37	___¹
17302	Santa Fe Reefer w/ ETD (Std. O), *90*	37	43	___¹
(17303)	C&O Reefer "7890" (Std. O), *93*	26	34	___¹
(17304)	Wabash Reefer "26269" (Std. O), *94*	27	33	___¹
(17305)	Pacific Fruit Express Reefer "459400" (Std. O), *94*	30	40	___¹
(17306)	Pacific Fruit Express Reefer "459401" (Std. O), *94*	24	32	___¹
(17307)	Tropicana Reefer "300" (Std. O), *95*	30	40	___¹
(17308)	Tropicana Reefer "301" (Std. O), *95*	24	32	___¹
(17309)	Tropicana Reefer "302" (Std. O), *95*	25	32	___¹
(17310)	Tropicana Reefer "303" (Std. O), *95*	27	35	___¹
17311	Railway Express Agency Reefer (Std. O), *96*	34	38	___¹
(17314)	Pacific Fruit Express Reefer "9800-198", *98*	—	37	___¹
(17315)	Pacific Fruit Express Reefer "9800-298", *98*	—	37	___¹
(17316)	NP Reefer "98583", *98*	—	50	___¹
(17317)	PRR Reefer FGE "91904", *96*	—	43	___¹
(17318)	UP Refrigerator Car "170650" (Std. O), *99*	—	55	___¹
(17319)	PFE Standard O Reefer 6-pack, *01*	—	300	___¹
(17331)	Hood's General American Milk Car "802" (Std. O), *02*	—	100	___¹
(17332)	Pfaudler General American Milk Car "501" (Std. O), *02*	—	80	___¹
(17334)	REA General American Milk Car "1741" (Std. O), *02*	—	100	___¹

		Exc	New	Cond/$
(17335)	New Haven General American Milk Car "102" (Std. 0), *02*	—	80	___[1]
(17336)	PFE Steel-sided Refrigerator Car "17760" (Std. 0), *03*		CP	___
(17337)	CN Steel-sided Refrigerator Car "209712" (Std. 0), *03*		CP	___
(17338)	Merchants Dispatch Transit Steel-sided Refrigerator Car "12322" (Std. 0), *03*		CP	___
(17339)	Burlington Steel-sided Refrigerator Car 74825" (Std. 0), *03*		CP	___
(17340)	White Bros. General American Milk Car "891" (Std. 0), *03*		CP	___
(17341)	Dairymen"s League General American Milk Car "779" (Std. 0), *03*		CP	___
(17342)	Miller Beer Steel-sided Refrigerator Car (Std. 0), *03 u*		CP	___
(17343)	Miller Beer Steel-sided Refrigerator Car (Std. 0), *03 u*		CP	___
(17349)	NYC General American Milk Car "6581" (Std. 0), *03*		CP	___
(17350)	Hood's General American Milk Car "503" (Std. 0), *03*		CP	___
(17360)	Hood's General American Milk Car "810" (Std. 0), *03*		CP	___
(17361)	Hood's General American Mi k Car "811" (Std. 0), *03*		CP	___
(17362)	Pfaudler General American Milk Car "502" (Std. 0), *03*		CP	___
(17363)	Pfaudler General American Milk Car "503" (Std. 0), *03*		CP	___
(17364)	REA General American Milk Car "1742" (Std. 0), *03*		CP	___
(17365)	REA General American Milk Car "1743" (Std. 0), *03*		CP	___
(17366)	NH General American Milk Car "103" (Std. 0), *03*		CP	___
(17367)	NH General American Milk Car "104" (Std. 0), *03*		CP	___
(17368)	White Brothers General American Milk Car "892" (Std. 0), *03*		CP	___
(17369)	White Brothers General American Milk Car "893" (Std. 0), *03*		CP	___
(17370)	Dairymen"s League General American Milk Car "780" (Std. 0), *03*		CP	___
(17371)	Dairymen"s League General American Milk Car "781" (Std. 0), *03*		CP	___

		Exc	New	Cond/$
(17372)	NYC General American Milk Car "6582" (Std. O), *03*		CP	___
(17373)	NYC General American Milk Car "6583" (Std. O), *03*		CP	___
(17374)	Hood's General American Milk Car (2nd version) "504" (Std. O), *03*		CP	___
(17375)	Hood's General American Milk Car (2nd version) "505" (Std. O), *03*		CP	___
17400	CP Rail Gondola w/ coal load (Std. O), *89*	41	44	___[1]
17401	Conrail Gondola w/ coal load (Std. O), *87*	34	40	___[1]
17402	Santa Fe Gondola w/ coal load (Std. O), *90*	25	31	___[1]
(17403)	Chessie System Gondola w/ coil covers "371629" (Std. O), *93*	25	26	___[1]
(17404)	Illinois Central Gulf Gondola w/ coil covers "245998" (Std. O), *93*	32	36	___[1]
(17405)	Reading Gondola w/ coil covers "24876" (Std. O), *94*	31	35	___[1]
(17406)	PRR Gondola w/ coil covers "385405" (Std. O), *95*	40	45	___[1]
(17407)	NKP Gondola w/ scrap load, *96*	—	33	___[1]
(17408)	Cotton Belt Gondola w/ scrap load "9820" (Std O), *97*	—	33	___[1]
(17410)	UP Gondola w/ scrap "903004" (Std. O), *99*	—	30	___[1]
(17413)	Service Center Gondola w/ parts load (SSS), *00*		CP	___
(17414)	Nickel Plate PS-5 Gondola "44801" (Std. O), *01–02*	—	40	___[1]
(17415)	Frisco PS-5 Gondola "61878" (Std. O), *01–02*	—	40	___[1]
(17416)	D&H Gondola w/ scrap "14011" (Std. O), *01*	—	35	___[1]
(17417)	BN Rotary Bathtub Gondola 3-pack, *01*	—	125	___[1]
(17421)	CSX Rotary Bathtub Gondola 3-pack, *01*	—	120	___[1]
(17425)	Western Maryland PS-5 Gondola "354903" (Std. O), *01–02*	—	40	___[1]
(17426)	Maine Central PS-5 Gondola "1116" (Std. O), *01–02*	—	40	___[1]
(17427)	CSX Rotary Bathtub Gondola Single Unit Add-on (Std. O), *02*	—	43	___[1]
(17428)	BN Rotary Bathtub Gondola Single Unit Add-on (Std. O), *02*	—	39	___[1]
(17429)	Conrail Rotary Bathtub Gondola 3-pack (Std. O), *02–03*	—	105	___[1]
(17433)	BNSF Rotary Bathtub Gondola 3-pack (Std. O), *02–03*	—	105	___[1]
(17439)	UP PS-5 Gondola "229606" (Std. O), *03*		CP	___
(17440)	Algoma Central PS-5 Gondola "801" (Std. O), *03*		CP	___

		Exc	New	Cond/$
(17441)	Conrail Rotary Bathtub Gondola "507673"(Std. 0), *03*		CP	___
(17442)	BNSF Rotary Bathtub Gondola "668330" (Std. 0), *03*		CP	___
(17443)	NS Rotary Bathtub Gondola 3-pack (Std. 0), *03*		CP	___
(17447)	UP Rotary Bathtub Gondola 3-pack (Std. 0), *03*		CP	___
(17455)	(See 52168)			
(17457)	GN PS-5 Gondola "72839" (Std. 0), *03*		CP	___
(17458)	Reading PS-5 Gondola "33267" (Std. 0), *03*		CP	___
17500	CP Flatcar w/ logs (Std. O), *89*	35	38	___[1]
17501	Conrail Flatcar w/ stakes (Std. O), *87*	37	45	___[1]
17502	Santa Fe Flatcar w/ trailer (Std. O), *90*	65	70	___[1]
17503	NS Flatcar w/ trailer (Std. O), *92*	60	70	___[1]
17504	NS Flatcar w/ trailer (Std. O), *92*	60	65	___[1]
17505	NS Flatcar w/ trailer (Std. O), *92*	55	60	___[1]
17506	NS Flatcar w/ trailer (Std. O), *92*	50	55	___[1]
17507	NS Flatcar w/ trailer (Std. O), *92*	55	60	___[1]
17508	BN I-Beam Flatcar w/ load (Std. O), *92*		NM	___
17509	Southerncar w/ load (Std. O), *92*		NM	___
(17510)	NP Flatcar w/ logs "61200" (Std. O), *94*	31	36	___[1]
(17511)	WM Flatcars w/ logs, set of 3 (Std. O), *95*	—	190	___[1]
17512	WM Flatcar w/ logs (Std. O), *95*	39	46	___[1]
17513	WM Flatcar w/ logs (Std. O), *95*	43	50	___[1]
17514	WM Flatcar w/ logs (Std. O), *95*	43	50	___[1]
17515	Norfolk Southern Flatcar w/ tractors (Std. O), *95*	24	43	___[1]
(17516)	T&P Flatcar w/ 2 Beechcraft Bonanzas "9823" (Std O), *97*	—	39	___[2]
(17517)	WP Flatcar w/ Ertl Caterpillar frontloader "9823" (Std O), *97*	—	42	___[1]
(17518)	PRR Flatcar w/ 2 Corgi Mack trucks "9823" (Std O), *97*	—	40	___[1]
(17522)	Flatcar w/ Plymouth Prowler, *98*	—	44	___[1]
(17527)	Flatcar w/ pair of Dodge Vipers, *98*	—	48	___[1]
(17529)	AT&SF Flatcar "90010" w/ Ford milk truck, *99*	—	46	___[1]
(17533)	MTTX Ford Flatcar w/ auto frames, *99*	—	38	___[1]
(17534)	Diamond T Flat "9823" w/ Mack trucks, *99*	—	65	___[1]
(17536)	Route 66 Flatcar w/ 2 luxury coupes "9823-3", *99*	—	37	___[1]
(17537)	Route 66 Flatcar w/ 2 touring coupes "9823-4", *99*	—	39	___[1]
(17538)	NYC Flatcar w/ Ford tow truck, *99*	—	46	___[1]
(17539)	Flatcar w/ 2 Corvettes "9823" (Std. O), *99*	—	70	___[1]
(17540)	Flatcar w/ 2 Corvettes "9823" (Std. O), *99*	—	70	___[1]

		Exc	New	Cond/$
(17546)	Lionel Lines Recovery Flatcar w/ rails "6424", *99*	—	50	___1
(17547)	Lionel Lines Recovery Flatcar w/ machinery "6429", *99*	—	50	___1
(17548)	Route 66 Flatcar w/ 2 luxury coupes "9823-6", *99*	—	43	___1
(17549)	Route 66 Flatcar w/ touring station wagon and trailer "9823-5", *99*	—	43	___1
(17550)	B&N Center Beam Flatcar w/ lumber load "6216" (Std O), *99*	—	39	___1
(17551)	NYC Flatcar w/ NYC Pickups, *99*	—	50	___1
(17553)	Trailer Train Flatcar w/ Combine "98102" (Std. O), *99*	—	125	___1
(17554)	GN Flatcar w/ logs "61042", *00*	—	38	___1
(17555)	Ford Mustang Flatcar w/ 2 cars (Std. O), *01*		CP	___
(17556)	Ford Mustang Flatcar w/ 2 cars (Std. O), *01*		NRS	___
(17557)	Rt. 66 Flatcar "9823-7" w/ black sedans, *99–00*	—	41	___1
(17558)	Rt. 66 Flatcar "9823-8" w/ brown sedans, *99*	—	40	___1
(17559)	Rt. 66 Flatcar w/ 2 wagons "9823-9" (Std. O), *01*	—	40	___1
(17560)	Rt. 66 Flatcar w/ 2 sedans "9823-10" (Std. O), *01*	—	40	___1
(17563)	Santa Fe Flatcar w/ railroad pick-up trucks "90011" (Std. O), *01*	—	49	___1
(17564)	West Side Lumber Shay Log Car 3-pack #2 (Std. O), *01*	—	105	___1
(17568)	PRR Flatcar w/ MOW pick-up trucks "470333" (Std. O), *02*	—	50	___1
(17571)	UP Flatcar w/ MOW pick-up trucks "909231" (Std. O), *03*		CP	___
(17572)	Pioneer Seed Flatcar with Peddle Cars, *02 u*		CP	___
(17573)	WM PS-4 Flatcar "2631" (Std. O), *03*		CP	___
(17574)	Santa Fe PS-4 Flatcar "90081" (Std. O), *03*		CP	___
(17575)	NYC PS-4 Flatcar "506098" (Std. O), *03*		CP	___
(17576)	Ontario Northland PS-4 Flatcar "2020" (Std. O), *03*		CP	___
17600	NYC Woodside Caboose (Std. O), *87 u*	40	47	___2
17601	Southern Woodside Caboose (Std. O), *88*	42	50	___1
17602	Conrail Woodside Caboose (Std. O), *87*	95	110	___1
17603	Rock Island Woodside Caboose (Std. O), *88*	28	60	___2
17604	Lackawanna Woodside Caboose (Std. O), *88*	40	44	___1
17605	Reading Woodside Caboose (Std. O), *89*	30	33	___2
17606	NYC Steelside Caboose w/ smoke (Std. O), *90*	70	75	___1

	Exc	New	Cond/$
17607 Reading Steelside Caboose w/ smoke (Std. O), *90*	55	65	____¹
17608 C&O Steelside Caboose w/ smoke (Std. O), *91*	65	65	____¹
17610 Wabash Steelside Caboose w/ smoke (Std. O), *91*	42	60	____¹
(17611) NYC Woodside Caboose "6003" (Std. O), *90 u, 91*	48	65	____²
17612 NKP Steelside Caboose w/ smoke (FF #6) (Std. O), *92*	65	70	____¹
(17613) Southern Steelside Caboose w/ smoke "7613" (Std. O), *92*	65	70	____¹
17615 Northern Pacific Woodside Caboose w/ smoke (Std. O), *92*	60	65	____¹
17617 D&RGW Steelside Caboose (Std. O), *95*	65	75	____²
17618 Frisco Woodside Caboose (Std. O), *95*	75	75	____¹
(17620) NP Woodside Caboose "1746", *98*	—	70	____¹
(17623) Farmrail EV Caboose, *99*	—	65	____¹
(17624) Conrail Extended Vision Caboose "6900", *99*	—	50	____¹
(17625) Burlington Northern Steel Sided Caboose "7606", *99*	—	65	____¹
(17626) Service Center E/V Caboose (SSS), *00*		CP	____
(17627) C&O E/V Caboose, *01*	—	65	____¹
(17628) BNSF E/V Caboose, *01*	—	65	____¹
(17629) Santa Fe E/V Caboose, *01*	—	65	____¹
(17630) UP E/V Caboose, *01*	—	75	____¹
(17631) Virginian B/W Caboose, *01*	—	70	____¹
(17632) CSX B/W Caboose, *01*	—	65	____¹
(17633) NYC B/W Caboose, *01*	—	75	____¹
(17634) Delaware & Hudson B/W Caboose, *01*	—	75	____¹
(17635) 100th Anniversary DC Gold Caboose "2000", *00*	—	300	____¹
(17636) NYC Die-cast Semi-scale Caboose "18096", *00-01*	—	110	____¹
(17637) NYC/P&LE Die-cast Semi-scale Caboose "21", *00*	—	110	____¹
(17638) Rock Island E/V Caboose "17011", Std. O, *02*	—	55	____¹
(17639) Chessie System E/V Caboose "3322", Std. O, *02*	—	55	____¹
(17640) CP Rail E/V Caboose "434604", Std. O, *02*	—	55	____¹
(17641) Soo Line E/V Caboose "2", Std. O, *02*	—	55	____¹
(17642) Conrail B/W Caboose "21023", Std. O, *02*	—	55	____¹
(17643) Nickel Plate Road B/W Caboose "480", *02*	—	55	____¹

		Exc	New	Cond/$
(17644)	Erie B/W Caboose "C307", Std. O, *02*	—	55	___ [1]
(17645)	N&W B/W Caboose "C-6", Std. O, *02*	—	55	___ [1]
(17646)	UP B/W Caboose "24555", Std. O, *02*	—	55	___ [1]
(17647)	B&O I-12 Caboose "C-2820" (Std. O), *03*		CP	___
(17648)	Chessie System I-12 Caboose "C-2800" (Std. O), *03*		CP	___
(17649)	Lionel Lines I-12 Caboose "7649" (Std. O), *03*		CP	___
(17650)	Rio Grande Extended Vision Caboose "01500" (Std. O), *03*		CP	___
(17652)	NYC B/W Caboose "20200" (Std. O), *03*		CP	___
(17653)	SP B/W Caboose "1337" (Std. O), *03*		CP	___
(17654)	Alaska E/V Caboose "989" (Std. O), *03*		CP	___
(17655)	WP B/W Caboose "448" (Std. O), *03*		CP	___
(17651)	BN E/V Caboose " 10531 " (Std. O), *03*		CP	___
(17664)	B&O I-12 Caboose "C-2824" (Std. O), *03*		CP	___
(17665)	Chessie System I-12 Caboose "C-2802" (Std. O), *03*		CP	___
(17700)	UP ACF 40-ton Stock Car "47456" (Std. O), *01–02*	—	70	___ [1]
(17701)	Rio Grande ACF 40-ton Stock Car "39269" (Std. O), *01–02*	—	60	___ [1]
(17702)	CP ACF 40-ton Stock Car "277083" (Std. O), *01–02*	—	70	___ [1]
(17703)	NYC ACF 40-ton Stock Car "23334" (Std. O), *01–02*	—	70	___ [1]
(17704)	B&O ACF 40-ton Stock Car "110234", (Std. O), *02*	—	40	___ [1]
(17705)	CB&Q ACF 40-ton Stock Car "52886", (Std. O), *02*	—	40	___ [1]
(17707)	Pennsylvania Stockcar "128994" (Std. O), *03*		CP	___
(17708)	CP Rail Stockcar "277313" (Std. O), *03*		CP	___
(17800)	Ontario Northland Ore Car "6126/6021", *00*	—	29	___ [1]
(17801)	CN Ore Car "6126/345165", *00*	—	43	___ [1]
(17802)	CP Ore Car "377249", *00*	—	25	___ [1]
(17803)	DMIR Ore Car "51456", *00*	—	25	___ [1]
(17804)	UP Ore Car "8023", *01*	—	29	___ [1]
(17805)	CP Rail Ore Car "377238", *01*	—	29	___ [1]
(17806)	UP Ore Car "27250", *03*		CP	___
(17807)	BN Ore Car "95887", *02*	—	25	___ [1]
17870	LCCA East Camden & Highland Boxcar (Std. O), *87 u*	42	45	___ [2]
(17871)	TTOS NYC Flatcar w/ Kodak and Xerox trailers "81487", *87 u*	330	375	___ [1]

		Exc	New	Cond/$
(17872)	TTOS Anaconda Ore Car "81988", *88 u*	70	95	___¹
17873	LCCA Ashland Oil 3-D Tank Car, *88 u*	55	65	___¹
(17874)	LOTS MILW Log Dump Car "59629", *88 u*	115	155	___¹
(17875)	LOTS PHD Boxcar "1289", *89 u*	55	65	___¹
17876	LCCA Columbia Newberry & Laurens Boxcar (Std. O), *89 u*	43	47	___²
(17877)	TTOS MKT 1-D Tank Car "3739469", *89 u*	55	70	___¹
17878	Gadsden Pacific Magma Ore Car w/ load, *89 u*	80	95	___¹
(17879)	TCA Valley Forge Dining Car "1989", *89 u*	65	65	___¹
17880	LCCA D&RGW Woodside Caboose (Std. O), *90 u*	65	70	___¹
17881	Gadsden Pacific Phelps-Dodge Ore Car w/ load, *90 u*	36	42	___¹
(17882)	LOTS B&O DD Boxcar w/ ETD "298011", *90 u*	60	70	___¹
(17883)	TCA New Georgia RR Passenger Car "1990", *90 u*	50	60	___¹
17884	TTOS Columbus & Dayton Terminal Boxcar (Std. O), *90 u*	36	47	___¹
17885	Artrain 1-D Tank Car, *90 u*	70	80	___¹
17886	Gadsden Pacific Cyprus Ore Car w/ load, *91 u*	35	39	___¹
17887	LCCA Conrail Flatcar w/ Armstrong Tile trailer (Std. O), *91 u*	44	75	___¹
17888	LCCA Conrail Flatcar w/ Ford New Holland trailer (Std. O), *91 u*	49	70	___¹
(17889)	TTOS SP Flatcar w/ trailer "15791" (Std. O), *91 u*	46	60	___¹
(17890)	LOTS CSX Auto Carrier "151161", *91 u*	85	90	___¹
17891	Artrain Grand Trunk Boxcar, *91 u*	85	110	___¹
(17892)	LCCA Conrail Flatcars w/ trailers (Std. O) (See 17887, 17888)			
(17893)	(See 8392)			
[17893]	LCAC BAOC 1-D Tank Car "914", *91 u*	—	85	___¹
(17894)	TTOS Southern Pacific Tractor, *91 u*	17	21	___¹
(17895)	LCCA Tractor, *91 u*	14	19	___¹
(17896)	LCCA Lancaster Lines Tractor, *91 u*	22	26	___¹
[17897]	VTC Passenger Cars (See 7692)			
(17898)	TCA Wabash Reefer "21596", *92 u*	45	55	___¹
(17899)	LCCA NASA Uni-body Tank Car "190" (Std. O), *92 u*	65	70	___²
17900	Santa Fe Uni-body Tank Car (Std. O), *90*	34	41	___¹
17901	Chevron Uni-body Tank Car (Std. O), *90*	29	35	___²
17902	NJ Zinc Uni-body Tank Car (Std. O), *91*	30	37	___¹
17903	Conoco Uni-body Tank Car (Std. O), *91*	28	34	___¹

		Exc	New	Cond/$
17904	Texaco Uni-body Tank Car (Std. O), *92*	35	44	___[1]
17905	Archer Daniels Midland Uni-body Tank Car (Std. O), *92*	36	46	___[1]
(17906)	SCM Uni-body Tank Car "78286" (Std. O), *93*	43	50	___[1]
17908	Marathon Oil Uni-body Tank Car (Std. O), *95*	43	50	___[1]
17909	Hooker Chemicals Uni-body Tank Car (Std. O), *96*	—	55	___[1]
(17910)	Sunoco Unibody Tank Car "7900", *97*	—	45	___[1]
(17913)	JM Huber Tankcar, *98*	—	37	___[1]
(17914)	Englehard Tank Car, *98*	—	45	___[1]
(17915)	Gulf Uni-Body Tank Car "8438", *00*	—	43	___[1]
(17916)	Burlington Uni-body Tank Car "130000", *00*	—	42	___[1]
(17918)	Southern Unibody Tank Car, *01*	—	32	___[1]
(17919)	Koppers Unibody Tank Car, *01*	—	39	___[1]
(17924)	Safety Kleen Unibody Tank Car "77603" (Std. O), *02*	—	40	___[1]
(17925)	Beefmaster Unibody Tank Car "120021" (Std. O), *02*	—	40	___[1]
(17926)	Cargill Unibody 1-D Tank Car "5836" (Std. O), *03*		CP	___
(17927)	Union Starch Unibody 1-D Tank Car "59137" (Std. O), *03*		CP	___
(17928)	Merck 1-D Tank Car "25421" (Std. O), *03*		CP	___
(17929)	Wyandotte Chemicals 1-D Tank Car "1325" (Std. O), *03*		CP	___
(18000)	PRR 0-6-0 "8977" 89, *91*	420	475	___[4]
(18001)	Rock Island 4-8-4 "5100", *87*	285	320	___[3]
(18002)	NYC 4-6-4 "785", *87 u*	540	590	___[4]
(18003)	Delaware Lackawanna & Western 4-8-4 "1501", *88*	285	345	___[2]
(18004)	Reading 4-6-2 "8004", *89*	215	220	___[2]
(18005)	NYC 4-6-4 "5340" w/ display case, *90*	890	1100	___[4]
(18006)	Reading 4-8-4 "2100", *89 u*	480	550	___[3]
(18007)	Southern Pacific 4-8-4 "4410", *91*	590	620	___[4]
(18008)	Disneyland 35th Anniversary 4-4-0 "4" w/ display case, *90*	225	260	___[1]
(18009)	NYC 4-8-2 "3000", *90 u, 91*	570	750	___[3]
(18010)	PRR 6-8-6 Steam Turbine "6200", *91–92*	1050	1350	___[1]
(18011)	Chessie System 4-8-4 "2101", *91*	600	690	___[2]
(18012)	NYC 4-6-4 "5340", *90*	710	1000	___[1]
(18013)	Disneyland 35th Anniversary 4-4-0 "4", *90*	200	255	___[1]
(18014)	Lionel Lines 2-6-4 "8014", *91*	125	165	___[1]
(18016)	Northern Pacific 4-8-4 "2626", *92*	345	395	___[1]
(18018)	Southern 2-8-2 "4501", *92*	940	980	___[2]

		Exc	New	Cond/$
18021	(See 18030)			
(18022)	Pere Marquette 2-8-4 "1201", *93*	550	650	___[1]
(18023)	Western Maryland Shay "6", *92*	1200	1550	___[3]
(18024)	Sears T&P 4-8-2 "907" w/ display case, *92 u*	730	780	___[2]
(18025)	T&P 4-8-2 "907" (See 18024), *92 u*			
(18026)	Smithsonian NYC Dreyfuss 4-6-4 "5450" (2-rail), *92 u*	—	2300	___[1]
(18027)	NYC Dreyfuss 4-6-4 "5450" (3-rail), *93 u*	—	1700	___[2]
(18028)	Smithsonian Pennsylvania 4-6-2 "3768" (2-rail), *93 u*	—	2500	___[1]
(18029)	NYC Dreyfuss 4-6-4 "5454" (3-rail) w/ operating roller base, *93 u*	1900	2150	___[1]
(18030)	Frisco 2-8-2 "4100", *93 u*	630	700	___[3]
(18031)	Bundesbahn BR-50 2-10-0 (2-rail), *93 u*		NRS	___
(18034)	Santa Fe 2-8-2 "3158", *94*	485	560	___[1]
(18035)	Reichsbahn BR-50 2-10-0 (2-rail), *93 u*		NRS	___
(18036)	French BR-50 2-10-0 (2-rail), *93 u*		NRS	___
(18040)	N&W 4-8-4 "612", *95*	780	870	___[3]
(18041)	Boston &Albany 4-6-4 "619", *95*		NM	___
(18042)	Boston &Albany 4-6-4 "618", *95*	305	295	___[1]
(18043)	Chesapeake &Ohio 4-6-4 "490", *95*	940	1100	___[3]
(18044)	Southern 4-6-2 "1390", *96*	—	300	___[1]
(18045)	"777" Commodore Vanderbilt, *96*	—	780	___[4]
(18046)	Wabash 4-6-4 "700", *96*	225	445	___[3]
(18049)	N&W Warhorse 4-8-2 "600", *96*	—	470	___[1]
(18050)	JC Penney 4-6-2 Steam "2055", *96*	320	355	___[1]
(18052)	"238E" Pennsylvania Torpedo, *97*	—	540	___[2]
(18053)	Berkshire Steam Locomotive 2-8-4 "726", *97*	—	910	___[3]
(18054)	NYC Switcher 0-4-0 "1665", black, *97*	—	140	___[1]
(18056)	"763E" NYC J1-e Hudson Steam Locomotive and Vanderbilt Tender, *97*	—	820	___[2]
(18057)	Century Steam Locomotive 6-8-6 "671", *97*	—	850	___[2]
(18058)	Hudson Steam Locomotive 4-6-4 "773", *97*	—	980	___[1]
(18059)	Western Maryland Baby Pacific 4-2 Loco Deluxe "209", *98*		NM	___
(18062)	AT&SF 4-6-4 Hudson L/T "3447", *97*	—	790	___[1]
(18063)	NYC Commodore Vanderbilt 4-6-4, *99*	—	1150	___[1]
(18064)	New York Central 4-8-2 Mohawk L-3A Steam Engine w/ Tender "3000", *98*	570	830	___[2]
(18067)	Commodore Vanderbilt Special Edition, *97*	1050	1300	___[2]
(18070)	Western Maryland Baby Pacific 4-2 Locomotive "208", *98*		NM	___

		Exc	New	Cond/$
(18071)	Southern Pacific Daylight Locomotive "4449", *98*	—	710	___2
(18072)	Lionel Lines Torpedo Engine w/ Tender, *98*	—	400	___2
(18079)	NYC Mikado 2-8-2 "1967", *99*	—	670	___1
(18080)	Denver & Rio Grande Mikado 2-8-2 "1210", *99*	—	700	___1
(18082)	NYC Hudson 4-6-4 "5404", *99*	—	220	___1
(18083)	C&O Hudson 4-6-4 "305", *99*	—	190	___1
(18084)	Santa Fe Hudson 4-6-4 "305", *99*	—	215	___1
(18085)	NH Pacific 4-6-2 "1334", *99*	—	275	___1
(18086)	NYC Pacific 4-6-2 "4929", *99*	—	265	___1
(18087)	Santa Fe Pacific 4-6-2 "3448", *99*	—	275	___1
(18088)	SP Pacific 4-6-2 "1407", *99*	—	350	___1
(18089)	CNJ Camelback 4-6-0 "771", *99*	—	405	___1
(18090)	LCCA D&RGW 4-6-2 "1990", *90 u*	270	330	___1
(18091)	PRR Camelback 4-6-0 "821", *99*	—	435	___1
(18092)	SP Camelback 4-6-0 "2283", *99*	—	440	___1
(18093)	C&NW Camelback 4-6-0 "3006", *99*	—	375	___1
(18094)	B&O E6 4-4-2 Atlantic, Command Control, *99–00*	—	350	___1
(18095)	Pennsylvania E6 4-4-2 Atlantic, Command Control, *99–00*	—	455	___1
(18096)	AT&SF E6 4-4-2 Atlantic, Command Control, *99–00*	—	435	___1
(18097)	CNJ Camelback 4-6-0 "770", *99*	—	330	___1
(18098)	PRR Camelback 4-6-0 "820", *99*	—	355	___1
(18099)	SP Camelback 4-6-0 "2282", *99*	—	370	___1
(18100)	Santa Fe F-3 A Unit "8100" (See 11711)			
(18101)	Santa Fe F-3 B Unit "8101" (See 11711)			
(18102)	Santa Fe F-3 A Unit Dummy "8102" (See 11711)			
(18103)	Santa Fe F-3 B Unit Dummy "8103", *91 u*	220	235	___2
(18104)	Great Northern F-3 A Unit Dummy "366A" (See 11724)			
(18105)	Great Northern F-3 B Unit Dummy "370B" (See 11724)			
(18106)	Great Northern F-3 A Unit Dummy "351C" (See 11724)			
(18107)	D&RGW Alco PA-1 ABA set "6001" and "6002", *92*	720	860	___3
(18108)	Great Northern F-3 B Unit "371B", *93*	95	105	___1
(18109)	Erie Alco A Unit "725A" (See 11734)			
(18110)	Erie Alco B Unit "725B" (See 11734)			
(18111)	Erie Alco A Unit Dummy "736A" (See 11734)			
(18112)	TCA F-3 A Unit "40" (See 11737)			

		Exc	New	Cond/$
(18113)	TCA F-3 B Unit (See 11737)			
(18114)	TCA F-3 A Unit Dummy "40" (See 11737)			
(18115)	Santa Fe F-3 B Unit, *93*	105	135	___[1]
(18116)	Erie-Lackawanna Alco PA-1 AA set "858"	465	740	___[3]
	and "859", *93*			
(18117)/(18118)	Santa Fe F-3 AA set "200", *93*	300	340	___[1]
(18119)/(18120)	UP Alco AA set "8119" and "8120", *94*	215	255	___[1]
(18121)	Santa Fe F-3 B Unit "200A", *94*	70	95	___[1]
(18122)	Santa Fe F-3 B Unit "200B", *95*	195	220	___[1]
(18123)	ACL F-3 A Unit "342" (See 11903)			
(18124)	ACL F-3 B Unit "342B" (See 11903)			
(18125)	Atlantic Coast Line F-3 A Unit Dummy "343"			
	(See 11903)			
(18128)	Santa Fe F-3 A Unit "2343", *96*	—	465	___[1]
(18129)	Santa Fe F-3 B Unit w/ RS II, *96*	—	325	___[1]
(18130)	Santa Fe F-3 Diesel Locomotive AB set, *96*	—	700	___[2]
(18131)	NP F-3 AB set, "2390A", "2390C", *97*	—	455	___[2]
(18132)	Santa Fe F-3 A Powered (See 18130)			
(18133)	Santa Fe F-3 A Dummy (See 18130)			
(18134)	Santa Fe F-3 A Unit Dummy "2343", *97*	—	190	___[1]
(18135)	NYC F-3 AA Diesel "2333", *97*	—	800	___[2]
(18136)	AT&SF F-3 B Unit w/ Railsounds "2343C", *97*	—	250	___[1]
(18138)	Milwaukee Road F3 A, "75A", (See 18140)			
(18139)	Milwaukee Road F3 B, "2378B", *98*		NRS	___
(18140)	Milwaukee Road F3 A-B Diesel Locomotive	—	670	___[2]
	"75A", *98*			
(18145)	NP F-3 A Unit "2390A", *97*	—	285	___[1]
(18146)	NP F-3 B Unit "2390C", *97*	—	150	___[1]
(18147)	NP F-3 AB Units "2390A, 2390C", *97*	500	570	___[2]
(18149)	Union Pacific Veranda Gas Turbine "61", *98*	—	890	___[1]
(18154)	Deluxe Santa Fe FT AA "168", *98–00*	—	375	___[1]
(18155)	Deluxe Santa Fe FT A Powered (See 18154)			
(18156)	Deluxe Santa Fe FT A Dummy (See 18154)			
(18157)	Santa Fe FT AA "158", *98–00*	—	210	___[1]
(18158)	Santa Fe FT A Powered (See 18157)			
(18159)	Santa Fe FT A Dummy (See 18157)			
(18160)	New York Central Deluxe FT AA "1603",	—	435	___[1]
	"2403", *98–00*			
(18161)	(See 18160)			
(18162)	(See 18160)			
(18163)	New York Central FT AA Unit, "1600",	—	300	___[1]
	"2400", *98–00*			
(18164)	(See 18163)			

		Exc	New	Cond/$
(18165)	(See 18163)			
(18166)	B&O FT AA, Command Control, *99–00*	—	375	___1
(18169)	B&O FT AA, Traditional, *99–00*	—	325	___1
(18178)	NYC F-3 B Unit Century Club, *98 u*	—	200	___1
(18189)	Army of Potomoc Operating Stock Car, *99*	—	45	___1
(18190)	McNeil's Rangers Operating Stock Car "2", *99*	—	45	___1
(18191)	WP F-3 A-A, *98*	—	850	___2
(18192)	WP F3 A Powered (See 18191)			
(18193)	WP F-3 A Dummy (See 18191)			
(18197)	WP F3 B-Unit "2355C", *99*	—	200	___1
(18198)	WP F3 B-Unit "2355C" Command Control, *99*	—	285	___1
(18200)	Conrail SD-40 "8200", *87*	210	235	___1
(18201)	Chessie System SD-40 "8201", *88*	305	355	___1
(18202)	Erie-Lackawanna SD-40 Dummy "8459", *89 u*	120	190	___1
(18203)	CP Rail SD-40 "8203", *89*	230	295	___2
(18204)	Chessie System SD-40 Dummy "8204", *90 u*	140	195	___1
(18205)	Union Pacific Dash 8-40C "9100", *89*	190	230	___4
(18206)	Santa Fe Dash 8-40B "8206", *90*	205	250	___2
(18207)	Norfolk Southern Dash 8-40C "8689", *92*	220	255	___1
(18208)	BN SD-40 Dummy "8586", *91 u*	155	225	___1
(18209)	CP Rail SD-40 Dummy "8209", *92 u*	185	250	___1
(18210)	Illinois Central SD-40 "6006", *93*	200	220	___1
(18211)	Susquehanna Dash 8-40B "4002", *93*	190	220	___1
(18212)	Santa Fe Dash 8-40B Dummy "8212", *93*	160	185	___1
(18213)	Norfolk Southern Dash 8-40C "8688", *94*	220	235	___2
(18214)	CSX Dash 8-40C "7500", *94*	270	290	___1
(18215)	CSX Dash 8-40C "7643", *94*	265	290	___2
(18216)	Conrail SD-60M "5500", *94*	330	355	___2
(18217)	Illinois Central SD-40 "6007", *94*	235	250	___1
(18218)	Susquehanna Dash 8-40B "4004", *94*	200	220	___1
(18219)	C&NW Dash 8-40C "8501", *95*	335	340	___1
(18220)	C&NW Dash 8-40C "8502", *95*	255	280	___2
(18221)	D&RGW SD-50 "5512", *95*	435	495	___1
(18222)	D&RGW SD-50 "5517", *95*	305	355	___2
(18223)	Milwaukee Road SD-40 "154", *95*	375	380	___1
(18224)	Milwaukee Road SD-40 "155", *95*	260	290	___1
(18226)	GE Dash 9 Diesel Locomotive, *97*	—	315	___2
(18228)	SP Dash 9 "8228", black, red nose, *97*	—	345	___2
(18229)	SP SD40 Diesel Warhorse "7333", *98*	—	450	___1
(18231)	BNSF Dash 9 Diesel Locomotive Deluxe "739", *98*	—	380	___2
(18232)	SOO Line SD-60 Diesel "5500", *97*	—	390	___1
(18233)	BNSF Dash 9 Diesel Locomotive "745", *98*	—	330	___1

		Exc	New	Cond/$
(18234)	BNSF Dash 9 "740" Command Control, *98–99*	—	405	___1
(18235)	BNSF Dash 9 Diesel Locomotive 2-pack "739", "740", *98*	—	710	___1
(18238)	Conrail SD70 "4145", *99–00*	—	300	___1
(18239)	(See 18229), *98*	—	400	___1
(18240)	Conrail Dash 8-40B "5065" Command Control, *98*	—	285	___1
(18241)	BN SD70 "9413", *99–00*	—	385	___1
(18245)	PRR Alco PA-1 AA "5750", *99*	—	540	___1
(18248)	PRR Alco PB-1 "5750B", *99*	—	250	___1
(18249)	Erie Alco PB-1 "850B", *00*	—	250	___1
(18250)	BNSF SD70 "9870", *99–00*	—	365	___1
(18251)	CSX SD60 "8701", *99–00*	—	350	___1
(18252)	Amtrak Dash 9, Command Control, *99*	—	285	___1
(18253)	BNSF Dash 9, Command Control, *99*	—	305	___1
(18254)	AT&SF Dash 9, Command Control, *99*	—	340	___1
(18255)	NS Dash 9, Commmand Control, *99*	—	315	___1
(18256)	Amtrak Dash 9, Traditional, *99*	—	190	___1
(18257)	BNSF Dash 9, Traditional, *99*	—	190	___1
(18258)	AT&SF Dash 9, Traditional, *99*	—	205	___1
(18259)	NS Dash 9, Traditional, *99*	—	215	___1
(18260)	Conrail SD70 "4144", *99–00*	—	265	___1
(18261)	BN SD60 "9412", *99–00*	—	255	___1
(18262)	BNSF SD70 "9869", *99–00*	—	250	___1
(18263)	CSX SD60 "8700", *99–00*	—	235	___1
(18264)	SD70M Southern Pacific "8238", *99–00*	—	245	___1
(18265)	SD70M Southern Pacific "9803", *99–00*	—	340	___1
(18266)	Norfolk Southern SD60 "6552", CC, *01–02*	—	400	___1
(18268)	Lionel Centennial SD90MAC "2000", Command Control, *00*	—	320	___1
(18269)	UP SD90MAC "8006", Command Control, *00*	—	345	___1
(18270)	UP SD90MAC "8007", Traditional, *00*	NM		___
(18271)	CP SD90MAC "9129", Command Control, *00*	—	315	___1
(18272)	CP SD90MAC "9130", Traditional, *00*	NM		___
(18273)	UP SD40MAC "8071", *99–00*	—	300	___1
(18274)	Burlington U30C "891"(CC), *01*	—	325	___1
(18276)	Seaboard U30C "7274", CC, *01*	—	295	___1
(18278)	UP U30C "2938", CC, *01*	—	305	___1
(18280)	Maersk SD70, CC, *00*	—	300	___1
(18281)	BNSF Dash 9-44CW "788", Command Control, *00*	—	340	___1
(18282)	BNSF Dash 9-44CW "789", Traditional, *00*	—	225	___1

		Exc	New	Cond/$
(18283)	CSX Dash 9-44CW "9019", Command Control, *00*	—	325	___1
(18284)	CSX Dash 9-44CW "9020", Traditional, *00*	—	300	___1
(18285)	UP Dash 9-44C "9659", CC, *01*	—	325	___1
(18286)	Amtrak Dash 8-32BWH "509", CC, *01*	—	325	___1
(18287)	CN Dash 9-44C "2529", CC, *01*	—	335	___1
(18288)	Odyssey System SD70, CC, *00u*	—	400	___1
(18290)	UP Dash 9-44CW "9717", CC, *01*	—	355	___1
(18291)	BNSF Dash 8-32BWH "580", CC, *02*	—	340	___1
(18292)	Chessie GE U30C Diesel "3312", CC, *02*	—	340	___1
(18293)	Santa Fe U30C, CC, *03*		CP	___
(18294)	Alaska SD70MAC "4005", CC, *01–02*	—	370	___1
(18295)	Conrail SD80MAC "7200", CC, *02–03*	—	355	___1
(18296)	CSX SD80MAC "801", CC, *02–03*	—	355	___1
(18297)	NYC SD80MAC "9914", CC, *02–03*	—	355	___1
(18298)	UP Desert Victory SD40-2 "3593", CC, *02–03*	—	340	___1
(18299)	CP Rail SD40-2 "5420", CC, *02–03*	—	355	___1
(18300)	PRR GG-1 "8300", *87*	460	520	___2
(18301)	Southern FM Trainmaster "8301", *88*	220	250	___3
(18302)	GN EP-5 "8302" (FF#3), *88*	245	320	___2
(18303)	Amtrak GG-1 "8303", *89*	405	475	___5
(18304)	Lackawanna MU Car set Powered and Dummy "2401" and "2402", *91*	455	520	___2
(18305)	Lackawanna MU Car set, Dummies "2400" and "2403", *92*	250	275	___1
(18306)	PRR MU Car set, Powered and Dummy "4574" and "483", *92*	285	345	___2
(18307)	PRR FM TrainMaster "8699", *94*	265	295	___2
(18308)	PRR GG-1 "4866", *92*	235	275	___2
(18309)	Reading FM Trainmaster "863", *93*	260	290	___2
(18310)	PRR MU Car set, Dummies "484" and "485", *93*	265	345	___1
(18311)	Disney EP-5 "8311", *94*	270	345	___3
(18313)	Pennsylvania GG-1 "4907", *96*	—	335	___2
(18314)	Pennsylvania GG-1 "2332", 5 gold stripes, *97*	—	660	___2
(18315)	Virginian E33 Recifier Electric "2329", *97*	—	255	___1
(18319)	New Haven EP-5 (Rectifier), *99*	—	320	___1
(18321)	CNJ Trainmaster "2341", *99*	—	415	___2
(18322)	Lackawanna Trainmaster "2321", *99*	—	475	___1
(18326)	PRR GG-1 Congressional, *00*		NRS	___
(18327)	Virginian 2331 FM Trainmaster, *99–00*	—	435	___2
(18328)	NH MU Commuter Set "4082/4083", CC, *00*	—	450	___1
(18331)	Reading MU Commuter Set "9109/10", CC, *00*	—	475	___1

		Exc	New	Cond/$
(18334)	NH MU Dummy Set "4084/5", CC, *01*	—	180	___¹
(18337)	Reading MU Dummy Set "9111/2", CC, *01*	—	220	___¹
(18340)	Lionel Century Club II FM Demo trainmaster,	—	900	___¹
	"TM-1", "TM-2", *00 u*			
(18343)	PRR GG-1 "2332", black, CC, *01*	—	460	___¹
(18344)	LI MU Powered Set "1163/4", CC, *01*	—	470	___¹
(18347)	IC MU Powered Set "1204/5", CC, *01*	—	470	___¹
(18350)	Archive Lionel EP-5 "2350", CC, *01*		NM	___
(18353)	Pennsylvania E-33 Rectifier "4403", CC, *02*	—	275	___¹
(18400)	Santa Fe Vulcan Rotary Snowplow "8400", *87*	165	215	___²
(18401)	Workmen Handcar, *87–88*	36	46	___²
18402	Lionel Lines Burro Crane, *88*	75	90	___²
18403	Santa Claus Handcar, *88*	29	39	___¹
18404	San Francisco Trolley "8404", *88*	75	125	___²
18405	Santa Fe Burro Crane, *89*	85	105	___²
18406	Lionel Track Maintenance Car, *89, 91*	46	60	___¹
(18407)	Snoopy and Woodstock Handcar, *90–91*	46	75	___¹
(18408)	Santa Claus Handcar, *89*	34	46	___¹
18410	PRR Burro Crane, *90*	110	115	___¹
18411	Canadian Pacific Fire Car, *90*	90	115	___¹
18412	Union Pacific Fire Car, *91*		NM	___
(18413)	Charlie Brown and Lucy Handcar, *91*	28	55	___¹
(18416)	Bugs Bunny and Daffy Duck Handcar, *92–93*	110	145	___¹
18417	Lionel Gang Car, *93*	60	75	___¹
(18419)	Lionelville Electric Trolley "8419", *94*	90	105	___²
(18421)	Sylvester and Tweety Handcar, *94*	48	65	___¹
(18422)	Santa and Snowman Handcar, *94*	39	46	___¹
(18423)	On-Track Step Van, *95*	28	35	___²
(18424)	On-Track Pick-up Truck, *95*	27	35	___²
(18425)	Goofy and Pluto Handcar, *95*	32	43	___¹
(18426)	Santa and Snowman Handcar, *95*	32	38	___¹
(18427)	Tie-Jector "55", *97*	—	65	___²
(18429)	Workmen Handcar, *96*	—	40	___¹
(18430)	Crew Car, *96*	—	37	___²
(18431)	Trolley Car, *96–97*	—	60	___¹
(18433)	Mickey and Minnie Handcar, *96–97*	—	46	___¹
(18434)	Porky and Petunia Handcar, *96*	—	33	___²
(18436)	Dodge Ram Track Inspection Vehicle, *97*	—	55	___²
(18438)	Pennsylvania High-rail Vehicle "49", *98*	—	45	___¹
(18439)	Union Pacific High-rail Maintenance Vehicle, *98*	—	41	___¹
(18440)	NJ Transit High-rail Inspection Vehicle, *98*	—	50	___¹
(18444)	Lionelville Fire Car (SSS), *98*	—	150	___¹
(18445)	NYC Fire Car, *98*	—	90	___¹

		Exc	New	Cond/$
(18446)	GN Rotary Snowplow "58", *99*	—	210	___ 2
(18447)	Executive Inspection Vehicle, *99*	—	135	___ 2
(18452)	Boston Trolley "3321", *99–00*	—	55	___ 1
(18454)	Blue Executive Inspection Car (#68), *00*	—	95	___ 2
(18455)	NYC Tie-Jector "X-2", *00–01*	—	70	___ 1
(18456)	Postwar Minuteman Motorized Unit "59", *01–02*	—	230	___ 1
(18457)	Postwar Handcar "65", *00–01*	—	45	___ 1
(18458)	D&RG Snowplow 53, *00*	—	185	___ 1
(18459)	Christmas Handcar, *01*	—	40	___ 1
(18461)	Lionel Track Cleaner, *02–03*		CP	___
(18463)	Hot Rod Inspection Vehicle, *01–02*	—	100	___ 1
(18464)	Postwar Track Ballast Tamper "54", *02–03*	—	170	___ 1
(18465)	Postwar Gang Car "50", *03*		CP	___
(18466)	UP Rotary Snow Plow, *01–02*	—	160	___ 1
(18468)	CN Railroad Speeder, *03*		CP	___
(18469)	Chessie System Railroad Speeder, *03*		CP	___
(18470)	Lionel Postwar Fire Car "52", *02*	—	125	___ 1
(18471)	UP GP-20 "1977", *03*		CP	___
(18473)	Lehigh Valley GP-20 "310", *03*		CP	___
(18476)	Mickey and Minnie Mouse Handcar, *03*		CP	___
(18474)	Postwar US Army Switcher "41", *03*		CP	___
(18475)	Toy Story Handcar, *03*		CP	___
(18481)	Christmas Yuletide Trolley, *03*		CP	___
(18500)	Milwaukee Road GP-9 "8500" (FF#2), *87*	200	225	___ 2
(18501)	WM NW-2 "8501" (FF#4), *89*	255	260	___ 2
(18502)	Lionel Lines 90th Anniversary GP-9 "1900", *90*	135	155	___ 1
(18503)	Southern Pacific NW-2 "8503", *90*	230	250	___ 3
(18504)	Frisco GP-7 "504" (FF#5), *91*	140	160	___ 2
(18505)	NKP GP-7 Powered and Dummy set "400" and "401" (FF#6), *92*	280	355	___ 1
(18506)	CN Budd RDC Powered and Dummy set "D202" and "D203", *92*	210	240	___ 3
(18507)	CN Budd RDC Baggage Powered "D202", *92*	50	75	___ 1
(18508)	CN Budd RDC Passenger Dummy "D203", *92*	125	150	___ 1
(18510)	CN Budd RDC Passenger Dummy "D200"	50	75	___ 1
(18511)	CN Budd RDC Passenger Dummy "D250"	50	75	___ 1
(18512)	CN Budd RDC Dummies set "D200" and "D250", *93*	110	170	___ 1
(18513)	NYC GP-7 "7420", *94*	125	145	___ 2
(18514)	Missouri Pacific GP-7 "4124", *95*	225	260	___ 1
(18515)	Lionel Steel Vulcan Diesel "57" (SSS), *96*	—	190	___ 1

		Exc	New	Cond/$
(18516)	Phantom III Locomotive, CC, *02*	—	300	___[1]
(18550)	JC Penney MILW GP-9 "8500" w/ display case, *87 u*	180	245	___[1]
(18551)	JC Penney Susquehanna RS-3 "8809" w/ display case, *89 u*	175	190	___[1]
(18552)	JC Penney DM&IR SD-18 "8813" w/ display case, *90 u*	165	190	___[1]
(18553)	Sears UP GP-9 "150" w/ display case, *91 u*	180	215	___[1]
(18554)	JC Penney GM&O RS-3 "721" w/ display case, *92–93 u*	200	230	___[1]
(18555)	Sears C&IM SD-9 "52", *92 u*	165	190	___[1]
(18556)	Sears Chicago & Illinois Midland Caboose and Freight Car set, *92 u*	145	155	___[1]
(18557)	Chessie System 4-8-4 "2101" w/ display case for export, *92 u*		NRS	___
(18558)	JC Penney MKT GP-9 "91" w/ display case, *94 u*	165	190	___[1]
(18562)	SP GP-9 "2380", *96*	—	215	___[1]
(18563)	NYC GP-9 "2380", *96*	—	215	___[1]
(18564)	CP GP-9 "2380", *97*	—	205	___[1]
(18565)	Milwaukee GP-9 "2338", *97*	—	220	___[1]
(18566)	CR SD-20 "8495" (SSS), *97*	—	155	___[1]
(18567)	PRR GP-9 "2028", *97*	—	225	___[1]
(18569)	Chicago Burlington & Quincy GP-9 Diesel "2380", *98*	—	245	___[2]
(18573)	Santa Fe GP-9 Diesel Freight "2380", *98*	—	155	___[1]
(18574)	Milwaukee Road GP-20 "975", *98*	—	250	___[1]
(18575)	Custom Series I GP-9 "2398", *98*	—	355	___[1]
(18576)	Southern Pacific GP-9 nonpowered B Unit "2385", *98*	—	135	___[1]
(18577)	New York Central GP-9 nonpowered B Unit "2385", *98*	—	145	___[1]
(18579)	Milwaukee GP-9 nonpowered "2384", *99*	—	135	___[1]
(18580)	Pennsylvania GP-9 B Unit "2027", *98*	—	145	___[1]
(18582)	Seaboard NW-2 Switcher, *98*	—	435	___[1]
(18583)	AEC-57 Switcher, *98*	—	245	___[1]
(18585)	Centennial SD40 "1999", *99*	—	570	___[1]
(18587)	Nickel Plate C-420 "577", CC, *99–01*	—	240	___[1]
(18588)	D&H C-420 "412", CC, *99–01*	—	240	___[1]
(18589)	LV C-420 "409", CC, *99–01*	—	265	___[1]
(18590)	Nickel Plate C-420 "578", Traditional, *99–01*	—	170	___[1]
(18591)	D&H C-420 "411", Traditional, *99–01*	—	170	___[1]
(18592)	LV C-420 "410", Traditional, *99–01*	—	165	___[1]

		Exc	New	Cond/$
(18595)	D&H RS-11 "5002", Traditional, *99–00*		NM	___
(18596)	D&H RS-11 "5001", CC, *99–01*	—	335	___¹
(18597)	NYC RS-11 "8011", Traditional, *99–00*		NM	___
(18598)	NYC RS-11 "8010", CC, *99–01*	—	330	___¹
(18599)	C&O GP-38 "3855", *99–00*	—	145	___¹
(18600)	ACL 4-4-2 "8600", *87 u*	65	75	___¹
(18601)	Great Northern 4-4-2 "8601", *88*	80	95	___¹
(18602)	PRR 4-4-2 "8602", *87*	75	85	___¹
(18604)	Wabash 4-4-2 "8604", *88–91*	65	75	___¹
(18605)	Mopar Express 4-4-2 "1987", *87–88 u*	75	120	___¹
(18606)	NYC 2-6-4 "8606", *89*	150	165	___¹
(18607)	Union Pacific 2-6-4 "8607", *89*	130	155	___¹
(18608)	D&RGW 2-6-4 "8608" (SSS), *89*	105	125	___¹
(18609)	Northern Pacific 2-6-4 "8609", *90*	150	170	___¹
(18610)	Rock Island 0-4-0 "8610", *90*	105	115	___¹
(18611)	Lionel Lines 2-6-4 "8611" (SSS), *90*	120	135	___¹
(18612)	C&NW 4-4-2 "8612", *89*	75	90	___¹
(18613)	NYC 4-4-2 "8613", *89 u*	75	95	___¹
(18614)	Circus Train 4-4-2 "1989", *89 u*	85	110	___¹
(18615)	GTW 4-4-2 "8615", *90*	70	85	___¹
(18616)	Northern Pacific 4-4-2 "8616", *90 u*	85	110	___¹
(18617)	Adolphus III 4-4-2, *89–92 u*	100	125	___¹
(18618)	B&O 4-4-2 "8618", *91*		NM	___
(18620)	Illinois Central 2-6-2 "8620", *91*	170	195	___¹
(18621)	Western Pacific 0-4-0 "8621", *92*		NM	___
(18622)	Union Pacific 4-4-2 "8622", *90–91 u*	65	80	___¹
(18623)	Texas & Pacific 4-4-2 "8623", *92*	80	110	___¹
(18625)	Illinois Central 4-4-2 "8625", *91 u*	70	95	___¹
(18626)	Delaware & Hudson 2-6-2 "8626", *92*	125	135	___¹
(18627)	C&O 4-4-2 "8627" or "8633", *92, 93 u, 94, 95 u*	75	95	___¹
(18628)	MKT 4-4-2 "8628", *92, 93 u*	70	85	___¹
(18630)	C&NW 4-6-2 "2903", *93*	330	355	___¹
(18632)	NYC 4-4-2 "8632", *93–95*	75	95	___¹
(18632)	C&O 4-4-2 Columbia "8632", *97–99*	75	95	___¹
(18633)	C&O 4-4-2 "8633", *94–95*	65	85	___¹
(18633)	Union Pacific 4-4-2 "8633", *93–95*	65	85	___¹
(18635)	Santa Fe 2-6-4 "8625", *93*	160	160	___¹
(18636)	B&O 4-6-2 "5300", *94*	330	350	___¹
(18637)	United Auto Workers 4-4-2 "8633", *93 u*	—	90	___¹
(18638)	Norfolk & Western 2-6-4 "638", *94*	170	220	___¹
(18639)	Reading 4-6-2 "639", *95*	130	155	___¹
(18640)	Union Pacific 4-6-2 "8640", *95*	110	130	___¹

		Exc	New	Cond/$
(18641)	Ford 4-4-2 "8641", *94 u*	65	85	___1
(18642)	Lionel Lines 4-6-2 "8642", *95*	110	130	___1
(18644)	AT&SF 4-4-2 Columbia "8644", *96–99*	75	90	___1
(18648)	Sears Zenith 4-4-2 "8632", *96 u*	—	100	___1
(18649)	Chevrolet 4-4-2 "USA-1", *96 u*	—	100	___1
(18650)	Lionel Lines 4-4-2 Columbia "X-1110", *96–99*	95	120	___1
(18653)	B&A 4-6-2 Pacific "2044", *97*	—	170	___1
(18654)	SP 4-6-2 Pacific "2044", *97*	—	150	___1
(18656)	Bloomingdale's 4-4-2 Columbia "8632", *96*	—	100	___1
(18657)	Sears Zenith 4-4-2 Columbia "8632", *96*	—	100	___1
(18658)	LL Little League 4-4-2 Columbia "X-1110", *97*	—	90	___1
(18660)	Canadian National 4-6-2 w/ Tender "2044", *98*	—	195	___1
(18661)	Norfolk & Western 4-6-2 w/ Tender "2044", *98*	—	170	___1
(18662)	Pennsylvania 0-4-0 Switcher, *98*	—	225	___1
(18666)	SP&S 4-6-2 Pacific "2044", *97*	—	200	___1
(18668)	Bloomingdale's 4-4-2 Columbia "8632", *97*	—	120	___1
(18669)	IC/JC Penney 4-6-2 Pacific "2099", *98*	—	235	___1
(18670)	D&H 4-4-2 Columbia "1400", *98*	—	80	___1
(18671)	N&W 4-4-2 Columbia "1201", *98*	—	70	___1
(18678)	Quaker Oats 4-4-2 Columbia "8632", *98*	—	150	___1
(18679)	JC Penney T&P 4-6-2 "2000", Traditional, *00 u*	—	250	___1
(18680)	Lionel RR Club Countdown 4-6-4 Hudson "2000", Traditional, *00 u*	—	260	___1
(18681)	PRR 4-4-2 Steam Engine "460", *99*	—	75	___1
(18682)	Santa Fe 4-4-2 Columbia "524", Traditional, *00–01*	—	70	___1
(18684)	LRRC Pacific 4-6-2 "1999", *99 u*	—	205	___1
(18689)	(See 18207)			
(18696)	ACL 4-6-4 "1800", *01*	—	120	___1
(18697)	Santa Fe 4-6-4 "3465", *01*	—	80	___1
(18699)	Alaska 4-4-2 "64", *01*	—	105	___1
(18700)	Rock Island 0-4-0T "8700", *87–88*	36	43	___1
(18702)	V&TRR 4-4-0 "8702" (SSS), *88*	140	170	___1
(18704)	Lionel Lines 2-4-0 "8704", *89 u*	36	43	___1
(18705)	"Neptune" 0-4-0T "8705", *90–91*	35	42	___1
(18706)	Santa Fe 2-4-0 "8706", *91*	36	43	___1
(18707)	Mickey's World Tour 2-4-0 "8707", *91, 92 u*	55	65	___1
(18709)	Lionel Employee Learning Center "Blue Engine" 0-4-0T, *92 u*	—	105	___1
(18710)	Southern 2-4-0 "2000", *93*	30	38	___1
(18711)	Southern 2-4-0 "2000", *93*	30	38	___1

		Exc	New	Cond/$
(18712)	Jersey Central 2-4-0 "2000", *93*	30	38	___¹
(18713)	Chessie System 2-4-0 "1993", *94–95*	30	38	___¹
(18716)	Lionelville Circus 4-4-0 "8716", *90–91*	90	110	___¹
(18718)	Lionel Lines 0-4-0 Dockside Switcher "8200", *97–98*	—	40	___¹
(18719)	Thomas the Tank Engine 0-6-0 "1", *97*	—	155	___¹
(18720)	Union Cavalry 4-4-0 General "1865", *99*	—	175	___¹
(18721)	Confederate States 4-4-0 General "1861", *99*	—	175	___¹
(18722)	Percy the Tank Engine "6", *99*	—	155	___¹
18799	Bethlehem Steel Diesel Switcher "44", *99*		CP	___
(18800)	Lehigh Valley GP-9 "8800", *87*	100	115	___¹
(18801)	Santa Fe U36B "8801", *87*	90	105	___¹
(18802)	Southern GP-9 "8802" (SSS), *87*	100	115	___¹
(18803)	Santa Fe RS-3 "8803", *88*	90	105	___²
(18804)	Soo Line RS-3 "8804", *88*	85	100	___¹
(18805)	Union Pacific RS-3 "8805", *89*	90	110	___¹
(18806)	New Haven SD-18 "8806", *89*	90	105	___¹
(18807)	Lehigh Valley RS-3 "8807", *90*	80	105	___¹
(18808)	ACL SD-18 "8808", *90*	95	120	___¹
(18809)	Susquehanna RS-3 "8809" (See 18551), *89 u*			
(18810)	CSX SD-18 "8810", *90*	95	130	___¹
(18811)	Alaska SD-9 "8811", *91*	135	190	___¹
(18812)	Kansas City Southern GP-38 "4000", *91*	115	140	___¹
(18813)	DM&IR SD-18 "8813" (See 18552), *90 u*	—	110	___¹
(18814)	D&H RS-3 "8814" (SSS), *91*	110	145	___¹
(18815)	Amtrak RS-3 "1815", *91, 92 u*	90	115	___¹
(18816)	C&NW GP-38-2 "4600", *92*	100	125	___¹
(18817)	UP GP-9 "150" (See 18553), *91 u*	—	160	___¹
(18818)	Lionel Railroader Club GP-38-2 "1992", *92 u*	160	190	___¹
(18819)	L&N GP-38-2 "4136", *92*	150	195	___¹
(18820)	WP GP-9 "8820" (SSS), *92*	105	120	___¹
(18821)	Clinchfield GP-38-2 "6005", *93*	125	150	___¹
(18822)	Gulf, Mobile & Ohio RS-3 "721" (See 18554), *92–93 u*			
(18823)	Chicago & Illinois Midland SD-9 "52" (See 18555), *92 u*			
(18824)	Montana Rail Link SD-9 "600", *93*	150	180	___¹
(18825)	Soo Line GP-38-2 "4000" (SSS), *93*	120	140	___¹
(18826)	Conrail GP-7 "5808", *93*	110	135	___¹
(18827)	"Happy Holidays" RS-3 "8827", *93*	155	265	___¹
(18830)	Budweiser GP-9 "1947", *93–94 u*	110	150	___¹
(18831)	SP GP-20 "4060", *94*	115	130	___¹
(18832)	PRR RSD-4 "8446", *95*	105	115	___¹

		Exc	New	Cond/$
(18833)	Milwaukee Road RS-3 "2487", *94*	100	110	___¹
(18834)	C&O SD-28 "8834", *94*	100	130	___¹
(18835)	NYC RS-3 "8223" (SSS), *94*	115	165	___¹
(18836)	CN/Grand Trunk GP-38-2 "5800", *94*	155	180	___¹
(18837)	"Happy Holidays" RS-3 "8837", *94–95*	155	200	___¹
(18838)	Seaboard RSC-3 "1538", *95*	120	155	___¹
(18840)	US Army GP-7 "1821", *95*	100	130	___¹
(18841)	Western Maryland GP-20 "27" (SSS), *95*	110	140	___¹
(18842)	JC Penney/B&LE SD-38 "868", *95 u*	—	285	___¹
(18843)	Great Northern RS-3 "197", *96*	—	130	___¹
(18844)	NdeM GP-38 "9288", *96*		NM	___
(18845)	D&RGW RS-3 "5204", *97*	—	105	___¹
(18846)	1997 Lionel Centennial Series GP-9, *98*	—	250	___¹
(18847)	Santa Fe H-12-44 Switcher "9087", *99*	—	460	___¹
(18848)	PRR H-12-44 Switcher "502", *99*	—	390	___¹
(18853)	Santa Fe JC Penney GP-9 "2370", *97u*	—	150	___¹
(18854)	Union Pacific GP-9 set "2380"-"2387" Dummy, *97*	—	450	___¹
(18855)	Union Pacific GP-9 Dummy (See 18854)			
(18856)	NJ Transit GP-38-2 "4303", *99*	—	370	___¹
(18857)	Union Pacific GP-9 "2397", *97*	—	240	___¹
(18858)	1998 Lionel Centennial GP-20 "1998", *98*	—	310	___²
(18859)	The Phantom II, *99*	—	340	___¹
(18860)	The Pratt's Hollow Collection I: The Phantom, *98*	—	400	___¹
(18864)	Southern Pacific GP-9 B Unit, *98*	—	110	___¹
(18865)	New York Central GP-9 B Unit, *98*	—	170	___¹
(18868)	NJ Transit GP-38-2 "4300", *98u*	—	140	___¹
(18870)	Pennsylvania GP-9 Diesel "2029", *98*	—	235	___¹
(18872)	Wabash GP-7 3-unit set "453, 454, 455", *99*	—	510	___¹
(18876)	C&NW H-12-44 Switcher "1053", *99*	—	415	___¹
(18877)	Union Pacific GP-9 nonpowered "2399", *99*	—	170	___¹
(18878)	Alaska GP-7 "1803", *99*	—	105	___¹
(18879)	B&O GP-9 "5616", *99*	—	260	___¹
(18881)	Custom GP-9 "5616", *99*	—	290	___¹
(18890)	LOTS UP RS-3 "8805", *89 u*	125	150	___¹
(18892)	Burlington GP-9 "2328", *99*	—	295	___¹
(18897)	Christmas GP-7 "1999", *99*	—	210	___¹
(18900)	PRR Diesel Switcher "8900", *88 u, 89*	26	34	___¹
(18901)/(18902)	PRR Alco AA set "8901" and "8902", *88*	110	130	___¹
(18903)/(18904)	Amtrak Alco AA set "8903" and "8904", *88–89*	90	130	___¹

		Exc	New	Cond/$
(18903)	Amtrak "Mopar Express", *99*	—	500	___1
(18905)	PRR 44-tonner "9312", *92*	90	105	___1
(18906)	Erie-Lackawanna RS-3 "8906", *91 u*	100	135	___1
(18907)	Rock Island 44-tonner "371", *93*	80	90	___1
(18908)/(18909)	NYC Alco AA set "8908" and "8909", *93*	105	115	___1
(18910)	CSX Diesel Switcher "8910", *93*	35	40	___1
(18911)	UP Diesel Switcher "8911", *93*	30	33	___1
(18912)	Amtrak Diesel Switcher "8912", *93*	31	35	___1
(18913)	Santa Fe Alco A Unit "8913", *93–94*	55	65	___1
(18915)	WM Alco A Unit "8915", *93*	60	75	___1
(18916)	WM Alco A Unit Dummy "8916", *93*	34	38	___1
18917	Soo Line NW-2, *93*	65	75	___1
(18918)	B&M NW-2 "8918", *93*	70	85	___1
(18919)	Santa Fe Alco A Unit Dummy "8919", *93–94*	33	44	___1
(18920)	Frisco NW-2 "254", *94*	65	75	___1
(18921)	C&NW NW-2 "1017", *94*	80	95	___1
(18922)	New Haven Alco A Unit "8922", *94*	75	105	___1
(18923)	New Haven Alco A Unit Dummy "8923", *94*	50	55	___1
(18924)	Illinois Central Diesel Switcher "8924", *94–95*	31	35	___1
(18925)	D&RGW Diesel Switcher "8925", *94–95*	32	35	___1
(18926)	Reading Diesel Switcher "8926", *94–95*	27	30	___1
(18927)	US Navy NW-2 "65-00637", *94–95*	75	85	___1
(18928)	C&NW NW-2 Calf, *95*	42	45	___1
(18929)	B&M NW-2 Calf, *95*	44	49	___1
(18930)	Crayola Diesel Switcher, *94 u, 95*	27	30	___1
(18931)	Chrysler Mopar NW-2 "1818", *94 u*	70	85	___1
(18932)	Jersey Central NW-2 "8932", *96*	—	55	___1
(18933)	Jersey Central NW-2 Calf "8933", *96*	—	50	___1
(18934)/(18935)	Reading Alco AA set "300" and "304", *95*	70	85	___1
(18936)	Amtrak Alco A Unit "8936", *95*	—	65	___1
(18937)	Amtrak Alco FA-2, nonpowered, *95–97*	—	43	___1
(18938)	US Navy NW-2 Calf, *95*	49	55	___1
(18939)	Union Pacific NW-2 Diesel Switcher set, *96*	—	130	___1
(18943)	Georgia Power NW-2 "1960", *95 u*	—	185	___1
(18946)	USC.G. NW-2 Switcher "8946", *96*	—	80	___1
(18947)	Port of Lionel City Alco FA-2 "2030", *97*	—	70	___1
(18948)	Port of Lionel City Alco FB-2 "2030B", *97*	—	55	___1
(18949)	NYC NW-2 "622", black, *97*		NM	___
(18951)	Erie NW-2 "6220", black, *97*		NM	___
(18952)	AT&SF Alco PA-1 "2000", *97*	—	240	___2
(18953)	NYC Alco PA-1 "2000", *97*	—	285	___2

		Exc	New	Cond/$
(18954)	AT&SF Alco FA-2 "212", powered, *97–99*	—	80	___1
(18955)	NJ Transit NW-2 Switcher "500", *96 u*	—	110	___1
(18956)	Dodge Motorsports "8956" NW-2, *96 u*	—	150	___1
(18959)	NYC NW-2 Switcher "622", *97*	—	450	___1
(18961)	Erie Alco PA-1"850", *98*	—	335	___1
(18965)	Santa Fe Alco PB1, *98*	—	235	___1
(18966)	New York Central Alco BP1 "20008", *98*	—	225	___1
(18971)	Alco A-Unit (nonpowered), *98*	—	65	___1
(18972)	Rock Island Alco FA AA, *98*		NM	___
(18973)	RI Alco FA-2 "2031", powered, *98–99*		NRS	___
(18974)	RI Alco FA-2 Dummy, *98–99*		NRS	___
(18975)	Southern 44-ton Switcher "1955", *99*	—	190	___1
(18978)	C&O NW-2 Switcher "624", *99–00*	—	375	___1
19000	Blue Comet Dining Car, *87 u*	65	85	___1
19001	Southern Dining Car, *87 u*	70	90	___1
19002	Pennsylvania Dining Car, *88 u*	29	45	___1
19003	Milwaukee Road Dining Car, *88 u*	29	44	___1
19010	B&O Dining Car, *89 u*	30	45	___1
(19011)	Lionel Lines Baggage Car "9011", *93*	250	320	___1
(19015)	Lionel Lines Passenger Car "9015", *91*	125	155	___1
(19016)	Lionel Lines Passenger Car "9016", *91*	90	110	___1
(19017)	Lionel Lines Passenger Car "9017", *91*	100	125	___1
(19018)	Lionel Lines Observation Car "9018", *91*	90	105	___1
(19019)	SP Baggage Car "9019", *93*	110	150	___1
(19023)	SP Passenger Car "9023", *92*	135	165	___1
(19024)	SP Passenger Car "9024", *92*	85	100	___1
(19025)	SP Passenger Car "9025", *92*	110	130	___1
(19026)	SP Observation Car "9026", *92*	85	100	___1
(19027)	Reading Baggage Car "9027", *92*		NM	___
(19031)	Reading Passenger Car "9031", *92*		NM	___
(19032)	Reading Passenger Car "9032", *92*		NM	___
(19033)	Reading Observation Car "9033", *92*		NM	___
(19038)	Adolphus Busch Observation Car, *92–93 u*	—	80	___1
(19039)	Pere Marquette Baggage Car, *93*	—	75	___1
(19040)	Pere Marquette Passenger Car "1115", *93*	—	75	___1
(19041)	Pere Marquette Passenger Car "1116", *93*	—	75	___1
(19042)	Pere Marquette Observation Car "36", *93*	—	75	___1
(19047)	Baltimore & Ohio Combination Car "9047", *96*	—	42	___1
(19048)	Baltimore & Ohio Passenger Car "9048", *96*	—	60	___1
(19049)	Baltimore & Ohio Dining Car "9049", *96*	—	42	___1
(19050)	Baltimore & Ohio Observation Car "9050", *96*	—	42	___1
(19056)	NYC Heavyweight Baggage Car, *96*	—	105	___1
(19057)	NYC Heavyweight Willow Run Coach, *96*	—	100	___1

(19058)	NYC Heavyweight Willow Trail Coach, *96*	—	75	_1
(19059)	NYC Heavyweight Seneca Valley Observation, *96*	—	100	_1
(19060)	Pullman Heavyweight set, *96*	—	315	_2
(19061)	Wabash Railway Passenger set, *97*	—	240	_1
(19062)	Wabash Railway "City of Columbia" Coach "2361", *97*	—	90	_1
(19063)	Wabash Railway "City of Danville" Coach "2362", *97*	—	75	_1
(19064)	Wabash REA Baggage Car "2360", *97*	—	75	_1
(19065)	Wabash "Windy City" Observation "2363", *97*	—	90	_1
(19066)	Commodore Vanderbilt Pullman Heavyweight 2-pack, *97*	—	190	_1
(19067)	Commodore Vanderbilt "Willow River" Pullman "2543", *97*	—	100	_1
(19068)	Commodore Vanderbilt "Willow Valley" Pullman "2544", *97*	—	100	_1
(19069)	Pullman Baby Madison set "9500-02", *97*	—	135	_1
(19070)	Baby Madison REA/Combo "9501", *97*	—	40	_1
(19071)	Baby Madison "Laurel Gap" Coach "9500", *97*	—	40	_1
(19072)	Baby Madison "Laurel Summit" Coach "9500", *97*	—	40	_1
(19073)	Baby Madison "Catskill Valley" Observation "9502", *97*	—	40	_1
(19074)	Legends of Lionel Madison set, *97*	—	435	_1
(19075)	Lionel Legends "Mazzone" Coach "2621", *97*	—	90	_1
(19076)	Lionel Legends "Caruso" Coach "2624", *97*	—	90	_1
(19077)	Lionel Legends "Raphael" Coach "2652", *97*	—	90	_1
(19078)	Lionel Legends "Cowen" Observation "2600", *97*	—	90	_1
(19079)	NYC Heavyweight Passenger Car set, *97*	—	345	_1
(19080)	NYC Heavyweight REA Baggage Car "2564", *97*	—	100	_1
(19081)	NYC Heavyweight "Park Place" Coach "2565", *97*	—	100	_1
(19082)	NYC Heavyweight "Star Beam" Coach "2566", *97*	—	100	_1
(19083)	NYC Heavyweight "Hudson Valley" Observation "2566", *97*	—	100	_1
(19087)	C&O Heavyweight Passenger Car 4-pack "2571-74", *97*	—	300	_1
(19088)	C&O Heavyweight Baggage Car "2571", *97*	—	100	_1
(19089)	C&O Heavyweight Sleeper Car "2572", *97*	—	100	_1
(19090)	C&O Heavyweight Diner Car "2573", *97*	—	115	_1
(19091)	C&O Heavyweight Observation Car "2574", *97*	—	100	_1

		Exc	New	Cond/$
(19093)	Commodore Vanderbilt Heavyweight Sleeper Cars 2-pack, *98*	—	190	___1
(19094)	Commodore Vanderbilt "Niagara Falls" Sleeper, *98*	—	70	___1
(19095)	Commodore Vanderbilt "Highland Falls" Sleeper, *98*	—	70	___1
(19096)	Legends of Lionel Madison Cars 2-pack, *98*	—	175	___1
(19097)	Lionel Legends "Bonnano" Coach "2653", *98*	—	90	___1
(19098)	Lionel Legends "Pagano" Coach "2654", *98*	—	90	___1
(19099)	Pennsylvania "Liberty Gap" Baggage Car "2623", *99*	—	85	___1
(19100)	Amtrak Baggage Car "9100", *89*	115	145	___1
(19101)	Amtrak Combination Car "9101", *89*	75	85	___1
(19102)	Amtrak Passenger Car "9102", *89*	75	85	___1
(19103)	Amtrak Vista Dome Car "9103", *89*	70	90	___1
(19104)	Amtrak Dining Car "9104", *89*	65	80	___1
(19105)	Amtrak Full Vista Dome Car "9105", *89 u*	70	80	___2
(19106)	Amtrak Observation Car "9106", *89*	75	90	___1
(19107)	SP Full Vista Dome Car, *90 u*	70	75	___3
(19108)	N&W Full Vista Dome Car "576", *91 u*	90	100	___1
(19109)	Santa Fe Baggage Car "3400", *91*	150	220	___1
(19110)	Santa Fe Combination Car "3500", *91*	115	165	___1
(19111)	Santa Fe Dining Car "601", *91*	110	155	___1
(19112)	Santa Fe Passenger Car, *91*	120	175	___1
(19113)	Santa Fe Vista Dome Observation Car, *91*	120	170	___1
(19116)	Great Northern Baggage Car "1200", *92*	95	110	___1
(19117)	Great Northern Combination Car "1240", *92*	75	85	___1
(19118)	Great Northern Passenger Car "1212", *92*	75	85	___1
(19119)	Great Northern Vista Dome Car "1322", *92*	75	85	___1
(19120)	Great Northern Observation Car "1192", *92*	75	85	___1
(19121)	Union Pacific Vista Dome Car "9121", *92 u*	105	120	___1
(19122)	D&RGW California Zephyr Baggage Car, *93*	120	155	___2
(19123)	D&RGW California Zephyr "Silver Bronco" Vista Dome Car, *93*	95	115	___1
(19124)	D&RGW California Zephyr "Silver Colt" Vista Dome Car, *93*	95	115	___1
(19125)	D&RGW California Zephyr "Silver Mustang" Vista Dome Car, *93*	100	125	___1
(19126)	D&RGW California Zephyr "Silver Pony" Vista Dome Car, *93*	95	115	___1
(19127)	D&RGW California Zephyr Vista Dome Observation Car, *93*	95	115	___1
(19128)	Santa Fe Full Vista Dome Car "507", *92 u*	175	185	___1

		Exc	New	Cond/$
(19129)	Illinois Central Full Vista Dome Car "9129", *93*	75	85	___¹
(19130)	Lackawanna Passenger Cars, set of 4, *94*	295	365	___¹
(19131)	Lackawanna Baggage Car "2000" (See 19130)			
(19132)	Lackawanna Dining Car "469" (See 19130)			
(19133)	Lackawanna Passenger Car "260" (See 19130)			
(19134)	Lackawanna Observation Car "789" (See 19130)			
(19135)	Lackawanna Combination Car "425", *94*	95	115	___¹
(19136)	Lackawanna Passenger Car "211", *94*	70	80	___¹
(19137)	New York Central Roomette Car, *95*	85	100	___¹
(19138)	Santa Fe Roomette Car, *95*	85	105	___²
(19139)	Norfolk & Western Baggage Car "577", *95*	120	155	___¹
(19140)	Norfolk & Western Combination Car "494", *95*	75	90	___¹
(19141)	Norfolk & Western Dining Car "495", *95*	120	155	___¹
(19142)	Norfolk & Western Passenger Car "538", *95*	75	95	___¹
(19143)	Norfolk & Western Passenger Car "537", *95*	75	95	___¹
(19144)	Norfolk & Western Observation Car "582", *95*	75	90	___¹
(19145)	Chesapeake & Ohio Combination Car "1403", *96*	—	85	___²
(19146)	Chesapeake & Ohio Passenger Car "1623", *96*	—	85	___¹
(19147)	Chesapeake & Ohio Passenger Car "1803", *96*	—	75	___¹
(19148)	C&O Chessie Club Coach "1903", *96*	—	75	___¹
(19149)	C&O Gadsby Kitchen Pass./Diner "1950", *96*	—	75	___¹
(19150)	Chesapeake & Ohio Observation Car "2504", *96*	—	65	___¹
(19151)	Norfolk & Western Duplex Roomette car, *96*	—	95	___²
(19152)	Union Pacific Duplex Roomette Car, *96*	—	70	___¹
(19153)	Chesapeake & Ohio Passenger Cars, set of 4, *96*	—	295	___²
(19154)	Atlantic Coast Line Passenger Cars set, *96*	—	310	___¹
(19155)	ACL Passenger/Combo "101", *96*	—	90	___¹
(19156)	ACL Talladega Diner, *96*	—	90	___¹
(19157)	ACL Moultrie Coach, *96*	—	90	___¹
(19158)	ACL Observation "256", *96*	—	90	___¹
(19159)	Norfolk & Western Passenger Cars, set of 4, *95 u*	300	370	___¹
(19160)	Super Chief REA Baggage Car, *96*	—	75	___¹
(19161)	Super Chief "Silver Sky" Coach, *96*	—	80	___¹
(19162)	Super Chief "Silver Mesa" Vista Dome, *96*	—	75	___¹
(19163)	Super Chief "Silver Rail" Observation, *96*	—	75	___¹
(19164)	Chesapeake & Ohio Passenger Cars, *96*	—	145	___¹
(19165)	Super Chief set, *96*	—	295	___¹
(19166)	NP Vista Dome set, *97*	—	340	___¹
(19167)	NP Pullman "2571", *97*	—	105	___¹

		Exc	New	Cond/$
(19168)	NP Pullman "2571", *97*	—	105	___¹
(19169)	NP Pullman "2570", *97*	—	95	___¹
(19170)	NP Pullman "2571", *97*	—	100	___¹
(19171)	NYC Streamlined Passenger set "2570-75", *97*	—	400	___¹
(19172)	NYC Aluminum Passenger Baggage "2570", *97*	—	85	___¹
(19173)	NYC Aluminum Passenger Diner "Manhattan Island", *97*	—	100	___¹
(19174)	NYC Aluminum Passenger Coach "Queensboro Bridge", *97*	—	100	___¹
(19175)	NYC Aluminum Passenger Observation "Windgate Brook", *97*	—	90	___¹
(19176)	AT&SF Indian Arrow Diner "2572", *97*	—	90	___¹
(19177)	AT&SF Grass Valley Coach "2573", *97*	—	90	___¹
(19178)	AT&SF Citrus Valley Coach "2574", *97*	—	90	___¹
(19179)	AT&SF Vista Heights "2575", *97*	—	90	___¹
(19180)	AT&SF Surfliner Passenger set "2572-75", *97*	—	300	___¹
(19181)	GN Empire Builder "Prairie View" Full Vista Dome, *98*	—	70	___¹
(19182)	GN Empire Builder "River View" Full Vista Dome, *98*	—	70	___¹
(19183)	GN Empire Builder Vista Dome Cars 2-pack, *98*	—	150	___¹
(19184)	Milwaukee Passenger set 4-pack, *99*	—	485	___¹
(19185)	Milwaukee Road Aluminum Passenger Coach "194 Red River Valley", *99*	—	125	___¹
(19186)	Milwaukee Road Aluminum Passenger Diner "170", *99*	—	110	___¹
(19187)	Milwaukee Road Aluminum Pass. Observation "186 Cedar Rapids", *99*	—	120	___¹
(19188)	Milwaukee Road Aluminum Passenger Baggage "1336", REA, *99*	—	110	___¹
(19194)	KCS Alum Passenger Car 4-pack, *00*	—	360	___¹
19200	Tidewater Southern Boxcar, *87*	11	19	___¹
19201	Lancaster & Chester Boxcar, *87*	40	65	___¹
19202	PRR Boxcar, *87*	28	34	___¹
19203	D&TS Boxcar, *87*	10	17	___¹
19204	Milwaukee Road Boxcar (FF #2), *87*	24	33	___¹
19205	Great Northern DD Boxcar (FF #3), *88*	22	28	___¹
19206	Seaboard System Boxcar, *88*	17	22	___¹
19207	CP Rail DD Boxcar, *88*	14	18	___¹
19208	Southern DD Boxcar, *88*	14	18	___¹
19209	Florida East Coast Boxcar, *88*	15	19	___¹
19210	Soo Line Boxcar, *89*	17	20	___¹

		Exc	New	Cond/$
19211	Vermont Railway Boxcar, *89*	20	23	___¹
19212	PRR Boxcar, *89*	22	26	___²
19213	SP&S DD Boxcar, *89*	18	21	___¹
19214	Western Maryland Boxcar (FF #4), *89*	24	28	___¹
19215	Union Pacific DD Boxcar, *90*	13	14	___¹
19216	Santa Fe Boxcar, *90*	15	19	___¹
19217	Burlington Boxcar, *90*	14	17	___¹
19218	New Haven Boxcar, *90*	14	17	___¹
19219	Lionel Lines 1900-1906 Boxcar w/ Diesel RailSounds, *90*	120	145	___¹
19220	Lionel Lines 1926-1934 Boxcar, *90*	27	30	___¹
19221	Lionel Lines 1935-1937 Boxcar, *90*	27	30	___¹
19222	Lionel Lines 1948-1950 Boxcar, *90*	27	30	___¹
19223	Lionel Lines 1979-1989 Boxcar, *90*	26	29	___¹
19228	Cotton Belt Boxcar, *91*	16	15	___¹
19229	Frisco Boxcar w/ Diesel RailSounds (FF #5), *91*	75	90	___¹
19230	Frisco DD Boxcar (FF #5), *91*	25	30	___¹
19231	TA&G DD Boxcar, *91*	17	20	___¹
19232	Rock Island DD Boxcar, *91*	17	19	___¹
19233	Southern Pacific Boxcar, *91*	17	22	___¹
19234	NYC Boxcar, *91*	65	75	___¹
19235	MKT Boxcar, *91*	55	65	___¹
19236	NKP DD Boxcar (FF #6), *92*	19	26	___¹
19237	C&IM Boxcar, *92*	14	19	___¹
19238	Kansas City Southern Boxcar, *92*	18	23	___¹
19239	Toronto, Hamilton & Buffalo DD Boxcar, *92*	14	19	___¹
19240	Great Northern DD Boxcar, *92*	14	18	___¹
19241	Mickey Mouse 60th Anniversary Hi-cube Boxcar, *91 u*	135	190	___¹
19242	Donald Duck 50th Anniversary Hi-cube Boxcar, *91 u*	125	160	___¹
(19243)	Clinchfield Boxcar "9790", *91 u*	38	41	___¹
(19244)	L&N Boxcar "9791", *92*	29	31	___¹
19245	Mickey's World Tour Hi-cube Boxcar, *92 u*	39	47	___²
19246	Disney World 20th Anniversary Hi-cube Boxcar, *92 u*	39	47	___¹
(19247)	6464 Series Boxcars, 1st Edition, set of 3, *93*	350	405	___²
(19248)	Western Pacific Boxcar "6464", *93*	75	85	___¹
(19249)	Great Northern Boxcar "6464", *93*	75	85	___¹
(19250)	M&StL Boxcar "6464", *93*	80	90	___¹
(19251)	Montana Rail Link DD Boxcar "10001", *93*	21	27	___¹
19254	Erie Boxcar (FF #7), *93*	21	25	___¹
19255	Erie DD Boxcar (FF #7), *93*	23	27	___¹

		Exc	New	Cond/$
19256	Goofy Hi-cube Boxcar, *93*	27	34	___¹
(19257)	6464 Series Boxcars, 2nd Edition, set of 3, *94*	135	150	___²
(19258)	Rock Island Boxcar "6464", *94*	28	35	___¹
(19259)	Western Pacific Boxcar "6464100", *94*	34	49	___¹
(19260)	Western Pacific Boxcar "6464100", *94*	39	55	___¹
19261	Perils of Mickey Hi-cube Boxcar I, *93*	31	33	___¹
19262	Perils of Mickey Hi-cube Boxcar II, *93*	31	33	___¹
19263	NYC DD Boxcar (SSS), *94*	36	42	___¹
19264	Perils of Mickey Hi-cube Boxcar III, *94*	31	35	___¹
19265	Mickey Mouse 65th Anniversary Hi-cube Boxcar, *94*	37	40	___¹
(19266)	6464 Series Boxcars, 3rd Edition, set of 3, *95*	90	95	___³
19267	NYC "Pacemaker" Boxcar "6464125", *95*	43	49	___¹
(19268)	Missouri Pacific Boxcar "6464150", *95*	37	41	___¹
(19269)	Rock Island Boxcar "6464", *95*	34	39	___¹
19270	Donald Duck 60th Anniversary Hi-cube Boxcar, *95*	36	40	___¹
19271	Minnie Mouse Hi-cube Boxcar, *95*	44	46	___¹
(19272)	6464 Series Boxcars, 4th edition, set of 3, *96*	90	130	___²
(19273)	BAR "State of Maine" Boxcar "6464275", *96*	—	32	___¹
(19274)	Southern Pacific "Overnight" Boxcar "6464225", *96*	—	32	___¹
(19275)	Pennsylvania Boxcar "6464", *96*	—	40	___¹
(19276)	"6464" Boxcar Series V "19277-79", *96*	—	85	___³
(19277)	Rutland Boxcar "6464-300" (Series V), *96*	—	32	___¹
(19278)	B&O Boxcar "6464-325" (Series V), *96*	—	30	___¹
(19279)	Central of Georgia "6464-375" (Series V), *96*	—	32	___¹
(19280)	Mickey's Wheat Hi-cube Boxcar, *96*	—	32	___¹
(19281)	Mickey's Carrots Hi-cube Boxcar, *96*	—	45	___¹
(19282)	Santa Fe "Super Chief" Boxcar "6464-196", *96*	—	27	___¹
(19283)	Erie Boxcar "6464-296", *96*	—	29	___¹
(19284)	Northern Pacific Boxcar "6464-396", *96*	—	38	___¹
(19285)	Bangor and Aroostook "State of Maine" Boxcar "6464-275", *96*	—	30	___¹
(19286)	Warner Bros. "All Abirrrrd" Boxcar, *96*	—	42	___¹
(19287)	NYC/PC Merger Boxcar "6464-125X", *97*	60	90	___¹
(19288)	PRR/CR Merger Boxcar "6464-200X", *97*	50	85	___¹
(19289)	Monon "Hoosier Line" Boxcar "6464", *97*	—	27	___¹
(19290)	Seaboard "Silver Meteor" Boxcar "6464", *97*	—	31	___¹
(19291)	GN Boxcar "6464-397", dark green, *97*	—	31	___¹
(19292)	"6464" Boxcar Series VI "19293-95", *97*	—	105	___¹
(19293)	MKT Boxcar Series VI "6464-350", *97*	28	36	___¹
(19294)	B&O Boxcar Series VI "6464-400", *97*	33	43	___¹

		Exc	New	Cond/$
(19295)	NH Boxcar Series VI "6464-425", 97	31	43	___¹
19300	PRR Ore Car, 87	16	21	___¹
19301	Milwaukee Road Ore Car, 87	24	30	___¹
19302	Milwaukee Road Quad Hopper w/ coal load (FF #2), 87	21	29	___¹
19303	Lionel Lines Quad Hopper w/ coal load, 87 u	20	28	___²
19304	GN Covered Quad Hopper (FF #3), 88	27	29	___¹
19305	Chessie System Ore Car, 88	17	23	___¹
19307	B&LE Ore Car w/ load, 89	17	23	___¹
19308	GN Ore Car w/ load, 89	17	22	___¹
19309	Seaboard Covered Quad Hopper, 89	17	22	___¹
19310	L&C Quad Hopper w/ coal load, 89	22	31	___¹
19311	SP Covered Quad Hopper, 90	14	19	___¹
19312	Reading Quad Hopper w/ coal load, 90	22	33	___¹
19313	B&O Ore Car w/ load, 90–91	20	25	___¹
19315	Amtrak Ore Car w/ load, 91	25	35	___¹
19316	Wabash Covered Quad Hopper, 91	21	29	___¹
19317	Lehigh Valley Quad Hopper w/ coal load, 91	55	65	___¹
19318	NKP Quad Hopper w/ coal load (FF #6), 92	29	33	___¹
19319	Union Pacific Covered Quad Hopper, 92	19	23	___¹
19320	PRR Ore Car w/ load, 92	21	26	___¹
19321	B&LE Ore Car w/ load, 92	21	26	___¹
19322	C&NW Ore Car w/ load, 93	27	34	___¹
19323	Detroit & Mackinac Ore Car w/ load, 93	20	25	___¹
19324	Erie Quad Hopper w/ coal load (FF #7), 93	23	26	___¹
(19325)	N&W 4-bay Hopper w/ coal "6446-1", 97	—	95	___¹
(19326)	N&W 4-bay Hopper w/ coal "6446-2", 96	—	65	___¹
(19327)	N&W 4-bay Hopper w/ coal "6446-3", 96	—	55	___¹
(19328)	N&W 4-bay Hopper w/ coal "6446-4", 96	—	55	___¹
(19329)	N&W 4-bay Hopper w/ coal "6436", 97	—	55	___¹
(19330)	Cotton Belt 4-bay Hopper w/ coal "64661", 98	—	45	___¹
(19331)	Cotton Belt 4-bay Hopper w/ coal "64662", 98	—	45	___¹
(19332)	Cotton Belt 4-bay Hopper w/ coal "64663", 98	—	45	___¹
(19333)	Cotton Belt 4-bay Hopper w/ coal "64664", 98	—	45	___¹
(19338)	Cotton Belt 4-bay Hopper 2-pack, 99	—	120	___¹
(19339)	Cotton Belt 4-bay Hopper "64469", 99		NRS	___
(19340)	Cotton Belt 4-bay Hopper "64470", 99		NRS	___
(19341)	LV 2-bay Hopper "6456", 99	—	30	___¹
(19344)	D&RGW 3-bay Cylindrical Hopper "15990", 99–00	—	49	___¹
(19345)	CN 3-bay Cylindrical Hopper "370708", 99–00	—	85	___¹
(19346)	PRR 4-bay Hopper w/ coal load "744433", 01		CP	___
(19347)	LV 2-bay Hopper "643657", 01		CP	___

		Exc	New	Cond/$
(19348)	Duluth, Missabe & Iron Range Ore Car "28000", *03*		CP	____
(19349)	US Steel Ore Car "19349", *03*		CP	____
(19350)	Postwar Alaska Quad Hopper "6636", *03*		CP	____
19400	Milwaukee Road Gondola w/ cable reels (FF #2), *87*	22	30	____[1]
19401	GN Gondola w/ coal load (FF #3), *88*	21	25	____[1]
19402	GN Crane Car (FF #3), *88*	41	55	____[1]
19403	WM Gondola w/ coal load (FF #4), *89*	19	23	____[1]
19404	Trailer Train Flatcar w/ WM trailers (FF #4), *89*	32	36	____[1]
19405	Southern Crane Car, *91*	50	80	____[1]
19406	West Point Mint Car, *91 u*	55	85	____[1]
19408	Frisco Gondola w/ coil covers (FF #5), *91*	28	32	____[1]
19409	Southern Flatcar w/ stakes, *91*	17	20	____[1]
19410	NYC Gondola w/ canisters, *91*	47	55	____[1]
19411	NKP Flatcar w/ Sears trailer (FF #6), *92*	47	60	____[2]
19412	Frisco Crane Car, *92*	49	65	____[1]
19413	Frisco Flatcar w/ stakes, *92*	17	22	____[1]
19414	Union Pacific Flatcar w/ stakes (SSS), *92*	19	23	____[1]
(19415)	Erie Flatcar w/ trailer "7200" (FF #7), *93*	28	35	____[1]
(19416)	ICG TTUX Flatcar set w/ trailers "19417" and "19418" (SSS), *93*	70	85	____[1]
19417/19418	ICG TTUX Flatcars w/ trailers (See 19416)			
19419	Charlotte Mint Car, *93*	32	39	____[2]
19420	Lionel Lines Vat Car, *94*	23	27	____[1]
19421	Hirsch Brothers Vat Car, *95*	24	29	____[1]
(19423)	Circle-L Racing Flatcar w/ stock cars "6424", *96*	—	29	____[1]
(19424)	Edison Electric Depressed-center Flatcar w/ transformer "6461", *97*	—	38	____[1]
(19425)	Artrain CSX Flatcar w/ trailer, *96 u*	—	80	____[1]
(19427)	Evans Auto Loader "6414", *99*	—	75	____[1]
(19428)	Evans Boat Loader "6414", *99*	—	70	____[2]
(19429)	Culvert Gondola "35621", *98–99*	—	50	____[1]
(19430)	AT&SF Flatcar w/ Beechcraft Bonanza "6411", *98*	—	43	____[1]
(19437)	LRRC Flatcar w/ trailer, *97 u*	—	65	____[1]
(19438)	Standard O Christmas Gondola, *98*	—	44	____[1]
(19439)	Flatcar w/ safes, *98*	—	35	____[1]
(19440)	Flatcar w/ FedEx trailer, *98*	—	34	____[1]
(19441)	Lobster Vat Car, *98*	—	28	____[1]
(19442)	Water Supply Flatcar w/ tank (SSS), *98*	—	35	____[1]
(19444)	Flatcar w/ VW Bug, *98*	—	50	____[1]

		Exc	New	Cond/$
(19445)	Borden Milk Tank Car "520", *99*	—	39	___1
(19446)	Pittsburg Paint Vat Car, *99*	—	39	___1
(19447)	Mama's Baked Beans Vat Car, *99*	—	35	___1
(19448)	Easter Gondola w/ candy "6462", *99*	—	30	___1
(19449)	Liquified Gas Tank Car "6469", *99*	—	32	___1
(19450)	Barrel Ramp Car "6343", *99*	—	36	___1
(19451)	Wheel Car "6262", *99*	—	32	___1
(19454)	PRR Flat Car w/ Gondola "6424", *99*	—	25	___1
(19455)	Lionel Lines Flatcar with Cooper-Jarrett trailers 6430, *99*	NRS		___
(19457)	Lionel Lines Extension Searchlight Car, *99*	—	40	___1
(19459)	Valentine Gondola w/ candy "6462", *99*	—	50	___1
(19471)	Mobil Flatcar w/ 2 trailers, *00 u*	—	95	___1
(19472)	Mobil Bulkhead Flatcar w/ tank, *00 u*	—	55	___1
(19473)	LRRC Log Dump Car, *99 u*	—	35	___1
(19474)	L&N Flatcar w/ die-cast trailer frames, *99*	—	30	___1
(19476)	Lionel Zoo 6462 Gondola w/ animals, *99–00*	—	43	___1
(19477)	Monday Night Football Flatcar w/ trailer, *01*	—	30	___1
(19478)	Culvert Gondola "6342", *99*	—	42	___1
(19479)	Borden's Milk Car "521", *00*	—	41	___1
(19480)	Valentine's Vat Car "6475", *99–00*	—	35	___1
(19481)	Easter Vat Car "2000", *99–00*	—	38	___1
(19482)	NYC Flat "6424" w/ 2 trailers, *00*	—	60	___1
(19483)	VW Beetle Flatcar "2000", *00*	—	47	___1
(19484)	Lionel 6264 Flatcar w/ timbers, *00*	—	30	___1
(19485)	PRR Culvert Gondola "347004", *01*	—	46	___1
19486	NYC Lumber Flat Car, *01*	—	40	___1
(19487)	Flat w/ airplane 6800, *00*	—	37	___1
19489	Evans Auto Loader "500085", *00*	—	50	___1
(19490)	Postwar Libby's Vat Car "6475", *01–02*	—	37	___1
(19491)	Christmas Vat Car, *01*	—	30	___1
(19492)	WM Skeleton Log Car 3-pack, *01*	—	90	___1
(19496)	Westside Lumber Skeleton Log Car 3-pack, *01*	—	105	___1
19500	Milwaukee Road Reefer (FF #2), *87*	34	44	___1
19502	C&NW Reefer, *87*	31	37	___1
19503	Bangor & Aroostook Reefer, *87*	25	28	___1
19504	Northern Pacific Reefer, *87*	17	20	___1
19505	Great Northern Reefer (FF #3), *88*	30	36	___1
19506	Thomas Newcomen Reefer, *88*	17	21	___1
19507	Thomas Edison Reefer, *88*	19	24	___1
19508	Leonardo da Vinci Reefer, *89*	19	24	___1
19509	Alexander Graham Bell Reefer, *89*	17	20	___1
19510	PRR Stock Car (FARR #5), *89 u*	25	26	___1

Exc New Cond/$

		Exc	New	Cond/$
19511	WM Reefer (FF #4), *89*	25	29	___¹
19512	Wright Brothers Reefer, *90*	17	21	___¹
19513	Ben Franklin Reefer, *90*	18	21	___¹
19515	Milwaukee Road Stock Car (FF #2), *90 u*	27	33	___¹
19516	George Washington Reefer, *89 u, 91*	14	19	___¹
19517	Civil War Reefer, *89 u, 91*	14	19	___¹
19518	Man on the Moon Reefer, *89 u, 91*	13	17	___¹
19519	Frisco Stock Car (FF #5), *91*	22	26	___¹
19520	CSX Reefer, *91*	15	19	___¹
19522	Guglielmo Marconi Reefer, *91*	19	23	___¹
19523	Dr. Robert Goddard Reefer, *91*	19	23	___¹
19524	Delaware & Hudson Reefer (SSS), *91*	28	31	___¹
19525	Speedy Alka Seltzer Reefer, *91 u*	31	34	___¹
19526	Jolly Green Giant Reefer, *91 u*	22	30	___¹
19527	Nickel Plate Road Reefer (FF #6), *92*	24	33	___¹
19528	Joshua L. Cowen Reefer, *92*	24	30	___¹
19529	A.C. Gilbert Reefer, *92*	21	25	___¹
19530	Rock Island Stock Car, *92 u*	34	39	___¹
19531	Rice Krispies Reefer, *92 u*	20	29	___¹
(19532)	Hormel Reefer "901", *92 u*	20	27	___¹
19535	Erie Reefer (FF #7), *93*	26	29	___¹
19536	Soo Line REA Reefer (SSS), *93*	26	31	___¹
19537	Kellogg's Corn Flakes Reefer, *93*		NM	___
(19538)	Hormel Reefer "102", *94*	24	28	___¹
19539	Heinz Reefer, *94*	26	31	___¹
(19540)	Broken Arrow Ranch Stock Car "3356", *97*	—	34	___¹
(19552)	Rutland Reefer "395" (Std O), *00*	—	41	___¹
(19553)	AT&SF Stock Car "23003", *00*	—	39	___¹
(19554)	Milk Car "36621", *00*	—	120	___¹
(19555)	Swift Reefer "5837", red, *01*	—	33	___¹
(19556)	Swift Reefer "1020", silver, *01*	—	32	___¹
(19557)	Circus Stock Car "6376", *00*	—	34	___¹
(19558)	Postwar MKT Stock Car "6556", *02*	—	24	___¹
(19560)	Lionel Archives NP DD Stock Car "6356", *02*	—	33	___¹
(19564)	Postwar Santa Fe Refrigerator Car "6672", *03*		CP	___
(19565)	Archive Burlington Refrigerator Car "6672", *03*		CP	___
(19599)	Old Glory Reefers, set of 3, *89 u, 91*	43	50	___¹
19600	Milwaukee Road 1-D Tank Car (FF # 2), *87*	40	48	___¹
19601	North American 1-D Tank Car (FF #4), *89*	30	32	___¹
19602	Johnson 1-D Tank Car (FF #5), *91*	24	31	___¹
19603	GATX 1-D Tank Car (FF #6), *92*	36	47	___¹
19604	Goodyear 1-D Tank Car (SSS), *93*	32	35	___¹
19605	Hudson's Bay 1-D Tank Car (SSS), *94*	30	34	___¹

		Exc	New	Cond/$
(19607)	Sunoco 1-D Tank Car "6315", 96	—	27	___1
(19608)	Sunoco Aviation Services 1-D Tank Car "6315" (SSS), 97	—	35	___1
(19611)	Gulf Oil 1-D Tank Car "6315", 98	—	28	___1
(19612)	Gulf Oil 3-D Tank Car "6425", 98	—	27	___1
(19614)	BASF 1-D Tank Car "UTLX 78252", 99–00	—	25	___1
(19615)	Vulcan Chemicals 1-D Tank Car, 99–00	—	25	___1
(19621)	Centennial 1-D Tank Car "6015-1", 99	—	40	___1
(19622)	Centennial 1-D Tank Car "6015-2", 99	—	46	___1
(19623)	Centennial 1-D Tank Car "6015-3", 99	—	42	___1
(19624)	Centennial 1-D Tank Car "6015-4", 99	—	40	___1
(19625)	Ethyl Tank Car " 6236", 01	—	31	___1
(19626)	Diamond Chemical Tank Car "19419", 01	—	27	___1
(19627)	Shell 1-D Tank Car "1227", 01	—	48	___1
(19628)	Lion Oil 1-D Tank Car"2256", 01	—	35	___1
(19629)	Lifesaver 1-D Tank Car, 01		NM	___
(19634)	General American Tank Car Corp. 1-D Tank Car, 01	—	30	___1
(19635)	US Army 1-D Tank Car "10936", 01	—	27	___1
(19636)	Hooker Chemicals 1-D Tank Car 10936, 01	—	40	___1
(19637)	GATX TankTrain Tank Car "44589", (Std. O), 02	—	60	___1
(19638)	CN TankTrain Tank Car "75571", (Std. O), 02	—	65	___1
(19639)	GATX TankTrain Tank Car 3-pack, (Std. O), 02	—	130	___1
(19644)	Union Texas 1-D Tank Car "9922", 02	—	33	___1
(19645)	Penn Salt 1-D Tank Car "4730", 02	—	33	___1
(19646)	CN Intermediate TankTrain Tank Car "75571", (Std. O), 03		CP	___
(19647)	GATX Intermediate TankTrain Tank Car "44589", (Std. O), 03		CP	___
19651	Santa Fe Tool Car, 87	26	31	___1
19652	Jersey Central Bunk Car, 88	18	23	___1
19653	Jersey Central Tool Car, 88	20	25	___1
19654	Amtrak Bunk Car, 89	20	23	___1
19655	Amtrak Tool Car, 90–91	19	24	___1
19656	Milwaukee Road Bunk Car w/ smoke, 90	40	50	___1
19657	Wabash Bunk Car w/ smoke, 91–92	36	41	___1
19658	Norfolk & Western Tool Car, 91	28	33	___1
(19660)	Lionel Mint Car, 98	—	50	___1
(19663)	Pratt's Hollow Bunk Car "5717", 99	—	43	___1
(19664)	Ambassador Award Bunk Car "1998", bronze, 99 u	—	375	___1
(19665)	Ambassador Engineer Bunk Car "1998", silver, 99 u	—	550	___1

		Exc	New	Cond/$
(19666)	Ambassador Engineer Bunk Car "1998", gold, *99 u*	—	460	___1
(19667)	Wellspring Gold Bullion Car, *99*	—	42	___1
(19669)	King Tut Museum Car "9660", *99*	—	60	___1
(19670)	NY Federal Reserve Bullion Car "6445", *00*	—	47	___1
(19671)	Lionel Model Shop Display Car "6445-01", *99–00*	—	55	___1
(19672)	Lionel Mines Mint Car, *00u*	—	250	___1
19673	Wellspring Capital Management Mint Car, *99 u*		CP	___
19674	Lionel Lines Platinum Car, *00*	—	43	___1
19675	Lionel Model Shop Display "6445-2", *01*	—	42	___1
19676	Philadelphia Mint Car, *01*	—	40	___1
19677	Ft. Knox Mint Car "6445", *00*	—	45	___1
(19678)	US Army Bunk Car, *02*	—	45	___1
(19679)	St. Louis Federal Reserve Mint Car, *02*	—	40	___1
(19681)	Area 51 Alien Suspension Car, *02*	—	41	___1
(19682)	Alaska Klondike Mining Co. Mint Car, *02*	—	40	___1
(19686)	Chicago Federal Reserve Mint Car "6445", *03*		CP	___
(19687)	UP Smoking Bunk Car "3887", *03*		CP	___
(19688)	Postwar Fort Knox Mint Car "6445", *02-03*		CP	___
(19689)	CIBRO TankTrain Tank Car 3-pack (Std. 0), *03*		CP	___
(19696)	US Savings Bond Mint Car, *03*		CP	___
19700	Chessie System E/V Caboose, *88*	55	65	___1
19701	Milwaukee Road NSC Caboose (FF #2), *88*	44	55	___1
19702	PRR N5C Caboose, *87*	40	49	___1
19703	Great Northern E/V Caboose (FF #3), *88*	55	65	___1
19704	WM E/V Caboose w/ smoke (FF #4), *89*	43	50	___1
19705	CP Rail E/V Caboose w/ smoke, *89*	46	50	___1
(19706)	UP E/V Caboose w/ smoke "9706", *89*	45	50	___2
19707	SP Work Caboose w/ searchlight and smoke, *90*	70	85	___1
(19708)	Lionel Lines B/W Caboose "1990", *90*	47	50	___1
19709	PRR Work Caboose w/ smoke, *89, 91*	70	80	___1
19710	Frisco E/V Caboose w/ smoke (FF #5), *91*	50	55	___1
19711	Norfolk Southern E/V Caboose w/ smoke, *92*	47	65	___1
19712	PRR N5C Caboose, *91*	47	55	___1
19714	NYC Work Caboose w/ searchlight and smoke, *92*	95	115	___1
(19715)	DM&IR E/V Caboose "C-217", *92 u*	55	65	___1
(19716)	Illinois Central E/V Caboose w/ smoke "9405", *93*	75	90	___1
(19717)	Susquehanna B/W Caboose "0121", *93*	44	55	___1

		Exc	New	Cond/$
(19718)	Chicago & Illinois Midland E/V Caboose "74", *92 u*	38	45	___¹
(19719)	Erie B/W Caboose "C-300" (FF #7), *93*	47	55	___¹
19720	Soo Line E/V Caboose (SSS), *93*	46	55	___¹
(19721)	GM&O E/V Caboose "2956", *93 u*	47	50	___¹
19723	Disney E/V Caboose, *94*	50	65	___¹
(19724)	JC Penney/MKT E/V Caboose "125", *94 u*	50	60	___¹
19726	NYC B/W Caboose (SSS), *95*	43	50	___¹
(19727)	Pennsylvania N5C Caboose "477938", *96*	—	28	___¹
(19728)	N&W B/W Caboose, *96*	—	75	___¹
(19732)	AT&SF B/W Caboose "6517", *96*	—	46	___¹
(19733)	New York Central Caboose "6357", *96*	—	34	___¹
(19734)	Southern Pacific Caboose "6357", *96*	—	31	___¹
(19736)	PRR N5C Caboose "6417" "Buffalo Zone", tuscan, *97*	—	32	___¹
(19737)	Lackawanna Searchlight Caboose "2420", *97*	—	85	___¹
(19738)	Conrail N5C Caboose "6417" (SSS), *97*	—	50	___¹
(19739)	NYC Woodside Caboose "6907", *97*	—	70	___¹
(19740)	Virginian N5C Caboose "6427", *97 u*	—	60	___¹
(19741)	Pennsylvania N5C Caboose "6417", *98*	—	55	___¹
(19742)	Erie B/W Caboose w/ Caboose Talk "C301", *98*	—	75	___²
(19748)	SP&S B/W Caboose "6517", *97 u*	—	50	___¹
(19749)	SP B/W Caboose "6517", *98*	—	100	___¹
(19750)	1998 Holiday Music B/W Caboose, *98*	—	165	___¹
(19751)	PRR Caboose N5C PRR "492418", *98*	—	39	___¹
(19752)	NP B/W Caboose "407", *98*	—	55	___¹
(19753)	UP E/V Caboose "25641", *98*	—	55	___¹
(19754)	NYC 7606 Caboose "20112", *98*	—	55	___¹
(19755)	Centennial Porthole Caboose, *99*	—	55	___¹
(19756)	Lionel Lines B/W Caboose, *99*	—	50	___¹
(19758)	DL&W Work Caboose "6419", *99*	—	55	___¹
(19759)	Corvette N5C Caboose, *99*	—	60	___¹
(19772)	Lionel Visitor's Center Vat Car, *99 u*	—	50	___¹
(19773)	Lionel Kids Club Barrel Ramp Car "6343", *96 u*		NRS	___
(19774)	LRRC Caboose Porthole "1999", *99 u*	—	55	___²
19775	LRRC Stock Car, *99*			
(19778)	Southern/Case Cutlery Woodside Caboose 1889 (Std. O), *99u*		NRS	___
(19779)	SP B/W Caboose "1908", *99*	—	55	___¹
(19780)	LV Porthole Caboose "641751", *99–00*	—	48	___¹
(19781)	Vapor Records Holiday Porthole Caboose "6417", *99–00*	—	42	___¹

		Exc	New	Cond/$
(19782)	NYC B/W Caboose "21719", *00*	—	75	___1
(19783)	Ford Mustang E/V Caboose, *01*		NRS	___
(19785)	SP B/W Caboose "6517", *00*	—	60	___1
(19786)	Pennsylvania RR E/V Caboose, *00u*	—	40	___1
(19787)	Pennsylvania RR E/V Caboose "477927", *01*	—	40	___1
(19790)	Postwar Lehigh Valley Caboose "6417", *02*	—	40	___1
(19792)	Postwar Erie B/W Caboose "C301", *03*		CP	___
19800	Circle L Ranch Operating Cattle Car, *88*	95	135	___1
19801	Poultry Dispatch Chicken Car, *87*	31	45	___1
19802	Carnation Milk Car, *87*	95	105	___1
19803	Reading Ice Car, *87*	42	50	___2
19804	Wabash Operating Hopper, *87*	27	35	___1
19805	Santa Fe Operating Boxcar, *87*	25	33	___1
19806	PRR Operating Hopper, *88*	35	42	___1
19807	PRR E/V Caboose w/ smoke, *88*	40	47	___3
19808	NYC Ice Car, *88*	43	50	___1
19809	Erie-Lackawanna Operating Boxcar, *88*	27	35	___1
19810	Bosco Milk Car, *88*	110	135	___2
19811	Monon Brakeman Car, *90*	55	60	___1
19813	Northern Pacific Ice Car, *89 u*	42	50	___1
19815	Delaware & Hudson Brakeman Car, *92*	45	55	___1
(19816)	Madison Hardware Operating Boxcar "190991", *91 u*	190	225	___2
19817	Virginian Ice Car, *94*	37	45	___1
(19818)	Dairymen's League Milk Car "788", *94*	85	105	___1
19819	Poultry Dispatch Car (SSS), *94*	36	43	___1
(19820)	Die-cast Metal Tender w/ RailSounds II, *95–96*	—	175	___1
(19821)	UP Operating Boxcar, *95*	35	41	___1
19822	Pork Dispatch Car, *95*	32	41	___1
19823	Burlington Ice Car, *94 u, 95*	40	47	___1
(19824)	US Army Target Launcher, *96*	—	29	___2
19825	EMD Generator Car, *96*	—	50	___2
(19827)	NYC Operating Boxcar, *97*	—	38	___1
(19828)	C&NW Animated Stock Car and Stockyard "3356", *96–97*	—	130	___1
(19830)	US Mail Operating Boxcar "3428", *97*	—	42	___1
(19831)	GM Generator Car w/ power pole and wire "3530", *97*	—	55	___1
(19832)	Lionel Cola Ice Car "6352", *97*	—	43	___1
(19833)	Railsounds II Tender "2426RS", *97*	—	240	___1
(19834)	LL 6-Wheel Crane Car "2460", *97*	—	55	___1
(19835)	FedEx Animated Boxcar "3464X", *97*	—	38	___1
(19837)	Bucyrus 6-Wheel Crane Car "2460", *99*	—	55	___1

		Exc	New	Cond/$
(19845)	Command Control Aquarium Car "3435", *98*	—	165	___¹
(19846)	Animated Giraffe Car "3376C", *98*	—	185	___¹
(19850)	Lionel RailSounds Stock Car "33760", *00*	—	130	___¹
(19853)	Firefighting Instruction Generator Car (SSS), *98*	—	60	___¹
(19854)	Lionelville Fire Car #1 (SSS), *98*	—	55	___¹
(19855)	Christmas "Aquarium" Car, *98*	—	60	___¹
(19856)	Mermaid Transport, *98*	—	65	___¹
(19857)	NYC Fire Instruction Car "19853", *98–99*	—	175	___¹
(19858)	Lionelville Operational Searchlight Car "19854", *99*	—	55	___¹
(19859)	REA Steam R/S Boxcar "6267", *99*	—	180	___¹
(19860)	Conrail Diesel R/S Boxcar "169671", *99*	—	140	___¹
(19864)	Animated Ostrich Boxcar "9700", *99*	—	34	___¹
(19867)	Operational Poultry Dispatch Car "3434", *99*	—	45	___¹
(19868)	Shark Aquarium Car "3435", *99*	—	190	___¹
(19869)	Alien Aquarium Car "3435", *99*	—	43	___¹
(19877)	AT&SF Operating Barrel Car, *99*	—	50	___¹
(19878)	Operating Helium Tank Flatcar "3362", *99*	—	34	___¹
19880	Lionel Lines Ext Searchlight Car, *00*	—	45	___¹
(19882)	Sanderson Farms Poultry Car "3434", *99*	—	49	___¹
(19883)	Lionel Lines Bucyrus Erie Crane Car "64608", *99*		NRS	___
19884	Atlantis Travel Aquarium Car, *00 u*	—	75	___¹
(19885)	3456 N&W Operating Hopper Car "22000", *00*	—	36	___¹
(19886)	Seaboard Boxcar w/ Steam RailSounds "16126", *00*	—	125	___¹
(19887)	SP Boxcar w/ Diesel RailSounds "651663", *00*	—	125	___¹
(19888)	Christmas Music Boxcar, *01*	—	85	___¹
(19889)	PRR B/W Caboose w/ Crewtalk "477719", *00*	—	155	___¹
(19890)	Santa Fe B/W Caboose w/ Crewtalk "999211", *00*	—	160	___¹
(19894)	Hood's Milk Car w/ platform, *03*		CP	___
(19896)	US Marines Missile Launch Sound Car "45", *03*		CP	___
(19899)	Pennsylvania Command Control Crane Car "19899", *03*		CP	___
19900	Toy Fair Boxcar, *87 u*	75	95	___¹
19901	"I Love Virginia" Boxcar, *87*	25	35	___¹
19902	Toy Fair Boxcar, *88 u*	70	90	___¹
19903	Christmas Boxcar, *87 u*	40	49	___¹
19904	Christmas Boxcar, *88 u*	36	49	___¹
19905	"I Love California" Boxcar, *88*	22	28	___¹
19906	"I Love Pennsylvania" Boxcar, *89*	22	27	___¹
19907	Toy Fair Boxcar, *89 u*	65	80	___¹

		Exc	New	Cond/$
19908	Christmas Boxcar, *89 u*	39	50	___²
19909	"I Love New Jersey" Boxcar, *90*	21	27	___¹
19910	Christmas Boxcar, *90 u*	28	33	___²
19911	Toy Fair Boxcar, *90 u*	85	110	___¹
19912	"I Love Ohio" Boxcar, *91*	21	26	___¹
(19913)	Christmas Boxcar, regular issue, *91*	40	50	___¹
19913	Christmas Boxcar for Lionel Employees, *91 u*	165	190	___¹
19914	Toy Fair Boxcar, *91 u*	65	80	___¹
19915	"I Love Texas" Boxcar, *92*	35	60	___¹
19916	Christmas Boxcar for Lionel Employees, *92 u*	280	325	___¹
19917	Toy Fair Boxcar, *92 u*	90	110	___¹
19918	Christmas Boxcar, *92 u*	65	85	___¹
19919	"I Love Minnesota" Boxcar, *93*	40	60	___¹
(19920)	Lionel Visitor's Center Boxcar, *92 u*	28	36	___¹
19921	Christmas Boxcar for Lionel Employees, *93 u*	160	190	___¹
19922	Christmas Boxcar, *93*	31	38	___¹
19923	Toy Fair Boxcar, *93 u*	70	105	___¹
19924	Lionel Railroader Club Boxcar, *93 u*	22	27	___²
19925	Learning Center Boxcar for Lionel Employees, *93 u*	125	135	___¹
19926	"I Love Nevada" Boxcar, *94*	21	26	___¹
(19927)	Lionel Visitor's Center Boxcar "1993", *93 u*	26	33	___¹
19928	Christmas Boxcar for Lionel Employees, *94 u*	300	350	___¹
19929	Christmas Boxcar, *94*	30	40	___¹
19930	Lionel Railroader Club Quad Hopper w/ coal load, *94 u*	26	28	___²
19931	Toy Fair Boxcar, *94 u*	70	100	___²
19932	Lionel Visitor's Center Boxcar, *94 u*	28	36	___¹
19933	"I Love Illinois" Boxcar, *95*	21	27	___¹
(19934)	Lionel Visitor's Center Boxcar "1995", *95 u*	25	33	___¹
(19935)	Lionel Railroader Club 1-D Tank Car "1995", *95 u*	25	32	___¹
19937	Toy Fair Boxcar, *95 u*	55	75	___¹
19938	Christmas Boxcar, *95*	29	37	___¹
19939	Christmas Boxcar for Lionel Employees, *95 u*	320	375	___¹
(19940)	Lionel Railroad Vat Car, *96 u*	—	33	___¹
19941	"I Love Colorado" Boxcar, *95*	23	30	___¹
19942	"I Love Florida" Boxcar, *96*	19	24	___¹
(19943)	"I Love Arizona" Boxcar, *96*	19	24	___¹
(19944)	Lionel Visitor's Center Tank Car, *96 u*	—	38	___¹
(19945)	Holiday Boxcar, *96*	—	31	___²
(19946)	Christmas Boxcar for Lionel Employees, *96 u*	—	200	___¹

		Exc	New	Cond/$
(19947)	Lionel Corporation Toy Fair Boxcar "9700", *96 u*	—	150	___1
(19948)	Visitors Center Flatar w/ trailer, *96 u*	—	41	___1
(19949)	"I Love NY" Boxcar "9700", *97*	—	39	___1
(19950)	"I Love Montana" Boxcar "9700", *97*	—	27	___1
(19951)	"I Love Massachusetts" Boxcar "9700", *98*	—	29	___1
(19952)	"I Love Indiana" Boxcar, "9700", *98*	—	31	___1
(19953)	LRRC Boxcar, *97 u*	—	45	___1
(19955)	Lionel Visitor's Center Gondola w/ coil covers, *98 u*	—	31	___1
(19956)	Toy Fair 9700 Boxcar "777", *98 u*	—	65	___1
(19957)	Ambassadore Caboose "1997", *97 u*	—	400	___1
(19958)	Ambassador Silver Caboose, "1998" (Std O), *98 u*	—	500	___1
(19959)	Ambassador Gold Caboose, "1998" (Std O), *98 u*	—	700	___1
(19960)	LOTS Western Pacific Boxcar "1952" (Std. O), *92 u*	60	75	___1
19961	Gadsden Pacific Inspiration Consolidated Copper Company Ore Car w/ load, *92 u*	36	40	___1
(19962)	Southwest TTOS SP 3-bay ACF Hopper "496035" (Std. O), *92 u*	50	65	___1
(19963)	TTOS Union Equity 3-bay ACF Hopper "86892" (Std. O), *92 u*	38	44	___1
(19964)	US JCI Senate Boxcar, *92 u*	70	95	___1
(19965)	LRRC Aquarium Car "3435", *99 u*	—	80	___1
(19966)	LRRC Gondola "9820" (Std O), *98 u*	20	32	___2
(19967)	Kids Club Animated Gondola, *98 u*	—	43	___1
(19968)	"I Love Maine" Boxcar "9700", *99*	—	500	___1
(19969)	"I Love Vermont" Boxcar "9700", *99*	—	700	___1
(19970)	"I Love New Hampshire" Boxcar "9700", *99*	—	34	___1
(19971)	"I Love Rhode Island" Boxcar "9700", *99*	—	34	___1
(19976)	Lionel Employee Holiday Boxcar "1999", *99 u*	—	180	___1
(19977)	Toy Fair Boxcar "9700", *99 u*	—	70	___2
(19978)	"Gold" Boxcar "1900-2000", *99–00*	—	60	___1
(19981)	Lionel Centennial Boxcar "1998-1", *99*	—	30	___1
(19982)	Lionel Centennial Boxcar "1998-2", *99*	—	30	___1
(19983)	Lionel Centennial Boxcar "1998-3", *99*	—	30	___1
(19984)	Lionel Centennial Boxcar "1998-4", *99*	—	30	___1
(19985)	I Love Georgia 9700 Boxcar, *99–00*	—	45	___1
(19986)	I Love North Carolina 9700 Boxcar, *99–00*	—	40	___1
(19987)	I Love South Carolina 9700 Boxcar, *99–00*	—	40	___1
(19988)	I Love Tennessee 9700 Boxcar, *99–00*	—	65	___1

		Exc	New	Cond/$
(19989)	Toy Fair Boxcar, *00 u*	—	70	___[1]
(19991)	LRRC Gold Club Boxcar, *00 u*	—	65	___[1]
(19992)	Western Union Tel. LRRC Tool Car "3550", *00 u*	—	55	___[1]
(19994)	LRRC Western Union Camp Car "1307", *01 u*	—	60	___[1]
19995	LRRC 25th Anniversary Boxcar (Std. O), *01*			
(19996)	Toy Fair 2001 Boxcar, *01u*	—	50	___[1]
(19997)	Lionel Employee 2001 Boxcar, *01u*	—	100	___[1]
(19998)	Christmas Boxcar, *01*	—	41	___[1]
(21029)	World of Little Choo Choo set, *94 u, 95*	36	43	___[1]
21596	(See 17898)			
(21719)	NYC B/W Caboose, *99*	—	70	___[1]
(21750)	Nickel Plate Rolling Stock 4-pack, *98*	—	160	___[1]
(21751)	PRR Rolling Stock 4-pack, *98*	—	170	___[1]
(21752)	Conrail Unit Trailer Train Set, *98*	—	390	___[1]
(21753)	1998 Service Station Fire Rescue Train set, *98*	450	500	___[1]
(21754)	BNSF 3-bay Covered Hopper 2-pack (Std. O), *98*	—	65	___[1]
(21755)	4-bay Covered Hoppers 2-pack, *98*	—	65	___[1]
(21756)	Overstamped 6464 Style Boxcars 2-pack, *98*	—	55	___[1]
(21757)	UP Freight Car set, *98*	—	190	___[1]
(21758)	Bethlehem Steel Service Station Exclusive "44", *99*	—	345	___[1]
(21759)	Canadian Pacific F3 Passenger set, *99*	—	1200	___[2]
(21761)	B&M Boxcar set 4-pack, *99*	—	180	___[1]
(21763)	New Haven Freight set, *99*	—	230	___[1]
(21766)	ACL Passenger Car set 2-pack, *99*	—	250	___[1]
(21769)	Centennial 1-D Tank Car Set 4-pack, *99*	—	180	___[1]
(21770)	NYC Reefer set 4-pack, *99*	—	175	___[1]
(21771)	D&RGW Stock Car Set 4-pack, *99*	—	275	___[1]
(21774)	Custom Series Consist I 3-pack "6424", *99*	—	150	___[1]
(21775)	Lionel Train Wreck Recovery set, *99*	—	205	___[1]
(21778)	AT&SF Trainmaster Freight set, *99*		NRS	___
(21779)	Seaboard Freight Car set, *99*	—	235	___[1]
(21780)	NYC Aluminum Pass Car set 2-pack, *99*	—	150	___[1]
(21781)	Case Cutlery Freight set, *99u*	—	1000	___[1]
(21782)	PRR Congressional set, *00*	—	910	___[1]
(21783)	Monday Night Football 2-pack, *01–02*	—	50	___[1]
(21784)	QVC PRR Coal Freight Steam set, *00 u*	—	395	___[1]
(21785)	QVC Gold Mine Freight Steam set, *00 u*	—	345	___[1]
(21786)	Santa Fe ABBA F3 Passenger set "200", *00*	—	1750	___[1]
(21787)	Blue Comet Steam Passenger set, *01–02*	—	1050	___[1]

		Exc	New	Cond/$
(21788)	Postwar Missile Launch Freight set, *02–03*	—	330	___ [1]
(21789)	NS GP-9 Flatcar set "102", SSS, CC, *01*	—	500	___ [1]
(21790)	CN TankTrain Dash 9 Diesel Freight set, *02*	—	540	___ [1]
(21791)	Freedom Train Diesel Passenger set w/RailSounds, *03*		CP	___
(21792)	C&O Coal Hopper 6-pack #2 (Std. O), *01*	—	145	___ [1]
(21793)	Virginian Coal Hopper 6-pack #2 (Std. O), *01*	—	160	___ [1]
(21794)	Pioneer Seed GP-7 Freight set, *01 u*	—	825	___ [1]
(21795)	Case Farmall Freight set, *01u*	—	830	___ [1]
(21796)	Lionel Centennial Freight set, *01 u*		CP	___
(21797)	SP Daylight Passenger set, *01*	—	690	___ [1]
(21900)	Union Civil War Train set, *99*	—	320	___ [1]
(21901)	Confederate Civil War Train set, *99*	—	320	___ [1]
(21902)	Construction Zone set, *99 u*	—	87	___ [1]
(21904)	Safari Adventure set, *99 u*	—	90	___ [1]
(21905)	NYC Flyer for Mass Merchants set, *99u*		CP	___
(21909)	AGFA Film Steam Freight set, *98 u*	—	1200	___ [1]
(21914)	Lionel Lines Freight set, *99*	—	105	___ [1]
(21916)	Lionel Village Trolley, *99*	—	70	___ [1]
(21917)	N&W Freight set, *99*	—	70	___ [1]
(21918)	Thomas Circus Play set, *00*	—	100	___ [1]
(21920)	Amtrak "Talgo" Passenger set, *99*		NM	___
(21922)	Erie Lackawanna Phoebe Snow Passenger set, *99*	—	1300	___ [1]
(21924)	Holiday Trolley set, *99*	—	65	___ [1]
(21925)	Thomas Tank Engine Island of Sodor Train set, *99–00*	—	150	___ [1]
(21932)	JC Penney NYC Freight Flyer Steam set, *00 u*	—	170	___ [1]
(21934)	Custom Series Consist II 3-pack "6424", *99*	—	150	___ [1]
(21936)	WB Looney Tunes set, *00 u*	—	290	___ [1]
(21944)	"Celebrate a Lionel Christmas" Steam set, *00–01*	—	145	___ [1]
(21945)	Christmas Trolley set, *00*	—	100	___ [1]
(21948)	NYC Freight Flyer set w/ air whistle, *00*	—	240	___ [1]
(21950)	Maersk SD70 Maxi-stack set, *00*	—	500	___ [1]
(21951)	World War II Troop Train set, *00*	—	425	___ [1]
(21952)	2000 Lionel Lines Service Station Special set, *00*	—	350	___ [1]
(21953)	Ford Mustang GP-7 CC set, *01*	—	340	___ [1]
(21955)	D&RG F3 AA Passenger set "5521", CC, *01*	—	1000	___ [1]
(21956)	New York Central Freight set "5412", *99–00*	—	390	___ [1]
(21969)	Lionel Village Trolley set, *00*	—	75	___ [1]
(21970)	SP RS-3 Diesel Freight set w/ horn, *00–01*	—	110	___ [1]
(21971)	Pennsylvania Flyer Steam set, *00*	—	150	___ [1]

		Exc	New	Cond/$
(21972)	Frisco GP-7 Diesel Freight set w/ horn, *00*	—	150	___¹
(21973)	AT&SF Passenger set w/ RailSounds, *00–01*	—	375	___¹
(21974)	AT&SF Passenger set w/ SignalSounds, *00–01*	—	240	___¹
(21975)	Burlington Steam Freight set w/ SignalSounds, *00*	—	275	___¹
(21976)	Centennial Steam Freight Starter set, *00*	—	575	___¹
(21977)	NYC Trainmaster Freight set, *99–00*	—	750	___¹
(21978)	AT&SF Trainmaster Freight set, *99–00*	—	500	___¹
(21981)	Pennsey NYC Flyer set, *00u*	—	150	___¹
(21988)	NYC Freight set w/ RailSounds, *00*	—	330	___¹
(21989)	Burlington Steam Freight set w/ RailSounds, *00—*	—	300	___¹
(21990)	NYC Flyer Freight set w/ RailSounds, *00*	—	175	___¹
(21999)	Whirlpool Steam Freight set, *00 u*	—	680	___¹
(22902)	Quonset Hut, *98–99*	—	22	___¹
(22907)	Die-cast Girder Bridge, *98–01*	—	10	___¹
(22910)	Gilbert Tractor-Trailer, *98*	—	20	___¹
(22914)	PowerHouse Lockon, *98–01*	—	21	___¹
(22915)	Municipal Building, *98–99*	—	30	___¹
(22916)	190-watt Power Accessory System, *98*	—	425	___¹
(22918)	The Lionel Locomotive Backshop, *98*	—	330	___²
(22919)	ElectroCouplers kit for GP-9, *98–00*	—	20	___¹
(22920)	Steam Service Siding, *98*	NM		___
(22922)	Intermodal Crane, *98*	—	185	___¹
(22929)	Lionel Factory, *98*	NM		___
(22931)	Die-cast Cantilever Signal Bridge, *98–03*	—	32	___¹
(22932)	High Tension Metal Wire Tower, *98*	NM		___
(22933)	Section Gang House, *98*	NM		___
(22934)	Walkout Cantilever Signal, *98–03*	—	38	___¹
(22935)	Hot Box Detector, *98*	NM		___
(22936)	3-piece Coaling Tower, *98*	—	65	___¹
(22938)	High Tension Plastic Tower, *98*	NM		___
(22939)	Transformer Substation, *98*	NM		___
(22940)	Mast Signal, *98–00*	—	37	___¹
(22942)	Accessories Box, *98–01*	CP		___
(22944)	Automatic Operating Semaphore, *98–03*	—	25	___¹
(22945)	Block Target Signal, *98–00*	—	39	___¹
(22946)	Automatic Crossing Gate and Railroad Crossing Signal, *98–99*	CP		___
(22947)	Auto Crossing Gate, *98–00*	—	36	___¹
(22948)	Gooseneck Street Lamps set of 2, *98–00*	—	230	___¹
(22949)	Highway Lights set of 4, *98–99*	CP		___
(22950)	Classic Street Lamps set of 3, *98–02*	CP		___
(22951)	Dwarf Signal, *98–00*	—	24	___¹

		Exc	New	Cond/$
(22952)	Classic Billboard set of 3, *98–00*		CP	____
(22953)	Linex Gasoline Tall Oil Tank, *98–99*	—	6	____[1]
(22954)	Linex Gasoline Wide Oil Tank, *98–99*	—	6	____[1]
(22955)	ElectroCouplers kit for J-class Tender and B&A Tender, *98–00*	—	20	____[1]
(22956)	ElectroCouplers kit for Switcher/NW2, *98*	—	20	____[1]
(22957)	ElectroCouplers kit for F3, *98–01*	—	20	____[1]
(22958)	ElectroCouplers kit for Dash 9, *98–01*	—	20	____[1]
(22959)	ElectroCoupler Conversion kit for Atlantic Steamer, *98–01*	—	13	____[1]
(22960)	TrainMaster Command Basic Upgrade kit, *98–01*	—	30	____[1]
(22961)	Standard GP-9 B Unit Upgrade kit, *98–01*	—	30	____[1]
(22962)	Deluxe GP-9 B Unit Upgrade kit (w/ black trucks), *98–01*	—	48	____[1]
(22963)	RailSounds Upgrade kit w/ Steam Railsounds, *98–01*	—	50	____[1]
(22964)	RailSounds Upgrade kit w/ Diesel Railsounds, *98–01*	—	50	____[1]
(22965)	Command Control Culvert Loader, *98–01*	—	245	____[1]
(22966)	Figure-8 Add-On Track Pack (O-27), *98–03*		CP	____
(22967)	Double-Loop Add-On Track Pack (O-27), *98–03*		CP	____
(22968)	Double-Loop Complete Track Pack (O-27), *98–03*	—	65	____[1]
(22969)	Deluxe Complete Track Pack (O gauge), *98–03*		CP	____
(22972)	Bascule Bridge, *98–99*	—	260	____[1]
(22973)	Lionel Corp Tractor-Trailer, *98*	—	14	____[1]
(22975)	Culvert Unloader CC, *99–00*	—	205	____[1]
(22979)	GP-9 B-Unit Deluxe Upgrade kit (w/ silver trucks), *98–01*		CP	____
(22980)	TMCC SC-2 Switch Controller, *99–03*	55	39	____[1]
(22982)	ZW Postwar Celebration Series Controller and Transformer set, *98*	—	260	____[1]
(22983)	180-watt PowerHouse Power Supply, *99–03*	—	65	____[1]
(22990)	Rt. 66 Autos on Flatcar 4-pack, *99*	—	28	____[1]
(22991)	Christmas Tree w/ Blue Comet Train, *99–00*	—	55	____[1]
(22993)	Rt. 66 Sinclair/Dino Cafe, *99–00*	—	290	____[1]
(22997)	Oil Drum Loader, *99–00*	—	115	____[1]
(22998)	Triple Action Magnetic Crane, *99*	—	200	____[1]
(22999)	Sound Dispatching Station, *99–00*	—	90	____[1]
(23000)	Operating Base Smithsonian NYC Dreyfuss Hudson (2-rail), *92 u*	—	190	____[1]

		Exc	New	Cond/$
(23001)	Operating Base NYC Dreyfuss Hudson (3-rail), *93 u*	—	190	___[1]
(23002)	Operating Base NYC Hudson, *92 u, 93–94*	—	190	___[1]
(23003)	Operating Base PRR B-6 Switcher, *92 u, 93–94*	—	190	___[1]
(23004)	Operating Base NP 4-8-4, *92 u, 93–94*	—	190	___[1]
(23005)	Operating Base Reading T-1, *92 u, 93–94*	—	190	___[1]
(23006)	Operating Base Chessie System T-1, *92 u, 93–94*	—	190	___[1]
(23007)	Operating Base SP Daylight, *92 u, 93–94*	—	190	___[1]
(23008)	Operating Base NYC L-3 Mohawk, *92 u, 93–94*	—	190	___[1]
(23009)	Operating Base PRR S-2 Turbine, *92 u, 93–94*	—	190	___[1]
(23010)	Left Remote Switch 31" "3010" (O), *95–99*	—	32	___[1]
(23011)	Right Remote Switch 31" "3011" (O), *95–99*	—	32	___[1]
(23012)	Operating Base F-3 ABA Diesels, *92 u, 93–94*	—	190	___[1]
(24102)	Industrial Water Tower, *03*		CP	___
(24103)	Double Floodlight Tower, *03*		CP	___
(24104)	Hobo Tower, *03*		CP	___
(24105)	Track Gang, *03*		CP	___
(24106)	Exploding Ammunition Dump, *02*	—	22	___[1]
(24107)	Missile Firing Range set, *02*	—	60	___[1]
(24108)	World War II Pylon, *03*		CP	___
(24109)	Santa Fe Railroad Tugboat, *03*		CP	___
(24110)	Pennsylvania Railroad Tugboat, *03*		CP	___
(24111)	Swing Bridge, *03*		CP	___
(24112)	Oil Field w/ bubble tubes, *03*		CP	___
(24113)	Lionelville Ford auto dealership, *03*		CP	___
(24114)	"AMC/ARC Gantry Crane, CC", *03*		CP	___
(24115)	"AMC/ARC Log Loader, CC", *03*		CP	___
(24117)	Covered Bridge, *02–03*		CP	___
(24122)	Lionelville People Pack, *03*		CP	___
(24123)	Passenger Station People Pack, *03*		CP	___
(24124)	Carnival People Pack, *03*		CP	___
(24131)	Dumbo Pylon, *03*		CP	___
(24134)	Bethlehem Steel Gantry Crane, *02*	—	145	___[1]
(24135)	Lionel Lighthouse, *02-03*		CP	___
(24137)	Mr. Spiff and Puddles Historic Layout, *03*		CP	___
(24138)	Playtime Playground Historic Layout, *03*		CP	___
(24139)	Duck Shooting Gallery Historic Layout, *03*		CP	___
(24140)	Charles Bowdish Homestead Historic Layout, *03*		CP	___
(24147)	Lionel Sawmill, *03*		CP	___
(24148)	Coal Tipple Coal Pack, *02*		CP	___
(24149)	NYC Hobo Hotel, *02*	—	37	___[1]
(24152)	Conveyor Lumber Loader, *03*		CP	___

		Exc	New	Cond/$
(24153)	Railroad Control Tower, *03*		CP	___
(24154)	Maiden Rescue, *03*		CP	___
(24173)	Derrick Platform "462", *03*		CP	___
(24504)	Santa Fe E6 A-A "14-15", CC, *03*		CP	___
(24507)	Milwaukee Road E6 A-A "15-16", CC, *03*		CP	___
(24511)	Burlington FT A-A set "113-A/D" w/ RailSounds, *03*		CP	___
(24516)	Santa Fe F3 B Unit, *03*		CP	___
(24517)	NYC F3 B Unit, *03*		CP	___
(24518)	WP F3 B Unit, *03*		CP	___
(24519)	B&O F3 B Unit, *03*		CP	___
(24520)	Alaska F3 A-A set, *03*		CP	___
(24521)	Alaska F3 B Unit (nonpowered), *03*		CP	___
(24522)	Alaska F3 B Unit, *03*		CP	___
(26000)	C&O Flatcar w/ pipes, *01*	—	20	___1
(26001)	BP Flatcar w/ trailers "6424", *01u*		NRS	___
(26002)	Monopoly Flatcar w/ airplane, *00u*		NRS	___
(26003)	Lackawanna Flatcar w/ NH trailer, *01*	—	60	___1
(26004)	Conrail Flatcar w/ trailer "71693", *01*	—	50	___1
(26005)	Nickel Plate Flatcar w/ trailer, *01*	—	50	___1
(26006)	Southern Flatcar w/ trailer "50126", *01*	—	50	___1
(26007)	NW Flatcar w/ trailer "203029", *01*	—	50	___1
(26008)	Farmall Flatcar, *01u*		NRS	___
(26011)	B&M Flatcar w/ bulkheads, *01u*		NRS	___
26013	CN Flatcar w/ Zamboni "26013", *01*	—	44	___1
(26014)	JC Penney Flatcar, *01u*		NRS	___
(26016)	Soo Line Flatcar w/ trucks, *01u*		NRS	___
(26017)	Soo Line Flatcar w/ trailer, *01u*		CP	___
(26018)	Soo Line Flatcar w/ trailer, *01u*		NRS	___
(26019)	Alaska Gondola "13801", *02*	—	30	___1
(26020)	Postwar Flatcar w/ submarine "3830", *02*	—	38	___1
(26021)	CN Flatcar w/ trailer features "685965", *02*	—	32	___1
(26022)	PFE Flatcar w/ trailer features "26022", *02*	—	32	___1
(26023)	Postwar Flatcar w/ bulldozer "6816", *02*	—	40	___1
(26024)	Postwar Flatcar w/ scraper "6817", *02*	—	40	___1
(26025)	Postwar Flatcar w/ rocket "6407", *02*	—	34	___1
(26026)	Postwar Flatcar w/ Mercury capsules 6413, *02*	—	75	___1
(26027)	Flatcar w/ US Army boat "6425", *02*	—	30	___1
(26028)	Conrail Well Car "768121", *02*	—	40	___1
(26033)	NYC Gondola "6462", *01*	—	30	___1
(26035)	Lionel Lines Flatcar w/ traffic helicopter, *01*	—	50	___1
(26039)	Lionel Lions Flatcar w/ Zamboni ice machines, *02*	—	39	___1

		Exc	New	Cond/$
(26526)	Santa Fe S/W Caboose "999471", *01*	—	28	___1
(26527)	Christmas Work Caboose w/ presents, *02*	—	32	___1
(26528)	PRR S/W Caboose "6257", *99*	—	21	___1
(26530)	LL S/W Caboose "6257", *99*	—	22	___1
(26532)	NYC S/W Caboose "296", *00*	—	20	___1
(26533)	SP S/W Caboose, *00*	—	20	___1
(26534)	PRR S/W Caboose "6257", *00*	—	20	___1
(26535)	Frisco S/W Caboose "1700", *00*	—	20	___1
(26536)	Centennial Express S/W Caboose, *00*	NRS		___
(26537)	Lionel Mines S/W Caboose, *00u*	—	45	___1
(26539)	Whirlpool S/W Caboose, *00u*	NRS		___
	ACL S/W Caboose "069", *01*	—	31	___1
	GN S/W Caboose "X66", *0u–01*	—	28	___1
	Alaska S/W Caboose "1084", *01*	—	25	___1
	Snap-On S/W Caboose, *00u*	NRS		___
	Pioneer Seed S/W Caboose, *00u*	NRS		___
	PRR S/W Caboose "4977947", *01*	—	20	___1
	NYC S/W Caboose "19293", *01*	—	20	___1
	Chessie System Center Cupola Caboose, *01*	—	25	___1
	Santa Fe S/W Caboose "999472", *01*	—	25	___1
	O Center Cupola Caboose "A918", *01*	—	30	___1
	Monopoly Short Line S/W Caboose, *00u*	NRS		___
	Center Cupola Caboose, *01*	—	35	___1
	all S/W Caboose, *01u*	NRS		___
	Center Cupola Caboose "518408", *01*	—	20	___1
	S/W Caboose, *01u*	—	20	___1
	Center Cupola Caboose, *01u*	—	20	___1
	Employee S/W Caboose "2001", *01u*	—	200	___1
	Caboose "731", *02*	—	25	1
	te S/W Caboose "1155", *02*			
	S/W Caboose "252",			

(26524) (26523) (26520) (26519) (26516) (26515) (26513) (26511) (26508) (26507) (26506) (2650...
Quaker ... NYC Emer... Alas... Safari RR Bob... Lionel Lines ... Christmas Work C... Bethlehem Steel Wor... Keebler Cheezit S/W Cab... NYC S/W Caboose "295" ... NRS 20

		Exc	New	Cond/$
(26042)	B&O Gondola w/ canisters "601272", *03*		CP	___
(26043)	Seaboard Flatcar w/ trailer "48109", *03*		CP	___
(26044)	NYC Flatcar w/ trailers "506089", *03*		CP	___
(26045)	Postwar Flatcar w/ big inch pipes "2411", *03*		CP	___
(26046)	Postwar Flatcar w/ cable reels "6561", *03*		CP	___
(26047)	Postwar Flatcar w/ transformer "2461", *03*		CP	___
(26048)	Lionel Postwar Flatcar w/ boat "6801", *02*	—	32	___1
(26049)	Steamboat Willie Flatcar w/ boat, *03*		CP	___
(26056)	Southern Flatcar w/ bulkheads "50125", *02*	—	19	___1
(26057)	SP Flatcar w/ tractors "599365", *02*	—	37	___1
(26058)	SP Flatcar w/ trailer frames "599366", *02*	—	35	___1
(26061)	Lionelville Tree Transport Gondola, *03*		CP	___
(26062)	NYC Gondola w/ cable reels "26062", *03*		CP	___
(26063)	Pennsylvania Flatcar w/ bulkheads "26063", *03*		CP	___
(26070)	Nestle Nesquik Flatcar w/ trailer "26070", *03*		CP	___
(26077)	Girl"s Lionel Lines Flatcar w/ autos "6424", *03*		CP	___
(26078)	Boy"s Lionel Lines Flatcar w/ boat "6801", *03*		CP	___
(26100)	PRR 1-D Tank Car, *00*	—	25	___1
(26101)	Lenoil 1-D Tank Car "6015", *00*	—	32	___1
(26102)	AEC Glow-in-Dark 1-D Tank Car, *00*	—	31	___1
(26103)	GATX Tank Train 1-D Tank Car "44588", *00*	—	34	___1
(26107)	BP Petroleum 3-D Tank Car, *00 u*	—	95	___1
(26108)	Lionel Visitor Center Searchlight Car "2000", *00u*	—	30	___1
(26109)	NYC/P&LE 1-D Tank Car, *00*	—	42	___1
(26110)	SP 3-D Tank Car "6415", *00–01*	—	15	___1
(26111)	Frisco Tank Car, *00*	—	25	___1
(26112)	Gulf Oil Tank Car, *00*	—	35	___1
(26113)	US Army Tank Car, *00*		CP	___
(26114)	Service Station Ltd. 1-D Tank Car (SSS), *00*	—	30	___1
(26115)	Lionel Celebrate 1-D Tank Car, *00 u*	—	65	___1
(26116)	Pepe La Pew 1-D Tank Car, *00 u*	—	90	___1
(26118)	NYC Tank Car "101900", *01*	—	25	___1
26119	Protex 3-D Tank Car "1054", *00*	—	32	___1
26120	KCS Tank Car "1229", *00*	—	37	___1
(26122)	Pioneer Seed Tank Car, *00u*	NRS		___
(26123)	Santa Fe Stock Car "23002", *01*	—	35	___1
(26124)	C&O 1-D Tank Car "X1019", *01*	—	30	___1
(26126)	Cheerios Boxcar, *98*	—	40	___1
26127	Wellspring Capital Management Clear 1-D Tank Car w/ confetti, *00 u*		CP	___
(26131)	Santa Fe 1-D Tank Car "335268, *02*	—	19	___1
(26132)	UP 1-D Tank Car "69015, *02*	—	35	___1

		Exc	New	Cond/$
(26133)	Tootsie Roll 1-D Tank Car "26133, *02*	—	35	[1]
(26136)	Southern 1-D Tank Car "8790011", *03*		CP	
(26137)	Jack Frost 1-D Tank Car "106", *03*		CP	
(26138)	Nestle Nesquick 1-D Tank Car "26138", *03*		CP	
(26139)	Lionel Lines Stockcar w/ horses "26139", *03*		CP	
(26141)	Whirlpool 1-D Tank Car, *03 u*		CP	
(26144)	Chessie System 1-D Tank Car "2233", *02*	—	19	[1]
(26145)	Do It Best 1-D Tank Car, *03 u*		CP	
(26146)	Do It Best 1-D Tank Car, *03 u*		CP	
(26147)	Lionel Archives Diamond Chemicals 1-D Tank Car "6315", *02*	—	33	[1]
(26149)	Egg Nog 1-D Tank Car, *03*		CP	
(26150)	Alaska 3-D Tank Car "26150", *03*		CP	
(26151)	NP Wood-sided Refrigerator Car "26151", *03*		CP	
(26164)	Girl's Lionel Lines 1-D Tank Car "6315", *03*		CP	
(26200)	NP Boxcar "18211", *98*	—	37	[1]
(26201)	Operation Lifesaver Boxcar, *98*	—	30	[1]
(26203)	D&H Boxcar "1829", *98*	—	25	[1]
(26204)	Alaska Boxcar "10806", *98–99*	—	35	[1]
(26205)	Rocky & Bullwinkle Boxcar "9700", *99*	—	36	[1]
(26206)	Curious George Boxcar "9700", *99*	—	40	[1]
(26208)	Vapor Records Boxcar #2, *98*	—	31	[1]
(26214)	Celebrate the Century Stamp Boxcar, *98 u*	—	90	[1]
(26215)	Glow-in-the-Dark AEC Boxcar, *98*	—	90	[1]
(26216)	Cheerios Boxcar "9700", *98 u*	—	90	[2]
(26218)	Quaker Oats Boxcar, *98 u*	—	375	[1]
(26219)	Ace Hardware Boxcar, *98 u*	NRS		
(26220)	Smuckers Boxcar "9700", *98 u*	—	75	[2]
(26222)	Penn Central Boxcar "125962", *99*	—	31	[1]
(26223)	FEC Boxcar "5027", *99*	—	31	[1]
(26224)	D&H Boxcar "9700", *99*	—	24	[1]
(26228)	Vapor Records Holiday Boxcar "9700", *99 u*	—	80	[1]
(26230)	Glow-in-the-Dark Boxcar II "9700", *99*	—	37	[1]
(26232)	Martin Guitar Lumber Boxcar "9823", *99*	—	31	[1]
(26234)	NYC Boxcar "9700", *99*	—	25	[1]
(26235)	Valentine Boxcar "9700", *99*	—	40	[1]
(26236)	Aircraft Boxcar "9700", *99*	—	31	[1]
(26237)	Boy Scout Boxcar "9700", *99*	—	90	[1]
(26238)	Detroit Historical Museum Boxcar "9700", *99*	—	32	[1]
(26239)	M.A.D.D Boxcar "9700", *99*	—	24	[1]
(26240)	Starter Set RailBox Boxcar "9700", *99–00*	—	33	[1]
(26241)	Starter Set Norfolk & Western "9700", *99–00*	—	15	[1]
(26242)	D.A.R.E Boxcar "9700", *99*	—	30	[1]

		Exc	New	Cond/$
(26243)	Lionel Christmas Boxcar "9700", *99*	—	39	[1]
(26244)	Woody Woodpecker Box Car "9700", *99*	—	38	
(26247)	Lionel Lines Boxcar "9700", *99*	—	38	
(26253)	Acme Explosives Boxcar "9700", *99u*	NRS		
(26254)	Keebler Boxcar "9700", *99u*	NRS		
(26255)	NYC Boxcar "200495", *99u*	—	30	
(26256)	Salvation Army Charity Boxcar "9700", *99*	—		
(26257)	Wheaties Boxcar "9700", *99*	—		
(26264)	Lionel Station Boxcar, *99*			
(26265)	NYC Pacemaker Boxcar "9700", *00*	—		
(26271)	Glow-in-the-Dark AEC Boxcar "9700-glo", *99*			
(26272)	Christmas Boxcar, *00*			
(26275)	Boy Scout Boxcar "9700", *00*			
(26276)	C&O 9700 Boxcar "23296", *99–00*			
(26277)	UP Boxcar "491050", *00*			
(26278)	Cap'n Crunch Christmas Boxcar, *99*			
(26280)	Tinsel Town Express Boxcar w/ musi			
(26284)	NY Toy Fair Preview Boxcar, *99 u*			
(26285)	NYC Pacemaker Boxcar "9700", *0*			
(26288)	AEC Glow-in-Dark 9700 Boxcar,			
(26290)	SP Boxcar, *00*			
(26291)	Pennsylvania Boxcar "47158			
(26292)	Frisco Boxcar "22015", *00*			
(26293)	Burlington Boxcar, *00*			
(26294)	Centennial Express Box			
(26295)	TrainMaster Boxcar, *9*			
(26296)	Service Station Ltd.			
(26298)	Taz Bobbing Boxca			
(26502)	UP B/W Caboose			
(26503)	AT&SF High-Cu			
(26504)	Mobil Oil S/W			
(5)	Lionelville Fl			
	N&W S/W			
	&H S/W			
	ka			

		Exc	New	Cond/$
(26710)	Southern Railroad Carsounds Stockcar, *99*	—	95	___[1]
(26712)	Churchill Downs Horse Car "6473", *99–00*	—	40	___[1]
(26713)	Shay Log Car 3-pack "9823", *99*	—	110	___[1]
(26714)	Westside Lumber Flatcar w/ logs (Std O), *99*	—	45	___[1]
(26715)	Westside Lumber Flatcar w/ logs (Std O), *99*	—	45	___[1]
(26716)	Westside Lumber Flatcar w/ logs (Std O), *99*	—	45	___[1]
(26717)	Orion Star 9600 Boxcar, *00*	—	30	___[1]
(26718)	Christmas RailSounds Boxcar, *00*	—	175	___[1]
(26719)	Bobbing Ghost Halloween 9700 Boxcar, *00*	—	40	___[1]
(26721)	Lionel Lines Coal Dump Car "3379", *00*	—	31	___[1]
(26722)	Lionel Lines Log Dump Car "3351", *00*	—	31	___[1]
(26723)	Lion Chasing Trainer Gondola "3444", *00*	—	49	___[1]
(26724)	Veterans Day 9700 Boxcar, *00*	—	70	___[1]
(26725)	NYC Jumping Hobo Boxcar "88160", *00*	—	50	___[1]
(26726)	T. Rex Bobbing Boxcar "9700", *00*	—	41	___[1]
(26727)	San Francisco City Lights Boxcar, *00*	—	55	___[1]
(26736)	Lionel Birthday Boxcar, *02 u*	—	43	___[1]
(26737)	Chasing Santa Operating Gondola "6462", *00 u*	—	65	___[1]
(26738)	Lionel Mines Gondola, *00u*		NRS	___
(26739)	Santa & Snowman Boxcar, *00*	—	46	___[1]
(26740)	Reindeer Car, *00*	—	49	___[1]
(26741)	Operating Santa Boxcar, *00*	—	49	___[1]
(26743)	Christmas Reindeer Car, *01*	—	55	___[1]
26745	Lionel Traveling Aquarium Car "506", *01*	—	70	___[1]
26746	Bobbing Vampire Boxcar, *01*	—	40	___[1]
26747	Halloween Bats Aquarium Car, *01*	—	45	___[1]
(26748)	T & P Operating "9699" Hopper Car, *01*	—	38	___[1]
26749	Alaska Log Dump Car, *01*	—	29	___[1]
(26750)	Carnegie Science Center Boxcar "9200", *99*	—	80	___[1]
26751	Chessie Coal Dump Car, *01*	—	27	___[1]
(26752)	Christmas Aquarium Car, *01*	—	55	___[1]
(26753)	Christmas Operating Dump Car, *01*	—	45	___[1]
(26757)	Operating Barrel Car "35621", *00*	—	50	___[1]
(26758)	AEC Nuclear Gondola "719766", *01*	—	70	___[1]
(26759)	Lionel Postwar Coal Dump Car "3459", *02*	—	55	___[1]
(26760)	Lionel Postwar Log Dump Car "3461", *02*	—	55	___[1]
(26761)	AEC Security Caboose 3535, *01*	—	60	___[1]
(26762)	Postwar Minuteman Car "3665", *01*	—	60	___[1]
(26763)	Postwar Exploding Boxcar "6448", *01*	—	40	___[1]
(26764)	Bethlehem Steel Operating Welding Car, *01*	—	50	___[1]
(26765)	Postwar Sheriff and Outlaw Car "3370", *01–02*	—	44	___[1]
(26766)	Priority Mail Operating Boxcar, *01–02*	—	43	___[1]

		Exc	New	Cond/$
(26768)	Postwar Searchlight Car "6520", *02*	—	50	___1
(26769)	Santa Fe Command Control Crane Car "199793", *03*		CP	___
(26770)	Wabash Brakeman Car 3424, *01*	—	65	___1
(26773)	Chessie Searchlight Car, *01*	—	20	___1
(26774)	Santa Fe Log Dump Car, *01*	—	25	___1
26775	US Army Searchlight Car, *00*	—	50	___1
26776	US Army Operating Boxcar "26413", *00*	—	50	___1
(26777)	United States Flag Boxcar, *01u*	—	250	___1
(26779)	Burlington Operating Hopper "189312", *02*	—	36	___1
(26780)	Postwar Bronx Zoo Giraffe Car "3376", *02*	—	36	___1
(26781)	Postwar Operating Radar Car "3540", *02*	—	32	___1
(26782)	Lenny the Lion Bobbing Head Car, *02*	—	38	___1
(26784)	Stingray Express Aquarium Car, *02*	—	40	___1
(26785)	Flatcar with Power Boat, *02*	—	25	___1
(26786)	Lionelville Operating Parade Car, *02*	—	40	___1
(26787)	Erie Jumping Hobo Boxcar, *01–02*	—	50	___1
(26788)	Christmas Music Boxcar, *02*	—	44	___1
(26789)	Kiss Kringle Chase Gondola, *02*	—	40	___1
(26790)	Christmas Lighted Boxcar, *02*	—	42	___1
(26791)	UP Animated Gondola, *02*	—	40	___1
(26792)	REA Operating Boxcar "6299", *03*		CP	___
(26793)	Alaska Extension Searchlight Car, *01*	—	44	___1
(26794)	Postwar PFE Ice Car "6352", *01–02*	—	60	___1
(26795)	NYC Stock Car w/ Cattle Sounds "3121", *02*	—	44	___1
(26796)	Lionel Farms Poultry Dispatch Car "26796", *01*	—	47	___1
(26797)	GN Log Dump Car "60011", *02*	—	50	___1
(26798)	Bethlehem Steel Coal Dump Car "26798", *02*	—	55	___1
(26905)	Bethlehem Steel Gondola w/ canisters "6462", *98*	—	30	___1
(26906)	Southern Pacific Flatcar w/ Corgi '57 Chevy "9823", *98*	—	36	___1
(26908)	T.T.U.X. w/ apple Trailers "6300", *98*	—	70	___1
(26913)	E. St. Louis Gondola "9820", *98*	—	30	___1
(26920)	UP Die-cast Ore Car "64861", *97*	—	55	___1
(26921)	UP Die-cast Ore Car "64862", *97*	—	55	___1
(26922)	UP Die-cast Ore Car "64863", *97*	—	55	___1
(26923)	UP Die-cast Ore Car "64864", *97*	—	55	___1
(26924)	UP Die-cast Ore Car "64865", *97*	—	55	___1
DX26925	(See 12810)			
(26925)	UP Die-cast Ore Car "64866", *97*	—	65	___1
(26926)	Union Pacific Die-cast Ore Car, *98*	—	55	___1
(26927)	Union Pacific Die-cast Ore Car, *98*	—	55	___1

		Exc	New	Cond/$
(26928)	Union Pacific Die-cast Ore Car, *98*	—	55	___1
(26929)	Union Pacific Die-cast Ore Car, *98*	—	50	___1
(26936)	Die-cast Tank Car 4-pack, *98*	—	355	___1
(26937)	Die-cast Hopper 4-pack, *98*	—	350	___1
(26938)	NYC Reefer, *99*	—	80	___1
(26940)	Rio Grande Stock Car "37710", *99*	—	80	___1
(26946)	D&H Semi-scale Hopper "9642"	—	100	___1
(26947)	Gulf Die-cast Tank Car, *98*	—	105	___1
(26948)	P&LE Die-cast Hopper, *98*	—	75	___1
(26949)	NP Flatcar w/ trailer "6424-2017", *98*	—	47	___1
(26950)	NP Flatcar w/ trailer "6424-2016", *98*	—	47	___1
(26951)	TTX Flatcar w/ PRR trailer "475185', *98*	—	65	___1
(26952)	J.B. Hunt TOFC Flatcar, *98*	—	40	___1
(26953)	J.B. Hunt TOFC Flatcar, *98*	—	40	___1
(26954)	J.B. Hunt TOFC Flatcar, *98*	—	40	___1
(26955)	J.B. Hunt TOFC Flatcar, *98*	—	40	___1
(26956)	C&O Gondola (O27), *98–99*	—	15	___1
(26957)	Delaware & Hudson Flatcar w/ stakes, *98*	—	20	___1
(26961)	Lionellville Fire Co. Flatcar, w/ ladder (SSS) load "6418-1", *98*	—	50	___1
(26971)	Lionel Steel 16-wheel Depressed Flatcar, *98*	—	140	___1
(26972)	Animated Pony Express Gondola, *98*	—	33	___1
(26973)	Getty Die-cast Tank Cars 3-pack, *98*	—	270	___1
(26974)	Getty Die-cast 1-D Tank Car "4003", *98*	—	80	___1
(26975)	Getty Die-cast 1-D Tank Car "4004", *98*	—	90	___1
(26976)	Getty Die-cast 1-D Tank Car "4005", *98*	—	80	___1
(26977)	Sinclair Die-cast Tank Cars 3-pack, *98*	—	265	___1
(26978)	Sinclair Tank Car UTLX "64026", *98*	—	105	___1
(26979)	Sinclair Tank Car UTLX "64027", *98*	—	85	___1
(26980)	Sinclair Tank UTLX "64028", *98*	—	90	___1
(26981)	Gulf Die-cast Tank Car 2-pack, *99*	—	140	___1
(26985)	B&O Die-cast Hoppers 2-pack "235154", *99*	—	165	___1
(26987)	Chessie System B&O Die-cast 4-bay Hopper "235154", *99*	—	90	___1
(26991)	Lionelville Ladder Firecar, Dept #2, *99*	—	47	___1
(26992)	NYC Reefer, *99*	—	85	___1
(26993)	NYC Reefer, *99*	—	85	___1
(26994)	NYC Reefer, *99*	—	110	___1
(26995)	Rio Grande Stock Car "37714", *99*	—	80	___1
(26996)	Rio Grande Stock Car "37715", *99*	—	80	___1
(26997)	Rio Grande Stock Car "37716", *99*	—	80	___1
(27104)	Wabash Cylindrical Hopper "33007" (Std. O), *03*	CP		___
(27105)	PC Cylindrical Hopper "884312" (Std. O), *03*	CP		___

No.	Description	Exc	New	Cond/$
(28000)	C&NW Hudson 4-6-4 "3005", *99*	—	205	___1
(28004)	B&O E6 4-4-2 Atlantic, Traditional, *99–00*	—	480	___1
(28005)	PRR E6 4-4-2 Atlantic, Traditional, *99–00*	—	345	___1
(28006)	AT&SF E6 4-4-2 Atlantic, Traditional, *99–00*	—	265	___1
(28007)	NYC Hudson 4-6-4 "5406", *99*	—	380	___1
(28008)	C&O Hudson 4-6-4 "306", *99*	—	345	___1
(28009)	Santa Fe Hudson 4-6-4 "3463", *99*	—	330	___1
(28011)	C&O 2-6-6-6 Allegheny Steam "1601", *99*	—	2000	___2
(28012)	Commodore Vanderbilt 4-6-4 Hudson, red, *00 u*	—	2000	___1
(28013)	NH Pacific 4-6-2 "1335", *99*	—	325	___1
(28014)	NYC Pacific 4-6-2 "4930", *99*	—	305	___1
(28015)	Santa Fe Pacific 4-6-2 "3449", *99*	—	340	___1
(28016)	Southern Pacific 4-6-2 "1408", *99*	—	345	___1
(28017)	Case Cutlery 4-6-2 Steamer, *99 u*	—	295	___1
(28018)	Reading Camelback "571", CC, *01*	—	440	___1
(28020)	Lionel Lines Pacific 4-6-2 "3344", *99*	—	250	___1
(28022)	West Side Lumber Shay "800", *99*	—	1200	___1
(28023)	PRR K4 4-6-2 Pacific, "1361", Command Control, *99*	—	400	___1
(28024)	Commodore Vanderbilt 4-6-4 Hudson, blue, *00 u*	—	2350	___1
(28025)	PRR K4 4-6-2 Pacific, Traditional, *99*	—	330	___1
(28026)	LL 4-6-2 Pacific, "1999", Command Control, *99*	—	325	___1
(28027)	NYC 4-6-4 Hudson "5413", *00*	—	690	___1
(28028)	Virginian 2-6-6-6 Allegheny "1601", *99*	—	1600	___2
(28029)	UP Big Boy 4-8-8-4 Articulated Steam Locomotive "4006", *99–00*	—	1550	___4
(28030)	NYC 4-6-4 Hudson "5450", gray, CC, *00*	—	315	___1
(28031)	NYC 4-6-4 Hudson "5451" gray, *00*		NM	___
(28032)	B&O 4-6-2 Pacific, Command Control, *00*	—	315	___1
(28033)	B&O 4-6-2 Pacific, Traditional, *00*	—	195	___1
(28034)	UP 4-6-2 Pacific, Command Control, *00*	—	320	___1
(28035)	UP 4-6-2 Pacific, Traditional, *00*	—	210	___1
(28036)	SP 2-8-0 Consolidation "2685", CC, *00–01*	—	400	___1
(28037)	SP 2-8-0 Consolidation "2686", Traditional, *00–01*	—	295	___1
(28038)	UP 2-8-0 Consolidation "324", CC, *00–01*	—	385	___1
(28039)	UP 2-8-0 Consolidation "326", Trad., *00–01*	—	250	___1
(28051)	B&O EM-1 2-8-8-4 Articulated Steam Locomotive "7617", *00*	—	1150	___1

		Exc	New	Cond/$
(28052)	N&W Class A 2-6-6-4 Articulated Steam Locomotive "1218", *00*	—	1100	___5
(28055)	GN 4-6-4 Hudson "1725", Traditional, *00–01*	—	158	___1
(28057)	SRR 4-8-2 Mountain "1491", CC, *00*	—	810	___1
(28058)	NH 4-8-2 Mountain "3310", CC, *00*	—	740	___1
(28059)	WP 4-8-2 Mountain "179", CC, *00*	—	860	___1
(28062)	Lionel Lines Gold-plated 700E J-1E 4-6-4 Hudson"1900" w/case, *00*	—	1350	___1
(28063)	PRR T-1 4-4-4-4 Duplex "5511", CC, *00*	—	1000	___1
(28064)	UP Challenger Coal Tender "3985", CC, *00 u*	1350	1800	___1
(28065)	NYC 4-6-4 Hudson w/ RailSounds "5412", *00*	—	290	___1
(28066)	B&O 4-6-2 President Polk, CC, *01*	—	710	___1
(28067)	Erie 4-6-2 "2934", CC, *01*	—	630	___1
(28068)	D&RG 4-6-4 Hudson "2001", Traditional, *01u*	—	300	___1
(28069)	Lionel Century Club NYC Niagara "6024", *00 u*	—	1000	___1
(28070)	SP Daylight 4-4-2 Atlantic "3000", CC, *01*	—	530	___1
(28071)	NP 4-4-2 Atlantic "604", CC, *01*	—	350	___1
(28072)	NYC 4-6-4 Hudson J3a "5444", CC, *01*	—	880	___1
(28074)	NP Berkshire "759", CC, *01*	—	1050	___1
(28075)	C&O 2-6-6-2 "1521", CC, *01*	—	860	___1
(28076)	NP 2-6-6-2 "921", CC, *01*	—	900	___1
(28077)	UP Lionmaster Challenger 4-6-6-4 "3983", CC, *01*	—	710	___1
(28078)	PRR J1a 2-10-4 "6465", CC, *01*	—	930	___1
(28079)	C&O Class T 2-10-4 "3004", CC, *01*	—	880	___1
(28080)	NYC 0-8-0 Yard Goat "7745", CC, *01–02*	—	540	___1
(28081)	C&O 0-8-0 Yard Goat "75", CC, *01–02*	—	520	___1
(28084)	NYC Dreyfuss 4-6-4 Hudson "5452", CC, *01–02*	—	850	___1
(28085)	N&W 2-8-8-2 Class Y6b Articulated "2200" Steam Locomotive, CC, *03*		CP	___
(28086)	PRR H9 Consolidation "1111", CC, *01*	—	480	___1
(28087)	UP Auxiliary Tender Yellow, CC, *01*	—	225	___1
(28088)	N&W Auxiliary Water Tender, CC, *01–02*	—	210	___1
(28089)	PRR T-1 4-4-4-4 Duplex "5511", 2-rail, *00*	—	1150	___1
(28090)	UP Challenger Oil Tender "3977", 2-rail, *00 u*	—	1800	___1
(28098)	NYC 4-6-0 Ten-Wheeler "1916", CC, *01–02*	—	490	___1
(28099)	UP Challenger Oil Tender "3977", CC, *00 u*	—	1700	___1
(28200)	D&H U30C "702", CC, *02*	—	400	___1
(28201)	UP SD90MAC "8049", *03*		CP	___
(28202)	Conrail SD80MAC "7203", *03*		CP	___

		Exc	New	Cond/$
(28203)	CSX SD80MAC "803", *03*		CP	
(28204)	NS SD80MAC "7201", *03*		CP	
(28205)	Chessie System SD9 "1833", CC, *03*		CP	
(28207)	Erie Lackawanna U33C Diesel "3304", CC, *02*	—	355	___1
(28208)	BN U33C Diesel "5734", CC, *02*	—	355	___1
(28211)	CP SD90MAC "9107", *03*		CP	
(28213)	Amtrak GE Dash 8 Diesel "516", CC, *02*	—	300	___1
(28214)	BNSF GE Dash 8 Diesel "582", CC, *02*	—	300	___1
(28215)	B&O EMD GP-30 Diesel "6939", CC, *02*	—	315	___1
(28216)	Reading EMD GP-30 Diesel "5513", CC, *02*	—	315	___1
(28217)	Rio Grande EMD GP-30 Diesel "3013", CC, *02*	—	315	___1
(28220)	Smuckers Box Car, *03*		CP	
(28228)	C&NW Dash 9-44CW "8669", CC, *03*		CP	
(28229)	SP Dash 9-44CW "8132", CC, *03*		CP	
(28292)	Chessie System U30C "3312", CC, *02*	—	300	___1
(28293)	Santa Fe U28CG "354", CC, *02*	—	355	___1
(28500)	Mopac GP-20 "2274", *99–00*	—	145	___1
(28501)	AT&SF Merger GP-9 "2924", Traditional, *99*	—	180	___1
(28502)	AT&SF Merger GP-9 "2925", Command Control, *99–00*	—	255	___1
(28503)	ACL GP-7, Command Control, *00*	—	250	___1
(28504)	ACL GP-7, Traditional, *00*	—	170	___1
(28505)	Monon C-420 "505", CC, *00–01*	—	230	___1
(28506)	Monon C-420 "506", Traditional, *00–01*	—	165	___1
(28507)	NH C-420 "2557", Traditional, *00–01*	—	240	___1
(28508)	NH C-420 "2556", CC, *00–01*	—	290	___1
(28509)	FEC GP-7 Triple Lashup "607/608/609", *99*	—	550	___1
(28514)	B&O GP-9 "6590", *00*	—	85	___1
(28515)	Lionel Service Station C-420, CC, *00*		CP	
(28517)	C&NW GP-7 "1518", CC, *00–01*	—	295	___1
(28518)	PRR EP5 Electric "2352", CC, *00*	—	405	___1
(28519)	NP GP-9 "2349", CC, *01*	—	295	___1
(28521)	SP RS-11"5725", CC, *01–02*	—	305	___1
(28522)	MP RS-11"4611", CC, *01–02*	—	285	___1
(28523)	SOO SD-40-2 "6622", CC, *01*	—	350	___1
(28524)	Chessie SD-40-2 "7616", CC, *01*	—	320	___1
(28527)	AEC GP-9 "2001", CC, *01*	—	295	___1
(28529)	Norfolk Southern GP-9, CC, *02*		CP	
(28530)	NP Alco S-4 Diesel "722", CC, *02*	—	285	___1
(28531)	Santa Fe Alco S-2 Diesel "2337", CC, *02*	—	285	___1
(28532)	LV Alco S-2 Diesel "150", CC, *02*	—	285	___1
(28533)	SAL Alco S-4 Diesel "1489", CC, *02*	—	285	___1
(28534)	Archive GTW GP-9 "4134", CC, *01*		NM	

		Exc	New	Cond/$
(28535)	US Army Transportation Corps GP-9, *02*		NM	___
(28536)	Rock Island GP-7 "1274", CC, *02–03*	—	230	___[1]
(28538)	WP S-2 "553", CC, *03*		CP	___
(28539)	B&O S-2 "9045", CC, *03*		CP	___
(28540)	UP SD40T-2 "4455", CC, *03*		CP	___
(28541)	SP SD40T-2 "8239", CC, *03*		CP	___
(28542)	Rio Grande SD40T-2 "5350", CC, *03*		CP	___
(28543)	Ontario Northland RS-3 "1308", *03*		CP	___
(28545)	NP RS-11 "900", CC, *03*		CP	___
(28612)	WP 4-4-2 Atlantic, Traditional, *02*	—	80	___[1]
(28615)	B&O 4-6-4 Hudson, Traditional, *02*	—	250	___[1]
(28616)	Nickel Plate 2-8-4 Berkshire, Traditional, *02*	—	190	___[1]
(28617)	Southern 2-8-4 Berkshire, Traditional, *02*	—	235	___[1]
(28625)	Wabash 4-4-2 Atlantic "8625", Traditional, *03*		CP	___
(28626)	Pennsylvania 4-6-4 Hudson "626", Traditional, *03*		CP	___
(28627)	C&O 2-8-4 Berkshire "2755" Traditional, *03*		CP	___
(28628)	L&N 2-8-4 Berkshire "1970" Traditional, *03*		CP	___
(28742)	B&O 4-6-0 Camelback "1630", CC, *03*		CP	___
(28743)	B&O 4-6-0 Camelback "1632", Traditional, *03*		CP	___
(28744)	D&H 4-6-0 Camelback "548", CC, *03*		CP	___
(28745)	D&H 4-6-0 Camelback "555", Traditional, *03*		CP	___
(28746)	Erie 4-6-0 Camelback "860", CC, *03*		CP	___
(28747)	Erie 4-6-0 Camelback "878", Traditional, *03*		CP	___
(28748)	Jersey Central 4-6-0 Camelback "772", CC, *03*		CP	___
(28749)	Jersey Central 4-6-0 Camelback "773", Traditional, *03*		CP	___
(28750)	Lackawanna 4-6-0 Camelback "690", CC, *03*		CP	___
(28751)	Lackawanna 4-6-0 Camelback "1031", Traditional, *03*		CP	___
(28752)	LIRR 4-6-0 Camelback "126", CC, *03*		CP	___
(28753)	LIRR 4-6-0 Camelback "127", Traditional, *03*		CP	___
(28754)	NYO&W 4-6-0 Camelback "249", CC, *03*		CP	___
(28755)	NYO&W 4-6-0 Camelback "253", Traditional, *03*		CP	___
(28756)	Pennsylvania-Reading 4-6-0 Camelback "6000", CC, *03*		CP	___
(28757)	Pennsylvania-Reading 4-6-0 Camelback "6001", Traditional, *03*		CP	___
(28758)	Susquehanna 4-6-0 Camelback "30", CC, *03*		CP	___
(28759)	Susquehanna 4-6-0 Camelback "36", Traditional, *03*		CP	___
(28800)	N&W GP-7 "507", *99–00*	—	70	___[1]
(28801)	Lionel Lines 44-ton Switcher, *99*	—	135	___[1]

		Exc	New	Cond/$
(28806)	Jersey Central Baby TrainMaster "1516", CC, *01*	—	350	___[1]
(28811)	Santa Fe Baby TrainMaster "3003", CC, *01*	—	315	___[1]
(28813)	Milwaukee Road Baby TrainMaster"406", CC, *01*	—	295	___[1]
(28815)	B&O GP-30 "6935", CC, *02*	—	310	___[1]
(28817)	Reading GP-30 "5513", CC, *02*	—	310	___[1]
(28819)	Rio Grande GP-30 "3013", CC, *02*	—	310	___[1]
(28821)	GT GP-7 "4438", *01*	—	100	___[1]
(28822)	SRR RS-3 "2127", *01*	—	70	___[1]
(28823)	Virginian Rectifier "234", *01*	—	170	___[1]
(28824)	Santa Fe FT nonpowered "172", *00*		NM	___
(28826)	Pioneer Seed GP-7 "2001", Traditional, *00u*		NRS	___
(28827)	Chessie GP-38, Traditional, *01*	—	100	___[1]
(28830)	Soo Line GP-9, Traditional, *01u*		CP	___
(28831)	Conrail U36B "2971", Traditional, *02*	—	100	___[1]
(28832)	Santa Fe RS-3 "2099", Traditional, *02*	—	70	___[1]
(28836)	NYC F-M H-16-44 Diesel "7000", CC, *02*	—	330	___[1]
(28837)	NH F-M H-16-44 Diesel "591", CC, *02*	—	325	___[1]
(28838)	UP F-M H-16-44 Diesel "1340", CC, *02*	—	325	___[1]
(28840)	Burlington GP-30 "945", CC, *03*		CP	___
(28841)	Seaboard GP-30 "1315", CC, *03*		CP	___
(28845)	Amtrak RS-3 "106", *03*		CP	___
(29000)	PRR Madison Coach "2622 Caleb Strong", *99*	—	80	___[1]
(29001)	PRR Madison Coach "2621 Villa Royal", *99*	—	80	___[1]
(29002)	PRR Madison Coach "2624 Philadelphia", *99*	—	80	___[1]
(29003)	PRR Madison Cars 4-pack, *98*	—	235	___[1]
(29004)	NYC Heavyweight Passenger set 2-pack, *99*	—	155	___[1]
(29007)	NYC Pullman Passenger Car 2-pack, *98u*	—	90	___[1]
(29008)	NYC Heavyweight Diner "383", *98*	—	90	___[1]
(29009)	NYC Heavyweight Combo Car "Van Twiller", *98*	—	90	___[1]
(29010)	C&O Heavyweight Passenger Set 2-pack, *99*	—	115	___[1]
(29011)	C&O Heavyweight Passenger Car (See 29010), *99*			
(29012)	C&O Heavyweight Passenger Car (See 29010), *99*			
(29039)	Lionel Lines Recovery Combo Car "9501", *99*		NRS	___
(29041)	Alaska Streamline Passenger (4-pack), *99–00*	—	230	___[1]
(29042)	Alaska Streamline Baggage "6310", *99–00*		NRS	___
(29043)	Alaska Streamline Coach "5408", *99–00*		NRS	___
(29044)	Alaska Streamline Vista Dome "7014", *99–00*		NRS	___
(29046)	B&O Streamline Passenger (4-pack), *99–00*	—	165	___[1]
(29047)	B&O Streamline Baggage, *99–00*		NRS	___

			Exc	New	Cond/$
(29048)	B&O Streamline Coach, *99–00*			CP	___
(29049)	B&O Streamline Vista Dome, *99–00*			NRS	___
(29050)	B&O Streamline Observation, *99–00*			NRS	___
(29051)	AT&SF Streamline Passenger (4-pack), *99–00*	—	200		___[1]
(29052)	AT&SF Streamline Baggage, *99–00*			NRS	___
(29053)	AT&SF Streamline Coach, *99–00*			NRS	___
(29054)	AT&SF Streamline Vista Dome, *99–00*			NRS	___
(29055)	AT&SF Streamline Obsevation, *99–00*			NRS	___
(29056)	NYC Streamline Passenger (4-pack), *99–00*	—	175		___[1]
(29057)	NYC Streamline Baggage, *99–00*			NRS	___
(29058)	NYC Streamline Coach, *99–00*			NRS	___
(29059)	NYC Streamline Vista Dome, *99–00*			NRS	___
(29060)	NYC Streamline Observation, *99–00*			NRS	___
(29061)	PRR Madison Passenger (4-pack), *99–00*	—	175		___[1]
(29062)	PRR Madison Baggage "Indian Point", *99–00*	—	50		___[1]
(29063)	PRR Madison Coach "Christopher Columbus", *99–00*	—	50		___[1]
(29064)	PRR Madison Coach "Andrew Jackson", *99–00*	—	50		___[1]
(29065)	PRR Madison Obsevation "Broussard", *99–00*	—	50		___[1]
(29066)	CNJ Madison Passenger (4-pack), *99–00*	—	195		___[1]
(29067)	CNJ Madison Baggage "420", *99–00*	—	50		___[1]
(29068)	CNJ Madison Coach "Beachcomber", *99–00*	—	50		___[1]
(29069)	CNJ Madison Coach "Echo Lake", *99–00*	—	50		___[1]
(29070)	CNJ Madison Observation "1178", *99–00*	—	50		___[1]
(29071)	NYC Baby Madison (4-pack), *00*	—	155		___[1]
(29072)	NYC Baby Madison Baggage "1001", *00*			NRS	___
(29073)	NYC Baby Madison Coach "1005", *00*			NRS	___
(29074)	NYC Baby Madison Coach "1006", *00*			NRS	___
(29075)	NYC Baby Madison Observation "1019 Detroit", *00*			NRS	___
(29076)	SR Baby Madison (4-pack), *00*	—	155		___[1]
(29077)	SR Baby Madison Baggage "702 Deleware", *00*			NRS	___
(29078)	SR Baby Madison Coach "800 North Carolina", *00*			NRS	___
(29079)	SR Baby Madison Coach "801 Maryland", *00*			NRS	___
(29080)	SR Baby Madison Observation "1100", *00*			CP	___
(29081)	AT&SF Baby Madison (4-pack), *00*	—	160		___[1]
(29082)	AT&SF Baby Madison Baggage/RPO "1765", *00*			NRS	___
(29083)	AT&SF Baby Madison Coach "3040" Chair, *00*			NRS	___
(29084)	AT&SF Baby Madison Coach "1535 Coach Club", *00*			NRS	___

		Exc	New	Cond/$
(29085)	AT&SF Baby Madison Observation "10", *00*		NRS	___
(29086)	Madison Set 3-pack, *99*	—	325	___ 1
(29090)	Lionel Liontech Madison Car "2656", *99*	—	75	___ 1
(29091)	Cowen Legends Madison Passenger "2657", *99–00*	—	70	___ 1
29108	Lionel Visitors Center Boxcar, *00*	—	30	___ 1
(29122)	Erie-Lackawanna F3 A-B Passenger set, *99*	—	1000	___ 2
(29123)	Erie-Lackawanna Aluminum Passenger Baggage "203", *99*	—	100	___ 1
(29124)	Erie-Lackawanna Aluminum Passenger Diner "770", *99*	—	100	___ 1
(29125)	Erie-Lackawanna Aluminum Passenger Coach "Eleanor Lord", *99*	—	100	___ 1
(29126)	Erie-Lackawanna Aluminum Passenger Obs. "789 Tavern Lounge", *99*	—	125	___ 1
(29127)	ACL Aluminum Baggage "152", *99*		NRS	___
(29128)	ACL Aluminum Coach "North Hampton", *99*		NRS	___
(29129)	Texas Special Passenger set 4-pack, *99*	—	650	___ 1
(29130)	Texas Special Aluminum "1200 Edward Burleson", *99*	—	100	___ 1
(29131)	Texas Special Aluminum "1201 David G. Burnett", *99*	—	100	___ 1
(29132)	Texas Special Aluminum "1202 J. Pinckney Henderson", *99*	—	100	___ 1
(29133)	Texas Special Aluminum "1203", *99*	—	100	___ 1
(29134)	WP Passenger Set 4-pack, *99*	—	485	___ 1
(29135)	Calif. Zephyr Aluminum Vista "Silver Poplar", *99*		NRS	___
(29136)	Calif. Zephyr Aluminum Vista "Silver Palm", *99*		NRS	___
(29137)	Calif. Zephyr Aluminum Vista "Silver Tavern", *99*		NRS	___
(29138)	Calif. Zephyr Aluminum Vista "Silver Planet", *99*		NRS	___
(29139)	Lionel Kughn Madison Car "2655", *99*	—	105	___ 1
(29140)	NYC Aluminum Sleeper "Castleton Bridge", *99*	—	120	___ 1
(29141)	NYC Aluminum Combine "Martin Van Buren", *99*	—	120	___ 1
(29142)	CP Aluminum Vista "Skyline 596", *99*		NRS	___
(29143)	CP Aluminum Observation "Banff Park", *99*		NRS	___
(29149)	CB&Q California Zephyr Aluminum Passenger Car 2-pack, *03*		CP	___

		Exc	New	Cond/$
(29152)	Santa Fe Super Chief Aluminum Passenger Car 2-pack, *03*		CP	___
(29155)	D&H Aluminum Passenger Car 2-pack, *03*		CP	___
(29158)	Southern The Southerner Aluminum Passenger Car 2-pack, *03*		CP	___
(29200)	LRRC Boxcar "9700", *98 u*	—	44	___ 2
(29202)	Santa Fe Map Boxcar "6464", *97 u*	—	75	___ 1
(29203)	Maine Central Boxcar "6464-597", *97 u*	—	30	___ 2
(29204)	Century Club Boxcar "1900-2000", *97 u*	—	550	___ 1
(29205)	MM Railroad Hi-cube Boxcar "9555", *97*	—	45	___ 1
(29206)	Vapor Records Boxcar (1st), *97*		NRS	___
(29209)	6464 Boxcar Series VII 3-pack, *98*	—	105	___ 1
(29210)	GN Boxcar "6464-50", *98*	—	39	___ 1
(29211)	B&M Boxcar "6464-450", *98*	—	33	___ 1
(29212)	Timken Boxcar "6464-500", *98*	—	35	___ 1
(29213)	AT&SF Grand Canyon Route 6464 Boxcar "6464-198", *98*	—	25	___ 1
(29214)	Southern Railway 6464 Boxcar "6464-298", *98*	—	31	___ 1
(29215)	Canadian Pacific 6464 Boxcar "6464-398", *98*	—	30	___ 1
(29217)	Airex Boxcar, *97 u*	—	80	___ 1
(29218)	Vapor Records Boxcar "6464-496", *97 u*	—	145	___ 2
(29220)	1997 Lionel Centennial Series High-Cube Boxcar 4-car set, *98*	—	120	___ 1
(29220)	GN Boxcar "6464-450", *98*	—	95	___ 1
(29221)	1997 Centennial Series High-Cube Boxcar "9697-1", *98*	—	50	___ 1
(29222)	1997 Centennial Series High-Cube Boxcar "9697-2", *98*	—	50	___ 1
(29223)	1997 Centennial Series High-Cube Boxcar "9697-3", *98*	—	50	___ 1
(29224)	1997 Centennial Series High-Cube Boxcar "9697-4", *98*	—	50	___ 1
(29225)	H.O.R.D.E. Music Festival Boxcar, *97*	47	55	___ 3
(29226)	Century Club Berkshire Boxcar, *97 u*	160	290	___ 2
(29227)	Century Club GG-1 Boxcar, *98 u*	—	65	___ 2
(29228)	Century Club Turbine Boxcar "671", *99 u*	—	60	___ 2
(29229)	Vapor Records Holiday Car, *98*	—	125	___ 1
(29231)	Animated Halloween Boxcar, *98*	—	34	___ 1
(29232)	Lenny the Lion Hi-Cube, *98*	—	75	___ 2
(29233)	CR Overstamp PC Boxcar "6464-598", *98*	—	50	___ 1
(29234)	CR Overstamp Erie Boxcar "6464-698", *98*	—	50	___ 1
(29235)	NYC Boxcar "6464-510", *99*	—	41	___ 1

		Exc	New	Cond/$
(29236)	Katy Boxcar "6464-515", *99*	—	41	___1
(29237)	M&StL Boxcar "6464-525", *99*	—	33	___1
(29248)	Century Club F3 Boxcar "2333", *99 u*	—	65	___1
(29250)	Phoebe Snow boxcar "6464-199", *99*	—	49	___1
(29251)	BN Boxcar "6464-299", *99*	—	38	___1
(29252)	CP Boxcar "6464-399", *99*	—	40	___1
(29253)	B&M Boxcar 6565 "76032", *99*	—	50	___1
(29254)	B&M Boxcar 6565 "76033", *99*	—	50	___1
(29255)	B&M Boxcar 6565 "76034", *99*	—	50	___1
(29256)	B&M Boxcar 6565 "76035", *99*	—	50	___1
(29257)	Southern Boxcar "9464-199", *99*	—	40	___1
(29258)	Reading Boxcar "9464-299", *99*	—	37	___1
(29259)	NP Bicentennial Boxcar "9464-399", *99*	—	40	___1
(29265)	Maine Central Boxcar "6565", *99*	—	39	___1
(29266)	Frisco Boxcar "6565", *99*	—	38	___1
(29267)	6464 Boxcar Series VIII 3-pack, *99*	—	105	___1
(29268)	Rio Grande Boxcar "6565", *99*	—	40	___1
(29271)	Lionel Cola Tractor-Trailer, *98*	—	10	___1
(29279)	JC/CR Boxcar "6464-28X", *99*	—	47	___1
(29280)	LV/CR Boxcar "6464-31X", *99*	—	47	___1
(29281)	Post-Merger Boxcar Conrail Overstamped CNJ & LV 2-pack set, *99*	—	70	___1
(29282)	Archive 2-pack "6464", *99*	—	105	___1
(29283)	NYC Boxcar "6464-900", *99*	—	55	___1
(29284)	GN Boxcar "6464/0000", *99*	—	40	___1
(29285)	Seaboard Boxcar, *99*	—	36	___1
(29286)	Overstamp Boxcars (2-pack), *99*	—	70	___1
(29287)	NH/PC Boxcar "6464-29X", *99*	20	35	___1
(29288)	RDG/CR Boxcar "6464-32X", *99*	—	41	___1
(29289)	6464- Boxcar Series IX (3-pack), *99–00*	—	75	___1
(29290)	D&RGW Boxcar "6464-650", *00*	—	48	___1
(29291)	AT&SF Boxcar "6464-700", *00*	—	45	___1
(29292)	NH Boxcar "6464-725", *00*	—	46	___1
(29293)	NH Boxcar "6464-425", *00*	—	95	___1
(29294)	Hellgate Bridge Boxcar "1900-2000", *99 u*	—	80	___4
(29295)	PRR 6565 "Don't Stand Me Still" Boxcar "24018", *99–00*	—	48	___1
(29296)	PRR 6565 "Merchandise" Boxcar "29296", *99–00*	—	40	___1
(29297)	PRR 6565 "No Damage" Boxcar "47158", *99–00*	—	45	___1
(29298)	Lionel Boxcar "6464-2000", *00*	—	40	___1

		Exc	New	Cond/$
(29400)	Bethlehem Steel Slag Car 3-pack (Std. O), *03*		CP	___
(29404)	Bethlehem Steel Hot Metal Car 3-pack (Std. O), *03*		CP	___
(29408)	PRR Coil Car, *01*	—	40	___[1]
(29411)	Sherwin-Williams Vat Car, *02*	—	35	___[1]
(29412)	Tabasco Brand Vat Car, *02*	—	27	___[1]
(29413)	Airex Boat Loader Car "29413", *02*	—	34	___[1]
(29414)	PRR Evans Auto Loader "480123", *01*	—	50	___[1]
(29415)	WM Skeleton Log Car 3-pack #2 (Std. O), *02*	—	90	___[1]
(29419)	West Side Lumber Skeleton Log Car 3-pack #2 (Std. O), *02*	—	90	___[1]
(29423)	Wellspring Capital Management Happy Holidays Vat Car, *03 u*		CP	___
(29424)	Meadow River Lumber Skeleton Log Car 3-pack (Std. O), *03*		CP	___
(29429)	Campbell's Soup Vat Car "29429", *03*		CP	___
(29430)	Meadow River Lumber Skeleton Log Car 3-pack, 2 (Std. O), *03*		CP	___
(29438)	UP TTUX Car, *03*		CP	___
(29439)	Lionel Postwar Evans Auto Loader "6414", *02*	—	43	___[1]
(29441)	UP Flatcar w/ grader "53471", *02*	—	43	___[1]
(29442)	CSX Flatcar w/ backhoe "600513", *02*	—	43	___[1]
(29453)	Elk River Lumber Skeleton Log Car 3-pack, 2 (Std. O), *03*		CP	___
(29457)	NS Flatcar w/ Caterpillar load "157590", *03*		CP	___
(29458)	BNSF Flatcar w/ Caterpillar load "922268", *03*		CP	___
(29459)	Archive Water Barrel Car "1878", *03*		CP	___
(29460)	Archive Lionel Lines Flatcar w/ piggyback trailers "3460", *03*		CP	___
(29461)	Postwar Flatcar w/ red-and-white airplane "6500", *03*		CP	___
(29462)	Postwar Flatcar w/ white-and-red airplane "6500", *03*		CP	___
(29463)	Postwar Evans Auto Loader "6414", *03*		CP	___
(29473)	Youngstown Sheet & Tube Slag Car 3-pack (Std. O), *03*		CP	___
(29477)	Youngstown Sheet & Tube Hot Metal Car 3-pack (Std. O), *03*		CP	___
(29481)	Cass Scenic Railroad Skeleton Log Car 3-pack (Std. O), *03*		CP	___
(29703)	PRR Porthole Caboose, *01*	—	45	___[1]
(29900)	"I Love Wisconsin" Boxcar "9700", *01*	—	34	___[1]

		Exc	New	Cond/$
(29901)	"I Love Kentucky" Boxcar "9700", *01*	—	23	___1
(29902)	"I Love Iowa Boxcar" "9700", *01*	—	28	___1
(29903)	"I Love Missouri Boxcar" "9700", *01*	—	28	___1
(29906)	"I Love Connecticut Boxcar" "9700", *02*	—	31	___1
(29907)	"I Love West Virginia Boxcar" "9700", *02*	—	31	___1
(29908)	"I Love Delaware Boxcar" "9700", *02*	—	31	___1
(29909)	"I Love Maryland Boxcar" "9700", *02*	—	40	___1
(29910)	Toy Fair Centennial Boxcar "9700", *03*		CP	___
(29912)	"I Love Alabama" Boxcar "9700", *03*		CP	___
(29913)	"I Love Mississippi" Boxcar "9700", *03*		CP	___
(29914)	"I Love Louisiana" Boxcar "9700", *03*		CP	___
(29915)	"I Love Arkansas" Boxcar "9700", *03*		CP	___
(29920)	"I Love North Dakota" Boxcar "9700", *03*		CP	___
(29921)	"I Love South Dakota" Boxcar "9700", *03*		CP	___
(29922)	"I Love Nebraska" Boxcar "9700", *03*		CP	___
(29923)	"I Love Kansas" Boxcar "9700", *03*		CP	___
(29949)	Weyerhaeuser Timber Skeleton Log Car 3-pack, 2 (Std. O), *03*		CP	___
(31700)	Postwar Girl's Train Freight set, *01*	—	500	___1
(31701)	Postwar Boy's Train Freight set, *02*	—	325	___1
(31704)	Alton Limited Steam Passenger set, *02*	—	630	___1
(31705)	50th Anniversary Hudson passenger set, *02*	—	1250	___1
(31706)	UP Burro Crane set, *02*	—	210	___1
(31707)	C&O Diesel Freight set, *03*		CP	___
(31708)	Postwar #1805 Land-Sea-Air Marines Missile Launch set, *03*		CP	___
(31710)	BN Coal Train Diesel Freight set w/ RailSounds, *03*		CP	___
(31711)	Postwar #1563W Wabash Diesel Freight set w/ RailSounds, *03*		CP	___
(31712)	UP Alco PA Diesel Passenger set w/ RailSounds, *03*		CP	___
(31713)	Southern Crescent Limited Steam Passenger set w/ RailSounds, *03*		CP	___
(31715)	Fire Rescue Steam Freight set, *02*	—	285	___1
(31716)	Fire Rescue Steam Freight set, *03*		CP	___
(31717)	CP Rail Snow Removal Train set, *03*		CP	___
(31718)	SP "Oil Can" TankTrain Freight set, *03*		CP	___
(31901)	Christmas Steam Freight set, *02*	—	145	___1
(31902)	PRR K4 Freight set, *01–02*	—	520	___1
(31904)	C&O Steam Freight set w/ RailSounds, *01*	—	400	___1
(31905)	NH RS-11 Freight set, CC, *01*	—	570	___1
(31907)	PRR Atlantic Freight set, *01u*	—	400	___1

		Exc	New	Cond/$
(31908)	Reading Hobo Express Freight set, *01u*	—	350	___[1]
(31909)	Santa Fe Shell Tank Car Freight set, *01u*	—	350	___[1]
(31910)	Soo Line Diesel Freight set, *01u*	—	350	___[1]
(31911)	Snap-On Anniversary Steam Freight set, *00 u*	—	450	___[1]
(31913)	PRR Steam Freight Flyer set, *01*	—	125	___[1]
(31914)	NYC Steam Freight Flyer set w/ Railsounds, *01–02*	—	170	___[1]
(31915)	Chessie GP-38 Freight set, *01–02*	—	155	___[1]
(31916)	Santa Fe Steam Freight set, *01*	—	300	___[1]
(31918)	C&O Steam Freight set w/ SignalSounds, *01*	—	315	___[1]
(31919)	T&P Steam Passenger set w/ RailSounds, *01*	—	185	___[1]
(31920)	LL Bean Freight set, *01u*	—	225	___[1]
(31923)	PRR Flyer Freight set, *01u*	—	130	___[1]
(31924)	UP RS-3 Freight set, *02*	—	95	___[1]
(31926)	Area 51 FA Freight set, *02*	—	135	___[1]
(31928)	UP General Freight set, *02*	—	160	___[1]
(31931)	Ballyhoo Circus Freight set, *02*	—	205	___[1]
(31932)	NYC FT Passenger set w/ RailSounds, *02*	—	285	___[1]
(31933)	Santa Fe Steam Freight set w/ RailSounds, *02*	—	320	___[1]
(31934)	Lionel 20th Century Express Steam Freight set, *00 u*		CP	___
(31936)	Pennsylvania Flyer Steam Freight set, *03*		CP	___
(31938)	Southern Diesel Freight set, *03*		CP	___
(31939)	Great Train Robbery Steam Freight set, *03*		CP	___
(31940)	NYC Flyer Steam Freight set w/ RailSounds, *03*		CP	___
(31941)	Winter Wonderland Railroad Christmas Train Steam Freight set, *03*		CP	___
(31942)	Norman Rockwell Christmas Train, *03*		CP	___
(31944)	NYC Limited Diesel Passenger set w/ RailSounds, *03*		CP	___
(31945)	Santa Fe Super Steam Freight set w/ RailSounds, *03*		CP	___
(31947)	World of Disney Steam Freight set, *03*		CP	___
(31950)	Kraft Holiday UP RS-3 Freight set, *02 u*		CP	___
(31952)	Great Northern Glacier Route Diesel Freight set, *03*		CP	___
(31953)	"Riding the Rails" Hobo Train Steam Freight set, *03*		CP	___
(31961)	Bloomingdales Pennsylvania Flyer Steam Freight set, *02 u*		CP	___
(31962)	GN Glacier Route Freight set, *03*		CP	___
(31963)	Riding the Rails Hobo Steam Freight set, *03*		CP	___
(32900)	DC Billboard Lionel, *99*	—	24	___[1]

		Exc	New	Cond/$
(32902)	Construction Zone Signs (6), *99–03*		CP	___
(32904)	Lionel Hellgate Bridge, *99*	—	485	___²
(32905)	Lionel Irvington Factory, *99–00*	—	300	___²
(32910)	Rotary Coal Dumper w/ Rotary Bathtub Gondola, *02*	—	350	___¹
(32919)	Animated Maiden Rescue, *99*	—	65	___¹
(32920)	Animated Pylon w/ airplane, *99*	—	130	___¹
(32921)	Electric Coaling Station "97", *99–01*	—	135	___¹
(32922)	Highway Barrels (6), *99–03*		CP	___
(32923)	Accessory Transformer, 36-watt, *99–03*		CP	___
(32929)	Icing Station with Santa, *99*	—	95	___¹
(32930)	ZW Controller w/ 2 180-watt transformers, *99–02*	—	325	___¹
(32933)	Christmas Stocking Hanger set (4-pc.), *99–00*	—	50	___¹
(32934)	Stocking Hanger, Gondola, *99–00*	—	15	___¹
(32935)	Stocking Hanger, Boxcar, *99–00*	—	15	___¹
(32960)	Hindenburger Cafe, *99*	—	160	___¹
(32961)	Route 66 U.F.O. Cafe, *99*	—	145	___¹
(32987)	Hobo Campfire, *99–00*	—	55	___¹
(32988)	#192 Railroad Control Tower, *99–00*	—	85	___¹
(32989)	#464 Sawmill, *99–00*	—	75	___¹
(32990)	Linex Oil Derrick, *99–00*	—	60	___¹
(32991)	WLLC Radio Station, *99*	—	65	___¹
(32996)	362 AT&SF Barrel Loader, "3562-25", *00*	—	115	___¹
(32997)	Aluminum Rico Station, *00*	—	225	___¹
(32998)	Lionel Hobby Shop, *99–00*	—	285	___¹
(32999)	Hellgate Bridge, *99–00*	—	315	___³
(33000)	Lionel Lines RailScope GP-9 "3000", *88–90*	165	230	___¹
(33002)	RailScope B&W TV, *88–90*	50	80	___¹
(33004)	NYC RailScope GP-9 "3004", *90*		NM	___
(33005)	Union Pacific RailScope GP-9 "3005", *90*		NM	___
(34108)	Lionelville Suburban House, *03*		CP	___
(34109)	Lionelville Large Suburban House, *03*		CP	___
(34110)	Lionelville Estate House, *03*		CP	___
(34111)	Lionelville Deluxe Fieldstone House, *03*		CP	___
(34112)	Lionelville Fieldstone House, *03*		CP	___
(34113)	Lionelville Large Suburban House, 2, *03*		CP	___
(34114)	Late Illuminated Station and Terrace "128", *03*		CP	___
(34117)	Early Illuminated Station and Terrace "128", *03*		CP	___
(36000)	Route 66 Flatcar w/ 2 red sedans, *98*	—	44	___¹
(36001)	Route 66 Flatcar w/ 2 wagons, *98*	—	47	___¹
(36002)	Pratt's Hollow Passenger Cars 4-pack, *98*	—	415	___¹

		Exc	New	Cond/$
(36006)	Uranium Flatcar "6508", *99*	—	60	___¹
(36016)	Flatcar w/ propellers, *98*	—	55	___¹
(36020)	Flatcar "TT-6424" w/ auto frames, *99*	—	37	___¹
(36021)	Alaska Flatcar w/ airplane "6424", *99*	—	33	___¹
(36024)	J.B. Hunt Flatcar w/ trailer "64245", *99*	—	40	___¹
(36025)	J.B. Hunt Flatcar w/ trailer "64246", *99*	—	50	___¹
(36026)	Flatcars w/ J.B. Hunt trailers 2-pack, *99*	—	80	___¹
(36027)	Tredegar Iron Works Flatcar w/ cannon, *99*	—	45	___¹
(36028)	Heavy Artillery Flatcar w/ cannon, *99*	—	45	___¹
(36029)	SP Auto Carrier "516712", *99*	—	40	___¹
(36030)	Troublesome Truck "1", *99*	—	31	___¹
(36031)	Troublesome Truck "2", *99*	—	31	___¹
(36032)	Christmas Gondola w/ presents "6462", *99*	—	44	___¹
(36036)	C&O Gondola, *99*		CP	___
(36038)	Construction Zone Gondola, *99u*		NRS	___
(36040)	Bethlehem Flatcar w/ block (SSS), *99*	—	75	___¹
(36041)	Bethlehem Ore Car (SSS), *99*	—	35	___¹
(36043)	Custom Consist Flatcar w/ pickup truck, *99*	—	40	___¹
(36044)	Custom Consist Flatcar w/ dragster, *99*	—	40	___¹
(36047)	Construction Zone Gondola, *99u*		NRS	___
(36048)	Construction Zone Gondola, *99u*		NRS	___
(36054)	Archaelogical Exp Gondola w/ eggs, *00 u*	—	55	___¹
(36055)	Flatcar w/ dragster, *01u*	—	30	___¹
(36056)	Flatcar w/ roadster, *01u*	—	30	___¹
(36059)	Season's Greetings Gondola, *99u*		CP	___
(36062)	NYC 6462 Gondola, *99–00*	—	19	___¹
(36063)	Conrail Gondola "604768", *99–00*	—	20	___¹
(36064)	Billboard Flatcar "6424", *00*	—	40	___¹
(36065)	Wabash Flat "25536" w/ Trailer, *00*	—	31	___¹
(36066)	Christmas Gondola w/ presents load, *00*	—	36	___¹
(36067)	King Auto Sales Flat w/ 2 cars "6424", *00*	—	41	___¹
(36068)	Pine Peak Tree Transport Gondola, *00*		NRS	___
(36079)	Service Station Ltd. Flatcar w/ trailer, *00*	—	35	___¹
(36082)	Whirlpool Flatcar w/ trailer, *00u*		NRS	___
(36083)	Santa Fe "168998" Gondola, *01*	—	17	___¹
36084	Grand Trunk Coil Car, *00*	—	37	___¹
36085	FEC Coil Car, *00*	—	33	___¹
36086	SP Flatcar w/ trailer, *01*	—	34	___¹
(36087)	Flatcar w/ wood whistle "6424", *01*	—	25	___¹
(36088)	Allis Chalmers Condenser Car "6519", *00*	—	34	___¹
36089	Frisco Flatcar w/ airplane, *00*	—	35	___¹
(36090)	TT Flat w/ Pepsi truck "6424", *01*	—	55	___¹
36091	Maersk Flat w/ die-cast tractors "250129", *00*	—	50	___¹

MODERN ERA 1970–2004   Exc New Cond/$

		Exc	New	Cond/$
36092	Maersk Flat w/ die-cast frames "250130", 00	—	50	___1
36093	Soo TT Auto Carrier "906760", 00	—	49	___1
(36094)	PC F-9 Well Car "768122", 01	—	41	___1
(36095)	Christmas Chase Gondola, 01	—	49	___1
(36098)	PRR Gondola "385186", 01	—	20	___1
(36200)	Quaker Life Cereal Boxcar, 00	420	475	___1
(36202)	Miniature Railroad & Village 80th Anniversary Boxcar, 00u		CP	___
(36203)	Whirlpool Boxcar, 00u		CP	___
(36205)	eBay Boxcar, 00	—	175	___1
(36206)	REA Boxcar, 01	—	25	___1
(36207)	Vapor Records Christmas Boxcar, 01	—	34	___1
(36208)	Father's Day Boxcar, 00	—	33	___1
(36210)	Burlington Hi-Cube Boxcar "19825", 01	—	40	___1
(36211)	NP "659999" Hi-Cube Boxcar, 01	—	33	___1
(36212)	Lionel Employee Christmas Boxcar, 00u	—	375	___1
(36213)	Vapor Records Christmas Boxcar, 00	—	35	___1
(36215)	Train Station 25th Anniversary Boxcar, 00 u	—	65	___1
(36218)	Snap-On Boxcar, 00u		NRS	___
(36220)	Pioneer Seed Boxcar, 00u		NRS	___
(36221)	PRR Boxcar "569356", 01	—	20	___1
(36222)	NYC Boxcar "162440", 01	—	20	___1
(36223)	Chessie System Boxcar, 01	—	20	___1
(36224)	Santa Fe Boxcar "16263", 01	—	20	___1
(36225)	C&O Boxcar "250549", 01	—	20	___1
(36226)	E-Hobbies Boxcar, 01u		CP	___
(36227)	Monopoly Community Chest Boxcar, 00u	—	50	___1
(36228)	Lionel Visitor Center Boxcar, 01u	—	40	___1
(36229)	Island Trains 20th Anniversary Boxcar, 01u	—	25	___1
(36232)	Farmall Boxcar, 01u		CP	___
(36234)	Carnegie Science Center Boxcar "9700", 01u		CP	___
(36236)	TM Books & Video I Love Lionel Boxcar "7474-1", 01u	—	50	___1
(36239)	LL Bean Boxcar, 01u		CP	___
(36240)	Do It Best Boxcar, 01u		CP	___
(36242)	Erie Lackawanna Boxcar "73113", 02	—	19	___1
(36243)	Christmas Boxcar "2002", 02	—	31	___1
(36244)	Teddy Bear Centennial Boxcar, 02	—	32	___1
(36245)	Lionel 20th Century Boxcar "1900-1925", 00 u		CP	___
(36246)	Lionel 20th Century Boxcar "1926-1950", 00 u		CP	___
(36247)	Lionel 20th Century Boxcar "1951-1975", 00 u		CP	___
(36248)	Lionel 20th Century Boxcar "1976-2000", 00 u		CP	___
(36253)	2003 O Gauge Christmas Boxcar, 03		CP	___

(36254)	Goofy Hi-Cube Boxcar, *03*		CP	___
(36255)	Donald Duck Hi-Cube Boxcar, *03*		CP	___
(36256)	GN Boxcar "6341", *03*		CP	___
(36264)	Santa Fe Boxcar "600196, *02*	—	18	___ [1]
(36265)	Angela Trotta Thomas "Window Wishing" Boxcar, *02*	—	34	___ [1]
(36267)	Mickey Mouse Hi-Cube Boxcar, *03*		CP	___
36270	Angela Trotta Thomas 10th Ann. Boxcar "Holidays", *02–03*		CP	___
(36305)	eBay Boxcar "9700", *00u*	—	100	___ [1]
(36701)	Baldwin Locomotive Works Operating Welding Car "36701", *02*	—	60	___ [1]
(36702)	Postwar Bosco Milk Car w/ platform "3672", *02*	—	105	___ [1]
(36703)	Lionel Postwar Circus Horse Car and Corral, *3366*	—	110	___ [1]
(36704)	Animated Reindeer Stockcar and Corral, *02*	—	115	___ [1]
(36718)	AEC Security Caboose, *02*	—	42	___ [1]
(36720)	Aladdin Aquarium Car, *03*		CP	___
(36721)	101 Dalmatians Animated Gondola, *03*		CP	___
(36722)	Peter Pan Bobbing Head Boxcar, *03*		CP	___
(36726)	Santa Fe Searchlight Car "36726", *03*		CP	___
(36727)	Weyerhaeuser Moe & Joe Flatcar, *03*		CP	___
(36728)	SP Walking Brakeman Boxcar 163143", *03*		CP	___
(36730)	US Army Missile Launch Sound Car "44", *03*		CP	___
(36731)	Motorized Aquarium Car "3435", *03*		CP	___
(36732)	C&NW Jumping Hobo Car, *03*		CP	___
(36733)	Christmas Music Boxcar, *03*		CP	___
(36734)	Santa Fe Operating Searchlight Car "20611", *02*	—	25	___ [1]
(36735)	WP Ice Car "7045", *02*	—	49	___ [1]
(36738)	T&P Poultry Dispatch Car "36738", *02*	—	50	___ [1]
(36739)	Postwar Lionel Lines Log Dump Car "3461", *03*		CP	___
(36740)	Postwar Lionel Lines Coal Dump Car "3469", *03*		CP	___
(36743)	Santa Claus Bobbing Head Boxcar, *03*		CP	___
(36744)	Little Mermaid Aquarium Car, *03*		CP	___
(36745)	Toy Story Animated Gondola, *03*		CP	___
(36758)	Patriotic Lighted Boxcar, *02*	—	45	___ [1]
(36760)	Lionel Archives B&O Sentinel Operating Brakeman Boxcar, "3424", *02*	—	65	___ [1]
(36761)	Wellspring Capital Management Illuminated Boxcar, *02 u*		CP	___
(36764)	West Side Lumber Log Dump Car "36764", *03*		CP	___

		Exc	New	Cond/$
(36765)	Alaska Coal Dump Car "401" Steam Locomotive, CC, *03*		CP	___
(36767)	Santa's Radar Tracking Car, *03*		CP	___
36769	Fourth of July Lighted Boxcar, *03*		CP	___
(36786)	Postwar MP Operating Boxcar "3494-150", *03*		CP	___
(36793)	Pennsylvania Derrick Car "36793", *03*		CP	___
(36794)	NYC Log Dump Car "36794", *03*		CP	___
(36795)	Southern Coal Dump Car "36795", *03*		CP	___
(36796)	GN Searchlight Car "36796", *03*		CP	___
(36797)	Operation Iraqi Freedom Minuteman Car "36797", *03*		CP	___
(36900)	Depressed Center Flatcar w/ backshop load, *99*	—	95	___[1]
(36913)	Allied Chemical 1-D Tank Car (2-pack), *00*	—	135	___[1]
(36914)	Allied Chemical Die-cast 1-D Tank Car, white "ACDX 68075", *00*	—	90	___[1]
(36915)	Allied Chemical Die-cast 1-D Tank Car, white "ACDX 68076", *00*	—	90	___[1]
(36916)	Allied Chemical 1-D Tank Car (2-pack), *00*	—	165	___[1]
(36917)	Allied Chemical Die-cast 1-D Tank Car, black "ACDX 65124", *00*	—	90	___[1]
(36918)	Allied Chemical Die-cast 1-D Tank Car, black "ACDX 65125", *00*	—	90	___[1]
(36927)	B&O DC Hopper 6-pack "435040/45", *01*	—	520	___[1]
(36935)	Maersk Maxi-Stack 2-pack "250131/2", *00*	—	90	___[1]
(36937)	SP Maxi-Stack "513957", *02*	—	70	___[1]
(38000)	Lionel Century Club II NYC Hudson 4-6-4 Empire State, *02 u*	—	900	___[1]
(38004)	Virginian 4-6-0 Ten-Wheeler "203", CC, *01–02*	—	570	___[1]
(38005)	Long Island 4-6-0 Ten-Wheeler "138", CC, *01–02*	—	530	___[1]
(38007)	UP Auxiliary Tender, black, CC, *01*	—	205	___[1]
(38008)	UP Auxiliary Tender, gray, CC, *01*	—	215	___[1]
(38009)	DRG 4-6-6-4 Challenger "3803", CC, *01*	—	1800	___[1]
(38010)	Clinchfield 4-6-6-4 Challenger "673", CC, *01*	—	1650	___[1]
(38012)	Wheeling & Lake Erie 2-6-6-2 "8005", CC, *01*	—	850	___[1]
(38013)	D&H 4-6-6-4 Lionmaster Challenger "1527", CC, *01*	—	760	___[1]
(38014)	DRG 4-6-6-4 Lionmaster Challenger "3800", CC, *01*	—	710	___[1]
(38016)	Southern 0-8-0 Yard Goat "6536", CC, *01–02*	—	530	___[1]
(38017)	CN 2-6-0 Mogul "86", CC, *03*		CP	___
(38018)	Wabash 2-6-0 Mogul "826", CC, *03*		CP	___

		Exc	New	Cond/$
(38019)	B&M 2-6-0 Mogul "1455", CC, 03		CP	___
(38020)	PRR 4-4-4-4 Lionmaster T1 Duplex "5514", CC, 02–03		CP	___
(38021)	WP 4-6-6-4 Challenger "402", CC, 02	—	690	___ [1]
(38022)	WM 4-6-6-4 Challenger "1206", CC, 02	—	690	___ [1]
(38023)	UP 4-6-6-4 Challenger "3976", CC, 02	—	690	___ [1]
(38025)	PRR 4-6-2 K4 Pacific "1361", CC, 02	—	900	___ [1]
(38026)	N&W 4-8-4 J Class Northern "606", CC, 02	—	1450	___ [1]
(38027)	Meadow River Lumber Co. Heisler Geared "6" Steam Locomotive, CC, 03		CP	___
(38028)	PRR 6-8-6 S2 Class "6200" Steam Turbine, 01	—	760	___ [1]
(38029)	UP 4-12-2 "9000", CC, 03		CP	___
(38030)	Santa Fe 2-8-8-2 "1795", CC, 03		CP	___
(38032)	Virginian 2-8-8-2 "741", CC, 03		CP	___
(38036)	Long Island 2-8-0 Consolidation, 01	—	390	___ [1]
(38037)	PRR-Reading Seashore 2-8-0 Consolidation "6072", CC, 01	—	495	___ [1]
(38038)	D&RG Auxilary Water Tender, 01	—	230	___ [1]
(38039)	Clinchfield Auxilary Water Tender, 01	—	220	___ [1]
(38040)	LV 4-6-0 Camelback, 01	—	450	___ [1]
(38042)	C&NW 4-6-0 Ten-Wheeler "361", CC, 02	—	450	___ [1]
(38043)	Frisco 4-6-0 Ten-Wheeler "719", CC, 02	—	425	___ [1]
(38044)	PRR 4-6-2 K4 Pacific "5385", CC, 02	—	920	___ [1]
(38045)	NYC 4-6-4 Lionmaster Hudson J-3a "5418", CC, 03		CP	___
(38046)	GN 0-8-0 "815", CC, 02	—	530	___ [1]
(38047)	N&W 0-8-0 "266", CC, 02	—	530	___ [1]
(38048)	Nickel Plate Road 0-8-0 "303", CC, 02	—	530	___ [1]
(38049)	N&W 2-6-6-4 Articulated Steam Locomotive "1234", CC, 02	—	690	___ [1]
(38050)	Nickel Plate 2-8-4 Berkshire "779", CC, 03		CP	___
(38051)	Erie 2-8-4 Berkshire "3315", CC, 03		CP	___
(38052)	Pere Marquette 2-8-4 Berkshire "1225", CC, 03		CP	___
(38053)	NYC 4-8-2 Mohawk L-2a "2793", CC, 03		CP	___
(38056)	Pennsylvania 4-8-2 Mountain M-1a "6759", CC, 03		CP	___
(38057)	Weyerhaeuser Timber Co. Shay, CC, 03		CP	___
(38061)	Cass Scenic RR Heisler Geared "6" Steam Locomotive, CC, 03		CP	___
(38062)	Lionel Lines 4-6-2 Pacific "8062", CC, 02-03		CP	___
(38065)	UP 2-8-8-2 Mallet "3672", CC, 02	—	1050	___ [1]
(38066)	Elk River Coal & Lumber Co. Shay, CC, 03		CP	___
(38067)	Milwaukee Road 4-6-2 Pacific "6316", CC, 03		CP	___

		Exc	New	Cond/$
(38068)	WM 4-6-2 Pacific "204", CC, *03*		CP	___
(38075)	UP 4-8-8-4 Lionmaster Big Boy "4024", CC, *03*		CP	___
(38085)	NYC 4-6-4 Lionmaster Hudson J-3a "5422", CC, *03*		CP	___
(38086)	B&A 4-6-4 Lionmaster Hudson "607", CC, *03*		CP	___
(38088)	NYC 2-6-0 Mogul "1924", CC, *03*		CP	___
(38100)	Texas Special F3 AB set "2245", *99*	—	760	___ [1]
(38103)	Texas Special F3 "2245", *99*	—	445	___ [1]
(38114)	AT&SF FT B Unit, *99–00*	—	150	___ [1]
(38115)	NYC FT B Unit, *99–00*	—	115	___ [1]
(38116)	B&O FT B Unit, *99–00*	—	115	___ [1]
(38144)	C&O F3 AA "7019/7021", *00*	—	780	___ [1]
(38147)	GN Alco FA-2 AA Diesel set, CC, *02*	—	405	___ [1]
(38150)	Platinum Ghost "2333", *99*	—	540	___ [3]
(38153)	Spirit of the Century "2333", *99*	—	1100	___ [1]
(38160)	Pennsylvania Alco FB-2 Unit, *02*	—	125	___ [1]
(38161)	MKT Alco FB-2 Unit, *02*	—	125	___ [1]
(38162)	Burlington FT B Unit, *01*		CP	___
(38167)	Burlington FT AA, *01*		CP	___
(38176)	Pennsylvania Alco FA-2 AA Diesel set, CC, *02*	—	405	___ [1]
(38182)	MKT Alco FA-2 AA Diesel set, CC, *02*	—	405	___ [1]
(38188)	Southern F3 ABA "2356", *00*	—	870	___ [1]
(38194)	GN Alco FB-2 Unit, *02*	—	125	___ [1]
(38196)	Santa Fe FT A Unit "171", *00*		CP	___
(38197)	SP F3 ABA "2387", *00*	—	640	___ [1]
[38356]	LOTS Dow Chemical 3-D Tank Car, *87*	75	95	___ [1]
(39008)	PRR Heavyweight Passenger Set (4-pack), *00*	—	190	___ [1]
(39009)	PRR Heavyweight Passenger set Combo "Indian Rock", *00*		NRS	___
(39010)	PRR Heavyweight Passenger set Coach "Andrew Carnegie", *00*		NRS	___
(39011)	PRR Heavyweight Passenger set Coach "Salmon P. Chase", *00*		NRS	___
(39012)	PRR Heavyweight Passenger set Observation "Skyline View", *00*		NRS	___
(39013)	B&O Heavyweight Passenger set (4-pack), *00*	—	400	___ [1]
(39016)	B&O Heavyweight Passenger set (4-pack), *00*	—	200	___ [1]
(39017)	B&O Heavyweight Passenger set Combo "Harper's Ferry", *00*		CP	___
(39018)	B&O Heavyweight Passenger set Coach "Youngstown", *00*		NRS	___
(39019)	B&O Heavyweight Passenger set Coach "New Castle", *00*		NRS	___

		Exc	New	Cond/$
(39020)	B&O Heavyweight Passenger set Observation "Chicago", *00*		NRS	___
(39028)	LL Madison Passenger set (3-pack), *00*	—	165	___[1]
(39029)	Lionel Lines Madison Passenger set Coach "Irvington 2625", *00*		NRS	___
(39030)	LL Madison Passenger set Coach "Madison 2627", *00*		NRS	___
(39031)	LL Madison Passenger set Coach "Manhattan 2628", *00*		NRS	___
(39032)	UP Madison Passenger Car 4-pack, *00*	—	244	___[1]
(39042)	N&W Heavyweight Passenger Car 4-pack, *00*	—	325	___[1]
(39047)	B&O Heavyweight Passenger Car 2-pack, *01*	—	200	___[1]
(39050)	PRR Heavyweight Passenger Car 2-pack, *01*	—	200	___[1]
(39053)	Alaska Streamliner Pass. Car 2-pack, *01*	—	90	___[1]
(39056)	NYC Streamliner Pass. Car 2-pack, *01*	—	75	___[1]
(39059)	Santa Fe Streamliner Pass. Car 2-pack, *01*	—	100	___[1]
(39062)	B&O Streamliner Pass. Car 2-pack, *01*	—	75	___[1]
(39065)	PRR Streamliner Pass. 4-pack, *01*	—	150	___[1]
(39079)	SP Heavyweight Passenger Car 2-pack, *01*		NM	___
(39082)	Blue Comet Heavyweight Pass. Car 2-pack, *02*	—	225	___[1]
(39085)	Freedom Train Heavyweight Passenger Car 3-pack, *03*		CP	___
(39092)	PRR 027 Streamline Passenger Car 2-pack, *01*		CP	___
(39099)	Alton Limited Heavyweight Passenger Car 2-pack, *03*		CP	___
(39100)	Congressional set "William Penn" Coach, *00*	—	100	___[1]
(39101)	Congressional set "Molly Pitcher" Coach, *00*	—	100	___[1]
(39102)	Congressional set "Betsy Ross" Vista Dome, *00*	—	100	___[1]
(39103)	Congressional set "Alexander Hamilton" Observation, *00*	—	100	___[1]
(39104)	Phoebe Snow StationSounds Car, *99*	—	215	___[1]
(39105)	Milwaukee Road Hiawatha StationSounds Car, *99*	—	195	___[1]
(39106)	CP Aluminum Passenger Car set (2-pack), *00*	—	190	___[1]
(39107)	CP Aluminum Passenger Coach "Blair Manor 2553", *00*		NRS	___
(39108)	CP Aluminum Passenger Coach "Craig Manor 2554", *00*		NRS	___
(39109)	Spirit of the Century Aluminum Passenger Car (4-pack), *99*	—	425	___[1]
(39110)	Spirit of the Century Full Vista Dome Car, *99–00*	—	100	___[1]

		Exc	New	Cond/$
(39111)	Spirit of the Century Full Vista Dome Car, 99–00	—	100	___[1]
(39112)	Spirit of the Century Full Vista Dome Car, 99–00	—	100	___[1]
(39113)	Spirit of the Century Skytop Observation Car, 99–00	—	100	___[1]
(39118)	Texas Special StationSounds Aluminum Pass "1203" "Garland", 99–00	—	255	___[1]
(39119)	Southern Aluminum Pass. Car set (4-pack), 00	—	350	___[1]
(39120)	Southern Aluminum Passenger Baggage "Grand Junction 1701", 00		NRS	___
(39121)	Southern Aluminum Passenger Coach "Charlottsville 812", 00		NRS	___
(39122)	Southern Aluminum Passenger Coach "Roanoke 814", 00	—	250	___[1]
(39123)	Southern Aluminum Passenger Observation "Memphis 1152", 00		NRS	___
(39124)	Amtrak Superliner Aluminum Passenger Car 4-pack, 02	—	355	___[1]
(39129)	Santa Fe Superliner Aluminum Passenger Car 4-pack, 02	—	355	___[1]
(39141)	Rock Island Aluminum Passenger Car 4-pack, 01	—	400	___[1]
(39146)	UP Aluminum Passenger Cars, 4-pack, 01	—	285	___[1]
(39151)	CP Aluminum Passenger Car 2-pack, 01	—	330	___[1]
(39154)	PRR Congressional Aluminum Passenger Car 2-pack, 02	—	150	___[1]
(39155)	PRR Congressional Baggage Car, 02		CP	___
(39156)	PRR Congressional Coach "Robert Morris", 02		CP	___
(39157)	Southern Aluminum Passenger Car 2-pack, 01	—	200	___[1]
(39160)	KCS Aluminum Passenger Car 2-pack, 01	—	190	___[1]
(39163)	E-L Aluminum Passenger Car 2-pack, 01	—	185	___[1]
(39166)	Texas Special Aluminum Passenger Car 2-pack, 01	—	430	___[1]
(39169)	ACL Aluminum Passenger Car 4-pack, 01	—	275	___[1]
(39179)	NP Aluminum Passenger Car 2-pack, 02	—	200	___[1]
(39182)	WP Aluminum Passenger Car 2-pack, 02	—	200	___[1]
(39185)	Rio Grande Aluminum Passenger Car 2-pack, 02	—	200	___[1]
(39194)	UP Aluminum Passenger Car 2-pack, 02	—	175	___[1]
(39197)	CP Aluminum StationSounds Car, 02	—	200	___[1]
(39198)	PRR Aluminum StationSounds Car, 02	—	200	___[1]

		Exc	New	Cond/$
(39200)	Hellgate Bridge Boxcar II "1900-2000", *00 u*	—	75	___[3]
(39201)	Century Club Hudson Boxcar "773", *00 u*	—	55	___[1]
(39202)	Lionel Centennial Boxcar "1900-2000", *00*	—	55	___[1]
(39203)	6464 Boxcar Series X 3-pack, *01*	—	85	___[1]
(39204)	New Haven Boxcar "6464-725", *01*	—	40	___[1]
(39205)	Alaska Boxcar "6464-825", *01*	—	50	___[1]
(39206)	NYC Boxcar "6464-900", *01*	—	40	___[1]
(39207)	UP Boxcar "508500", red, *00*	—	50	___[1]
(39208)	UP Boxcar "903658", silver, *00*	—	45	___[1]
(39209)	UP Boxcar "500200", yellow, *00*	—	42	___[1]
(39210)	6530 Fire Fighting Car, *00*	—	40	___[1]
(39211)	6464 Archive 2 Boxcar 3-pack, *00*	—	75	___[1]
(39215)	LCC II Boxcar, *01u*	—	75	___[1]
(39216)	PRR DD Boxcar "47211", *01*	—	40	___[1]
(39217)	LCC II Boxcar, *00u*	—	75	___[1]
(39218)	LCC II Member Boxcar, gold, *01u*	—	100	___[1]
(39220)	B&LE Heavyweight Boxcar "82101", *01*	—	41	___[1]
(39221)	L&N Heavyweight Boxcar "109829", *01*	—	42	___[1]
(39222)	Conrail Heavyweight Boxcar "269198", *01*	—	42	___[1]
(39223)	Postwar 6464 Boxcar Series 3-pack, *02*	—	100	___[1]
(39227)	Postwar 6468 Automobile Boxcar 3-pack, *01*	—	95	___[1]
(39236)	Postwar WP Boxcar "6464-250", *01*	—	45	___[1]
(39238)	Elvis Boxcar, *03*		CP	___
(39239)	P&LE Boxcar "22300, *02*	—	35	___[1]
(39240)	Pennsylvania Boxcar "118747", *02*	—	35	___[1]
(39241)	PC Boxcar "252455", *02*	—	35	___[1]
(39242)	Archive 6464 Boxcar Series 3-pack, *03*		CP	___
(39247)	Postwar NYC DD Boxcar "6468", *02-03*		CP	___
39249	Christmas Boxcar, *03*		CP	___
(39250)	Campbell's Kids Centennial Boxcar, *03*		CP	___
(39257)	Boy's WP Boxcar "6464-100", *03*		CP	___
(39258)	Elvis Presley Boxcar, 2, *03*		CP	___
(39259)	Buick Centennial Boxcar, *03*		CP	___
(51007)	LCC II UP M-10000 set, *00u*	—	900	___[1]
51200	(See 17510)			
(51201)	Lionel Lines Rail Chief Passenger set, *90*	—	480	___[1]
(51220)	NYC "Imperial Castle" Passenger Car, *93 u*	—	500	___[1]
(51221)	NYC "Niagara County" Passenger Car, *93 u*	—	500	___[1]
(51222)	NYC "Cascade Glory" Passenger Car, *93 u*	—	500	___[1]
(51223)	NYC "City of Detroit" Passenger Car, *93 u*	—	500	___[1]
(51224)	NYC "Imperial Falls" Passenger Car, *93 u*	—	500	___[1]
(51225)	NYC "Westchester County" Passenger Car, *93 u*	—	500	___[1]

		Exc	New	Cond/$
(51226)	NYC "Cascade Grotto" Passenger Car, *93 u*	—	500	___[1]
(51227)	NYC "City of Indianapolis" Passenger Car, *93 u*	—	500	___[1]
(51228)	NYC "Manhattan Island" Observation Car, *93 u*	—	500	___[1]
(51229)	NYC Dining Car "680", *93 u*	—	500	___[1]
(51230)	NYC Baggage Car "5017", *93 u*	—	500	___[1]
(51231)	NYC "Century Club" Passenger Car, *93 u*	—	500	___[1]
(51232)	NYC "Thousand Islands" Observation Car, *93 u*	—	500	___[1]
(51233)	NYC Dining Car "684", *93 u*	—	500	___[1]
(51234)	NYC Baggage Car "5020", *93 u*	—	500	___[1]
(51235)	NYC "Century Tavern" Passenger Car, *93 u*	—	500	___[1]
(51236)	NYC "City of Toledo" Passenger Car, *93 u*	—	500	___[1]
(51237)	NYC "Imperial Mansion" Passenger Car, *93 u*	—	500	___[1]
(51238)	NYC "Imperial Palace" Passenger Car, *93 u*	—	500	___[1]
(51239)	NYC "Cascade Spirit" Passenger Car, *93 u*	—	500	___[1]
(51240)	NYC Dining Car "681", *93 u*	—	500	___[1]
(51241)	NYC "City of Chicago" Passenger Car, *93 u*	—	500	___[1]
(51242)	NYC "Imperial Garden" Passenger Car, *93 u*	—	500	___[1]
(51243)	NYC "Imperial Fountain" Passenger Car, *93 u*	—	500	___[1]
(51244)	NYC "Cascade Valley" Passenger Car, *93 u*	—	500	___[1]
(51245)	NYC Dining Car "685", *93 u*	—	500	___[1]
51300	Shell Semi-Scale 1-D Tank Car "8124", *91*	—	155	___[2]
(51301)	Lackawanna Semi-Scale Reefer "7000", *92*	250	290	___[1]
(51401)	PRR Semi-Scale Boxcar "100800", *91*	145	165	___[1]
(51402)	C&O Semi-Scale Stock Car "95250", *92*	190	185	___[1]
51501	B&O Semi-Scale Hopper "532000", *91*	105	110	___[1]
(51502)	Lionel Lines Steel Die-cast Ore Car "6486-3" (SSS), *96*	—	80	___[1]
(51503)	Lionel Lines Steel Die-cast Ore Car "6486-1" (SSS), *96*	—	80	___[1]
(51504)	Lionel Lines Steel Die-cast Ore Car "6486-2" (SSS), *96*	—	80	___[1]
(51600)	NYC Depressed Center Flatcar w/ transformer "6418", *96*	—	125	___[1]
51701	NYC Semi-Scale Caboose "19400", *91*	—	135	___[1]
(51702)	PRR N-8 Caboose "478039", *91–92*	250	320	___[1]
52000	Detroit-Toledo TCA Flatcar w/ trailer, *92 u*	80	95	___[1]
52001	NETCA B&M Quad Hopper w/ coal load, *92 u*	50	75	___[1]
[52002]	VTC Passenger Cars (See 7692)			
52003	Ozark TCA "Meet Me in St. Louis" Flatcar w/ trailer, *92 u*	—	395	___[1]

		Exc	New	Cond/$
[52004]	LCAC Algoma Central Gondola w/ coil covers "9215", *92 u*	75	95	___[1]
[52005]	LCAC Canadian National F-3 B Unit "9517", *93 u*	—	30	___[1]
[52006]	LCAC CP Boxcar "930016" (Std. O), *93 u*	—	145	___[1]
[52007]	NLOE Long Island RS-3 "1552", *92 u*	120	250	___[1]
[52008]	TCA Bucyrus Erie Crane Car "1993X", *93 u*	55	60	___[1]
(52009)	Sacramento Valley TTOS Western Pacific Boxcar "64641993", *93 u*	41	45	___[2]
(52010)	TTOS Weyerhaeuser DD Boxcar "838593" (Std. O), *93 u*	49	59	___[2]
52011	Gadsden Pacific Tucson, Cornelia & Gila Bend Ore Car w/ load, *93 u*	31	40	___[1]
52013	Artrain Norfolk Southern Flatcar w/ trailer (Std. O), *92 u*	175	275	___[1]
(52014)	LOTS BN TTUX Flatcar set w/ N&W trailers "637500A" and "637500B", *93 u*	155	190	___[1]
52016	NETCA B&M Gondola w/ coil covers, *93 u*	55	65	___[1]
52018	Lakes & Pines TCA 3M Boxcar, *93 u*	—	450	___[1]
[52019]	NLOE Long Island Boxcar "8393", *93 u*	30	47	___[1]
[52020]	NLOE Long Island B/W Caboose "8393", *93 u*	60	75	___[1]
(52021)	TTOS Weyerhaeuser tractor and trailer, *93 u*	24	31	___[1]
52022	TTOS Union Pacific Boxcar, *93 u*	—	400	___[1]
(52023)	LCCA D&TS 2-bay ACF Hopper "2601" (Std. O), *93 u*	38	42	___[3]
52024	Artrain Conrail Auto Carrier, *93 u*	95	105	___[1]
(52025)	LCCA Madison Hardware tractor and trailer, *93 u*	21	25	___[2]
[52026]	NLOE Long Island Flatcar w/ Grumman trailer "8394", *94 u*	230	330	___[1]
52027	Gadsden Pacific Pinto Valley Mine Ore Car w/ load, *94 u*	29	32	___[1]
(52028)	TTOS Ford Cars, set of 3, *94 u*	65	75	___[1]
(52029)	TTOS Ford 1-D Tank Car "12" (O27), *94 u*	30	35	___[1]
(52030)	TTOS Ford Gondola "4023", *94 u*	23	29	___[1]
(52031)	TTOS Ford Hopper "1458" (O27), *94 u*	28	33	___[1]
(52032)	TTOS Ford 1-D Tank Car "14" w/ Kughn inscription (O27), *94 u*	75	105	___[1]
(52033)	Wolverine TTOS Lionel Lines tractor and trailer (See 52040)			
(52034)	Wolverine TTOS Grand Trunk Flatcar "52040" (See 52040)			
(52035)	TCA Yorkrail GP-9 "1750", shell only, *94 u*	44	55	___[1]

		Exc	New	Cond/$
(52036)	TCA 40th Anniversary B/W Caboose, *94 u*	46	55	___1
(52037)	TCA Yorkrail GP-9 "1754", *94 u*	155	190	___1
(52038)	LCCA Southern Hopper w/ coal load "360794" (Std. O), *94 u*	38	42	___1
(52039)	LCCA "Track 29" Bumper, *94 u*	—	15	___1
52040	Wolverine TTOS GTW Flatcar w/ Lionel Lines tractor and trailer, *94 u*	55	60	___2
(52041)	LOTS BN TTUX Flatcar set w/ Conrail trailers "637500D" and "637500E", *94 u*	70	90	___2
(52042)	LOTS BN TTUX Flatcar w/ CN trailer "637500C", *94 u*	55	65	___1
[52043]	NETCA LL Bean Boxcar "1994", *94 u*	85	115	___1
(52044)	Eastwood Vat Car, *95 u*	—	45	___1
[52045]	TCA Penn Dutch Milk Car "61052", *94 u*	—	90	___1
(52046)	TTOS ACL Boxcar "16247", *94 u*	—	110	___1
(52047)	Southwest TTOS Cotton Belt Woodside Caboose w/ smoke "1921" (Std. O), *93–94 u*	70	75	___1
(52048)	LOTS CN tractor and trailer "197993", *94 u*	32	35	___1
52049	Artrain BN Gondola w/ coil covers, *94 u*	55	70	___1
[52050]	Schuylkill Haven Borough Day SP-type Caboose "1994", *94 u*	—	37	___1
(52051)	TCA Baltimore & Ohio "Sentinel" Boxcar "6464095", *95 u*	45	49	___2
[52052]	TCA 40th Anniversary Boxcar, *94 u*	—	80	___1
52053	TTOS Carail Boxcar, *94 u*	50	55	___1
52054	Carail Boxcar, *94 u*		NRS	___
(52055)	LCCA Sovex tractor and trailer, *94 u*	22	28	___1
(52056)	LCCA Southern tractor and trailer "206502", *94 u*	22	27	___1
(52057)	TTOS Western Pacific Boxcar "64641995", *95 u*	47	50	___2
(52058)	Central California TTOS Santa Fe Boxcar "64641895", *95 u*	39	55	___1
(52059)	Eastern TCA Clinchfield Quad Hopper w/ coal load "16413", *94 u*	95	125	___1
[52060]	VTC Tender w/ whistle "7694", *94 u*	—	70	___1
[52061]	NLOE Long Island Stern's Pickle Products Vat Car "8395", *95 u*	—	155	___1
(52062)	TCA "Skytop"Observation Car "1995", *95 u*	430	250	___3
(52063)	TCA New York Central "Pacemaker" Boxcar "6464125", *95 u*	—	375	___1
(52064)	TCA Missouri Pacific Boxcar "6464150", *95 u*	—	360	___1

Exc New Cond/$

		Exc	New	Cond/$
(52065)	Penn-Dutch Grain Operating Boxcar "9028", *96u*	—	100	___[1]
(52066)	TrainMaster Tractor and Trailer, *94 u*	—	115	___[1]
(52067)	LOTS Burlington Ice Car "50240", *95 u*	—	55	___[2]
(52068)	Toy Train Parade TTOS Contadina Boxcar "16245", *94 u*	—	50	___[1]
52069	Carail Tractor and Trailer, *94 u*	—	65	___[1]
52070	Knoebel's Boxcar, *95 u*	—	55	___[1]
52071	Gadsden Pacific Copper Basin Railway Ore Car w/ load, *95 u*	—	32	___[1]
[52072]	NLOE Grumman Tractor, *94 u*	—	60	___[1]
(52073)	Southwest TTOS Pacific Fruit Express Reefer "459402" (Std. O), *95 u*	—	60	___[1]
(52074)	LCCA Iowa Beef Packers Reefer "197095" (Std. O), *95 u*	—	37	___[2]
52075	United Auto Workers Boxcar, *95 u*	—	85	___[1]
[52076]	NLOE Long Island Observation Car "8396", *96 u*	—	350	___[1]
(52077)	Pacific Northwest TCA Great Northern Hi-cube Boxcar "9695", *95 u*	—	460	___[1]
(52078)	TTOS Southern Pacific SD-9 "5366", *96 u*	—	250	___[2]
(52079)	TTOS SP B/W Caboose "1996", *96 u*	—	55	___[1]
[52080]	NETCA Boston & Maine Flatcar w/ trailer "91095", *95 u*	—	250	___[1]
(52081)	C&NW Boxcar "6464555", *96u*	—	80	___[1]
52082	Steamtown Lackawanna Boxcar, *95 u*	—	100	___[1]
(52083)	Eastwood Chemicals Flatcar w/ tanker "16380", *95 u*	—	45	___[1]
(52084)	TTOS Union Pacific I-Beam Flatcar w/ load "16380", *95 u*	—	170	___[1]
(52085)	TCA Full Vista Dome Car "1996", *96 u*	—	130	___[2]
(52086)	Canadian TTOS Pacific Great Eastern Boxcar "64641972", *96 u*	—	60	___[1]
(52087)	TTOS New Mexico Central Boxcar "64641996", *96 u*	—	60	___[1]
[52088]	Desert TCA 25th Anniversary On-Track Step Van, *96 u*	—	140	___[1]
52089	Gadsden Pacific SMARRCO Ore Car w/ load, *96 u*	—	30	___[1]
(52090)	LCCA Pere Marquette DD Boxcar (Std. O), *96 u*	—	39	___[1]
(52091)	LCCA Lenox Tractor and Trailer, *95 u*	—	18	___[1]
(52092)	LCCA Iowa Interstate Tractor and Trailer, *95 u*	—	20	___[1]
(52093)	Lone Star TCA Boxcar "6464696", *96 u*	—	70	___[1]

		Exc	New	Cond/$
(52096)	Dept. 56 Snow Village Boxcar "9756", *95u*	—	80	___1
52097	Artrain Chessie System Reefer, *95 u*	—	75	___1
(52098)	National Bureau of Standards Boxcar (Std. O), *96u*	—	70	___1
(52099)	MP TOFC Flatcar, *96 u*	—	80	___1
52100	Grand Rapids Station Platform, *96*		CP	___
52100	LCCA Station Platform, *98*		CP	___
(52101)	Chicagoland RR Club Maxistack Flatcar "64287", *97 u*	—	80	___1
(52102)	Chicagoland RR Club AT&SF E/V Caboose "999758", *96 u*	—	75	___1
(52103)	Chicagoland RR Club AT&SF E/V Caboose "999556", *96 u*	—	75	___1
52104	St. Louis LRRC T&T, *96 u*		CP	___
(52105)	Superstition Mountain Operating Gondola "61997", *97 u*	—	80	___1
(52106)	TCA "City of Phoenix" Dining Car "1997", *97u*	—	100	___1
(52107)	LCCA Pickup Truck, *96 u*	—	50	___1
(52108)	LCCA Step Van, *96 u*	—	50	___1
(52110)	CSPM&O Boxcar, *97 u*	22	60	___1
52111	NETCA Ben & Jerry's TOFC Flatcar w/ tractor, *94*	—	350	___1
(52112)	NLOE LIRR Aluminum Passenger Car "9733", *97 u*	—	300	___1
(52113)	NDG&W 3-bay Hopper, *97 u*	—	55	___1
(52114)	NYC TOFC Flatcar, *97 u*	—	70	___1
(52115)	LCAC Wabash Lake Auto Carrier "9519", *98 u*	—	100	___1
(52116)	Milwaukee Road Flatcar w/ Tractor and Trailer "194797", *97 u*	—	60	___1
(52117)	St. Louis LRRC Wabash TOFC Flatcar, *97 u*	—	65	___1
(52118)	TCA D&RGW Boxcar "5477097", *97 u*	—	70	___1
(52119)	TCA Museum 20th Anniversary Boxcar, *97 u*		NRS	___
(52120)	Shedd Aquarium Car "3435-557", *98 u*	—	75	___1
(52121)	Mobilgas 1-D Tank Car "238" (Std. O), *97u*	—	75	___1
(52122)	NLOE Meenan Oil 1-D Tank Car, *97 u*; "9883", *98 u*	—	60	___1
(52123)	Long Island RR "Ronkonkoma" Full Vista Dome "9783", *97u*	—	300	___1
(52123)	Long Island RR "Hicksville" Dining Car "9883", *98u*	—	300	___1
(52124)	El Paso & South Western Ore Car w/ load, *97u*	—	40	___1
(52125)	(See 2346)			
(52126)	MILW Boxcar w/ CTT logo "21027", *97 u*	—	60	___1

Exc New Cond/$

(52127)	Southern TCA Hopper (Std. O) "360997", *98 u*	—	70	___1
(52128)	TCA Pennsylvania Dutch Boxcar "91653", *97 u*	—	80	___1
52129	Lighted Billboard LOTS, *97*		CP	___
(52130)	Hot Wheels TOFC Flatcar "21697", *97 u*	—	60	___1
52131	LCCA Airplane Blue, *98*		CP	___
(52132)	Knoebel's #2, *99 u*	—	75	___1
(52133)	Knoebel's Boxcar, *98 u*	—	75	___1
(52134)	Knoebel Phoenix #4 Boxcar, *00 u*	—	75	___1
(52135)	Santa Fe Refrigerator Car "22739", *98u*	—	60	___1
52136A	Christmas Special Tractor and Trailor, *97*		CP	___
52136B	Frisco Special Tractor and Trailer, *98*		CP	___
(52137)	Red Wing Shoes Boot Oil Tank Car, *98*	—	50	___1
52138	LCCA Airplane Orange, *98*		CP	___
(52139)	Dept. 56 S/W Caboose "6256", *97u*	—	65	___1
(52140)	Artrain UP Bunk Car, *97 u*	—	100	___1
(52141)	Zep Boxcar, *96*	—	70	___1
52142	Mass Central Maxi-Stack Flatcar, *98u*	—	120	___1
(52143)	TCA "City of Providence" Coach "1998", *98u*	—	140	___1
(52144)	NLOE LIRR/Grumman TOFC Flatcar "8398", *98 u*	—	110	___1
(52145)	Long Island RR "Jamaica" Coach "99831", *99u*	—	300	___1
(52145)	Long Island RR "Penn Station" Coach "99832", *99u*	—	300	___1
(52146)	Ocean Spray Plug Door Refrigerator Car "OSCX 1998", *98u*	—	115	___1
(52147)	Frisco/Campbell 66 TOFC Flatcar, *98 u*; "52148-558", *99 u*	—	75	___1
(52148)	REA/Santa Fe Operating Boxcar "52148-558", *99u*	—	70	___1
(52149)	TTOS Conrail Flatcar w/ shovel, *98 u*	—	45	___1
(52150)	Frisco/Campbell 66 TOFC Flatcar, *98 u*	—	150	___1
(52151)	Amtrak Express Baggage Boxcar "71998" (Std. O), *98u*	—	60	___1
(52152)	Ben Franklin Philadelphia Woodside Refrigerator Car, *98u*	—	120	___1
52153	6414 Auto set (4-pack), *98*		CP	___
(52154)	Pacific Fruit Express Refrigerator Car "459403" (Std. O), *98u*	—	70	___1
(52155)	TCA "City of San Francisco" Baggage Car "1999", *99u*	—	140	___1
(52157)	Holly Bros. 3-D Tank Car "6156", *98 u*	—	70	___1
(52158)	Monopoly Mint Car "M-0539", *98*	—	180	___1

Exc New Cond/$

		Exc	New	Cond/$
(52159)	Monopoly Depressed Center Flatcar w/ transformer, *98*	—	95	____¹
(52160)	Monopoly Water Works Tank Car, *98*	—	95	____¹
(52161)	Monopoly SP-type Caboose "M-1006", *98*	—	55	____¹
(52162)	LOTS BMandO DD Boxcar "24580", *99 u*	—	65	____¹
(52163)	Milwaukee LRC Milwaukee Road DD Boxcar "194798", *99 u*	—	60	____¹
(52164)	SP Ore Car w/ load, *98u*	—	40	____¹
(52165)	Artrain S/W Caboose, "6256", *97u*	—	75	____¹
(52166)	NLOE LIRR/Northrop TOFC Flatcar "8399", *99 u*	—	110	____¹
(52167)	AT&SF Navajo TOFC Flatcar "83199", *99 u*	—	70	____¹
(52168)	Carail Flatcar with Trailer "17455", *99u*	—	85	____¹
(52169)	Zep Manufacturing Co. Flatcar w/ trailer "62734", *99u*	NRS		____
(52170)	CLRC SP Operating Boxcar, *99 u*	—	65	____¹
(52171)	CLRC UP Operating Boxcar, *99 u*	—	65	____¹
(52172)	L&N Boxcar, *99 u*	—	65	____¹
52173	Long Island RR F3 AA Shells, *00*		CP	____
(52174)	REA Baggage Car "0083", *00u*		CP	____
(52175)	Dept. 56 4-6-4 Hudson, *99 u*	—	430	____¹
(52176)	Fort Worth & Denver Boxcar "8277", *99u*	—	60	____¹
(52177)	Arizona Southern RR Ore Car w/ load, *99u*	—	40	____¹
(52178)	CLRC Burlington Route Operating Boxcar, *00 u*	—	65	____¹
(52179)	CLRC ACL Operating Boxcar, *00 u*	—	65	____¹
(52180)	Milwaukee Road Flatcar w/ trailer "194799", *99 u*	—	70	____¹
(52181)	Monopoly set 2 (4-pack), *99*	—	345	____¹
(52182)	Monopoly Railroads Boxcar "M0636", *99 u*	—	80	____¹
(52183)	Monopoly Jail Car "M-1131", *99*	—	70	____¹
(52184)	Monopoly Free Parking Flat w/ 2 autos, *99*	—	75	____¹
(52185)	Monopoly Chance Gondola "M-0893", *99*	—	60	____¹
(52186)	Grucci Fireworks Boxcar "2000", *00u*	—	75	____¹
(52187)	Madison Hardware Flatcar w/ 2 trailers "1909-1999", *99*	—	80	____¹
(52188)	Carail Aquarium w/ 2 autos, 25th Anniversary, *99*	—	70	____¹
(52189)	Monopoly 4-6-4 Hudson "1999", *99*	—	430	____¹
(52190)	St. Louis LRRC IC TOFC Flatcar, *00 u*	—	80	____¹
(52191)	TCA "City of Grand Rapids" Sleeper/Roomette "2000", *00u*	—	140	____¹
(52192)	TTOS SP Crane & Gondola 2-pack, *00 u*		CP	____
(52193)	TTOS SP Crane, *00 u*	—	50	____

		Exc	New	Cond/$
(52194)	TTOS SP Gondola, *00 u*	—	35	___[1]
(52195)	LCCA CP Maxistack Flatcar "200030", *00 u*	—	100	___[1]
(52196)	LOTS CP Maxistack Flatcar "524115", *00 u*	—	90	___[1]
(52197)	Artrain GP-38 "2380", *00 u*	—	250	___[1]
(52198)	Frisco Boxcar "5477000", *00u*		CP	___
52199	Real Plastic Snow 4-bay Hopper "6756", *00*		CP	___
(52205)	SP Overnight Merchandise Service Boxcar 5-pack "6464-2000", *00u*		CP	___
52206	LCCA SD-40 w/ E/V Caboose "2000", *00 u*		CP	___
52207	Lionel Lines SD40, Traditional, *00*		CP	___
(52208)	Lionel Lines E/V Caboose, *00u*		CP	___
(52209)	World's Fair Sleeper/Roomette Car "0183", *01u*		CP	___
52210	Rico Station, *00*		CP	___
(52212)	Berkshire Brewing Reefer, *00 u*	—	200	___[1]
(52213)	BHP Copper Ore Car, *00u*	—	40	___[1]
(52215)	C&NW Cylindrical Hopper (Std. O), *01u*	—	60	___[1]
(52216)	C&NW Cylindrical Hopper (Std. O), *02u*	—	60	___[1]
52217	LCCA/LOTS 2000 Convention Billboard, *00*		CP	___
(52218)	Monopoly 4-4-2 Steam Freight set, *00 u*	—	325	___[1]
(52219)	Monopoly 4-6-4 Bronze Hudson "2000", *00 u*	—	530	___[1]
(52220)	TCA "City of Chattanooga" Vista Dome "2001", *01u*	—	140	___
(52221)	Norfolk Southern Boxcar "2001", *01u*	—	50	___
(52222)	SP Daylight Flatcar w/ trailer, *01u*	—	50	___
52223	CLRC Santa Fe REA Operating Boxcar, *00 u*		CP	___
52224A	SP Flatcar w/ Navajo tractor and trailer, *01*		CP	___
52224B	SP Flatcar w/ Trailer Flatcar Service tractor and trailer, *01*		CP	___
(52225)	Monopoly 4-6-4 Pewter Hudson "2001", *01 u*	—	400	___[1]
(52226)	Angela Trotta Thomas Boxcar "2000", *01u*	—	100	___[1]
52227	Artrain Space Boxcar, *01 u*		CP	___
(52228)	Milwaukee Road 1-D Tank Car, *00u*		CP	___
(52229)	Milwaukee Road 1-D Tank Car, *00u*		CP	___
(52230)	Milwaukee Road 1-D Tank Car 2-pack, *00u*		CP	___
(52231)	British Columbia RR 1-D Tank Car, *00u*		CP	___
(52232)	Central RR of Long Island Boxcar, *01u*		CP	___
(52234)	WM F9 Well Car w/ transformer, *01u*	—	60	___[1]
(52235)	World's Fair Vista Dome Car "0283", *02u*		CP	___
(52236)	Moxie Boxcar, *01u*		CP	___
52237	Lionel Gondola "2002", yellow, *01*		CP	___
52238	Lionel Gondola "2002", red, *01*		CP	___
52239	Lionel Gondola "2002", silver, *01*		CP	___
52240	Lionel Gondola 3-pack "2002", *01*		CP	___

		Exc	New	Cond/$
52241	Lionel Gondola "2002", black, *02*		CP	___
52242	Lionel Gondola "2002", blue, *02*		CP	___
52243	National Toy Train Museum 1-D Tank Car 1954, *01*		CP	___
(52243)	National Toy Train Museum 1-D Tank Car "1954" (Std. O), *01u*		CP	___
52244	Louisville & Nashville Horse Car, *01*		CP	___
(52246)	Milwaukee Road DD Boxcar "194701", *01u*		CP	___
(52248)	Tombstone & Southern RR Ore Car, *01u*	—	40	___1
(52249)	Knoebels Amusement Park 75th Anniversary Boxcar "9700", *01u*	—	75	___1
(52250)	TCA "City of Chicago" Combo Car "2002", *02u*	—	130	___1
(52251)	PRR Customized Mail/Cargo Car, *01u*	—	50	___1
52253	San Pedro Boxcar, *02*		CP	___
52254	Happy Holidays Gondola "6462-56", *01*		CP	___
(52255)	Lionel Lines Artrain 30th Anniversary Flatcar w/ billboard, *01*	—	100	___1
(52256)	New York & Atlantic Ry. Boxcar "8302", *02u*		CP	___
52257	Season's Greetings Gondola "4002", *01*		CP	___
52258	UP Flatcar w/ UP tractor and trailer, *02*		CP	___
(52259)	MP GP-20 "28500", Traditional, *01u*		CP	___
(52260)	LOTS Baltimore Aquarium Car, *01 u*	—	110	___1
(52261)	Schlitz Beer/URT Refrigerator Car "92132", *02u*		CP	___
52263	World's Fair Combine Car "0383", *02*		CP	___
(52264)	Durango & Silverton Operating Hopper "9325", *02u*		CP	___
52265	Milwaukee Road/Zoological Society of Milwaukee Aquarium Car "4701", *02*		CP	___
52266	PRR "Coal Goes to War" Hopper "707025", *02*		CP	___
52267	PRR "Coal Goes to War" Hopper "707026", *02*		CP	___
(52270)	Jenney Mfg. Co. Tank Car, *02u*		CP	___
(52271)	National Toy Train Museum Wheel Car "1957", *02u*		CP	___
52272	Lionel Gondola "2002" Gold, *02*		CP	___
52273	LCCA Subcar, *02*		CP	___
52274	"City of Los Angeles" RPO Car "2003", orange, *03*		CP	___
52276	California Gold Mint Car "2003", *03*		CP	___
52277	Carnegie Science Center 10th Anniversary Boxcar "9700", *02*		CP	___
52279	D&N Ore Care, *02*		CP	___
52280	LOTS Product Mint Car, *02*		CP	___
52282	Western Pacific Feather Boxcar "2003", red, *03*		CP	___
52287	Minute Man Operating Boxcar, *03*		CP	___
52295	National Toy Train Museum Gondola w/ pipes, *03*		CP	___

		Exc	New	Cond/$
52296	Flatcar w/ tractor and tanker, *03*		CP	___
(52299)	UP Las Vegas Jackpot Security Transport "2003", *03 u*		CP	___
52306	NE Trans TOFC, *03*		CP	___
(62162)	Automatic Crossing Gate and Signal "262", *99–03*	—	34	___ [1]
(62180)	Railroad Signs (14), *99–03*	—	4	___ [1]
(62181)	Telephone Pole set "150", *99–03*	—	5	___ [1]
(62283)	Die-cast illuminated bumpers "260", *99–03*	—	15	___ [1]
(62709)	Rico Station kit, *99–00*		CP	___
(62716)	Short Extension Bridge, *99–03*	—	7	___ [1]
(62900)	Lockon, *99–03*		CP	___
(62901)	Ives Track Clips (O-27) (12), *99–03*	—	5	___ [1]
(62905)	Lockon w/ wires, *99–03*		CP	___
(62909)	Smoke Fluid, *99–03*		CP	___
(62927)	Lubrication/Maintenance set, *99–03*	—	10	___ [1]
(62985)	The Lionel Train Book, *99–03*	—	12	___ [1]
(65014)	Half-Curved Track 27" (O27), *99–02*		CP	___
(65019)	Half-Straight Track (O27), *99–03*		CP	___
(65020)	90° Crossover (O27), *99–03*		CP	___
(65021)	Left Manual Switch 27" (O27), *99–03*		CP	___
(65022)	Right Manual Switch 27" (O27), *99–03*		CP	___
(65023)	45° Crossover (O27), *99–03*		CP	___
(65024)	Straight Track 35" (O27), *99–03*		CP	___
(65033)	Curved Track 27" (O27), *99–03*		CP	___
(65038)	Straight Track 9" (O27), *99–03*		CP	___
(65041)	Insulator Pins (12) (O27), *99–03*		CP	___
(65042)	Steel Pins (12) (O27), *99–02*		CP	___
(65049)	Curved Track 42" (O27), *99–03*		CP	___
(65113)	Curved Track 54" (O27), *99–03*		CP	___
(65121)	Left Remote Switch 27" (O27), *99–03*		CP	___
(65122)	Right Remote Switch 27" (O27), *99–03*		CP	___
(65149)	Remote Uncoupling Section (O27), *99–03*		CP	___
(65165)	Right Remote Switch 72" (O), *99–03*		CP	___
(65166)	Left Remote Switch 72" (O), *99–03*		CP	___
(65167)	Right Remote Switch 72" (O27), *99–03*	—	15	___ [1]
(65168)	Left Remote Switch 42" (O27), *99–03*	—	15	___ [1]
(65500)	Straight Track 10" (O), *99–03*		CP	___
(65501)	Curved Track 31" (O), *99–03*		CP	___
(65504)	Half-Curved Track 31" (O), *99–03*		CP	___
(65505)	Half-Straight Track (O), *99–03*		CP	___
65514	Half Curved Track (O-27), *99–03*		CP	___
(65523)	Straight Track 40" (O), *99–03*		CP	___

		Exc	New	Cond/$
(65530)	Remote Uncoupling Section (O), *99–03*		CP	___
(65540)	90° Crossover (O), *99–03*		CP	___
(65543)	Insulator Pins (12) (O), *99–03*		CP	___
(65545)	45° Crossover (O), *99–03*		CP	___
(65551)	Steel Pins (12) (O), *99–03*		CP	___
(65554)	Curved Track 54" (O), *99–03*		CP	___
(65572)	Curved Track 72" (O), *99–03*		CP	___
[80948]	LOTS Michigan Central Boxcar, *82 u*	125	200	___ 1
(81024)	Christmas Train set, *02–03*		CP	___
(81027)	Thomas the Tank Engine set, *01–03*		CP	___
[86009]	LCAC CN Bunk Car, *86 u*	—	100	___ 1
[87010]	LCAC CN Express Reefer, *87 u*	—	100	___ 1
(87024)	2003 Large Scale Christmas Boxcar, *03*		CP	___
[88011]	LCAC CN Woodside Caboose (Std. O), *88 u*	—	440	___ 1
(99000)	Keebler Elf in Express Steam Freight, *99 u*	—	900	___ 1
(99001)	Mickey's Holiday Express Freight set, *99u*		CP	___
(99002)	Looney Tunes S/W Caboose, *99u*		CP	___
(99006)	Keebler Flatcar w/ bulkheads, *99u*		CP	___
(99007)	Smuckers Fudge 1-D Tank Car, *99 u*	—	80	___ 1
(99008)	Mickey's Merry Christmas Boxcar "9700", *99u*		CP	___
(99009)	Mickey's Holiday Express S/W Caboose, *99u*		CP	___
(99013)	Case Cutlery Tank Car "1889", *00u*		CP	___
(99014)	Case Cutlery Gondola "1889", *00u*		CP	___
(99015)	Case Cutlery Boxcar "1889", *00u*		CP	___
(99018)	Case Cutlery Rolling Stock 3-pack, *00u*		CP	___
[121315]	LOTS PRR Hi-cube Boxcar, *84 u*	95	195	___ 1
[830005]	LCAC CN Boxcar, *83 u*		NRS	___
[840006]	LCAC Canadian Wheat Board Covered Quad Hopper, *84 u*	—	125	___ 1
[900013]	LCAC CN Flatcar w/ trailers, *90 u*	—	205	___ 1
Not Assigned	Disney Pluto Chase Gondola "3444", *00 u*	—	100	___ 1
Not Assigned	Disney Mickey Millennium Steam Freight set, *00 u*	—	375	___ 1
Not Assigned	e-Hobbies Boxcar, *00 u*	—	50	___ 1
Not Assigned	NY Toy Fair Boxcar, *01 u*	—	70	___ 1
Not Assigned	NY Toy Fair Loco Puzzle, *01 u*		CP	___
Not Assigned	Pacific Fruit Express Reefer "459403", *98*		NRS	___
Not Assigned	FEC Flatcar w/ Ertl dump truck "6434", *98*		NRS	___
Not Assigned	Lionel Const. Depressed Flatcar w/ Ertl Uniloader "6461", *98*		NRS	___
Not Assigned	Plasticville USA. Boxcar "9741", *01u*		CP	___
UCS	Remote Control Track (O), *70*	4	7	___ 1

	Exc	New	Cond/$
[No Number] Pacific Northwest TCA F-3 AA, shells only, *74 u*	—	60	___¹
[No Number] LCCA Lionel Lines Tender only, *76–77 u*	22	26	___¹
[No Number] Lone Star TCA Texas Special F-3 A Unit, shell only, *81 u*		NRS	___
No Number L.A.S.E.R. Playmat, *81–82*	—	8	___¹
No Number Cannonball Freight Playmat, *81–82*	—	8	___¹
No Number Black Cave Flyer Playmat, *82*	—	8	___¹
[No Number] Lone Star TCA Texas Special F-3 B Unit, shell only, *82 u*		NRS	___
No Number Station Platform, *83–84*	—	8	___¹
No Number Rocky Mountain Platform, *83–84*	—	8	___¹
No Number Commando Assault Train Playmat, *83–84*	—	8	___¹
[No Number] Sacramento-Sierra TCA Lionel Lines Tender, shell only, *84 u*		NRS	___
No Number B&A Hudson and Standard O cars set, *86 u*	1500	1700	___¹
No Number The Blue Comet set, *78–80, 87 u*	560	620	___¹
No Number Burlington "Texas Zephyr" set, *80, 80 u*	980	1150	___¹
No Number Jersey Central set, *86*	345	370	___¹
No Number Chessie System Special set, *80, 86 u*	560	620	___¹
No Number Chicago & Alton Limited set, *81, 86 u*	560	620	___¹
No Number Favorite Food Freight set, *81–82*	240	285	___¹
No Number The General set, *77–80*	215	250	___¹
No Number Great Northern set (FARR #3), *81, 81 u*	620	690	___¹
No Number Illinois Central "City of New Orleans" set, *85, 87, 93*	790	940	___¹
No Number Joshua Lionel Cowen set, *80, 80 u, 82*	540	560	___¹
No Number Lionel Lines set, *82–84 u, 86, 86–87 u, 94–95*	530	620	___¹
No Number Mickey Mouse Express set, *77–78, 78 u*	1100	1900	___¹
No Number The Mint set, *79 u, 80–83, 84 u, 86 u, 87, 91 u, 93*	940	1050	___¹
No Number NYC "20th Century Limited" set, *83, 83 u, 95*	980	1150	___¹
No Number N&W "Powhatan Arrow" set, *81, 81 u, 82 u, 91 u*	1450	1700	___¹
No Number PRR set, *79–80, 79–80 u, 81 u, 83 u*	1200	1350	___¹
No Number PRR set (FARR #5), *84–85, 89 u*	600	660	___¹
No Number Rock Island & Peoria set, *80–82*	210	285	___¹
No Number Santa Fe set (FARR #1), *79, 79 u*	460	580	___¹
No Number Southern set (FARR #4), *83, 83 u*	620	690	___¹
No Number Southern Crescent Limited set, *77–78, 87 u*	540	600	___¹

No Number Southern Pacific Daylight Diesel set,   2150 2300 ____1
  82–83, 82–83 u, 90 u
No Number The Spirit of '76 set, *74–76*   570   620 ____1
No Number Toys "R" Us Thunderball Freight set, *75 u*   NRS ____
No Number Union Pacific set (FARR #2), *80, 80 u*   540   580 ____1
No Number Union Pacific "Overland Route" set,   770   980 ____1
  84, 92 u
No Number Wabash set (FF #1), *86, 87*   790   940 ____1
No Number Amtrak Passenger set, *89, 89 u*   640   770 ____1
No Number Baltimore & Ohio set, *94, 96*   NRS ____
No Number C&NW Passenger set, *93*   385   460 ____1
No Number Chesapeake & Ohio set, *95–96*   NRS ____
No Number D&RGW "California Zephyr" set, *92, 93*   1250 1050 ____1
No Number Erie-Lackawanna Passenger set, *93, 94*   940   980 ____1
No Number Erie set (FF #7), *93*   385   460 ____1
No Number Frisco set (FF #5), *91*   405   425 ____1
No Number Great Northern "Empire Builder" set, *92, 93* 690 730 ____1
No Number Illinois Central "City of New Orleans"   980 1150 ____1
  set, *85, 87, 93*
No Number Illinois Central set, *91–92, 95*   230   250 ____1
No Number Lionel Lines Madison Car set, *91, 93*   560   620 ____1
No Number The Mint set, *79 u, 80–83, 84 u, 86 u,*   940 1050 ____1
  87, 91 u, 93
No Number Milwaukee Road set (FF #2), *87, 90 u*   380   405 ____1
No Number Missouri Pacific set, *95*   —   390 ____1
No Number Norfolk & Western "Powhatan Arrow"   325   390 ____1
  Passenger set, *95*
No Number Nickel Plate Road set (FF #6), *92*   385   460 ____1
No Number New Haven set, *94–95*   —   400 ____1
No Number Northern Pacific set, *90–92*   190   250 ____1
No Number New York Central set, *89, 91*   240   270 ____1
No Number Pennsylvania set, *87–90, 95*   240   270 ____1
No Number Pere Marquette set, *93*   720   770 ____1
No Number SP Daylight Steam set, *90, 92, 93*   790   940 ____1
No Number Santa Fe "Super Chief" set, *91, 91 u,*   1400 1700 ____1
  92 u, 93, 95
No Number Union Pacific set, *94*   430   500 ____1
No Number Wabash set (FF #1), *86, 87*   790   940 ____1
No Number Western Maryland set (FF #4), *89*   345   405 ____1

Section 4
MODERN TINPLATE

O GAUGE CLASSICS

1-263E	Lionel Lines "Blue Comet" 2-4-2 (See 51004)			
44E	(See 51100)			
350E	Lionel Lines "Hiawatha" 4-4-2 (See 51000)			
882	Lionel Lines Combination Car (See 51000)			
883	Lionel Lines Passenger Car (See 51000)			
884	Lionel Lines Observation Car (See 51000)			
892	(See 51202)			
893	(See 51203)			
894	(See 51204)			
895	(See 51205)			
1612	Lionel Lines Passenger Car (See 51004)			
1613	Lionel Lines Passenger Car (See 51004)			
1614	Lionel Lines Baggage Car (See 51004)			
1615	Lionel Lines Observation Car (See 51004)			
8814	(See 51400)			
8816	(See 51500)			
8817	(See 51700)			
8820	(See 51800)			
(51000)	Milwaukee Road "Hiawatha" set, *88 u*	—	900	___ 2
(51001)	Lionel #44 Freight Special set, *89*	—	700	___ 1
(51004)	Blue Comet set, *91*	—	1500	___ 1
(51100)	Lionel Lines Electric "44E" (See 51001), *89*			
(51201)	Rail Chief Passenger Cars, set of 4, *90*	—	500	___ 2
(51202)	Lionel Lines Combination Car "892" (See 51201)			
(51203)	Lionel Lines Passenger Car "893" (See 51201)			
(51204)	Lionel Lines Passenger Car "894" (See 51201)			
(51205)	Lionel Lines Observation Car "895" (See 51201)			
(51400)	Lionel Lines Boxcar "8814" (See 51001), *89*			

281

(51500)   Lionel Lines Hopper "8816" (See 51001), *89*
(51700)   Lionel Lines Caboose "8817" (See 51001), *89*
(51800)   Lionel Lines Searchlight Car "8820"
              (See 51001), *89*

STANDARD GAUGE CLASSICS

1-44   (See 13805)
1-214   (See 13605)
1-215   (See 13303)
1-318E   Lionel Lines Electric (See 13001)
1-381E   (See 13102)
1-384E   (See 13101)
1-390E   (See 13100)
1-400E   (See 13103)
1-408E   (See 13107)
1-4390   American Flyer "West Point" Baggage Car (See 13003)
1-4391   American Flyer "Academy" Passenger Car (See 13003)
1-4392   American Flyer "Army/Navy" Observation Car (See 13003)
1-4689   (See 13109)
2-390E   (See 13106)
2-400E   (See 13108)
7E   (See 13104)
8   (See 13803)
9   (See 13803)
126   (See 13801)
183   (See 13413)
184   (See 13414)
185   (See 13415)
200   (See 13900)
201   (See 13901)
323   (See 13400)
324   (See 13401)
325   (See 13402)
326   (See 13416)
327   (See 13417)
328   (See 13418)
437   (See 13804)

		Exc	New	Cond/$
1115	(See 13800)			
1217	(See 13702)			
1412	(See 13404)			
1413	(See 13405)			
1414	(See 13407)			
1416	(See 13406)			
1420	(See 13409)			
1421	(See 13410)			
1422	(See 13411)			
1423	(See 13425)			
1512	(See 13300)			
1513	(See 13600)			
1517	(See 13700)			
1520	(See 13200)			
2412	(See 13421)			
2413	(See 13422)			
2414	(See 13423)			
2416	(See 13424)			
4400C	(See 51900)			
5130	Lionel Lines Flatcar w/ lumber (See 13001)			
5140	Lionel Lines Reefer (See 13001)			
5150	Lionel Lines "Shell" Tank Car (See 13001)			
5160	Lionel Lines Caboose (See 13001)			
(13001)	1-318E Freight Express Train set, *90–91*	—	960	___[1]
(13002)	Fireball Express set, *90 u*	—	1600	___[1]
(13003)	American Flyer "Mayflower" Passenger Car set, *92*	—	2000	___[1]
(13004)	Milwaukee Road Hiawatha Passenger Set, *01–02*	—	1900	___
(13008)	NYC CommodoreVanderbilt Passenger Set, *02*	—	1500	___
(13100)	Lionel Lines 2-4-2 "1-390E", *88 u*	—	610	___[1]
(13101)	Lionel Lines 2-4-0 "1-384E", *89 u*	—	650	___[1]
(13102)	Lionel Lines Electric "1-381E", *89 u*	—	880	___[1]
(13103)	Lionel Lines "Blue Comet" 4-4-4 "1-400E", *90*	—	1200	___[1]
(13104)	Lionel Lines "Old #7" 4-4-0 "7E", *90*	—	800	___[1]
(13106)	Lionel Lines "Fireball Express" 2-4-2 "2-390E" (See 13002)			

			Exc	New	Cond/$
(13107)	Lionel Lines Electric "1-408E", *91*		—	880	___¹
(13108)	Lionel Lines 4-4-4 "2-400E", *91*		—	1100	___¹
(13109)	American Flyer "Mayflower" Electric "1-4689", *92*		—	2500	___¹
(13200)	Lionel Lines Searchlight Car "1520", *89 u*		—	110	___¹
(13300)	Lionel Lines Gondola "1512", *89 u*		—	75	___¹
(13303)	Lionel Lines Sunoco Tank Car "1-215", *92*		—	135	___¹
(13400)	Lionel Lines Baggage Car "323", *88 u*		—	155	___¹
(13401)	Lionel Lines Passenger Car "324", *88 u*		—	135	___¹
(13402)	Lionel Lines Observation Car "325", *88 u*		—	135	___¹
(13403)	Lionel Lines State Passenger Car set, *89 u*		—	1100	___¹
(13404)	Lionel Lines "California" Passenger Car "1412" (See 13403)				
(13405)	Lionel Lines "Colorado" Passenger Car "1413" (See 13403)				
(13406)	Lionel Lines "New York" Observation Car "1416" (See 13403)				
(13407)	Lionel Lines "Illinois" Passenger Car "1414", *90*		—	450	___¹
(13408)	Lionel Lines "Blue Comet" Passenger Car set, *90*		—	1500	___¹
(13409)	Lionel Lines "Faye" Passenger Car "1420" (See 13408)				
(13410)	Lionel Lines "Westphal" Passenger Car "1421" (See 13408)				
(13411)	Lionel Lines "Tempel" Observation Car "1422" (See 13408)				
(13412)	Lionel Lines "Old #7" Passenger Car set, *90*		—	800	___¹
(13413)	Lionel Lines Combination Car "183" (See 13412)				
(13414)	Lionel Lines Passenger Car "184" (See 13412)				
(13415)	Lionel Lines Observation Car "185" (See 13412)				
(13416)	Lionel Lines "New Jersey" Baggage Car "326" (See 13002)				
(13417)	Lionel Lines "Connecticut" Passenger Car "327" (See 13002)				

		Exc	New	Cond/$
(13418)	Lionel Lines "New York" Observation Car "328" (See 13002)			
(13420)	Lionel Lines State Passenger Car set, *91*	—	1300	___[1]
(13421)	Lionel Lines "California" Passenger Car "2412" (See 13420)			
(13422)	Lionel Lines "Colorado" Passenger Car "2413" (See 13420)			
(13423)	Lionel Lines "Illinois" Passenger Car "2414", *92 u*	—	450	___[1]
(13424)	Lionel Lines "New York" Observation Car "2416" (See 13420)			
(13425)	Lionel Lines "Barnard" Passenger Car "1423", *91 u*	—	1500	___[1]
(13600)	Lionel Lines Cattle Car "1513", *89 u*	—	90	___[1]
13601	Season's Greetings Boxcar, *89 u*	—	105	___[1]
13602	Season's Greetings Boxcar, *90 u*	—	95	___[1]
13604	Season's Greetings Boxcar, *91 u*	—	115	___[1]
(13605)	Lionel Lines Boxcar "1-214", *92*	—	135	___[1]
(13700)	Lionel Lines Caboose "1517", *89 u*	—	105	___[1]
(13702)	Lionel Lines Caboose "1217", *91*	—	115	___[1]
(13800)	Lionelville Passenger Station "1115", *88 u*	—	390	___[1]
(13801)	Lionelville Station "126", *89 u*	—	290	___[1]
(13802)	Lionel Runabout Boat, *90*	—	360	___[1]
(13803)	Lionel Racing Automobiles "8" and "9", *91*	—	900	___[1]
(13804)	Lionelville Switch Tower "437", *91*	—	400	___[1]
(13805)	Lionel Racing Boat "1-44", *91*	—	360	___[1]
(13807)	Racing Automobiles Straight Track, *91 u*	NRS	___	
(13808)	Racing Automobiles Inner Radius Curve Track, *91 u*	NRS	___	
(13809)	Racing Automobiles Outer Radius Curve Track, *91 u*	NRS	___	
(13900)	Electric Rapid Transit Trolley "200", *89 u*	—	280	___[1]
(13901)	Electric Rapid Transit Trolley Trailer "201", *89 u*	—	130	___[1]
(51900)	Signal Bridge and Control Panel "4400C", *89 u*	—	399	___[1]

Section 5
LARGE SCALE

(See 85120)
(See 85115)
(See 85117)
(See 85121)
(See 85122)
(See 85100)
(See 85101, 85124)
(See 85112)
(See 87400)
(See 87401)
(See 87404)
(See 85006)
(See 85007)
(See 87700)
(See 87701, 87724)
(See 87709)
(See 85008, 87712)
(See 85013)
(See 85003)
(See 85005)
(See 55000, 85000)
(See 85001)
(See 85102)
(See 85103)
(See 85104)
(See 85105)
(See 85106)
(See 85107)
(See 85108)
(See 85109)
(See 85110)
(See 85111)
(See 85113)
(See 85114)
(See 86000)

(See 86001)
(See 86002)
(See 86003)
(See 86004)
(See 86005)
(See 87402)
(See 87403)
(See 87405)
(See 87406)
(See 87407)
(See 87500)
(See 87501)
(See 87502)
(See 87503)
(See 87504)
(See 87508)
(See 87702)
(See 87703)
(See 87704)
(See 87705)
(See 87706)
(See 87707)
(See 87708)
(See 87711)
(See 87713)
(See 87716)
(See 87800)
(See 87806)
(See 87808)

		Exc	New	Cond/$
(55000)	Lionel Lines RailScope 0-4-0T "5000", *88–90*	150	230	___
(81000)	Gold Rush Special set, *87–90*	—	160	___
(81001)	Thunder Mountain Express set, *88–89*	—	200	___
(81002)	Frontier Freight set, *88–89*	—	175	___
(81003)	Great Northern set, *90*		NM	___
(81004)	North Pole Railroad set, *89–91*	—	165	___
(81006)	Union Pacific Limited set, *90–91*	100	220	___
(81007)	Disney Magic Express set, *90*	—	250	___

		Exc	New	Cond/$
(81008)	Walt Disney World set, *91*		NM	___
(81011)	Thomas the Tank Engine set, *93 u*	110	130	___
(81014)	James and Troublesome Trucks set, *94–95*	85	130	___
(81016)	Thomas the Tank Engine Deluxe set, *94–95*	—	180	___
(81017)	Ornament Express set, *94–95*	—	150	___
(81019)	Christmas Train set, *98–01*			___
(81024)	Silver Bell Express Christmas Train set, *02–03*		CP	___
(81027)	Thomas the Tank Engine set, *01–03*		CP	___
(81050)	Gold Rush Special set w/ mailer, *87 u*		NRS	___
(81051)	Spiegel PRR set, *87 u*		NRS	___
(81054)	Gold Rush Special set w/o transformer, *90 u*		NRS	___
(81057)	North Pole Railroad set w/ mailer, *90 u*		NRS	___
(81059)	JC Penney Thomas the Tank Engine set, *94 u*	125	150	___
(81061)	Thomas the Tank Engine set, *95*	—	130	___
(81064)	Gold Rush set, *99*		NM	___
(82000)	Straight Track, *87–96, 02*		CP	___
(82001)	Curved Track (4.3' diameter), *87–96, 02–03*		CP	___
(82002)	Straight Track, box of 4, *87–96*	—	9	___
(82003)	Curved Track 4.3', box of 4, *87–96*	—	9	___
(82004)	Curved Track, (5.3'), *88–03*		CP	___
(82006)	35" Straight Track, *88–96*	—	12	___
(82007)	Right-hand Remote Switch, *89–03*		CP	___
(82008)	Left-hand Remote Switch, *89–03*		CP	___
(82010)	Thomas Track Pack, *94–95*	—	40	___
(82011)	Thomas Left Manual Switch, *94–95*	—	18	___
(82012)	Thomas Right Manual Switch, *94–95*	—	18	___
(82013)	Thomas Curved Track 4.3', box of 4, *94–95*	—	9	___
(82014)	Thomas Straight Track, box of 4, *94–95*	—	9	___
(82015)	Right Manual Switch, *95–96*	—	18	___
(82016)	Left Manual Switch, *95–96*	—	18	___
(82101)	Lockon w/ wires, *88–96, 02–03*		CP	___
(82102)	Conversion Rail Joiners (6), *88–96*	—	3	___
(82103)	Conversion Knuckle Couplers (2), *88–91*	—	5	___
(82104)	Water Tower kit, *88–89*	—	50	___
(82105)	Engine House kit, *88–89*	—	125	___
(82106)	Watchman Shanty kit, *88–89*	—	65	___
(82107)	Passenger and Freight Station kit, *88–89*	—	100	___

		Exc	New	Cond/$
(82108)	Manual Uncoupler, *88–96*	—	5	___
(82109)	Brass Pins (12), *88–96*	—	5	___
(82110)	Lumber Shed kit, *89*	—	65	___
(82111)	Freight Platform kit, *89*	—	90	___
(82112)	Figure set (6), *89–96*	—	9	___
(82115)	RailSounds Control Box, *90–95*	—	20	___
(82115)	Wooden Vehicle Assortment, *89*		NM	___
(82116)	DC Converter Box, *91 u, 92–96*	—	40	___
(82116)	1936 Ford Pickup, *89*		NM	___
(82117)	Crossing Gate and Signal, *91*		NM	___
(82117)	1928 Ford Model A Coupe, *89*		NM	___
(82118)	1936 Ford "Woody" Station Wagon, *89*		NM	___
(82120)	Thomas Sound System, *94–95*	—	5	___
(82121)	Thomas Play Pack, *94–95*	—	70	___
(82122)	Thomas Building Pack, *94–95*	—	27	___
(85000)	Seaboard System GP-9 "5000", *90–91*	—	315	___
(85001)	Conrail GP-7 "5001", *90–91*	—	315	___
(85003)	BN GP-20 "2003", *91 u, 92–94*	—	365	___
(85005)	BN GP-20 Dummy "2004", *92–94*	—	225	___
(85006)	Union Pacific GP-20 "485", *93–95*	—	265	___
(85007)	Union Pacific GP-20 Dummy "486", *93–95*	—	235	___
(85008)	Santa Fe GP-9 "712", *95*		NM	___
(85013)	Santa Fe GP-9 Dummy "722", *95*		NM	___
(85014)	Pennsylvania GP-9 Diesel, "7151", *98*	—	375	___
(85015)	Milwaukee Road GP-20 Diesel, "971", *98*	—	375	___
(85100)	Pennsylvania 0-6-0T "100", *87*	—	110	___
(85101)	D&RG 0-6-0T "101", *87–90*	—	100	___
(85102)	New York Central 4-4-2 "5102", *88*	150	200	___
(85103)	Santa Fe 4-4-2 "5103", *88*	—	200	___
(85104)	Santa Fe 0-4-0T "5104", *88–89*	—	90	___
(85105)	Pennsylvania 0-4-0T "5105", *88–89*	—	90	___
(85106)	Chessie System 4-4-2 "5106", *89*	—	190	___
(85107)	Great Northern 4-4-2 "5107", *89*	—	200	___
(85108)	B&O 0-4-0T "5108", *89*	—	95	___
(85109)	Canadian Pacific 0-6-0T "5109", *89*	—	100	___
(85110)	PRR 4-4-2 "5110", *90, 94–95*	160	350	___
(85111)	Great Northern 0-4-0T "5111", *90*		NM	___
(85112)	RI&P 0-6-0T "112", *90*		NM	___

Exc New Cond/$

		Exc	New	Cond/$
(85113)	Union Pacific 0-4-0T "5113", *90–91*	—	100	___
(85114)	North Pole Railroad 0-4-0T "5114", *89–91*	—	105	___
(85115)	Disneyland 0-6-0T "3", *90*	—	110	___
(85117)	Disney World 0-6-0T "4", *91*		NM	___
(85120)	Thomas the Tank Engine 0-6-0T "1", *93 u, 94–95*	—	65	___
(85121)	James the Red Engine 2-6-0 "5", *94–95*	—	70	___
(85122)	Ornament Express 0-6-0T "8", *94–95*	—	75	___
(85124)	D&RG 0-6-0T "101", *95*	—	40	___
(86000)	PRR Passenger Car "6000", *88–89*	—	65	___
(86001)	PRR Observation Car "6001", *88–89*	—	65	___
(86002)	Union Pacific Passenger Car "6002", *90–91*	—	65	___
(86003)	Union Pacific Observation Car "6003", *90–91*	—	65	___
(86004)	Disney World Passenger Car "6004", *91*		NM	___
(86005)	Disney World Observation Car "6005", *91*		NM	___
(86006)	"Annie" Passenger Car, *93 u, 94–95*	—	55	___
(86007)	"Clarabel" Passenger Car, *93 u, 94–95*	—	55	___
87000	New York Central Boxcar, *89*	—	45	___
87001	Pennsylvania Boxcar, *88*	—	45	___
87002	Santa Fe Boxcar, *88*	—	45	___
87003	Great Northern Boxcar, *89*	—	45	___
87004	Southern Boxcar, *90*	—	50	___
87005	Northern Pacific Boxcar, *90*	—	50	___
87006	Christmas Boxcar, *89 u*	—	75	___
87007	Christmas Boxcar, *90 u*	—	80	___
87009	Western Pacific Boxcar, *91*	—	50	___
87013	Christmas Boxcar, *95*	—	35	___
(87015)	Christmas Boxcar, *96*	—	45	___
(87016)	Union Pacific Boxcar, "507406", *98*	—	45	___
(87017)	Large Scale Christmas Boxcar, "9700", *98*	—	45	___
(87018)	Large Scale Christmas Boxcar "7001", *00*	—	40	___
(87021)	Happy Holidays 1999 Boxcar "7001", *99*	—	45	___
(87022)	Christmas Boxcar, *01*		NRS	___
(87023)	2002 Large Scale Christmas Boxcar, *02*	—	50	___
87024	2003 Large Scale Christmas Boxcar, *03*		CP	___
87100	Union Pacific PFE Reefer, *88*	—	50	___
87101	Pennsylvania Reefer, *88*	—	50	___
87102	Chesapeake & Ohio Reefer, *89*	—	50	___

		Exc	New	Cond/$
87103	Tropicana Reefer, *90*	—	55	___
87104	Gerber Reefer, *90*	—	55	___
87105	Seaboard Reefer, *89*	—	50	___
87107	A&P Reefer, *91*	—	60	___
87108	Pacific Fruit Express Reefer, *95*	—	35	___
87018	Large Scale Christmas Boxcar, *00*	—	45	___
87109	Santa Fe Reefer, *95*	—	35	___
(87110)	Pennsylvania Reefer, "91910", *98*	—	44	___
(87111)	NYC Refrigerator Car "78903", *99*	—	44	___
87200	Buford and Roscoe Handcar, *89–90*	—	70	___
87201	Milwaukee Road Ore Car, *89*	—	35	___
87202	Chessie System Ore Car, *89*	—	35	___
87203	Santa and Snowman Handcar, *90*	—	85	___
87204	Northern Pacific Ore Car, *90*	—	40	___
87205	Pennsylvania Ore Car, *90*	—	40	___
87207	Mickey & Donald Handcar, *91, 95*	—	75	___
87208	Wile E. Coyote & Roadrunner Handcar, *92*	—	100	___
87210	Santa Fe Ore Car, *95*	—	40	___
(87212)	Santa and Snowman Handcar, "Tinsel Town", *99*		NRS	___
(87214)	Ontario Northland Ore Car "6071", *99*	—	44	___
87216	Mickey Mouse and Goofy Handcar, *03*		CP	
(87400)	PRR Gondola "400", *87*	—	35	___
(87401)	D&RG Gondola "401", *87–90*	—	30	___
(87402)	Santa Fe Gondola "7402", *88*	—	35	___
(87403)	New York Central Gondola "7403", *88*	—	35	___
(87404)	Disneyland Gondola "404", *90*	—	40	___
(87405)	Chessie System Gondola "7405", *89*	—	35	___
(87406)	Southern Gondola "7406", *89*	—	35	___
(87407)	MKT Gondola "7407", *90*	—	40	___
(87410)	Ornament Express Gondola w/ ornaments, *94–95*	—	35	___
(87411)	"Troublesome Trucks" Gondola, *94–95*	—	20	___
(87500)	D&RG Flatcar "7500", *88*	—	35	___
(87501)	Pennsylvania Flatcar "7501", *88*	—	35	___
(87502)	Santa Fe Flatcar "7502", *88–89*	—	30	___
(87503)	ICG Flatcar "7503", *89*	—	30	___
(87504)	Union Pacific Flatcar "7504", *89*	—	30	___

		Exc	New	Cond/$
87505	Soo Line Flatcar w/ logs, *90*	—	45	___
87507	Great Northern Flatcar, *90*		NM	___
(87508)	Merry Christmas Lines Flatcar, *89–91*	—	35	___
87600	Alaska Tank Car, *89*	—	55	___
87601	Santa Fe Tank Car, *89*	—	50	___
87602	Gulf Tank Car, *90*	—	55	___
87603	Borden Tank Car, *90*	—	55	___
87604	Shell Tank Car, *91*	—	65	___
87612	Santa Fe Tank Car, *95*	—	40	___
(87614)	GATX Tank Train SD Tank Car "44589", *99*	—	44	___
(87700)	Pennsylvania Caboose "700", *87*	—	50	___
(87701)	D&RG Caboose "701", *87–90*	—	50	___
(87702)	Santa Fe Caboose "7702", *88*	—	45	___
(87703)	New York Central Caboose "7703", *88*	—	45	___
(87704)	Santa Fe Bobber Caboose "7704", *88–89*	—	40	___
(87705)	Great Northern Caboose "7705", *89*	—	50	___
(87706)	Chessie System Caboose "7706", *89*	—	50	___
(87707)	B&O Bobber Caboose "7707", *89*	—	40	___
(87708)	Canadian Pacific Bobber Caboose "7708", *89*	—	45	___
(87709)	Disneyland Caboose "709", *90*	—	50	___
(87010)	CN LCAC Reefer, *96*	—	150	___
(87711)	Great Northern Bobber Caboose "7711", *90*		NM	___
(87712)	RI&P Caboose "712", *90*		NM	___
(87713)	Pennsylvania Caboose "7713", *90*	—	50	___
(87716)	North Pole Railroad Bobber Caboose "7716", *89–91*	—	45	___
(87722)	Ornament Express Bobber Caboose, *94–95*	—	40	___
(87724)	D&RG Caboose "701", *95*	—	20	___
(87800)	NYC Searchlight Car "7800", *89–90*	—	85	___
87802	Conrail Boxcar w/ ETD, *90–91*	—	70	___
87803	Seaboard Boxcar w/ ETD, *90–91*	—	70	___
(87806)	REA Boxcar w/ Steam RailSounds, *91*		NM	___
(87808)	Union Pacific Searchlight Car "7808", *95*	—	70	___
87809	Railbox Boxcar, *95*	—	45	___

UNCATALOGED CLUB CARS AND SPECIAL PRODUCTION

ARTRAIN

____	**9486**	GTW "I Love Michigan" Boxcar, *87*
____	**17885**	Artrain 1-D Tank Car, *90*
____	**17891**	Grand Trunk Boxcar, *91*
____	**19425**	Artrain 25th Anniversary CSX Flatcar w/ trailer, *97*
____	**52013**	Norfolk Southern Flatcar w/ trailer (Std O), *92*
____	**52024**	Conrail Auto Carrier, *93*
____	**52049**	Burlington Northern Gondola w/ coil covers, *94*
____	**52097**	Chessie System Reefer, *95*
____	**52140**	Union Pacific Bunk Car, *97*
____	**(52165)**	SP Caboose "6256", *97*
____	**(52197)**	Santa Fe GP38 Diesel Locomotive, *00*
____	**(52227)**	Artrain Space Boxcar, *01 u*
____	**(52255)**	Lionel Lines Artrain USA 30th Anniversary Flatcar w/ billboard, *01*

CARNEGIE SCIENCE CENTER

____	**(26750)**	Great Miniature Railroad and Village Boxcar "9700", *99*
____	**(36202)**	Great Miniature Railroad and Village 80th Anniversary Boxcar "9700", *00*
____	**(36234)**	Great Miniature Railroad and Village Boxcar "9700", *01*
____	**(52277)**	Carnegie Science Center 10th Anniversary Boxcar "9700", *02*

CHICAGOLAND RAILROAD CLUB

____	**(52081)**	C&NW Boxcar "6464555", *96*
____	**(52101)**	BN Maxi-Stack Flatcar w/ containers "64287", *97*
____	**(52102)**	Santa Fe E/V Caboose "999556" w/ black roof, *96*
____	**(52103)**	Santa Fe E/V Caboose "999758" w/ red roof, *96*
____	**(52120)**	Shedd Aquarium Car "3435-557", *98*
____	**(52148)**	REA/Santa Fe Boxcar "52148-558", *99*
____	**(52170)**	SP Operating Boxcar "52170-561", *99*
____	**(52171)**	UP Operating Boxcar "52171-561", *99*
____	**(52178)**	Burlington Operating Boxcar "52178-559", *00*
____	**(52179)**	ACL Operating Boxcar "52179-500", *00*

UNCATALOGED CLUB CARS AND SPECIAL PRODUCTION

____	**(52215)**	CLRC CNW 3-Bay Cyl. Hopper, *01 u*
____	**(52216)**	C&NW Cylindrical Hopper (Std. O), *02*
____	**(52223)**	CLRC Santa Fe REA Operating Boxcar, *00 u*
____	**(52251)**	PRR Customized Mail/Cargo Car, *01*
____	**(52259)**	MP GP20 "28500", Traditional, *01*
____	**(52279)**	D&N Ore Car, *02*
____	**(52280)**	LOTS Product Mint Car, *02*
____	**52282**	Western Pacific Feather Boxcar (red) "2003", *03*
____	**(52287)**	Minute Man Operating Boxcar, *03*
____	**(52295)**	National Toy Train Museum Gondola w/ pipes, *03*
____	**(52296)**	Flatcar w/ tractor and tanker, *03*
____	**(52299)**	UP Las Vegas Jackpot Security Transport "2003", *03*
____	**52306**	NE Trans TOFC, *03*
____	**Not Assigned** CLRC MILW Fuel SD Tank Car "907797", *01 u*	
____	**Not Assigned** CLRC MILW Water SD Tank Car "908309", *01 u*	

CLASSIC TOY TRAINS

____	**(52126)**	MILW Boxcar w/ CTT Logo "21027", *97*

DEPT. 56

____	**(16270)**	Heritage Village Boxcar, *98*
____	**(52096)**	Snow Village Boxcar "9756", *95*
____	**(52139)**	Dept. 56 S/W Caboose "6256", *97*
____	**(52157)**	Dept. 56 Holly Brothers 3-D Tank Car, *98 u*
____	**(52175)**	4-6-4 Hudson "NO. 56" Steam Locomotive, CC, *99*
____	**(52199)**	Real Plastic Snow 4-bay Hopper "6756", *00*
____	**(52253)**	San Pedro Boxcar, *02*
____	**(52254)**	Happy Holidays Gondola "6462-56", *01*
____	**(52272)**	Lionel Gondola "2002" Gold, *02*
____	**52273**	LCCA Subcar, *02*
____	**(52274)**	"City of Los Angeles" RPO Car "2003", *03*
____	**(52275)**	Western Pacific Feather Boxcar "2003", orange, *03*
____	**(52276)**	California Gold Mint Car "2003", *03*

EASTWOOD AUTOMOBILIA

____	**(16275)**	Eastwood Radio Flyer Boxcar "16275", *96*
____	**(16757)**	Johnny Lightning Auto Carrier "3435", *96*
____	**[16985]**	Eastwood Flatcar w/ 2 Ford vans, *97*
____	**(26002)**	Monopoly Flatcar w/ airplane, *00*
____	**(26554)**	Monopoly Short Line S/W Caboose, *00*

UNCATALOGED CLUB CARS AND SPECIAL PRODUCTION

____	**(36227)**	Monopoly Community Chest Boxcar, *00*
____	**(52044)**	Eastwood Vat Car, *95*
____	**(52083)**	Eastwood PRR Flat w/ tanker, "21697", *95 u*
____	**(52130)**	Eastwood Hot Wheels TOFC w/ tank trailer, *97*
____	**(52158)**	Monopoly Mint Car "M0539", *98*
____	**(52181)**	Monopoly Rolling Stock 4-pack, *99*
____	**(52182)**	Monopoly Railroads Boxcar "M0636", *99*
____	**(52183)**	Monopoly Railroads Jail Car "M1131", *99*
____	**(52184)**	Monopoly Railroads Flatcar w/ autos, *99*
____	**(52185)**	Monopoly Railroads Gondola "M0893", *99*
____	**(52218)**	Monopoly Railroads Steam Freight set, *00*

HOUSTON TINPLATE OPERATORS SOCIETY (HTOS)

____	**(8901)**	Miracle Petroleum 1-D Tank Car, *01*
____	**(8999)**	Lone Star Aquarium Car, *99*
____	**Not Assigned**	Sam Houston Mint Car "8901", *00*

INLAND EMPIRE TRAIN COLLECTORS ASSOC. (IETCA)

____	**[1979]**	IETCA Boxcar, *79*
____	**[1980]**	IETCA SP-type Caboose, *80*
____	**[1981]**	IETCA Quad Hopper, *81*
____	**[1982]**	IETCA 3-D Tank Car, *82*
____	**[1983]**	IETCA Reefer, *83*
____	**[1986]**	IETCA Bunk Car, *86*
____	**[7518]**	IETCA Carson City Mint Car, *84*

LIONEL CENTRAL OPERATING LINES (LCOL)

____	**[1981]**	LCOL Boxcar, *81*
____	**[1986]**	LCOL Work Caboose, shell only, *86*
____	**[5724]**	Pennsylvania Bunk Car, *84*
____	**[6508]**	Canadian Pacific Crane Car, *83*
____	**[9184]**	Erie B/W Caboose, *82*
____	**[9475]**	D&H "I Love NY" Boxcar, *85*

LIONEL COLLECTORS ASSOCIATION OF CANADA (LCAC)

____	**[5710]**	Canadian Pacific Reefer, *83*
____	**[5714]**	Michigan Central Reefer, *85*
____	**[6100]**	Ontario Northland Covered Quad Hopper, *82*
____	**[8103]**	Toronto, Hamilton & Buffalo Boxcar, *81*

UNCATALOGED CLUB CARS AND SPECIAL PRODUCTION

____	[8204]	Algoma Central Boxcar, *82*
____	[8507]/[8508]	Canadian National F-3 AA, shells only, *85*
____	[8912]	Canada Southern Operating Hopper, *89*
____	[9413]	Napierville Junction Boxcar, *80*
____	[9718]	Canadian National Boxcar, *79*
____	[17893]	BAOC 1-D Tank Car "914", *91*
____	[52004]	Algoma Central Gondola w/ coil covers "9215", *92*
____	[52005]	Canadian National F-3 B unit "9517", *93*
____	[52006]	Canadian Pacific Boxcar "930016" (Std O), *93*
____	(52115)	Wabash Lake Railway 2-tier Auto Carrier "WL 9519", *98*
____	(52125)	Toronto, Hamilton & Buffalo Gondola 2-pack "2346-2354", *99*
____	[86009]	Canadian National Bunk Car, *86*
____	[87010]	Canadian National Express Reefer, *87*
____	[88011]	Canadian National Woodside Caboose (Std O), *88*
____	[830005]	Canadian National Boxcar, *83*
____	[840006]	Canadian Wheat Board Covered Quad Hopper, *84*
____	[900013]	Canadian National Flatcar w/ trailers, *90*

LIONEL COLLECTORS CLUB OF AMERICA (LCCA)

LCCA National Convention Cars

____	6112	Commonwealth Edison Quad Hopper w/ coal load, *83*
____	6323	Virginia Chemicals 1-D Tank Car, *86*
____	(6567)	Illinois Central Gulf Crane Car "100408", *85*
____	7403	LNAC Boxcar, *84*
____	(8068)	Rock Island GP-20 "1980", *80*
____	9118	Corning Covered Quad Hopper, *74*
____	9155	Monsanto 1-D Tank Car, *75*
____	9212	Seaboard Coast Line Flatcar w/ trailers, *76*
____	X9259	Southern B/W Caboose, *77*
____	9358	Sands of Iowa Covered Quad Hopper, *80*
____	9435	Central of Georgia Boxcar, *81*
____	9460	D&TS DD Boxcar, *82*
____	[9701]	Baltimore & Ohio DD Boxcar, *72*
____	9727	TA&G Boxcar, *73*
____	9728	Union Pacific Stock Car, *78*
____	9733	Airco Boxcar w/ tank, *79*
____	17870	East Camden & Highland Boxcar (Std O), *87*
____	17873	Ashland Oil 3-D Tank Car, *88*
____	17876	Columbia, Newberry & Laurens Boxcar (Std O), *89*
____	17880	D&RGW Woodside Caboose (Std O), *90*

UNCATALOGED CLUB CARS AND SPECIAL PRODUCTION

____	**17887**	Conrail Flatcar w/ Armstrong Tile trailer (Std O), *91*
____	**17888**	Conrail Flatcar w/ Ford New Holland trailer (Std O), *91*
____	**(17899)**	NASA Uni-body Tank Car "190" (Std O), *92*
____	**(18090)**	D&RGW 4-6-2 "1990", *90*
____	**(52023)**	D&TS 2-bay ACF Hopper "2601" (Std O), *93*
____	**(52038)**	Southern Hopper w/ coal load "360794" (Std O), *94*
____	**(52074)**	Iowa Beef Packers Reefer "197095" (Std O), *95*
____	**(52090)**	Pere Marquette DD Boxcar "71996" (Std O), *96*
____	**(52107)**	LCCA On-Track Pick-Up, orange, *96 u*
____	**(52108)**	LCCA On-Track Van, blue, *96 u*
____	**(52110)**	CStPM&O Boxcar "71997" (Std O), *97*
____	**(52151)**	Amtrak Express Baggage Boxcar "71998" (Std O), *98*
____	**(52176)**	Fort Worth & Denver Boxcar "8277" (Std O), *99*
____	**(52195)**	CP Maxi-stack Flatcar "200030", *00 u*
____	**(52206)**	LCCA SD-40 w/ E/V Caboose "2000", *00 u*
____	**(52244)**	Louisville & Nashville Horse Car "2001", *01*
____	**(52266)**	PRR "Coal Goes To War" Hopper "707025", *02*
____	**(52267)**	PRR "Coal Goes To War" Hopper "707026", *02*

LCCA Meet Specials

____	**[6014-900]**	Frisco Boxcar (O27), *75-76*
____	**6483**	Jersey Central SP-type Caboose, *82*
____	**[9016]**	Chessie System Hopper (O27), *79-80*
____	**[9036]**	Mobilgas 1-D Tank Car (O27), *78-79*
____	**[9142]**	Republic Steel Gondola w/ canisters, *77-78*
____	**[No Number]**	Lionel Lines Tender only, *76-77*

Other LCCA Production

____	**[9739]**	D&RGW Boxcar, *78*
____	**[9771]**	Norfolk & Western Boxcar, *77*
____	**(17895)**	LCCA Tractor, *91*
____	**(17896)**	Lancaster Lines Tractor, *91*
____	**(29232)**	Lenny the Lion Hi-cube, signed by Lenny Dean, *99*
____	**(52025)**	Madison Hardware Tractor and Trailer, *93*
____	**(52039)**	"Track 29" Bumper, *94*
____	**(52055)**	SOVEX Tractor and Trailer, *94*
____	**(52056)**	Southern Tractor and Trailer "206502", *94*
____	**(52091)**	Lenox Tractor and Trailer, *95*
____	**(52092)**	Iowa Interstate Tractor and Trailer, *95*
____	**(52100)**	LCCA Station Platform, *98*
____	**(52100)**	Grand Rapids Station Platform, *96*
____	**(52107)**	On-Track Pick-Up Truck, orange, *96*
____	**(52108)**	On-Track Step Van, blue, *96*

UNCATALOGED CLUB CARS AND SPECIAL PRODUCTION

___ **(52131)** LCCA Airplane, blue *98*
___ **(52138)** LCCA Airplane, orange *98*
___ **(52152)** Philadelphia Reefer, *98*
___ **(52153)** 6414 Auto set (4-pack), *98*
___ **(52207)** Lionel Lines SD40, Traditional, *00*
___ **(52257)** Seasonís Greetings Gondola, *01*
___ **Not Assigned** RJ Corman RR Boxcar "4002", *01*

LIONEL KIDS CLUB (LKC)

___ **6464-2003** Maddox Retirement Boxcar "02", *02*
___ **(19695)** Western Union 1-Dome Tank Car, *03*
___ **(19773)** LKC Barrel Ramp Car "6343", *99*
___ **(36769)** Fourth of July Lighted Boxcar, *03*

LIONEL OPERATING TRAIN SOCIETY (LOTS)

LOTS National Convention Cars

___ **[303]** Stauffer Chemical 1-D Tank Car, *85*
___ **[3764]** Kahn Boxcar, *81*
___ **[6111]** L&N Covered Quad Hopper, *83*
___ **[6211]** C&O Gondola w/ canisters, *86*
___ **[9414]** Cotton Belt Boxcar, *80*
___ **(16812)** Grand Trunk 2-bay ACF Hopper "16812" (Std O), *96*
___ **(16813)** Pennsylvania Power & Light Co. Hopper
w/ coal load (Std O), *97*
___ **(17874)** Milwaukee Road Log Dump Car "59629", *88*
___ **(17875)** PHD Boxcar "1289", *89*
___ **(17882)** B&O DD Boxcar w/ ETD "298011", *90*
___ **(17890)** CSX Auto Carrier "151161", *91*
___ **(18890)** Union Pacific RS-3 "8805", *90*
___ **(19960)** Western Pacific Boxcar "1952" (Std O), *92*
___ **[38356]** Dow Chemical 3-D Tank Car, *87*
___ **(52014)** BN TTUX Flatcar set w/ N&W trailers "637500A/B", *93*
___ **(52041)** BN TTUX Flatcar set w/ Conrail trailers
"637500D/E", *94*
___ **(52067)** Burlington Ice Car "50240", *95*
___ **(52135)** AT&SF Reefer "22739", *98*
___ **(52162)** GM&O DD Boxcar "24580", *99*
___ **[52196]** CP Maxi-stack Flatcar w/ 2 containers "524115", *00*
___ **(52234)** WM F9 Well Car w/ Transformer, *01*

UNCATALOGED CLUB CARS AND SPECIAL PRODUCTION

____	**(52261)**	Schlitz Beer/URT Refrigerator Car "92132", *02*
____	**[80948]**	Michigan Central Boxcar, *82*
____	**[121315]**	Pennsylvania Hi-cube Boxcar, *84*

Other LOTS Production

____	**[1223]**	Seattle & North Coast Hi-cube Boxcar, *86*
____	**(12958)**	LCCA/LOTS Banquet Water Tower, *00*
____	**(52042)**	BN TTUX Flatcar w/ Canadian National trailer "637500C", *94*
____	**(52048)**	Canadian National Tractor and Trailer "197993", *94*
____	**(52129)**	Lighted Billboard (Scranton), *97*
____	**(52217)**	LCCA/LOTS 2000 Convention Billboard, *00*
____	**(52260)**	National Aquarium in Baltimore Car "2001", *01*
____	**Not Assigned**	LOTS WM F-9 Well Car w/ transformer, *01 u*

LIONEL CENTURY CLUB (LCC)

____	**(14532)**	LCC II PRR Sharknose AA set, *00*
____	**(18053)**	Lionel Century Club Berkshire Steam Locomotive 2-8-4 "726", *97*
____	**(18057)**	Lionel Century Club Steam Locomotive 6-8-6 "671", *98*
____	**(18058)**	Lionel Century Club Hudson Steam Locomotive 4-6-4 "773", *97*
____	**(18135)**	Lionel Century Club NYC F-3 AA Diesel "2333", *97*
____	**(18178)**	Lionel Century Club NYC F-3 B-Unit, *99*
____	**(18314)**	Lionel Century Club PRR GG-1 "2332", *97*
____	**(18340)**	LCC II FM Demo Train Master set, "TM-1", "TM-2", *00*
____	**(28069)**	LCC II NYC 4-8-6 Niagara "6024" Steam Locomotive, CC, *00*
____	**(29204)**	Lionel Century Club Boxcar "1900-2000", *96*
____	**(29226)**	Lionel Century Club Berkshire Boxcar, *97*
____	**(29227)**	Lionel Century Club GG-1 Boxcar, *98*
____	**(29228)**	Lionel Century Club Turbine Boxcar "671", *99*
____	**(29248)**	Lionel Century Club F3 Boxcar "2333", *99*
____	**(38000)**	Lionel Century Club II NYC 4-6-4 Hudson Empire State Express Steam Locomotive, *00*
____	**(39215)**	Lionel Century Club II Niagara Boxcar, *01*
____	**(39217)**	Lionel Century Club 2 Boxcar, *00 u*
____	**(39218)**	Lionel Century Club 2 Gold Boxcar, *00 u*
____	**(39249)**	Christmas Boxcar, *03*
____	**(51007)**	Lionel Century Club 2 UP M1000 Passenger set, *00 u*

LIONEL RAILROADER CLUB (LRRC)

____	**0780**	LRRC Boxcar, *82*
____	**0781**	LRRC Flatcar w/ trailers, *83*
____	**0782**	LRRC 1-D Tank Car, *85*
____	**0784**	LRRC Covered Quad Hopper, *84*
____	**(12875)**	LRRC Tractor and Trailer, *94*
____	**(12921)**	LRRC Illuminated Station Platform, *95*
____	**16800**	LRRC Ore Car, *86*
____	**16801**	LRRC Bunk Car, *88*
____	**16802**	LRRC Tool Car, *89*
____	**16803**	LRRC Searchlight Car, *90*
____	**16804**	LRRC B/W Caboose, *91*
____	**(18680)**	LRRC Countdown Hudson 4-6-4 "2000", *00*
____	**(18684)**	LRRC Pacific 4-6-2 "1999", *99*
____	**(18818)**	LRRC GP-38-2 "1992", *92*
____	**(19437)**	LRRC Flatcar w/ Inside Track trailer "1997", *97*
____	**(19473)**	LRRC Operating Log Dump Car "3351", *99*
____	**(19774)**	LRRC Caboose Porthole "1999", *99*
____	**(19775)**	LRRC Stock Car, *99*
____	**19924**	LRRC Boxcar, *93*
____	**19930**	LRRC Quad Hopper w/ coal load, *94*
____	**(19935)**	LRRC 1-D Tank Car "1995", *95*
____	**(19940)**	LRRC Vat Car, *96*
____	**(19953)**	LRRC Lionel Corporation Boxcar "6464-97", *97*
____	**(19965)**	LRRC Aquarium Car "3435", *99*
____	**(19966)**	LRRC Gondola "9820" (Std O), *98*
____	**(19978)**	LRRC Membership Kit, *99-00*
____	**(19991)**	LRRC Gold Member Boxcar, *00*
____	**(19992)**	LRRC Western Union Tool Car "3550", *00*
____	**(19994)**	Western Union Sleeping Car "1307", *01*
____	**(19995)**	LRRC 25th Anniversary Boxcar (Std. O), *01*
____	**(28062)**	LRRC Century 4-6-4 Hudson "2000", *00*
____	**(29200)**	LRRC Lionel Corporation Boxcar "9700", *96*

LIONEL RAILROAD CLUB—MILWAUKEE

____	**[52116]**	Milwaukee Road Flatcar w/ tractor and trailer "194797", *97*
____	**(52163)**	Milwaukee Road DD Boxcar "194798", *98*
____	**(52180)**	Milwaukee Road Flatcar w/ trailer "194799", *00*

UNCATALOGED CLUB CARS AND SPECIAL PRODUCTION

___ **(52230)** Milwaukee Road 1-D Tank Car 2-pack, *00*
___ **(52246)** Milwaukee Road DD Boxcar "194701", *01*
___ **(52265)** Milwaukee Road/Zoological Society of Milwaukee
Aquarium Car "4701", *02*

NASSAU LIONEL OPERATING ENGINEERS (NLOE)

___ **[8389]** Long Island Boxcar, *89*
___ **[8390]** Long Island Covered Quad Hopper, *90*
___ **[8391A]** Long Island Bunk Car, *91*
___ **[8391B]** Long Island Tool Car, *91*
___ **[8392]** Long Island 1-D Tank Car, *92*
___ **[52007]** Long Island RS-3 "1552", *93*
___ **[52019]** Long Island Boxcar "8393", *93*
___ **[52020]** Long Island B/W Caboose "8393", *93*
___ **[52026]** Long Island Flatcar w/ Grumman trailer "8394", *94*
___ **[52061]** Long Island Stern's Pickle Products Vat Car "8395", *95*
___ **[52072]** Grumman Tractor, *94*
___ **[52076]** Long Island Observation Car "8396", *96*
___ **(52112)** Long Island Full Vista Dome Aluminum Passenger
Car "9783", *97*
___ **(52122)** NLOE Meenan Oil 1-D Tank Car "8397" (Std O.), *97*
___ **(52123)** Long Island Aluminum Diner Car, "9883", *98*
___ **(52144)** LIRR Flatcar w/Grumman Van (TT), *99*
___ **(52145)** Long Island Aluminum Passenger Coaches,
"9983-1/9983-2", *99*
___ **(52166)** Long Island Flatcar w/ Grumman trailer "8398", *98*
___ **(52173)** Long Island RR F3 AA Shells, *00*
___ **(52174)** REA Baggage Car "0083", *00*
___ **[52186]** Grucci Fireworks Boxcar, *00*
___ **(52209)** World's Fair Sleeper/Roomette Car "0183", *01*
___ **(52232)** Central RR of Long Island Boxcar, *01*
___ **(52235)** World's Fair Vista-Dome Car "0283", *02*
___ **(52256)** New York & Atlantic Ry. Boxcar "8302", *02*
___ **(52263)** World's Fair Combine Car "0383", *02*

ST. LOUIS LIONEL RAILROAD CLUB (ST. LOUIS LRRC)

___ **(52099)** MP Flatcar w/ St. Louis LRRC trailer, *96*
___ **(52104)** St. Louis LRRC T&T, *96 u*

UNCATALOGED CLUB CARS AND SPECIAL PRODUCTION

____	**(52117)**	Wabash Flatcar w/ REA Tractor and Trailer, *97*
____	**(52136A)**	Christmas Special Tractor and Trailer, *97*
____	**(52136B)**	Frisco Special Tractor and Trailer, *98*
____	**(52147)**	Frisco Campbell TOFC Flatcar (TT), *98*
____	**(52150)**	Frisco Campbell TOFC Flatcar (TT), *98*
____	**(52167)**	AT&SF TOFC Flatcar w/ Navajo trailers "831999", *99*
____	**(52190)**	IC TOFC Flatcar w/ Trailers, *00*
____	**(52222)**	SSW (Cotton Belt) Flatcar w/SP tractor and trailer, *01*
____	**(52224A)**	SP Flatcar w/ Navajo tractor and trailer, *01*
____	**(52224B)**	SP Flatcar w/ Trailer Flatcar Service tractor and trailer, *01*
____	**(52258)**	UP Flatcar with UP tractor and trailer, *02*

TRAIN COLLECTORS ASSOCIATION (TCA)

TCA National Convention Cars

____	**(0511)**	TCA St. Louis Baggage Car "1981", *81*
____	**5734**	TCA REA Reefer, *85*
____	**6315**	TCA Pittsburgh 1-D Tank Car, *72*
____	**6464-1970**	TCA Chicago Boxcar, *70*
____	**6464-1971**	TCA Disneyland Boxcar, *71*
____	**6926**	TCA New Orleans E/V Caboose, *86*
____	**(7205)**	TCA Denver Combination Car "1982", *82*
____	**(7206)**	TCA Louisville Passenger Car "1983", *83*
____	**(7212)**	TCA Pittsburgh Passenger Car "1984", *84*
____	**7812**	TCA Houston Stock Car, *77*
____	**(8476)**	TCA 4-6-4 "5484", *85*
____	**(9123)**	TCA Dearborn Auto Carrier "1973" (3-tier), *73*
____	**9319**	TCA Silver Jubilee Mint Car, *79*
____	**(9544)**	TCA Chicago Observation Car "1980", *80*
____	**9611**	TCA Boston Hi-cube Boxcar, *78*
____	**9774**	TCA Orlando Southern Belle Boxcar, *75*
____	**(9779)**	TCA Philadelphia Boxcar "9700-1976", *76*
____	**9864**	TCA Seattle Reefer, *74*
____	**(11737)**	TCA 40th Anniversary F-3 ABA set "40", *93*
____	**(17879)**	TCA Valley Forge Dining Car "1989", *89*
____	**(17883)**	New Georgia Railroad Passenger Car "1990", *90*
____	**(17898)**	Wabash Reefer "21596", *92*
____	**(52008)**	Bucyrus Erie Crane Car "1993X", *93*
____	**(52035)**	Yorkrail GP-9 "1750", shell only, *94*
____	**(52036)**	TCA 40th Anniversary B/W Caboose, *94*
____	**(52037)**	Yorkrail GP-9 "1754", *94*

UNCATALOGED CLUB CARS AND SPECIAL PRODUCTION

	(52062)	TCA "Skytop" Observation Car "1995", *95*
____	**(52062)**	TCA "Skytop" Observation Car "1995", *95*
____	**(52085)**	TCA Full Vista Dome Car "1996", *96*
____	**(52106)**	TCA City of Phoenix Diner "1997", *97*
____	**(52142)**	TCA Mass. Central Maxi-stack "5100-01", *98*
____	**(52143)**	TCA City of Providence Passenger Car "1998", *98*
____	**(52155)**	TCA City of San Francisco Baggage Car "1999", *99*
____	**(52191)**	TCA Duplex Aluminum Passenger "City of Grand Rapids", *00 u*
____	**(52198)**	TCA Frisco Boxcar "5477000", *00 u*
____	**(52210)**	TCA Rico Station, *00 u*
____	**(52220)**	City of Chattanooga Vista Dome Car "2001", *01*
____	**(52221)**	TCA Norfolk Southern Boxcar "2001", *01*
____	**(52250)**	City of Chicago Combo Car "2002", *02*

TCA Museum-Related Cars

____	**[1018-1979]**	Mortgage Burning Hi-cube Boxcar, *79*
____	**[5731]**	L&N Reefer, *90*
____	**[7780]**	TCA Museum Boxcar, *80*
____	**[7781]**	Hafner Boxcar, *81*
____	**[7782]**	Carlisle & Finch Boxcar, *82*
____	**[7783]**	Ives Boxcar, *83*
____	**[7784]**	Voltamp Boxcar, *84*
____	**[7785]**	Hoge Boxcar, *85*
____	**[9771]**	Norfolk & Western Boxcar, *77*
____	**(16811)**	Rutland Boxcar "5477096", *96*
____	**[52045]**	Penn Dutch Milk Car "61052", *94*
____	**[52051]**	Baltimore & Ohio "Sentinel" Boxcar "6464095", *95*
____	**[52052]**	TCA 40th Anniversary Boxcar, *94*
____	**(52063)**	NYC "Pacemaker" Boxcar "6464125", *95*
____	**(52064)**	Missouri Pacific Boxcar "6464150", *95*
____	**(52065)**	Penn-Dutch Grain Operating Boxcar "9208", *01*
____	**(52118)**	Rio Grande Boxcar "5477097", *97*
____	**(52119)**	TCA Museum 20th Anniversary Boxcar, *97*
____	**(52128)**	Pennsylvania Dutch Pretzels Boxcar, *99*
____	**(52172)**	L&N Share the Freedom Boxcar "5477099", *99*
____	**(52198)**	Frisco Boxcar "5477000", *00*
____	**(52226)**	Angela Trotta Thomas Boxcar "2000", *01*
____	**(52242)**	Lionel Gondola "2002", blue, *02*
____	**(52243)**	National Toy Train Museum 1-D Tank Car 1954, *01*
____	**(52271)**	National Toy Train Museum Wheel Car "1957", *02*

UNCATALOGED CLUB CARS AND SPECIAL PRODUCTION

TCA Bicentennial Special Set

____	**1973**	TCA Bicentennial Observation Car, *76*
____	**1974**	TCA Bicentennial Passenger Car, *76*
____	**1975**	TCA Bicentennial Passenger Car, *76*
____	**1976**	TCA Bicentennial U36B, *76*

Atlantic Division TCA

____	**[1980]**	Atlantic Division Flatcar w/ trailers, *80*
____	**[6101]**	Burlington Northern Covered Quad Hopper, *82*
____	**[9186]**	Conrail N5C Caboose, *79*
____	**[9193]**	Budweiser Vat Car, *84*
____	**[9466]**	Wanamaker Boxcar, *83*
____	**[9788]**	Lehigh Valley Boxcar, *78*
____	**[No Number]**	Pennsylvania Reading Seashore Bunk Car, *85*

Desert Division TCA

____	**[52088]**	Desert Division 25th Anniversary On-Track Step Van, *96*
____	**(52105)**	TCA Superstition Mountain Operating Gondola "61997", *97*

Dixie Division TCA

____	**(52127)**	TCA Dixie Division 10th Anniversary Southern 3-bay Hopper "360997", *98*

Eastern Division TCA

____	**(52059)**	Clinchfield Quad Hopper w/ coal load "16413", *94*

Eastern Division TCA—Washington, Baltimore and Annapolis Chapter

____	**[9412]**	Richmond, Fredericksburg, & Potomac Boxcar, *79*
____	**[9740]**	Chessie System Boxcar, *76*
____	**[9771]**	Norfolk & Western Boxcar, *78*
____	**[9783]**	B&O "Time-Saver" Boxcar, *77*

Ft. Pitt Division TCA

____	**[1984-30X]**	Heinz Ketchup Boxcar, *84*

Great Lakes Division TCA

____	**[9740]**	Chessie System Boxcar, *76*
____	**[1983]**	Churchill Downs Boxcar, *83*
____	**[1983]**	Churchill Downs Reefer, *83*

Great Lakes Division TCA—Detroit-Toledo Chapter

____	**[8957]**	Burlington Northern GP-20, *80*

UNCATALOGED CLUB CARS AND SPECIAL PRODUCTION

____ **[8958]** Burlington Northern GP-20 Dummy, *80*
____ **[9119]** Detroit & Mackinac Covered Quad Hopper, *77*
____ **[9272]** New Haven B/W Caboose, *79*
____ **[9401]** Great Northern Boxcar, *78*
____ **[9730]** CP Rail Boxcar, *76*
____ **52000** Detroit-Toledo Division Flatcar w/ trailer, *92*

Great Lakes Division TCA—Three Rivers Chapter
____ **[9113]** Norfolk & Western Quad Hopper, *76*

Great Lakes Division TCA—Western Michigan Chapter
____ **[9730]** CP Rail Boxcar, *74*

Lake & Pines Division TCA
____ **52018** 3-M Boxcar, *93*

Lone Star Division TCA
____ **[7522]** New Orleans Mint Car w/ coin, *86*
____ **(52093)** Lone Star Division Boxcar "6464696", *96*

Lone Star Division TCA—North Texas Chapter
____ **[9119]** Detroit & Mackinac Covered Quad Hopper, *78*
____ **[9184]** Erie B/W Caboose, *77*
____ **[9739]** D&RGW Boxcar, *76*
____ **[No Number]** Texas Special F-3 A unit, shell only, *81*
____ **[No Number]** Texas Special F-3 B unit, shell only, *82*

METCA
____ **[10]** Jersey Central F-3 A unit, shell only, *71*
____ **[9272]** New Haven B/W Caboose, *79*
____ **[9754]** New York Central "Pacemaker" Boxcar, *76*

Midwest Division TCA
____ **[4]** C&NW F-3 A unit, shell only, *77*
____ **[00005]** Midwest Division Covered Quad Hopper, *78*
____ **[1287]** C&NW Reefer, *84*
____ **[1988]** Illinois Central Boxcar, *88*
____ **[7600]** Frisco "Spirit of '76" N5C Caboose "00003", *76*
____ **[9725]** Midwest Division Stock Car "00002", *75*
____ **[9872]** PFE Reefer "00006", *79*
____ **(52237)** Lionel Gondola "2002", yellow, *01*
____ **(52238)** Lionel Gondola "2002", red, *01*
____ **(52239)** Lionel Gondola "2002", silver, *01*

UNCATALOGED CLUB CARS AND SPECIAL PRODUCTION

____ **(52240)** Lionel Gondola 3-pack "2002", *01*
____ **(52241)** Lionel Gondola "2002", black, *02*
____ **Not Assigned** Lionel Gondola "2002", blue, *02*
____ **Not Assigned** Lionel Gondola "2002", gold, *02*

Midwest Division TCA Museum Express

____ [9264] Illinois Central Gulf Covered Quad Hopper, *78*
____ [9289] Chicago & North Western N5C Caboose, *80*
____ [9785] Conrail Boxcar, *77*
____ [9786] Chicago & North Western Boxcar, *79*

NETCA

____ [1203] Boston & Maine NW-2, shell only, *72*
____ [5710] Canadian Pacific Reefer, *82*
____ [5716] Vermont Central Reefer, *83*
____ [6124] Delaware & Hudson Covered Quad Hopper, *84*
____ [8051] Hood's Milk Boxcar, *86*
____ [9181] Boston & Maine N5C Caboose, *77*
____ [9400] Conrail Boxcar, *78*
____ [9415] Providence & Worcester Boxcar, *79* .
____ [9423] NYNH&H Boxcar, *80*
____ [9445] Vermont Northern Boxcar, *81*
____ [9753] Maine Central Boxcar, *75*
____ [9768] Boston & Maine Boxcar, *76*
____ [9785] Conrail Boxcar, *78*
____ 52001 Boston & Maine Quad Hopper w/ coal load, *92*
____ 52016 Boston & Maine Gondola w/ coil covers, *93*
____ [52043] L.L. Bean Boxcar "1994", *94*
____ [52080] B&M Flatcar w/ trailer "91095", *95*
____ (52111) Ben & Jerry's NETCA Flatcar w/ trailer TOFC, *96*
____ (52146) Ocean Spray Plug Door Reefer "OSCX 1998", *98*
____ (52212) Berkshire Brewing Refrigerator Car, *00*
____ (52236) Moxie Boxcar, *01*
____ (52270) Jenney Mfg. Co. Tank Car, *02*

Ozark Division TCA—Gateway Chapter

____ [5700] Oppenheimer Reefer, *81*
____ [9068] Reading Bobber Caboose, *76*
____ [9601] Illinois Central Gulf Hi-cube Boxcar, *77*
____ [9767] Railbox Boxcar, *78*
____ 52003 "Meet Me In St. Louis" Flatcar w/ trailer, *92*

UNCATALOGED CLUB CARS AND SPECIAL PRODUCTION

Pacific Northwest Division TCA

____ **(52077)** Great Northern Hi-cube Boxcar "9695", *95*
____ **[No Number]** Pacific Northwest Division F-3 AA, shells only, *74*

Rocky Mountain Division TCA

____ **1971-1976** Rocky Mountain Division Reefer, *76*

Sacramento—Sierra Chapter TCA

____ **[6401]** Virginian B/W Caboose, *84*
____ **[9301]** US Mail Operating Boxcar, *76*
____ **[9414]** Cotton Belt Boxcar, *80*
____ **[9427]** Bay Line Boxcar, *81*
____ **[9444]** Louisiana Midland Boxcar, *82*
____ **[9452]** Western Pacific Boxcar, *83*
____ **[9705]** D&RGW Boxcar, *75*
____ **[9723]** Western Pacific Boxcar, *73*
____ **[9726]** Erie-Lackawanna Boxcar, *79*
____ **[9730]** CP Rail Boxcar, *77*
____ **[9785]** Conrail Boxcar, *78*
____ **[No Number]** Lionel Lines Tender, shell only, *84*

Southern Division TCA

____ **[1976]** Florida East Coast F-3 ABA, shells only, *76*
____ **[1986]** Southern Division Bunk Car, *86*
____ **[6111]** L&N Covered Quad Hopper, *83*
____ **[9287]** Southern N5C Caboose, *77*
____ **[9352]** Trailer Train Flatcar w/ circus trailers, *80*
____ **[9403]** Seaboard Coast Line Boxcar, *78*
____ **[9405]** Chattahoochie Boxcar, *79*
____ **[9443]** Florida East Coast Boxcar, *81*
____ **[9471]** ACL Boxcar, *84*
____ **[9482]** Norfolk & Southern Boxcar, *85*
____ **[16606]** Southern Searchlight Car, *88*

TOY TRAIN OPERATING SOCIETY (TTOS)

TTOS National Convention Cars

____ **[1984]** TTOS Sacramento Northern Boxcar, *84*
____ **[1985]** TTOS Snowbird Covered Quad Hopper, *85*
____ **6076** Santa Fe Hopper (O27), *70*
____ **6582** TTOS Portland Flatcar w/ wood load, *86*

UNCATALOGED CLUB CARS AND SPECIAL PRODUCTION

____	[9326]	Burlington Northern B/W Caboose, *82*
____	9347	TTOS Niagara Falls 3-D Tank Car, *79*
____	[9355]	Delaware & Hudson B/W Caboose, *82*
____	[9361]	Chicago & North Western B/W Caboose, *82*
____	[9382]	Florida East Coast B/W Caboose, *82*
____	9512	TTOS Summerdale Junction Passenger Car, *74*
____	9520	TTOS Phoenix Combination Car, *75*
____	9526	TTOS Snowbird Observation Car, *76*
____	9535	TTOS Columbus Baggage Car, *77*
____	9678	TTOS Hollywood Hi-cube Boxcar, *78*
____	9868	TTOS Oklahoma City Reefer, *80*
____	[9883]	TTOS Phoenix Reefer, *83*
____	(17871)	NYC Flatcar w/ Kodak and Xerox trailers "81487", *87*
____	(17872)	Anaconda Ore Car "81988", *88*
____	(17877)	MKT 1-D Tank Car "3739469", *89*
____	17884	Columbus & Dayton Terminal Boxcar (Std O), *90*
____	(17889)	Southern Pacific Flatcar w/ trailer "15791" (Std O), *91*
____	(19963)	Union Equity 3-bay ACF Hopper "86892" (Std O), *92*
____	(52010)	Weyerhaeuser DD Boxcar "838593" (Std O), *93*
____	(52029)	Ford 1-D Tank Car "12" (O27), *94*
____	(52030)	Ford Gondola "4023", *94*
____	(52031)	Ford Hopper "1458" (O27), *94*
____	(52057)	Western Pacific Boxcar "64641995", *95*
____	(52087)	New Mexico Central Boxcar "64641996", *96*
____	(52114)	NYC Flatcar w/ Gleason & "SABIB" trailers, *97*
____	(52149)	Conrail Flatcar w/ Blum coal shovel, *98*
____	(52192)	TTOS SP Crane & Gondola 2-pack, *00 u*
____	(52193)	SP Crane Car "SPMW 6060", *00*
____	(52194)	SP Gondola "7111", *00*
____	(52231)	British Columbia RR 1-D Tank Car, *01*

TTOS Division Cars

____	(52009)	Sacramento Valley Division Western Pacfic Boxcar "64641993", *93*
____	52040	Wolverine Division GTW Flatcar w/ LL tractor and trailer, "52033", *94*
____	(52058)	Central California Division Santa Fe Boxcar "64641895", *95*
____	(52086)	Canadian Division Pacific Great Eastern Boxcar "64641972", *96*

UNCATALOGED CLUB CARS AND SPECIAL PRODUCTION

Southwest Division TTOS Cal-Stewart

____ **(19962)** Southern Pacific 3-bay ACF Hopper
"496035" (Std O), *92*

____ **(52047)** Cotton Belt Woodside Caboose w/ smoke
"1921" (Std O), *93-94*

____ **(52073)** Pacific Fruit Express Reefer "459402" (Std O), *95*

____ **(52098)** National Bureau of Standards Boxcar (Std O), *96*

____ **(52121)** Mobilgas Tank Car "238" (Std O), *97*

____ **(52154)** Pacific Fruit Express Reefer "459403" (Std O), *98*

____ **(52205)** SP Overnight Merchandise Service Boxcar 5-pack, *00*

____ **(Not Assigned)** SP Boxcars, 5-Car Set "6400-2000", *00*

TTOS New Mexico Division Cars

____ **(52264)** Durango & Silverton Operating Hopper "9325", *02*

Other TTOS Production

____ **[1983]** TTOS Phoenix 3-D Tank Car, *83*

____ **(17894)** Southern Pacific Tractor, *91*

____ **(52021)** Weyerhaeuser Tractor and Trailer, *93*

____ **52022** Union Pacific Boxcar, *93*

____ **(52032)** Ford 1-D Tank Car "14" w/ Kughn inscription (O27), *94*

____ **(52046)** ACL Boxcar "16247", *94*

____ **52053** TTOS Carail Boxcar, *94*

____ **(52068)** Toy Train Parade TTOS Contadina Boxcar "16245", *94*

____ **(52078)** Southern Pacific SD-9 "5366", *96*

____ **(52079)** Southern Pacific B/W Caboose "1996", *96*

____ **(52084)** Union Pacific I-Beam Flatcar w/ load "16380", *95*

____ **(52113)** Northeastern Division Genesee & Wyoming RR 3-Bay
ACF Hopper "10000" (Std O), *97*

TOY TRAIN OPERATING MUSEUM

Gadsden Pacific Ore Cars

____ **17878** Magma Ore Car w/ load, *89*

____ **17881** Phelps-Dodge Ore Car w/ load, *90*

____ **17886** Cyprus Ore Car w/ load, *91*

____ **19961** Inspiration Consolidated Copper Co. Ore Car
w/ load, *92*

____ **52011** Tucson, Cornelia & Gila Bend Ore Car w/ load, *93*

____ **52027** Pinto Valley Mine Ore Car w/ load, *94*

____ **52071** Copper Basin Railway Ore Car w/ load, *95*

UNCATALOGED CLUB CARS AND SPECIAL PRODUCTION

____	**52089**	SMARRCO Ore Car w/ load, *96*
____	**(52124)**	EPSW Ore Car w/ load, *97*
____	**(52164)**	SP Ore Car w/ load, *98*
____	**(52177)**	Arizona Southern Ore Car w/ load, *99*
____	**(52213)**	TTOS GPD Ore Car BHP Copper, *00 u*
____	**(52248)**	Tombstone & Southern RR Ore Car, *01*

VIRGINIA TRAIN COLLECTORS (VTC)

____	**[7679]**	VTC Boxcar, *79*
____	**[7681]**	VTC N5C Caboose, *81*
____	**[7682]**	VTC Covered Quad Hopper, *82*
____	**[7683]**	Virginia Fruit Express Reefer, *83*
____	**[7684]**	Vitraco 3-D Tank Car, *84*
____	**[7685]**	VTC Boxcar, *85*
____	**[7686]**	VTC GP-7, *86*
____	**[7692-1]**	VTC Baggage Car (O27), *92*
____	**[7692-2]**	VTC Combination Car (O27), *92*
____	**[7692-3]**	VTC Dining Car (O27), *92*
____	**[7692-4]**	VTC Passenger Car (O27), *92*
____	**[7692-5]**	VTC Vista Dome Car (O27), *92*
____	**[7692-6]**	VTC Passenger Car (O27), *92*
____	**[7692-7]**	VTC Observation Car (O27), *92*
____	**[52060]**	VTC Tender w/ whistle "7694", *94*

Section 7
LIONEL CATALOGS 1945–2003

					Exc	New
___	**1945**	Consumer Catalog	8½" x 11"	4 pages		NRS
___	**1946**	Consumer Catalog	8⅜" x 11¼"	20 pages	50	75
___	**1947**	Consumer Catalog	11¼" x 7⅝"	32 pages	30	45
___	**1948**	Consumer Catalog	11¼" x 8"	36 pages	30	45
___	**1949**	Consumer Catalog	11¼" x 8"	40 pages	75	100
___	**1950**	Consumer Catalog	11¼" x 8"	44 pages	45	75
___	**1951**	Consumer Catalog	11¼" x 7¾"	36 pages	25	45
___	**1952**	Consumer Catalog	11¼" x 7¾"	36 pages	20	35
___	**1953**	Consumer Catalog	11¼" x 7⅝"	40 pages	20	30
___	**1954**	Consumer Catalog	11¼" x 7⅝"	44 pages	20	30
___	**1955**	Consumer Catalog	11¼" x 7⅝"	44 pages	20	30
___	**1956**	Consumer Catalog	11¼" x 7⅝"	40 pages	12	24
___	**1957**	Consumer Catalog	11¼" x 7½"	52 pages	10	20
___	**1958**	Consumer Catalog	11¼" x 7⅝"	56 pages	10	15
___	**1959**	Consumer Catalog	11" x 8½"	56 pages	10	15
___	**1960**	Consumer Catalog	11" x 8⅜"	56 pages	6	10
___	**1961**	Consumer Catalog	8½" x 11"	72 pages	6	10
___	**1962**	Consumer Catalog	8½" x 11"	100 pages	8	12
___	**1963**	Consumer Catalog	8⅜" x 10⅞"	56 pages	4	6
___	**1964**	Consumer Catalog	8⅜" x 10⅞"	24 pages	4	6
___	**1965**	Consumer Catalog	8½" x 10⅞"	40 pages	4	6
___	**1966**	Consumer Catalog	10⅞" x 8⅜"	40 pages	4	6
___	**1967**	Same Catalog as 1966			4	6
___	**1968**	Consumer Catalog	8½" x 11"	8 pages	4	6
___	**1969**	Consumer Catalog	11" x 8½"	8 pages	3	5
___	**1970**	Consumer Catalog w/ foldout poster	8½" x 11"	8 pages	3	5
___	**1971**	Consumer Catalog	8½" x 11"	12 pages	3	5
___	**1972**	Consumer Catalog	8½" x 11"	16 pages	3	5
___	**1973**	Consumer Catalog	8½" x 11"	16 pages	2	4
___	**1974**	Consumer Catalog	8½" x 11"	20 pages	2	4
___	**1975**	Consumer Catalog	8½" x 11"	24 pages	2	4
___	**1976**	Consumer Catalog	8½" x 11"	24 pages	2	4
___	**1977**	Consumer Catalog	8½" x 11"	24 pages	2	4
___	**1978**	Consumer Catalog	8½" x 11"	24 pages	2	4
___	**1979**	Consumer Catalog	8½" x 11"	24 pages	2	4
___	**1980**	Consumer Catalog	8½" x 11"	28 pages	2	4
___	**1981**	Consumer Catalog	5½" x 7"	32 pages	1	2

	Year	Description	Size	Pages	Exc	New
___	1982	Traditional Series Consumer Catalog	8½" x 11"	20 pages	2	4
___	1982	Collector Series Consumer Catalog	8½" x 11"	12 pages	2	4
___	1983	Traditional Series Consumer Catalog	8½" x 11"	20 pages	2	3
___	1983	Collector Series Consumer Catalog	8½" x 11"	16 pages	2	3
___	1984	Traditional Series Consumer Catalog	8½" x 11"	20 pages	2	3
___	1984	Collector Series Consumer Catalog	8½" x 11"	16 pages	2	3
___	1985	Traditional Series Consumer Catalog	8½" x 11"	20 pages	2	3
___	1985	Collector Series Consumer Catalog	8½" x 11"	12 pages	2	3
___	1986	Traditional Series Consumer Catalog	8½" x 11"	16 pages	2	3
___	1986	Collector Series Consumer Catalog	8½" x 11"	16 pages	2	3
___	1986	Stocking Stuffers Brochure	8½" x 11"	4 pages	2	3
___	1987	Consumer Catalog	8½" x 11"	40 pages	3	4
___	1987	Large Scale Brochure	11" x 8½"	6 pages	1	2
___	1987	Stocking Stuffers Brochure	8½" x 11"	4 pages	2	3
___	1988	Consumer Catalog	8½" x 11"	40 pages	2	3
___	1988	Large Scale Catalog	8½" x 11"	16 pages	1	2
___	1988	Classics Brochure	8½" x 11"	4 pages	1	2
___	1988	Hiawatha Brochure	8½" x 11"	4 pages	2	3
___	1988	Stocking Stuffers Flyer	8½" x 11"	1 page	2	3
___	1989	Pre-Toy Fair Consumer Catalog	8½" x 11"	20 pages	2	3
___	1989	Toy Fair Consumer Catalog	8½" x 11"	28 pages	2	3
___	1989	Pre-Toy Fair Classics Brochure	8½" x 11"	4 pages	1	2
___	1989	Toy Fair Classics Brochure	8½" x 11"	4 pages	1	2
___	1989	Large Scale Catalog	8½" x 11"	20 pages	1	2
___	1989	Stocking Stuffers Brochure	8½" x 11"	4 pages	2	3

	Year	Description	Size	Pages	Exc	New
___	1990	Book 1 Consumer Catalog	8½" x 11"	20 pages	2	4
___	1990	Book 2 Consumer Catalog	8½" x 11"	36 pages	2	3
___	1990	Large Scale Catalog	8½" x 11"	16 pages	1	2
___	1990	Stocking Stuffers Brochure	8½" x 11"	6 pages	2	3
___	1991	Book 1 Consumer Catalog	8½" x 11"	24 pages	2	4
___	1991	Book 2 Consumer Catalog	8½" x 11"	60 pages	2	3
___	1991	Stocking Stuffers Brochure	8½" x 11"	6 pages	2	3
___	1992	Book 1 Consumer Catalog	8½" x 11"	32 pages	2	4
___	1992	Book 2 Consumer Catalog	8½" x 11"	48 pages	2	3
___	1992	Stocking Stuffers Brochure	8½" x 11"	8 pages	2	3
___	1993	Book 1 Consumer Catalog	8½" x 11"	32 pages	2	4
___	1993	Book 2 Consumer Catalog	8½" x 11"	52 pages	2	3
___	1993	Stocking Stuffers/ 1994 Spring Releases Catalog	8½" x 11"	28 pages	2	3
___	1994	Consumer Catalog	8½" x 11"	64 pages	3	4
___	1994	Thomas the Tank Engine Catalog	8½" x 11"	8 pages	1	2
___	1994	Trainmaster Transformer Catalog	8½" x 11"	8 pages	1	2
___	1994	Stocking Stuffers/ 1995 Spring Releases Catalog	8½" x 11"	32 pages	2	3
___	1994	Preschool Brochure	8½" x 11"	4 pages	1	2
___	1994	Crayola Brochure	8½" x 11"	4 pages	1	2
___	1994	Gift Collection Catalog	8½" x 11"	12 pages	1	2
___	1995	Consumer Catalog	8½" x 11"	88 pages	3	4
___	1995	Stocking Stuffers/ 1996 Spring Releases Catalog	8½" x 11"	32 pages	2	3
___	1996	Consumer Catalog	8½" x 11"	24 pages	2	3
___	1996	Consumer Catalog Illustrated	10" x 8"	24 pages	2	3
___	1996	Accessories Catalog	10" x 8"	32 pages	2	3
___	1997	Heritage Catalog	10" x 8"	12 pages	2	3

	Year	Catalog	Size	Pages	Exc	New
___	1997	Century Club Catalog	10" x 8"	16 pages	2	3
___	1997	Classic I Catalog	10" x 8"	24 pages	2	3
___	1997	Classic II Catalog	10" x 8"	36 pages	2	3
___	1997	Lionel Brochure	10" x 8"	4 pages	2	3
___	1997	Fall '97 Heritage II Catalog	10" x 8"	12 pages	2	3
___	1998	Classic Catalog	8½" x 9"	76 pages	2	3
___	1998	Heritage Catalog	11" x 8½"	24 pages	2	3
___	1998	Legendary Trains Catalog	10⅞" x 8½"	64 pages	2	3
___	1998	Gilbert American Flyer Trains Brochure	8½" x 11"	4 pages	1	2
___	1999	Classic Trains Catalog Volume 1	8¼" x 10½"	63 pages	2	3
___	1999	Classic Trains Catalog Volume 2	8¼" x 10½"	45 pages	2	3
___	1999	Heritage Catalog	11" x 8½"	26 pages	2	3
___	1999	Classic Trains Catalog Volume 3	8¼" x 10¾"	58 pages	2	3
___	2000	Classic Trains Catalog Volume 1	8" x 10¾"	110 pages	2	3
___	2000	Classic Trains Catalog, Volume 2	8" x 10¾"	85 pages	2	3
___	2001	Classic Trains Catalog, Volume 1	8" x 10¾"	122 pages	2	3
___	2001	Classic Trains Catalog Volume 2	8" x 10¾"	122 pages	2	3
___	2001	Challenger Brochure	8½" x 11"	4 pages	1	2
___	2001	Hiawatha Brochure	11" x 8½"	4 pages	1	2
___	2002	Classic Trains Catalog Volume 1	8" x 10¾"	122 pages	2	3
___	2002	Classic Trains Catalog, Volume 2	8" x 10¾"	110 pages	2	3
___	2003	Classic Trains Catalog, Volume 1	8" x 10¾"	132 pages		CP
___	2003	Classic Trains Catalog, Volume 2	8" x 10¾"	152 pages		CP

ABBREVIATIONS
Pocket Guide Descriptions

A	diesel A unit
AA	two diesel A units
AAR	Association of American Railroads (truck type)
AC	alternating current
acc.	accessory
ACF	hopper type
Alco	diesel type
Alco A	diesel type
Alco FA-2A	diesel type
Alco FA-2B	diesel type
Anniv.	Anniversary
appro.	approaches
auto.	automatic
B	diesel B unit
Bag.	baggage
Bldg.	building
Blvd.	boulevard
Box.	boxcar
b/w	black and white
B/W	bay window
bump.	bumper(s)
Cab.	caboose
cata.	catalog
CC	command control
cent.	central
chem.	chemical
con.	connection
cont.	control
Conv.	conversion
CP	current production
C.V.	Commodore Vanderbilt
Dash 8	diesel type
Dash 9	diesel type
DC	direct current
DD	double-door
dep.	depressed
d.p.d.t.	double-pole, double-throw switches
dir.	direct
dum.	dummy
dz.	dozen
elec.	electric
electr.	electronic
EP-5	electric type locomotive
ETD	end-of-train device
Exp.	express
ext.	extended
E/V	extended vision
F-3	diesel type
F.A.O.S.	F A O Schwarz
FARR	Famous American Railroad Series
FF	Fallen Flag Series
Flat.	flatcar
FM	Fairbanks-Morse
GG-1	electric type locomotive
GE	switcher type
Gen.	General, steam type
Gon.	gondola
GP-7	diesel type
GP-9	diesel type
GP-20	diesel type
GP-35	diesel type
GP-38-2	diesel type
Hi-cube	boxcar type
Hop.	hopper
HS	heat-stamped
illum.	illuminated
ins.	insulated, insulator
lett.	lettering
litho.	lithographed
low-cup.	low-cupola
maint.	maintenance
man.	manual
MB	multi-block door
mech.	mechanical
merch.	merchandise
MU	multiple unit (commuter cars)
N5C	caboose type
N8	caboose type
NBA	National Basketball Assoc.

NHL	National Hockey League		**St.**	state
NM	not manufactured		**Sta.**	station
NW-2	diesel type		**Std.**	Standard gauge (2⅛" between outside rails)
O	Lionel gauge (1¼" between outside rails)		**Std. O**	Standard O (scale length and dimension)
OO	Lionel Gauge (¾" between outside rails)		**Steam**	steam engine
Obs.	observation		**str.**	straight
oper.	operating		**Sup.**	super
or.	orange		**S/W**	square window
pass.	passenger		**Switch.**	switcher
pc(s).	piece(s)		**Tdr.**	tender
port.	porthole		**TOFC**	flatcar type
pow.	power, powered		**TT**	TruTrack
pr.	pair		**TTUX**	flatcar type
Pull.	Pullman		**Trk.**	track
Quad	quad hopper		**Trans.**	transformer
Rad.	radius		***u* or uncat.**	uncataloged
R.C.	remote control		**U36B**	diesel type
RDC	diesel-powered passenger unit		**U36C**	diesel type
rect.	rectifier		**V. D.**	Vista Dome
rectifier	electric type locomotive		**w/**	with
Reefer	refrigerator car		**w/o**	without
Refrig.	refrigerator		**whl.**	wheel
rem.	remote		**1-D**	one dome
rnd.	round		**2-D**	two dome
RS	rubber-stamped		**3-D**	three dome
RS-3	diesel type			
RSC-3	diesel type			
RSD-4	diesel type			
SB	single-block door			
SD-9	diesel type			
SD-18	diesel type			
SD-24	diesel type			
SD-28	diesel type			
SD-38	diesel type			
SD-40	diesel type			
SD-50	diesel type			
SD-60M	diesel type			
sec.	section			
SP	caboose type			
spec.	special			
SSS	Service Station Special			

Railroad Name Abbreviations

ACL	Atlantic Coast Line
ACY	Akron, Canton, and Youngstown
ALASK	Alaska Railroad
AT&SF (ATSF)	Atchison, Topeka, and Santa Fe
B&A	Boston and Albany
BAOC	British American Oil Co.
BAR	Bangor and Aroostook
B&LE	Bessemer and Lake Erie
B&M	Boston and Maine
BN	Burlington Northern
B&O	Baltimore and Ohio
C&A	Chicago and Alton
C&IM	Chicago and Illinois Midland
CB&Q (CBQ)	Chicago, Burlington, and Quincy
CCC&StL	Cleveland, Cincinnati, Chicago, and St. Louis
CN	Canadian National
CNJ	Central of New Jersey
C&NW (CNW)	Chicago and North Western
C&O	Chesapeake and Ohio
CP	Canadian Pacific
CRI&P	Chicago, Rock Island, and Peoria
CSt PM&O	Chicago, St. Paul, Minneapolis, and Omaha
D&H	Delaware and Hudson
DL&W	Delaware, Lackawanna, and Western
DM&IR	Duluth, Missabe, and Iron Range
D&RG	Denver and Rio Grande
D&RGW	Denver and Rio Grande Western
DT&I	Detroit, Toledo, and Ironton
D&TS	Detroit and Toledo Shore Line
EJ&E	Elgin, Joliet, and Eastern
EMD	Electro-Motive Division
Erie-Lack.	Erie-Lackawanna
FEC	Florida East Coast
GM&O	Gulf, Mobile, and Ohio
GN	Great Northern
GTW	Grand Trunk Western
IC	Illinois Central
ICG	Illinois Central Gulf
IETCA	Inland Empire Train Collectors Association
L&C	Lancaster and Chester
Lack	Lackawanna
LCAC	Lionel Collectors Association of Canada
LCCA	Lionel Collectors Club of America
LCOL	Lionel Central Operating Lines
LL	Lionel Lines
L&N	Louisville and Nashville
LNAC	Louisville, New Albany, and Corydon
LOTS	Lionel Operating Train Society
LRRC	Lionel Railroader Club

LV	Lehigh Valley
MD&W	Minnesota, Dakota, and Western
METCA	New York Metropolitan Division TCA
MKT	Missouri, Kansas, Texas (KATY)
MNS (MN&S)	Minneapolis, Northfield, and Southern
MP (MoPac)	Missouri Pacific
MPA	Maryland and Pennsylvania (Ma and Pa)
MILW	Milwaukee Road
M&StL	Minneapolis and St. Louis
NC&StL	Nashville, Chattanooga, and St. Louis
NdeM	Nacionales de Mexico Railway
NETCA	New England Division Train Collectors Association
NH	New Haven
NKP	Nickel Plate Road
NLOE	Nassau Lionel Operating Engineers
NP	Northern Pacific
N&W	Norfolk and Western
NYC	New York Central
NYNH&H	New York, New Haven, and Hartford
ON	Ontario Northland
PC	Penn Central
P&E	Peoria and Eastern
PFE	Pacific Fruit Express
PHD	Port Huron and Detroit
P&LE	Pittsburgh and Lake Erie
PRR	Pennsylvania Railroad
REA	Railway Express Agency
RF&P	Richmond, Fredericksburg, and Potomac
RI	Rock Island
RI&P	Rock Island and Peoria
SCL	Seaboard Coast Line
SMARRCO	San Manuel Arizona Railroad Company
SP	Southern Pacific
SP&S	Spokane, Portland, and Seattle
SUNX	Sunoco
TA&G	Tennessee, Alabama, and Georgia
TCA	Train Collectors Association
T&P	Texas and Pacific
TP&W	Toledo, Peoria, and Western
TTOS	Toy Train Operating Society
UP	Union Pacific
USMC	United States Marine Corps
VTC	Virginia Train Collectors
V&TRR	Virginia and Truckee Railroad
Wab.	Wabash
W&ARR (W&A)	Western and Atlantic Railroad
WB&A	Washington, Baltimore, and Annapolis Chapter TCA
WM	Western Maryland
WP	Western Pacific